9/11 THE AWFUL TRUTH

.

9/11 The Awful Truth

AN ACCOUNT OF THE
CONSPIRACY BEHIND
THE 9/11 ATTACK ON
AMERICA, THE
ENSUING COVER-UP,
AND THE PILLARS OF
LAW AND JOURNALISM
THAT SUSTAIN IT TO
THIS DAY

INTRODUCTION BY
DENNIS CUNNINGHAM

Contents

Woe unto you, ye lawyers! Ye have not entered in at the Gates of Knowledge, and them that would enter have ye hindered...

Jesus of Nazareth, Luke, 12:24 (Gideon)

INTRODUCTION

The law case which is a story within the story told in this book was built on a shocking accusation about the events of September 11, 2001— a full-bore Conspiracy Theory in every way—alleging that the attack in its essence was an "inside job", in which the vice president, the secretary of defense, the top military chief and other U.S. officials high and low were variously involved in aiding and abetting the hijackers in a variety of ways, thereby helping and enabling the infamous Attack on America to succeed. Part and parcel of the plot was also, naturally, that they and others subsequently by various ways and means would carry on a cover-up; as they have done. The accusation was and remains based primarily on undeniable, publicly established facts, as intrepid readers will realize, and—once you get past the horrors of the Very Idea of such a heinous plot, and the seeming impossibility of such great iniquity, and treason, and above all, the culprits getting away with it—there is copious additional evidence, and powerful inferences, which, in the view of many sober and reputable, open-minded people, form an overwhelming case.

As lawyers, we came to believe, from careful research, investigation and analysis, and so alleged in our complaint, that the attack was indeed a "false flag" action— with whatever amount of witting or unwitting involvement of the nineteen Arab guys, et al (Osama, Al Qaeda, ISI, Mossad, whoever)—that was permitted and facilitated, where not engineered outright, by Americans, including these leading officials, to ensure its success. We said their purpose was to generate the great public fear and fervor of "a new Pearl Harbor", in the spirit and cover of which they could then swiftly bring about huge, jarring, radical alterations in the Country's military and foreign policy—and domestic political and police, or (what came to be known as) "homeland security" programs, actions, plans, laws, and secret operations—to say nothing of super-aggressive supporting propaganda activities in all spheres. We said the official Commission carried out a whitewash, and issued a report full of falsehood, as part of the cover-up.

Only think: was it not indeed an expansive and fecundating sequel, all told, to the first-stage *coup d'etat*, accomplished in the 2000 election via *Bush v. Gore*? Was there not a profound, double disaster in American history in those few months, which we lived through, definitively book-ending the days of our grown-up years, us older ones, with the coup that occurred on November 22, 1963...?

But many Americans, probably a good majority, would regard such a theory as far-fetched, and hare-brained; and members of the Establishment—including the judges in our case—also uniformly find it outrageous, and despicable; unimaginable on its face, and so beneath serious consideration. Some people even believe that to seriously suggest the possibility is altogether unacceptable, and that questions and disputes such as those David Ray Griffin has been raising now for many [several] years, shouldn't be allowed, should be classified as an offense of some kind, and forbidden, even punished. Indeed, that was exactly the position of the judges in our case, in the United States Court of Appeals for the Second Circuit, who indeed punished us severely, as Bill describes here, with a $15,000 fine—as seen in their wretched Orders—for daring to utter it.

Generally, there are two or three forms of automatic response people typically have to the "false flag" conspiracy theory: 'They would never do such a thing, the very idea is outrageous'; or, 'They could never have gotten away with it; somebody would have told'; or, obtusely, as from the late, eminent commentator, Alexander Cockburn, 'The U.S. Government is too incompetent; they never could have pulled it off.' In each case, there is a reflexive reaction, or snap judgment, often colored with scorn or anger, or both; but at bottom, "Don't trouble me with facts" is the order of the day.

The Nobel laureate Daniel Kahnemann has written of what he calls "cognitive illusions". A cognitive illusion is a belief in something one instinctively feels sure of, but which is in fact false, where the illusion of assured truth—though in a given case unfounded—actually stems from an abiding belief in the reliability of one's own judgment. So it is here: people feel they just know it couldn't have happened. Or, as in one striking variation, a woman said she didn't want to even talk about it, because, "I don't want to live in a country where that could happen..." The cognitive illusion is a simple, pre-emptive negation: No way.

Actually, everyone pretty much starts right there, or did start there, back in 2001, because, coming out of the shock and horror and astonishment at what had occurred, the population was bombarded with the trumped-up, trumpeted official version: nineteen suicide bombers, fanatical Islamic "jihadists" who "hate us for our freedoms", were sent by the terrorist evil genius, Osama bin Laden, to hijack the four planes and crash them into the buildings, which spectacularly collapsed—except that on the fourth plane the passengers heroically fought back, resulting in a fatal crash in a country field—and now, the President said, "We are at war." It's to be a War on Terror, global in scope, which may well take a generation to win, or indeed may never end. That was the explanation, and the outlook, and the entire content of public discourse: an immediate world-wide war against the 'terrorists and those who harbor them'; and we were sending an invading army to central Asia forthwith. Who can forget this stunning turn of events?

Everything was changed, and the portents in our own country were ominous indeed, and soon blossomed hideously in sweeping round-ups of Arab-Americans, U.S. military invasion of Afghanistan, a torture prison at Guantanamo, the Patriot Act, "renditions", and a war of mass murder and lies against Iraq: Shock and Awe, Abu Ghraib, Fallujah, Haditha, uncounted other American atrocities, and a full civil war, still continuing, between local Arab peoples who had previously lived at peace together for centuries. These horrors, in the stunned, freaked-out atmosphere that blew up, literally, unstoppably, in those first days, flowed directly from and were enabled by this veritable Pearl Harbor moment in the life of the nation. These and so many more: only think for yourself of what happened and has happened since, and is still going forward, militarily and otherwise, world-wide—and is even today being extended and refocused in mounting provocations against Russia, and the ominous "Pacific Pivot" of our country's death-dealing, nuclear armadas, in an aggressive close encirclement of China—to confront the two ultimate 'adversaries' who haunt the febrile, jut-jawed, neocon dreams of all-out war.

So, anyone who comes merely to question the official version, or major parts of it, let alone conspiracy theorists of whatever school, must first set aside the overweening official account—which is of course much more elaborate, in its lying way, than what is stated here—which we set out to expose, and did substantially expose, in our lawsuit. And it should help to keep in mind that the weird, implausible alternative to the "false flag" conspiracy, surely equally hard to swallow if you think about it, is that the attack succeeded because of widespread, eerily fortuitous, across-the-board bungling—time-coordinated blunders at all stations, on that day and for weeks and months beforehand—which has never been plausibly described, let alone explained, by half. Moreover, no one has given or taken any blame for any of it; and no one at the Top, including our defendants, has ever shown any interest in finding out who in fact was responsible for any of it.

We took that as a completely unnatural and 'implausible' response to what occurred, and rich fodder for an inference of the defendants' guilt. Apparently, however, the Country was so quickly swept up in public horror and alarm—and a universal rage, instantly mobilized against this mortal enemy, the former CIA 'asset' bin Laden, and "Al Qaeda", a hostile terrorist army drawn from among more than a billion Muslims, world-wide—that the question was never really raised in the Public Mind, and certainly not in the Public Media. The many questions, that is, of how the horrific attack could ever have come about successfully against our vaunted, heroically expensive national defenses? *How did it happen, and who was responsible for the lapses?*

It is amazing that these questions were not faced—and that a patent whitewash was purveyed and sold, and bought and swallowed whole instead. But the fact is that, rather than attending to the obvious questions, the nation plunged or was plunged and driven ahead into an enormous change of life; and particularly, into war—wildly expensive, ultra-modern, high-tech war—involving lawless invasion and occupation, and slaughter and destruction, brought to many millions of plainly innocent fellow humans, all of very different faith and culture and history, unto their uncounted tens and hundreds of thousands of wrongful deaths; plus violent upheaval, dispossession, mass imprisonment, torture; and a vast, awful ruination in their own ancient, distant country. It was, and remains, a ghastly, aggravated, profoundly criminal, aggressive war—"the paramount international crime" under the Nuremberg Laws—against people halfway around the world, who our country and its buccaneer military and business partners had already bled and tyrannized behind the similarly phony, trumped-up "First Gulf War," for twelve years...

And our own country meanwhile roared ahead into a maelstrom of high-level corporate and banking crookedness, reactionary packing of the courts and agencies, and relentless expansion of the manifold "security" apparatus; and a political and economic morass soon developed that has only gotten worse since that day. And that—"as all sentient beings know"—is what happened in the country and the world after 9/11, as a result of 9/11. We know it was brought about by a political leadership cabal in Washington, who seized the moment, and drove events as they progressed; and that there was a political movement in the country that reveled in all of it, and still does, and that stays well in the mix as the country itself continues to play out the political, military and economic gambits, foreign and domestic, that exploded out of the Horrific Attack.

And that movement has deep roots, and had proclaimed itself and its belief in the need for America to make such wars, especially in west and central Asia, where the oil and gas is, well before 9/11. They—that "neo-conservative" movement, with our two leading defendants, Cheney and Rumsfeld at the center of it—had stated clearly their core belief that America must have "full spectrum dominance" over all the nations and peoples of the world; and therefore must control the oil in the 'Middle East' and the Caspian basin (and keep China away from it), and that "we" must send, and use, great armies, navies and air forces—now including death-dealing robot "drones"—to secure and maintain our dominance.

This was the position of the "Project for a New American Century", a 'neocon' think tank cohort, developed to defend and promote U.S. military-industrial interests in the backwash of the Cold War's end. They put it in a formal statement of policy, "Rebuilding America's Defenses", published in 1998; but they conceded there that the American Public was in no frame of mind to share their outlook, or accept their program, and would require a shocking stimulus—"a catastrophic and catalyzing event, like a new Pearl Harbor", they called it—before it would ever accept or support the broad military-foreign policy-energy industry endeavor the Neocons saw as vital to America's future.

Given that perspective, is it really so impossible that, fully in power, true believers in this viewpoint would be willing to see an actual new Pearl Harbor come about; or that they might be moved, once they were aware that an attack plan was afoot, to take various measures designed to ensure that it would succeed, to that end? Do we Remember the Maine? The Reichstag fire? The Gulf of Tonkin?

Normally, in a case raising claims of serious official wrongdoing, the first question is, obviously, What is the evidence? That vital question is screened, however, as noted, by the cognitive illusion that the supposed conspiracy—and the intentional acts and omissions which would have carried it forward—simply, *a priori,* absolutely could not have occurred. In a majority of cases, apparently— including the entire Establishment, journalistic and otherwise, as recounted here—these illusions served and still serve as an effective excuse for refusing to examine the evidence, and instead dismissing the possibility of this great treason, out of hand, and generally with anger, scorn, and condescension.

So one must risk this opprobrium, and perhaps undertake 'a willing suspension of disbelief', to cross into the "country where that could happen", and so learn the evidence, and consider the objective implications of known and apparent facts, and unanswered questions. Once the jump is made, however, and the mind is opened, the evidence is sobering indeed, and profound attendant political questions arise, and loom. Whether it changes your mind or not, no one who surveys the material reasonably will fail to see that the truth has not been told, and that a fully independent and complete investigation absolutely must occur if anything close to the truth is to be found out.

In this book, Bill Veale tells the story of his own passage from skepticism and doubt to the farther shores of conviction, on the main points of what is known as '9/11 Truth'. Thence he was impelled into action, as a seasoned lawyer and investigator, concerned not only with the facts and evidence of what happened but with the sources and modes, and malign, misleading effects, of the dictated official version—i.e. the cover-up—especially as they reflected the continuing conspiracy. In particular, he has explored the near-universal self-enforcement of the cover-up throughout the American journalistic establishment.

One thing he learned right away is that, despite all the resistance, reluctance, and refusal, there is a vast population of "truthers" in the country—including Lawyers for 9/11 Truth, Architects and Engineers for 9/11 Truth, Pilots for 9/11 Truth, Scholars for 9/11 Truth, Scientists for 9/11 Truth, and many, many more. As *Time* Magazine reported on 9/6/2006:

"A Scripps-Howard poll of 1,010 adults last month found that 36% of Americans consider it 'very likely' or 'somewhat likely' that government officials either allowed the attacks to be carried out or carried out the attacks themselves. Thirty-six percent adds up to a lot of people. This is not a fringe phenomenon. It is a mainstream political reality. Although the 9/11 Truth Movement, as many conspiracy believers refer to their passion, has been largely ignored by the mainstream media, it is flourishing on the Internet."

Indeed it is a very broad movement, encompassing many points of view about many different phases of the known and possible facts, as Bill soon found out. The one thing everyone agrees on is that the official explanation(s)—in and out of the official 9/11 Commission Report—are a crock; and that a completely independent inquiry, with full and complete subpoena access to the documentary, photographic and physical evidence, and the sworn testimony of all concerned, must be had, if anything approaching the truth is ever to be publicly established. That was the strategic point we meant to push with our lawsuit, which, theoretically, could have yielded just such an investigation if it had been allowed to proceed. That just such an investigation could not be tolerated by the Powers that Be, however—and the great likelihood that such a lawsuit would thus be quashed in the courts, by hook or crook—was clear to us, I'm sure. But, in light of the evidence and the plain reality of the cover-up, that was basically irrelevant to our commitment to raise the issues, despite how forcefully they had been shunned, suppressed, and pushed beyond the pale of the respectable world.

Bill Veale is a shrewd, indefatigable lawyer, retired from a lifetime in the trenches as a big city public defender, who did every type of case from the death penalty on down. He was a top supervisor of other lawyers in the Contra Costa County (CA) Public Defender's Office, and, for eleven years, a lecturer in criminal trial practice at Boalt Hall (the UC Berkeley law school). When he dug into the accumulated independent evidence and information about 9/11, and read David Ray Griffin's books, and others, he realized the factual basis of a conspiracy case was deeply present, as he describes. Then he met April Gallop, a survivor of the Pentagon blast, whose office was in the ground floor area where the plane supposedly hit. She was there that morning, and by a fluke had her two-month old son, Elisha, with her; and both of them were hurt when a big explosion collapsed the walls and ceiling around them. Knocked out momentarily, she recovered, grabbed the baby from the rubble, and made her way out through a wide opening where the building's front wall was blown off. She saw no sign of a crashed airliner, and it was plain from her location that if one had crashed where they said it did, she and her child would have been killed.

Bill thought she had a case, and, on the good word of my late and deeply lamented old comrade, Susan Jordan—that I was someone who had substantial experience suing cops and government officials for violating civil rights—he came to talk to me about it. On my office wall—skeptic that I was myself, from the beginning (and before the beginning)—I had pinned up a page from the Web that showed three views of the south tower exploding, with smoke and dust billowing out. He sat down and looked up and saw it and smiled, "I came to the right place."

And it was indeed up my alley, and something of a dream case, really, and potentially a righteous capstone to a long career of fighting the Man. Here after all was apparently the all-time Man, who had stolen the election, and then evidently went completely berserk—to the point of mass murder, as subsequent activities in Afghanistan and Iraq had confirmed—and was here very much exposed. When Bill showed me the evidence, I jumped at it, and we agreed to begin the project together. We went to Virginia to talk to April Gallop.

III.

At an absolute minimum, US Army Specialist 4 April Gallop, the 125 people who died at the Pentagon on 9/11, and many others who were injured, should have and clearly could have been warned, and evacuated to safety, well before the hijacked airliner supposedly hit. But they were not evacuated, or even warned, and it strongly appeared that the reason involved, *at best,* an enormous, nefarious dereliction of duty, which had been swept under the rug. Published FAA records made it clear that flight controllers had first put out an alert regarding the wayward plane, Flight 77, heading back towards Washington, at least a half-hour before it supposedly crashed at the Pentagon. The plane was plainly visible on radar during a long approach, and the country was known to be under attack. It was indubitable that, whatever the timeline was, the vaunted defenses at 'the most powerfully fortified building in the world' had failed completely.

April had tried to raise questions about the failure. She and others had been heavily indoctrinated about the strength and power of the defense system at the giant fortress, after being assigned there, and they had been subjected to repeated evacuation drills over the preceding several months—to the point where many were disgruntled over the frequent interruptions of their work. Her fellow surviving denizens of the blown-up section of the building, however—being dependent on the Army and the Government for ongoing medical and other benefits and support in the aftermath, and obviously for their jobs—were frightened by the questions she had begun to raise, and they shunned her; and her own ongoing medical and housing benefits began to be suspiciously disrupted. She tried to raise her questions about how or why the defenses failed, at a special session of the 9/11 Commission, reserved for survivors, where they could forward questions through assigned Commission members (hers was Jamie Gorelick), and Rumsfeld had agreed to appear and respond. In the event, however, the Secretary in his inimitable style made rambling, unresponsive answers, choked with irrelevancies and hyperbole, and the Commissioners made no effort to pin him down; the answer was, there was no answer.

But she had a case, and that stonewalling performance by Rumsfeld bolstered it. Cheney was evacuated, at the White House, with others, and was heard by Transportation Secretary Norman Mineta, in the White House bunker, affirming an apparent standdown order to the military as the plane approached. Mineta reported this, but his testimony was ignored—not followed up by the Commission and left out of its Report—and Cheney was never questioned about it. Rumsfeld and Myers, acting Chair of the Joint Chiefs, had both given accounts in which each one said he knew nothing of the attack until the plane hit—Myers claimed he wasn't even in the building—but the counter-terrorism chief Richard Clarke said in his book he saw them both taking their seats in the Pentagon teleconference room, for an urgent meeting on the crisis, shortly after the second tower was hit in New York, at 9:03 a.m., and there was no question that the country was under attack. The Pentagon was hit at 9:37.

In the aftermath of the horrific attack, President Bush, then-NSA Chief Condoleezza Rice and other leading figures insisted to Congress, the Commission and the Public that no one in Government had ever imagined that terrorists might hijack planes and fly them into buildings as living bombs, and Gen. Myers testified sheepishly that the Air Force had focused exclusively on possible attacks from outside the country. But it was shown that, in fact, at least four or five agencies, including the National Reconnaisance Center, the CIA, and the Pentagon itself, had planned and trained for precisely such a possibility, and indeed a large-scale, multi-force training exercise premised on that very possibility was planned for October, 2001.

And there is no picture, not one, showing a crashed airliner at the Pentagon, and many which show the clear absence of one. And these show also that, in the first half-hour afterwards, before that whole section of the building fell in on itself so cleanly, the front was blown off on the ground floor only. The facade above it is intact, and no wrecked plane is present. Further, it has emerged that some 80-odd videotapes, from fixed surveillance cameras at various spots on or near the building—all rapidly collected by FBI agents in the first hours after the attack— are being withheld by the Justice Department from Freedom of Information Act disclosure. Just five frames have been released, from two viewpoint-redundant cameras, which show only an ambiguous silver streak, not recognizable as an airliner, headed towards the wall just before a big explosion that appears to begin at ground level.

We learned further that the radar record showed Flight 77 making a precipitous, aeronautically fantastic, 8000-foot dive, in a spiraling three-quarter turn over Washington, before supposedly leveling off just a few feet above the ground (and so by then hidden from the radar), and crashing into the building right where April Gallop worked—where the financial records were kept. Experienced pilots said only an unusually skilled and experienced—and reckless—pilot, or a programmed auto-pilot, could have made the dive in such a big plane, and the supposed flight path along the ground was shown to be wholly implausible and self-contradictory—and at odds with data from the Flight 77 "black box", released by the NTSB to Pilots for 9/11 Truth. The weirdness of this hugely difficult and unlikely, swooping turn, to get to an obscure rear part of the building, rather than aiming straight down at the roof, or the exposed front side, where Rumsfeld and the top generals and admirals were publicly known to have their river-view offices on the third (middle) floor, was patent. And flight instructors said the man the FBI named as the hijacker pilot, one Hani Hanjour —how they knew it was him has never been disclosed—was altogether incompetent as a pilot, couldn't fly even a small Cessna safely, to the point where they refused to go up with him, and recommended that his license be revoked.

There is more to this part, some discussed below, and within, but it was quite clear that April had a hell of a case, based on an obvious pack of lies, covering a clear-cut conspiracy. And, for all the sarcasm of the district judge in dealing with it, Rumsfeld did announce on September 10, 2001, that $2.3 trillion ---a word rarely seen in those times but omnipresent now---was missing from Pentagon accounts, and being hunted for. You will be unable to find any record of subsequent press coverage of that issue, however, or of the promised search for those funds, because there was none. And the plaintiff did work in the financial administration section, and that is what was blown up, and she barely escaped alive, with her baby...

IV

So we went ahead, on our considered information and beliefs about the facts and evidence as we were coming to know them, and the inferences, and we formulated and put forth our theories of diabolical plotting by Cheney and Rumsfeld, et al. We charged them, finally, and General Myers and others unknown, with facilitation, enablement and perhaps some participation, in what was in essence a "false flag" attack on America on 9/11, absolutely an inside job. We said it was done with the awful purpose of sowing great fear in the American population, and a great rage for retaliation, and revenge, which would allow the cabal (as the Bush Administration inner circle in fact called themselves, at least for a time while they were riding high) to launch the murderous, lunatic military adventures wet-dreamed of by the PNAC.

For the whole world had been changed, utterly—had it not?—not so much by the attack as by the madly disproportionate, clearly pre-ordained U.S. response, regardless of what exactly happened on 9/11, and exactly who did what to make it happen or let it happen. Yet there was never any serious independent public inquiry to determine the truth about what happened, from all the facts, let alone assign blame for the disastrous breakdown of the country's defenses. Instead —and only after stout, prolonged resistance, obstruction and manipulation by the Bush Administration—a Commission was formed which then carried out a patently fraudulent, high-level whitewash, and cover-up, that persists to this day. So, what really happened has not been publicly examined, and the merits of the conspiracy theory have not been tested. The evidence of it, in the framework of a full and fair investigation, was what we hoped against hope to push forward by forcing the issue in a lawsuit...

We struggled early over the proper scope of the case we would initiate, and specifically whether we would or could or should include claims in the Complaint about the collapse of the towers in New York—which was probably of livelier interest over all, not least because so many people of substance had voiced and subscribed to the many issues arising from conflicts between the official version and the known facts, and relevant science. We knew we shouldn't over-reach, since the towers were a separate aspect of the apparent conspiracy, only indirectly related to our client's injuries and loss of rights through some over-arching hub of evil intention, and, one assumes, command. In the end, knowing that all of the matters in Manhattan would come up in discovery, and could at any rate be part of an Amended Complaint, we left it out.

But, anyone who buys the explanation that the two towers collapsed because airplanes crashed into them and caused fires, hasn't really watched the collapses —let alone interrogated or even lightly parsed the official, "scientific" explanation, that gravity done it. It is said that both buildings (never mind the third, which wasn't even hit by a plane) came down—indeed, disintegrated, identically, a half-hour apart, as they do before your eyes in the videos—because crucial internal structural members were weakened by the fires left over from the plane crashes, and the weight of the upper sections did the rest. This adamant official fantasy has about as much substance as the canard that Saddam Hussein was behind the attack.

Only look at the pictures. You don't see "a plane fly into a building and the building falls down". You see a plane fly into a building and cause a big, flashing explosion, which results in a fire. The jet fuel is consumed in and just after the explosions from the initial impacts, producing white smoke, but the resulting fire—black smoke now, trailing in the sky from burning draperies, desks, panels and other building contents—lasts for an hour. Then, quite suddenly, right before your eyes, an enormous explosion occurs, or a group of explosions. Huge burgeoning clouds of white smoke and dust plow out and up into the air, and billow downwards, and the building almost instantly crumbles into shards, including innumerable 30-foot segments of the massive interior steel columns, some even square-cut, well fitted for the trucks which showed up so quickly to haul them away...

And it happened twice, the exact same way: 25 minutes later you see the other, north building—which was actually hit first, 17-18 minutes earlier than the south one, that fell first—also go down. Uncannily, the north tower is also suddenly enveloped in the same huge, billowing explosions, and also totally crumbles straight down to the ground, at close to free fall speed, exactly as the first one did.

And these explosions were so powerful that huge portions of the buildings' walls and floors were blown into a heavy dust, which spread everywhere, blanketing all of lower Manhattan, inches thick, and blew all the way into the middle of Brooklyn. That is, the composite construction materials, concrete, plaster, gypsum, etc, were *pulverized,* by high explosives. What else in this world could have produced the awful, fine, ingestible, toxic dust, which lingered in the air for days, and embedded itself in the lungs and sinuses of thousands of responders and site workers, who were falsely told the air was safe to breathe?

"Many have fallen, more will..."

And dozens of them, firefighters, EMTs and others, denizens of the buildings, have testified to hearing and feeling big explosions inside the towers in the moments before they fell, long after the planes hit. They have been ignored. The New York Times went to Court to get the statements released, and apparently put them on line, but never reported about what the people said.

The WTC towers were blown up, friends, massively bombed; anyone can see it: open eyes will feed an open mind. Chunks of debris were blown hundreds of feet out from the buildings; and incandescent pools of molten metal were left in the ruins—white hot, runny and dripping when uncovered in the wreckage and finally exposed to the air—*even weeks later.* No way in life could the fires you saw before the collapses cause that. And certainly no plane crash caused the stunning meltdown of WTC Building Seven, also plainly evident on television, at about 5:30 that afternoon, seven hours after the second tower fell; and no fire did either. Building Seven descended in a well-coordinated flow, flawlessly executed, flat, symmetrical, amazingly quick, and clearly recognizable—as it was indeed explicitly recognized by each of the big three network news mediators, Rather, Jennings and Brokaw—as a programmed sequence of explosives, 'like the demolitions of big buildings we've all seen on television..'

People were warned well beforehand to get away from the building, and there are reports that word was out as early as noon-time that day, and even before, that the building was coming down. Strikingly, there were offices of the CIA, the FBI, the Secret Service, the SEC—reportedly its investigative headquarters, with all its files—and the City's Disaster Command Post, just set up that morning in Building Seven. All of them were completely destroyed.

The National Institute of Standards and Technology (NIST)—a branch of the Commerce Department that was formerly the Bureau of Standards, which was co-opted into the 9/11 cover-up to provide an official source for the baseless pretense that structural members, softened by fire, gave way to cause the identical collapses of the towers—waited eight years before announcing a similarly fanciful story for the fall of Building Seven. The absurdity of this purported explanation for the smooth disappearance of the 47-story structure—which NIST itself said had a less than 25 percent chance of being accurate—remains one of the very most glaring signs of cynical falsehood in the official 9/11 reports.

No steel-framed skyscraper was ever brought down by fire, before or since, even fires that raged for many hours; and these towers were massively built, to stand against high winds, and carefully engineered to withstand a crash from a large airliner. Dust samples from at least four widely separated locations have now, since we filed, been conclusively shown to contain traces of "nanothermite", a military-grade incendiary substance that instantly burns at 5000 degrees when ignited, and easily and quickly cuts steel. More than 2100 architects, engineers, scientists and other experts who studied the evidence have signed petitions rejecting all or part of the official government explanation of the collapses, and demanding independent, science-based investigation.

Certainly there is no question but that literally dozens of increasingly pointed warnings—specifically that a terrorist attack by bin Laden's forces was imminent, and likely would involve hijacking, and possibly planes flown into buildings—were received by our Government from various foreign intelligence services and others over the course of 2001, through August. It is also clearly established that these warnings were presented to and studiously ignored by the high command of the Bush regime—including by the president himself, at his ranch, on August 6—and dismissed from its serious attention. And it is indisputable that normal operation of the nation's air defense system, and ground defenses at the Pentagon also, failed completely on 9/11. But the top commanders—in keeping with their indifference beforehand—have never provided reasonable answers, or required answers from their subordinates, regarding how this failure came about, after so many years of assiduous training, practice and expense. No responsibility has ever been fixed; and official explanations have been palpably inadequate, contradictory and fraudulent. The 9/11 Commission Report in particular is shot through with glaring omissions, distortions and outright lies, and its partisan provenance has been exposed.

Only think, it is established beyond doubt that the warnings were ignored (leaving aside the bald-faced lie by President Bush, in his rigged "interview"with the co-chairs of the 9-11 Commission—and not challenged or even acknowledged by them—that there simply were no warnings). Likewise, it cannot be denied that the defenses did not operate; and Richard Clarke's testimony that the active counter-terrorism operations he supervised during the Clinton administration were basically shut down by the Bush Cabal, in early 2001, has not been contradicted.

The rule of Occam's Razor ought to apply: the simplest, most logical explanation is probably right. So,

+ Nineteen Arab guys supposedly known as terrorist suspects or associates—fifteen of them Saudis and none of the rest from Afghanistan, Iraq, Pakistan,Yemen, Libya, Syria, Somalia, Iran or any other place where the U.S. has subsequently been making open or secret war—were able to enter the United States, live in various places, move around at will, get airplane flight training for several of them, hang out at strip clubs or whorehouses or whatever, and then book airline flights in groups of five, under their own supposed names, and board the planes, with weapons, all on the same morning; *because the anti-terrorist forces were looking the other way*; and,

+ The squads of high-performance fighter-interceptor jets which have so expensively guarded U.S. airspace for so long, which at least up to June, 2001, would normally scramble about twice a week, to check on wayward airliners and other in-flight 'emergencies'—going routinely, we learned, from FAA phone call to 29,000 feet in less than three minutes, with a top speed of 1800 m.p.h.—were nowhere to be found on that morning, *because the orders for them to launch were withheld, delayed and misdirected;* and,

+ the super-built towers exploded into enormous clouds of toxic dust, and crumbled instantly into mountains of cut pillars and beams, and ruined concrete, laced with pools of molten steel that was still liquid many days later, *because large quantities of high explosives and nanothermite were detonated inside them; and,*

+ there is no demonstrable evidence of airliner wreckage at the Pentagon, and it is obvious that pre-set explosives, and/or possibly a missile, did the damage; and 80-some tapes from video surveillance cameras surrounding the building have been suppressed by the FBI, *because no airliner hit the Pentagon;* and,

+ debris from Flight 93 was found spread as far as eight miles from the Shanksville crash site, an engine a mile away, and nothing but a hole in the ground at the site *because the plane was hit by a U.S. military air-to-air missile while still at altitude*; and,

+ officials at the highest level of our government ignored many strong warnings of an imminent attack, planned and realized enormous military adventures, and political and other benefits from its occurrence—as a new Pearl Harbor—and were altogether uninterested afterwards in determining what went wrong with U.S. defenses, and who was responsible, *because they were in on it...*

And so forth. In such circumstances, as the late Judi Bari pointed out, "You're either a conspiracy theorist or a coincidence theorist."

All of it was stated in our pleadings—and is spelled out far more cogently in David Ray Griffin's several books on the subject, which have been our guide throughout. Of course, it is shocking and horrifying and scandalous to contemplate this interpretation of the facts, and the mind recoils—often with loathing, invective and unbridled ridicule about conspiracy theories and tinfoil hats, etc, as noted, and reported in this book—from the mere suggestion of such monstrous treason. But, there is an enormous body of evidence, and science, going far beyond this brief sketch, catalogued extensively by Griffin and others and made out at length in our case, which shows clearly— especially when taken with the clearly stated longing of the neocon brain trust for a new Pearl Harbor—that the inside job/false flag theory is far and away the most likely explanation for what happened. And certainly, for all that happened next...

For we all do now undeniably live in the grim new world these defendants and their cohorts brought about, playing on the horror and trauma and fear and rage of 9/11, with the bogus "war on terror" they initiated on 9/12; and we are stuck with that world, and in it, like it or not. It brought a decade and more of war—now expanded to five or six countries, and features a twice-renewed "Patriot" Act, a new Department of "Homeland" Security; torture and "rendition" of prisoners, "targeted" assassinations (i.e, officially sanctioned drone and death squad murders); negation of *habeas corpus*, and Fourth Amendment protections against wiretapping, "black bag" entries and infiltration by provocateurs; pervasive official secrecy and stonewalling; and as we have now learned, universal government surveillance and recording of all electronic communications. And all of it is compounded on enormous corruption and thievery at the highest levels, at huge net loss to the country, and its taxpayers—let alone the Constitution—which has accompanied these misbegotten adventures.

All these things have become enduring facts of our national life, comprehensively affirmed, extended and stoutly defended on all sides by the successor regime of Barack Obama & Co., leaving no reasonable prospect that any of it will be counteracted or rolled back in the foreseeable future—at least without a great upheaval in the way things are now arranged.

On the Law side, I can say after forty-some years prosecuting civil rights cases in the federal courts that we presented a totally solid, perfectly viable federal civil rights complaint. Under any remotely fair and reasonable application of well-worn, elementary rules of civil justice and procedure—scandal and outrage aside—it should have entitled us to full discovery and a jury trial. The chance that the law would be followed, however, in the specific premises of this case, *qua* case—simply to allow us to go forward with Discovery, and begin a long struggle with the Government over disclosures, and testimony—as opposed to it being twisted, manipulated and plain ignored, in order to squash the case, and bar any discovery, was virtually nil in light of the stakes; I guess we knew that.

This was a case where the Rule of Law would be made to take a back seat to the rule of power, and the needs of power in maintaining its rule. A determination that such a case could go forward, like any other, on our concrete, good faith factual allegations showing apparent complicity in the attack, and conspiracy, would have given us access to all the documentary evidence: radar tapes and logs, phone and radio records and read-outs, and other records of every type, and orders, procedures, manuals, personnel records, and all the physical evidence and photos and tapes, et cetera, much of which has yet to be accounted for. We would also have been entitled to conduct sworn interrogations of all the relevant actors, supervisors, commanders, responders, survivors, investigators, evaluators, analysts and experts, in depositions. That is, there would have been a full, real investigation of all the evidence which could possibly help prove the defendants' liability; everything in the open, the way it's done in any civil case, simple as that.

But this would have been a calamity for the rulership of our country, not just the culprits, because, even if no conspiracy could be shown, the bungling and malfeasance was so extreme, and widespread, and the indifference of top-ranked officials to finding out the causes afterwards was so palpable. An honest accounting would have been unbearable, and there was really no chance it would be allowed to happen. When you read what we said in our Complaint that we could show about what happened (and didn't happen), you'll see why. The people in the system, or in charge of the system, absolutely needed to avoid that, and so we were cut off at the pass by then-U.S. District Court Judge Denny Chin's ruling, granting the Government's motion to dismiss.

The warp and woof of his decision was simply that the Very Idea: that such important high officials could commit such heinous high treason, was beyond outrageous, unspeakable, and unacceptable; so much so that he would and did find the lawsuit frivolous on its face, "even assuming the factual allegations in the complaint are true."!

Now, normally, if you come into court with a written complaint in which you reasonably allege the existence or occurrence of facts, involving wrongful conduct by official defendant(s) that caused injury to the plaintiff, and loss of her rights, your assertions of fact are taken as true, by rule, and you now have a working case. There may be lots of reasons it's a loser, and this may be possible to determine simply; but it may not be. If there is a 'material' dispute about the 'operative' facts— what truly happened, who did what to whom, or who is otherwise responsible by act or omission for a loss of rights—the plaintiff is entitled to have a jury decide those issues, in a trial; and to prepare for trial she is allowed Discovery of all relevant documents and records, and information known to the defendants or others, to learn about and prepare the evidence the jury will hear and see. That's the fundament of our civil court system, as refined over generations in Anglo-American law.

But it so happened, ironically, that our then-brand-new Supreme Court had just rolled out one of its new, radically revisionary doctrines of law, on this very subject: the adequacy and properly non-"conclusory" quality of the factual allegations in a complaint in federal court, which will or won't support the plaintiff's right to go forward and have discovery and trial. Just as we were filing our case, they changed the law in a great big way (and no, we don't say that was also part of the conspiracy; however, it surely was part of their own conspiracy, meaning the reactionary cohort on the Court, without a doubt...). An Arab-American man, Iqbal, jailed in the sweeps after 9/11, in which thousands of U.S. Muslims were rounded up and imprisoned as possible terrorists, claimed he was abused and punished in jail for no reason except that he was a Muslim. He sued all the officials involved, including then-U.S. Attorney General John Ashcroft, and Director Robert Mueller of the FBI, as the highest chiefs of the police forces that wronged him. He alleged that, as top commanders, they must have ordained the maltreatment he received, because he was a Muslim, in violation of his rights.

The two high officials appealed to the same 2nd Circuit US Court of Appeals, in New York, where our case was later decided; unsuccessfully. At the time, before 2008, the long-standing law was that if you make a reasonably cogent allegation that someone wronged you, it is taken as true, and they are summoned to come in to the court and answer; admit or defend. They may make short work of your case, but they have to deal with it. It is, or was, "the accepted rule that a complaint should not be dismissed for failure to state a claim unless it appears beyond doubt that the plaintiff can prove no set of facts in support of his (*sic*) claim which would entitle him to relief." The Court had firmly reset this rule in 1957, in *Conley v. Gibson*, 355 U.S. 41 (1957).

Nothing daunted, Ashcroft and Mueller then petitioned the U.S. Supremes, arguing that, instead, such a case should be peremptorily thrown out of court, because Iqbal's claim that they ordained the discriminatory treatment he received was not accompanied by allegations of fact—such as time and place and circumstance, which of course Iqbal had no way of knowing—sufficient to show that such an 'ordainment' actually occurred. Iqbal had relied instead on the logical inference that they must have ordained it, because it happened at the hands of officers under their command. Now, however, rather than make the normal response of denying knowledge, and passing the buck down the chain of command, the two high chiefs said the allegation was "conclusory", and that they should not be required by law to meet it with any defense at all; but rather that it should be dismissed, out of hand.

Out of the blue, the High Court agreed. In another of its already-infamous, unlooked-for radical departures from long-held precedent, it set a broad new rule: a new complaint is to be reviewed by the judge, who is to discount any "conclusory" allegations, and permit the case to go forward only if he or she finds that the remaining assertions of fact will still, in his or her mind, support a "plausible" claim for relief. Needless to say, this is an entirely different, much narrower standard, and a very slippery, hugely subjective, manipulable rule.

The district court here followed only the last part of it—not troubling to analyze, but only to ridicule and mostly ignore our allegations of fact, collectively, as can be seen—saying it granted him unbridled power to throw out any case he would find "implausible". This he promptly did, citing *Ashcroft v. Iqbal*, and dismissing our complaint as "frivolous", period—because he found it outrageous. Tellingly, he first took care to explain away April Gallop's own direct, absolutely non-conclusory, factual assertion—which was absolutely entitled to be taken as true under *Iqbal* or *Conley* or any rule—that she herself had witnessed first-hand (and was alive only because of) precisely, the fact that no airliner crashed into the Pentagon, at that part where her office was, at the time on 9/11 when a large explosion occurred in the area that caused her office walls and ceiling to fall around her. She alleged she was injured and then made her way outside to safety before that section of the building collapsed, and that there was no sign of a crashed airliner—no wreckage, no bodies, no burning fuel—as witness the fact that she had lived to tell about it.

Judge Chin was absolutely prohibited by elementary rules of Due Process from ruling on the validity of this totally concrete averment of fact—usurping the fact-finding function at the start of the case, as he did, and discounting it as evidence, as he did—as if he himself were the Jury. But he did it, bit the bullet for

the team, as it were, where—as with April's claim that she should have been evacuated—it formed a perfectly valid, otherwise absolutely undismissible minimum case, under any rule; he did it brazenly...

This was glaring, but hardly came as a surprise. For the Court to outrightly weigh and dispose of first-hand allegations of fact on a motion to dismiss—summarily quashing a Complaint which contained more than a hundred additional, highly specific, concrete allegations of fact—was a naked misappropriation of his authority, in the service of his outrage, and of the Rulership's urgent need. As can be seen, he dealt with all of it scornfully, but knew he had to dispose of April's first-hand fact claim specifically, so he Just Did It. And he also slyly defused another fundamental, undeniably concrete allegation of fact, by saying we had claimed that the defendants "missed" the many dire warnings they were given of the impending attack. In fact, we had asserted clearly, and crucially, that they ignored the warnings, knowingly. It's one disingenuous thing to ignore 98% of the fact claims, then illicitly, impatiently, decide the one that can't be ignored; it's just plain dishonest to change and stultify another key point by misstating it.

So, if one were playing the federal civil rights case game straight, it was a seriously flawed decision, for the illicit fact judgment, and generally under *Iqbal*, and it left us with a very 'plausible' appeal, on multiple grounds of straight-up law, and open questions about what is or isn't frivolous, and why, now that *Iqbal* is the new pleading rule. I mean—cognitive illusions about dastardly conspiracies aside—any independent lawyer reads the pleadings and says other- wise is crooked too, if not just obtuse, I'd have to say...

In any case, playing it straight, we filed an appeal. Like the complaint, it was chock-full of detailed, concrete allegations of fact, and statements of the inferences, that supported our conspiracy claim. The judges in the Court of Appeals hated it even worse. To make short reference to a story Bill spells out richly within, they roundly, railingly, affirmed the district court decision dismissing the case—even going so far as to specifically regurgitate the corrupt (insulting, demeaning, sexist) rationale for disregarding April's first-hand assertions. Invoking their supposed "inherent power"—where they certainly knew and intended that we would have no real recourse against it—they fined us, $15,000 USD, for fil- ing an appeal they said we should have known was "frivolous" and should not have been filed. Where neither the district court or the Government had said anything at all about sanctions, the higher Court sanctioned us on its own motion, quia volo, for a supposed affront to it alone, i.e. them, the three higher judges.

Of the three, two were among the members of the Court who had an unprecedented public shit-fit over the supposedly lenient sentence given to the distinguished civil rights lawyer, Lynne Stew- art—on her conviction in 2005, for supposedly aiding terrorism by passing a message from jail for her accused terrorist client—and or- dered the trial judge to resentence her, as she struggled with cancer, under prison medicine, at age 70-plus, to at least ten years instead of the 30 months he had prescribed. Two of them were also on the panel of the Court that reversed three jury verdicts in favor of the Attica Brothers, finally won twenty years after the five-day prison- ers' rebellion at Attica in 1971, awarding damages to the class of hundreds of prisoners who had been shot, beaten, stripped naked and tortured when the prison was retaken in an armed assault. They ruled, after 20 years of litigation, that the group of prisoners was not a proper class. In fact, it was a perfect, textbook, plaintiff class, and the ruling was a cynical, opportunistic, essentially crooked, perversion of the law, which just happened to save the State of New York several tens of millions of dollars the prisoners stood to collect based on those verdicts.

The one of the three who was on both those earlier panels was a cousin of George Bush, John Walker, a key hatchet-man on the Court, appointed by the father and also most recently on the panel that suspended the historic New York City injunction against stop and frisk.

In other words, we fell in among fixers. As in the Attica case, this was naked ruling-class power at work, nothing more or less, doing what it felt had to be done to maintain itself. In that respect sort of like the edicts of the defendants et al. to invade countries, start torturing prisoners, etc.; as part of the post-NPH dispensation. It's all part of Bill's story; you can read it here—and in the pleadings and decisions in the Appendix, and at 911justice.org. In the meantime, we wear the sanction as truly a badge of honor, against the crypto-proto-neo-piggo Fascismo which has crept and swilled over the land since the Day of Infamy, and wait in the time left to see if any force will begin to arise from among the People that will stop it.

People can read Bill Veale's whole story here, recounting heroic and definitely ongoing efforts of one aroused citizen, possessed of top-notch professional investigation chops, to put the American Establishment to the test over truth and falsehood about the 9/11 attack, in light of the complete, actual evidence: the known facts, the plain contradictions, the myriad unanswered questions, and the evident cover-up. As with the Kennedy Assassination—surely the most significant parallel to 9/11 as a secret *coup d'état, a*nd its counterpart in pretty much bracketing the period in which the great

American experiment in democratic self-rule appears to have failed definitively—the effort to expose the truth about such a cataclysmic, "game-changing" event is a continuing saga, however mortally discouraging it may be.

In it, one thing is clear: if there is to be any chance at all for the Republic to survive the profound and devastating changes in U.S. policy and action, and governance, for which the New Pearl Harbor on 9/11 opened the way, we'll need a lot more people seeing as clearly, speaking as fearlessly, and working as hard as Bill Veale has in this case. As the Dalai Lama says, it's time to put aside your personal desires and ambitions and help save the World. That's what Bill Veale has done: Live like him.

Dennis Cunningham

1

Life-Changing, In Bold Type

THE GROUND SHOOK. Buildings shook. Cameras shook. My life shook, but not immediately. At that moment on the morning of 9/11/2001, my world-view was cast in some considerable tension with the mainstream of American life. I was, in fact, a dissident with regard to large swathes of American foreign policy. That being said, however, life as a whole, with regard to most of the remainder of my existence was pretty much as Mother said it was; just as it was broadcast on CNN; just as it existed in the minds of everyone I knew; just as it existed in the minds of most of humanity with a few notable exceptions.

It isn't as if I had swallowed even the bulk of the New York Times stories I had read for so many years. My coming to consciousness in the early 80's taught me that very little produced by the mainstream news can be taken without question. So much represents the drum-beat of the world's state departments and security services, with some notable exceptions. There is a concrete agenda

1

that requires daily maintenance for the understanding of events. If reality gets in the way or threatens to, the apparats of information have their ways of making it conform.

Were one to take a step back and ask, "What, in the last 70 years of American history, rules out the possibility that the government of the United States, or agents of it, would, or could, or actually did help to enable the attacks of 9/11?", the correct answer would surely be, "nothing." I mean, there was the assassination of JFK, if nothing else. But though I certainly hope and believe I'd have answered that question correctly had it been asked of me that morning, I was no more inclined to think along those lines than any of my compatriots.

When I learned of the attacks, I was with my 11-year-old daughter. We were running up at the track that morning when a friend told us about it—and then we went home to see buildings fall on TV. I was, for the next three and a half years, an adherent of the Osama Bin Laden version of the story. It is true I thought at the same time that if the U.S. had pursued a marginally more enlightened policy toward Israel and the Middle East, the terrorists might have had a harder time recruiting misguided and pathologically misinformed suicidal zealots. And I said as much to an old friend at the office; he was visibly disturbed by my words. That was my initiation into the nether world of impermissible thought, whose deep penetration and scale was inconceivable for me at that time. In fact, I could no more have understood the power and effect of the idea of impermissible thought at that time than flown one of those airplanes myself.

So now, having immersed myself in impermissible thought for close to a decade, I have come to write about the experience. What you will find here is written with sadness and some considerable anger, but with a lawyer's concern for the precision of truth. I seek to tell this story now because everyone should know what happened. If the knowledge impels action or if it doesn't, I will have done all I thought I could.

The bare bones of what I have done these last 9 years include learning all I could about what happened; writing letters to powerful people in government and the media; engaging in extended email exchanges with a high official of the CIA and a reporter from the New York Times; wearing out the subject with friends and family, giving speeches to small gatherings; and most importantly, filing a lawsuit in federal court accusing Dick Cheney, Donald Rumsfeld, and General Richard Myers of mass murder and treason, and conspiracy to commit those crimes.

My life has been as a trial lawyer, giving speeches for a living. A part of what I have written about this struggle has been in the form of speeches, because at some point, it seemed like running for office made the most sense. What follows here will drift in and out of public address form, depending on what is being covered at the moment, how I thought about it then, and what felt best as the fingers hit the keyboard now as I write this book.

If I had run for office, it would have been to be a United States Senator. I might have begun by saying something like this: My name is Bill Veale. I have decided to run for the U.S. Senate, and I am seeking your support. After a lot of reading, thought, study, and commiseration, I have come to the conclusion that the attacks of 9/11 were, in their essence, an inside job controlled by those at the highest levels of the U.S. government. I have done my best as a private citizen to demand action from my elected representatives and from opinion leaders throughout the country. There has been no satisfactory response; in fact, there has been what I regard as an apathetic silence, almost without exception. Since no one else has seen fit to make the events of 9/11 the focus of a Senatorial campaign, and because Senator Dianne Feinstein's response to my entreaties has demonstrated ignorance, or apathy, or heaven forbid, complicity, I have decided to give the people of the State of California the chance to elect a leader who thinks their government has betrayed them in the most unspeakable manner, and who thinks that the fight to expose and bring to justice all those responsible is more important than anything else that he is capable of.

Any reasonable person would ask why I feel up to such a challenge. The answer proceeds with uncertainty as the forces arrayed against this endeavor are the most formidable ever assembled on the planet. They are more powerful than any one person's ability to conceive of, much less prevail against. The only force equal to that which currently wields power would be an outraged, demanding, and united people. To the extent that my qualifications bear on this struggle, they consist of thirty-one years as a public defender in Contra Costa County, California. I have never been afraid to be a leader when it was necessary; this has been true all of my life in one small way or another. I grew up in the country outside of Baltimore, was fortunate to receive an education at a private high school there, went to college at the University of Virginia, and law school at the University of Maryland. I moved to California in 1973, passed the Bar and began my life's work as a public defender. I was supervising a branch of the office by the age of 33. In 1993 I was chosen to lead the first Alternate Defender Office in the country to handle felony cases. I retired as Chief Assistant Public Defender at the end of March, 2006, having defended many, many cases, including some where the prosecution sought the death penalty. I taught Criminal Trial Practice at Boalt Hall School of Law at the University of California for eleven years.

I have spent my life trying to get people to do things they haven't wanted to do, from prosecutors to judges to juries to colleagues to students to clients, and, of course, my own children. I have been speaking in public for three decades as part of making a living. I have been analyzing evidence and conducting investigations for all that time. And of all of the capacities missing in the U.S. Senate, the ability and the willingness to get to the bottom of things, seems to me the most pronounced. Just to pick one glaring example, the Joint Congressional investigation into the attacks of 9/11, had it been carried out honestly, should have been equal to the task but instead became an impoverished embarrassment. I would hope my tenacity in the face of obstruction and dishonesty would cause me to be relentless in the pursuit of truth. The citizens of this State and nation deserve no less.

I am convinced, after hours and hours of reading and study and analysis, reluctantly, in disbelief, with unnerving convulsions of rethinking, that the single most outrageous atrocity ever committed on American soil took place with the connivance of, if not at the instigation of, some of those in high places in the U.S. Government itself. No one should take my word for such an idea, experienced trial lawyer or not. I ask each person to consider the facts, to do as much studying as they are able to do. The books and the scholarly articles are available to all. I will, however, seek to give a synopsis of the evidence which I have found convincing, which I in turn conveyed to Senator Feinstein seeking some sort of response. None came.

So how does one go about this, exactly? I guess I can do no more than attempt to lead in the direction of water and leave the drinking or the not drinking to you. The 9/11 catastrophe, as the slightest effort will confirm, is the most massive accumulation of information about a five-hour period of time that any of us have ever been given the occasion to think about. There is not a human being on the face of this earth who was not in some way a witness to what took place on 9/11. There are also the worldwide consequences of the crime, two wars, for example, one of which clearly constituted the war crime of aggression, the waging of war without justification. There were also innumerable other breaches of the sovereignty of other nations. Those occurred wherever and whenever a critical combination of forces within the US intelligence community determined, by whatever means they deemed fitting, that an enemy to America, or someone those forces deemed to be such, deserved capture, or torture, or death.

The amount of possible information bearing on this crime is virtually unquantifiable. What has been studied to this day by government and private citizens is vast; what has yet to be done by an honest investigation will be monumental in scope. I cannot produce, here and now, the entirety of the case that establishes the complicity of members of the U.S. Government in this atrocity. What I will do is attempt to provide enough information so that if those hearing or reading fail to look into it in the future, it cannot be blamed on the person responsible for these words. In truth, I do want action, even if it is only to ask an acquaintance if they think that any of this could be true.

So, as they said in church when I was a child, here beginneth the lesson. And I will begin with the actions and words of the principal defendant in the federal lawsuit that I helped file: former Vice President Dick Cheney. When allegations of criminal activity are made, it is fundamental to examine the whereabouts and activities of the defendants around the time of the crime. Of course, there are plenty of instances where the hand of the principal actor is hidden, and there is nothing of interest in his or her actions at the moment of the crime, because all was done before when orders were given to those wielding the weapons. Think of the top-level organized crime figures in this regard. They are unlikely to carry guns, but their participation and guilt is not diminished by this. This may be true of some conspirators in the crime but not all of them.

2

Vice President Dick Cheney, for example

It is actually quite productive to examine the actions of our former vice president at the time of the crime, and not a bit surprising to learn that there is controversy surrounding them. Perhaps you will remember the name of Norman Mineta; he was the only Democrat in the Bush cabinet and was Secretary of Transportation. For many years he was a congressman from San Jose, California, where the local international airport is named after him. When the second airplane hit the South Tower in Manhattan, he was called to the White House. There he met Counter-terrorism Chief Richard Clarke, a holdover from the Clinton Administration. Clarke directed Mineta to the Presidential Emergency Operations

Center (PEOC) where he said he arrived between 9:15 and 9:20 AM. According to Mineta who testified to these facts before the 9/11 Commission, when he arrived in the "bunker," as it is called, Cheney was already there and giving orders.

As a person with my background in the criminal law, I'd like to add that it is of key importance that Cheney claims not to have been in the room at 9:15, or in the next 45 minutes. It is also key to understand that two further statements by him some eight years apart are completely consistent with Mineta's testimony and have him sitting there at the table entirely in charge. We are confronted immediately not just by a conflict of statements between two powerful men, but a conflict of statements by the man accused. Criminal investigators will feel the bells chiming, and the hairs on the backs of their necks stand up. What is it that Mineta observes, that Cheney, at least at one point, says is impossible because he wasn't even in the room?

Mineta testified that Cheney was informed by a young man of the approach of a plane. It became clear that it was the plane that is supposed to have hit the Pentagon. This young man would stick his head in the room and give information to the vice president and then leave. "The plane is fifty miles out", he said. This was repeated as thirty, then ten. When he said the plane was ten miles out, the young man inquired of Cheney, "do the orders still stand?" According to Mineta, Cheney "whipped his neck around and said, 'of course they still stand; have you heard anything to the contrary?'" Within minutes, a small section of the Pentagon was dust, rubble, and destruction.

For the moment, let's leave aside the question of whether or not American Airlines Flight 77 actually hit the suggested target. It is undeniable that it was a principal instrument of the attack on the Pentagon, whether it hit the building or was simply a decoy. What we do know is that a well-renowned public official of high office gave testimony under oath that the vice president was apparently confirming orders concerning the airplane that succeeded in either crashing into or overflying the Pentagon as a part of a terrorist attack.

We do not know, beyond inference, what the orders were, to which the young man referred. It's hard to conceive, however, of more than two possibilities. First, the plane was to be shot down because it was part of the attacks on our country that very morning. Second, that it should be allowed to proceed unmolested---for our defensive forces to stand down, at least with regard to that airplane. Let us look briefly at each of these possibilities. If the orders were to shoot the plane down, an entirely reasonable possibility given the state of crisis that morning, which were not carried out, how would we know it? Well, our nation has a rich and lengthy military history, which includes Boards of Inquiry that are assembled when orders in the military are not followed successfully. It is axiomatic that there is no better way to ensure discipline and learn from mistakes than to investigate failures thoroughly and determine their causes.

No matter how one chooses to look at it, when people started dying in the Pentagon, by simple supposition the most well defended building on the planet, it was because our defenses were not activated. Whether that failure was the result of gross negligence or because they were maliciously sabotaged would have been the question before any theoretical Board of Inquiry. Following the military investigation, the truth is determined, blame is assigned, demotions are ordered, or, in the most extreme instance, prosecutions are initiated. For those who recall the My Lai massacre in Vietnam, then-Colonel Colin Powell was the officer charged with investigating that episode and recommending action to the chain of command. No one familiar with that history should have been optimistic about any "truths" that might be found, to be sure. Powell's investigation into My Lai allowed the world to continue ignorant of

Operation Speedy Express, the US Army directive to kill everything that moved within that designated area. But there was an investigation. That is the way we do it in this country.

Does anyone reading this, or in this world, know who was the investigator, like Colin Powell, for 9/11? ...That's because there wasn't one. Not only were there no Courts Martial for the failures, almost every officer of any significance was later promoted for, or in spite of, their service that day. There will be many who will jump to the conclusion of conspiracy simply because of what I have said so far; I urge you not to do that. This nation needs open minds at this moment, minds that suspend judgment until all that can be known is known.

The second possibility with regard to the orders that Cheney gave or confirmed, is that they were instructions to let the plane fly without opposition, a directive to our forces of defense to stand down. In that case, it's fair to say, Cheney gave or confirmed orders that allowed American Flight 77 to approach or strike the Pentagon. He allowed the crime to be accomplished with the devastation with which we are all familiar.

3

Destruction at the Pentagon and in New York

The devastation that occurred at this nation's military headquarters itself requires some analysis. From what we understand of terrorism the point of the bloodshed is to make the perceived oppressor suffer the gravest possible injury. The attack on the Pentagon demands our attention for a number of reasons, but among them is the fact that it appears that the pilot of the airplane, according to the official FBI account an Egyptian named Hani Hanjour, made a near miraculous maneuver for an airplane of that size.

According to radar analysis, he executed a spiraling dive of some 330 degrees and 7000 ft in 2 1/2 minutes. He managed to pilot that plane in such a way that it hit an area of the building that had been recently reinforced so as to better withstand attack, a section of the building that housed a small fraction of the personnel working elsewhere at the Pentagon, thus resulting in the deaths of just 125 people of whom only one was a flag officer. That puzzling maneuver allowed the airplane to avoid flying into the roof of the building, the largest possible target, thus not killing a much larger part of the 20,000 occupants on that day. And, as well, Hanjour avoided flying into the office of Secretary of Defense Donald Rumsfeld and those of the other very top brass.

Shouldn't everyone be given pause considering these facts? What would it mean to this country if, upon reading these words, about just these facts, one were to take the time to look them up for oneself, to determine if further investigation is warranted? Further investigation will take you to New York, to the destruction of not two but three World Trade Center buildings, to the finding of explosive residue in the dust there, to the work of eminent physicists and architects and engineers, and to elaborate efforts at cover-up, the hallmark of criminal activity on the part of government agents.

I will begin the discussion of the evidence in Manhattan by highlighting the efforts of a group known as Architects and Engineers for 9/11 Truth. Richard Gage is an architect who has designed multi-million-dollar buildings in San Francisco. Today as a result of his efforts, over 2100 architects and engineers have signed on to his call for a new investigation because the physical, architectural, engineering, construction facts of the matter demonstrate that the three buildings brought down that day did not collapse because of fire or airplanes crashing into them or any combination of those conditions. According to these men and women who construct as a profession, for a living, and have made their identities known, thus wagering their good names and reputations on their conclusions, those three buildings were demolished by controlled demolition, as it appeared to Dan Rather, Peter Jennings, and Tom Brokaw who all said, "just like we have all seen so many times on television," when Building 7 collapsed in 6.3 seconds at 5:20 PM that day.

Expert opinions such as these are extremely important, but even more important is the corroboration of those views provided by the work of chemical physicists who have studied samples of dust and debris taken from independent and separate sources at Ground Zero. Again, staking their reputations on their claims, Professor Steven Jones, formerly of Brigham Young University and Neils Harrit of the University of Copenhagen, and others, published their finding of a substance known as nano thermite in the samples of dust and debris. Nano thermite is a substance which, when ignited, can create temperatures as high as 5000 degrees Fahrenheit, enabling it to cut through steel instantaneously. It is a substance ideally suited for controlled demolition, and with its confirmed presence in the ruins becoming an integral part of the evidence in this case, we have what amounts to DNA showing governmental complicity in the attacks. Not only is nano thermite a substance developed in military laboratories and not generally available for civilian use, but that 3rd building to be destroyed that day, Building 7, housed such governmental agencies as the FBI, the CIA, the SEC, and the DIA. The only way you can get into that building is by having your identity confirmed by elaborate governmental security requirements.

Reading this must be hard; harder for some than others, but hard nonetheless. It is impossible for me to know how any particular reader might be reacting to this information, but one sure possibility involves denial. In some cases, it is impressively fortified to the point of impregnability. For those experiencing something along those lines at the moment, the next words won't be read because the book will be closed. If this were a listening experience, the remnants of an old newspaper or racing form may have been retrieved from a pocket, and the listening stopped all together. In any event, there is a battle under way, an active struggle against every idea to which breath is given or image created on the page, defenses formed in the mind, of this beloved country whose agents are here accused of the most unimaginable atrocity and betrayal. I urge you to soldier on with this study to learn about, possibly, the most important piece of evidence that to this moment has been ignored by all who wish it did not exist.

4

Molten Metal

Found in the debris at Ground Zero, particularly in the basements of the Towers and Building 7, was molten metal. Molten metal is metal that has melted due to being subjected to very high temperatures. The importance of this point is that those temperatures are not achieved when you set fire to jet fuel or office furniture, or building materials or any of the other things that were consumed in Manhattan that day. Ordinary office fires or jet fuel fires, so-called hydrocarbon fires, under normal conditions burn to about 1700 degrees Fahrenheit.? Steel, though it may begin to weaken at less than that temperature, will not melt until it reaches 2800 degrees Fahrenheit. The difference in the temperature of a jet fuel fire and the temperature required to melt steel, therefore, is about 1000 degrees Fahrenheit. There is simply no way, consonant with the laws of physics as we know them, to bridge that gap given the conditions of that day without an explosive compound like nano thermite. Simply no way.

Those who labor on behalf of the "Official Story" find in molten metal their most formidable opponent. Those who deign to discuss temperatures at all seem heartened to point out that weak steel can make buildings fall down without the tremendously high temperatures that lead to melting. Even though it misses the point of explaining the phenomenon of molten metal, the fact is fairly stated, and with a click or two at ae911truth.org one can see what such buildings look like when the dust has settled. They look like buildings, mostly as they were built, lying on their side or at some alarming angle. When steel weakens, it does not do so symmetrically and universally throughout the entirety of the structure. Where the weakness first becomes acute, that portion fails, and the rest of the building falls in the direction of the weakness. The building itself remains whole. This is just one of the many important arguments for controlled demolition that the architects and engineers set out to such devastating effect.

But can anyone be sure that there was, in fact, molten metal at Ground Zero? Absolutely, and without question. If there is certainty about anything regarding the attacks of 9/11, and I contend that there is a great deal of certainty, it is the fact of the existence of molten metal at Ground Zero. We know of its existence because of eyewitness testimony by firefighters and rescue workers and inspectors from Johns Hopkins University. We know of its existence because of still, color photographs taken in the days and weeks following the event, showing a range of temperatures from bright orange-hot to pale yellow-really hot. We know of its existence because of videotaped footage of large pieces of steel being lifted from the ruins with the ends dripping as if in a foundry. We know of its existence because of videotaped footage of the 83rd floor of the North Tower just before its demolition where metal is pouring off the side of the building.

Honest defenders of the government's story have no choice, assuming they wish to engage, but to explain the existence of molten metal. If there is evasion or denial, it is an admission that the existence of molten metal conclusively proves the fact of controlled demolition. Let me give an analogy. Suppose a detective investigating a death finds a bullet inside the victim. Now, bullets do not always kill. There are those among us who are living with bullets in their bodies that doctors have decided it was best to let be. It may turn out that such was the case with the hypothetical victim of my analogy, but one thing is for certain: if the detective does not include a paragraph in his report which explains why that bullet had nothing to do with this person's demise, he or she will be fired or back on patrol in a heartbeat.

5

Investigators of 9/11

The crime of 9/11 has had a number of investigators, one of which was the National Institute of Standards and Technology, an agency of the Department of? Commerce. NIST did many things that are scientifically indefensible, but there are two that blare louder than all of the rest: its failure to explain the molten metal found in the rubble at Ground Zero, choosing simply to omit any reference, and thereby deny its existence, and its failure to test that rubble for the presence of explosives, particularly nano thermite.

Another investigator in the case of 9/11 is now the dean of the Rutgers University School of Law. His name is John Farmer, and he was Senior Counsel to the 9/11 Commission. He wrote a book published in 2009 called the Ground Truth, the Untold Story of America Under Attack on 9/11. The story he chose to tell is a penetrating indictment of the military in the aftermath of the event. However, it is also a deft and precisely sculpted effort at misdirection. "Look here, Ladies and Gentlemen, here is the crux of the matter", and while he utters those words, he turns his back on every single piece of evidence that any detective in his or her first year of work would be fixated on.

The book he wrote might be thought of little help to people who want to look at the matter without preconception, because Dean Farmer has no interest in how the Towers fell, the fact that Building 7 fell, in any of the photographs, or stories of firefighters, or seismographic evidence, chemical analysis of samples of dust, or the sworn testimony of Secretary Norman Mineta. He makes no reference to NIST, or any of the work done by that group, some but not all of which was completed by the time his book was published. His interest is not in discussing 9/11, but rather in finding fault with the agents of government who were inaccurate, in fact lying, when they testified before the 9/11 Commission.

And of course, he would be. He was in large measure responsible for the investigation, and it would be quite something for him to disavow his own crowning achievement. I asked him for an interview in 2009 or so, but he declined. Is it possible that he conducted himself with integrity in producing the work for which he is responsible? Probably. Many of us, maybe the majority of people in this country are incapable of conceiving that our leaders were involved in the matters of which I accuse them. It is a bedrock instinct that this nation is good; therefore, our leaders are good; therefore, it is folly to think otherwise, and any evidence of a different view may, and in fact must be disregarded because it is unworthy of thought.

If one of Farmer's staff attorneys walked into his office with pages of statements by firefighters reporting explosions before and as the towers were falling to the ground, he would have used whatever tone came most naturally to him, and told them that this is a serious investigation being conducted here; if the staffer wants to cavort with the fanciful and deranged, they will need to find a new position. That attitude is one that would undoubtedly express itself in meetings within the Commission so staffers would be unlikely to bother to knock on the door in the first place.

Which brings me to an important observation. It's true that adherents of the "Official Story," have much they can cling to, to reinforce their certainty. It is irrefutably true that the 9/11 Truth Movement, in the first instance requires no more than that the fundamental laws of physics be in good working order. Nevertheless, in addition, marching along beside those bulwarks of human understanding, are many quite striking, or unusual facts or sets of circumstance which must have been grounded in reality as well.

The first of these is that a substantial number of people, probably at least 25, maybe many more, had to be willing to join a conspiracy by which they would participate in mass murder and treason. This is a large number; but history shows that powerful forces have never had difficulty recruiting others to do their bidding. Ideology is a compelling force; the proximity to power has a command of its own; money is abundant; and the ability to enforce silence is strong, through verbal or physical intimidation.

The second hard-to-swallow fact is the enormity of the task of preparing the Twin Towers and Building 7 for demolition. This would be a monumental undertaking that involved many people, a lot of time, and tons of explosives, not to mention access to the buildings. It may or may not be important that two of the directors of the companies responsible for security at the World Trade Center, Securacom, or its subsequent identity Stratesec, were Marvin Bush, the president's brother, and a most fascinatingly involved individual with a Bush family name and extensive Bush connections,

Wirt Walker. Whether important or not, it does not seem implausible that paid operatives could infiltrate a security company, put up repair signs and then do the work at night. There are reports of power being shut off the weekend before the attack, and countless instances of elevators closed off to normal use for maintenance or repair. There is no doubt that the demolition was a sophisticated operation that would have taken months to plan and prepare for. Part of that time could have been spent filling the buildings with explosives.

6

Hard to Believe, or Just Hard to Swallow?

It is with some significant fear and reluctance that I address the next item on the chart of the farfetched. I have been told that it is a matter that has the capacity to delegitimize everything else that I may say. The idea is that the phenomenon to be discussed is so outside of the common experience that its consideration must be some sort of delusion. Other reactions are mild by comparison, underscoring the wide variety of human experience which sculpts our view of reality. The reader thus prepared, the issue involves the possibility of faked telephone calls, with the use of what is called voice-morphing technology. Is everyone with me? To be maybe a little bit more helpful, the essential premise is that on some level, the Official Story needed to be sold. Our lives and our minds are controlled by the narrative that successfully captures the territory. The narrative is most always made up of stories to which the average person can relate. Apparently, the conspirators felt that telling the tale through phone calls by the victims would be an effective way to control the psychological terrain.

Many people around the world went to the movie, United 93. There depicted larger than life was the hijacking of the fourth plane that supposedly crashed in Pennsylvania. Though most central to the action were seatback airphones with which United 93 was indisputably equipped, also shown were passengers, calling loved ones on cellphones. The overwhelming force of the evidence is that such calls were a technological impossibility in 2001. Experiments done by a scholar in Canada and a Japanese television station prove that you might be able to have a conversation of some undetermined length up to about 6000 ft, maybe 8000, using the phones and the technology available in 2001. But higher than that, nothing worked at all. The speed of the planes appears to be inconsistent with the required handshakes between cell towers. In addition, the amount of insulation in the planes prohibits the signal from being properly relayed.

The point is that cellphones, a large part of the lore of 9/11 thanks to Hollywood and books and articles by media and survivors, with recipients of calls like Deena Burnett from her husband, Tom, actually remembering seeing her husband's cell number on her caller ID, cannot bear the scrutiny of historical investigation. It appears there is something wrong there. But even when the focus moves to the seatback airphones, the questions do not disappear. There is, for another example, Todd Beamer. He, in the movie and in all of the newspapers, organized the heroic storming of the cockpit with the now iconic exhortation "Let's Roll!" that foiled the hijackers' strategy and plunged the plane into the ground, according to the Official Story. Why would that Todd Beamer decline to have his call to a GTE airphone operator--- that stayed connected for an inordinately long period of time to the shock of the operator whose knowledge of disconnections that morning was fresh and well-stocked--- transferred so that he could talk to his wife? Because she was pregnant, and he didn't want to upset her? Questions upon questions refuse to relent. But in spite of them, surely, government defenders assert, the various wives and mothers and operators cannot have been part of the plot. I certainly doubt it, but the reason I am able to feel that way, with a modicum of comfort, is because of the existence of voice-morphing technology, and another frightening possibility that I will address shortly.

To the extent that this seems crazy to some readers, it is simply due to unfamiliarity with the subject matter. The majority of people have spent no time whatever considering the ways and means of advanced technology that might be used in a battlefield or intelligence context. Our defense research and development budget is pretty much all of the evidence anyone needs for the fact that a segment of the population spends most of their time thinking about nothing else. Voice-morphing is the product of a great deal of very highly paid thought.

It is the technological ability to hijack a person's voice and use it by way of a computer program, to communicate with the unknowing receiver of the call. To give you an idea of the technology, its inventors, in a demonstration to military officials, were able to put treasonous words in the mouth of a general who was at that moment sitting at the table in the room.

Virtually every person who thought they received a cellphone call from any of those hijacked jets was the victim of some sort of fraud. How do we know that? First and foremost, as set out above, because cellphone technology in 2001 did not permit calls above

6000 feet in altitude. The bulk of the calls we know about would have taken place when the planes were higher than 30,000 feet. Secondly, because the FBI says so.

You may recall the story of Barbara Olson, the wife of the Solicitor-General of the U.S. and a CNN television news personality. According to her husband, she was aboard American Flight 77, the plane said to have crashed into the Pentagon. Again, according to her husband, she called him twice from the airplane on her cellphone and told him of the hijacking by "Middle Eastern men". The calls, according to Ted Olson, lasted a minute and then two or three minutes. This was a crucial element of the story first conveyed to the world, of the terrorist plot that killed 3000 people and rearranged each of our lives forever.

Now it is not unimportant that as Solicitor General Olson told his tale, he told it a number of different ways, including assertions that they were seatback airphone calls, and not cell phone calls, and then that he simply didn't know which they were. Which may be entirely reasonable under the circumstances. Could it actually have been a seatback airphone call? Everyone concedes that American Airlines had decided to discontinue seatback phone service on their 757's before 9/11, and since the disconnection, according to at least one American Airlines maintenance mechanic, was a simple matter taking no more than a half an hour, it seems there was no seatback airphone service available to Ms. Olson.

But, because nothing in this case is simple or uncontroversial, some investigators have asserted that some of the fleet of 757's had not yet undergone the process of decommissioning those phones by 9/11. Authors Summers and Swan, in *The Eleventh Day*, state in footnote 114 on page 476 that, "...analysis indicates that such phones were still in use on some flights as late as March 2002." Analysis by whom, of what, we are not told. Where, for example, did the March

2002 date come from? Did someone find a 757 where the airphones still worked at that time? Not that anyone has written about. If they did, does that establish that Flight 77's airphones were operational? The answer is "no." In addition it is important to note that the discontinuance of the service has been affirmed by at least one pilot and a number of flight attendants. But, the last known word from an American Airlines official on the subject is that records of the conversion or disconnection have not been found, so it is assumed not to have happened. Maybe we will learn more considering this controversy in the future, or maybe we won't.

But I have digressed. The necessity to be wary under circumstances such as these is not the point presently being addressed. Under consideration now is the reality of any of these phone calls, and with regard to that the FBI was, at one time, quite clear. Which is to say that no word from that agency, for a period of three years, undercut in the slightest the widespread knowledge that it was cellphone communications that gave us the story, the inside-with-the-harrowing-details story of the hijackings.

Since then, there have been some corrections. For example, that agency has established through phone records that no cellphone call by Barbara Olson to her husband was ever connected. There was no conversation from her phone to his, or vice versa. The FBI phone records, admitted into evidence at the trial of Zacarias Moussaoui, the so-called twentieth hijacker, document only one call shown in the record as lasting zero seconds, thus forever giving the lie to Ted Olson's wrenching rendition of events. If only the matter could be anywhere near that simple.

There do appear to have been calls to the Justice Department by someone claiming to be Barbara Olson. These are attested to by individuals who received them at Ted Olson's office. If the 757 in question still had undisconnected seatback airphones, by no means even a probability at this point, it is theoretically possible that those calls actually came from Ms. Olson. As set forth above, there are good reasons to question that conclusion. And then there is the further question of what difference does it make. Does any of this make Ted Olson a complicit member of the conspiracy? Given his inconsistent reporting surrounding extremely important events that played such a pivotal role in the crime, he may properly be a suspect, but there is no reason to adopt the interpretation that he is a participant in the crime when we know of voice-morphing technology, by which conversations between husband and wife could have been arranged by computer without Mrs. Olson's participation and without Mr. Olson's knowledge.

7

Those Phone Calls, A Frightening Possibility

Some may question the ability of anyone to accurately dupli-cate the way husbands and wives talk to each other; may think that the recipient of the call would know or feel that something was not right. There are two possibilities. The first is that receivers of these calls had no reason to be wary since the call itself established a frightening circumstance that would cause one to naturally make al-lowances. The second response draws us to the record of the calls themselves. One of note is Mark Bingham's call to his mother. He is recorded as saying, "Mom, it's Mark Bingham." How many of us have used our last name when calling our mother? The whole cat-alogue of calls from the planes presents problem or peculiarity af-ter problem or peculiarity. According to phone records, at least two calls lasted until well after the planes from which they were made had crashed. The landscape, actual and otherwise, is strewn with examples like this where heads are scratched and shook, foreheads are creased with incomprehension, and answers dissolve as soon as they take form. Every side of this controversy must think and re-think, stay with it all until the matter comes to rest. Which requires that we summon the necessary hard bark and grit to think about another possibility that involves the last moments of our once-air-borne passenger victims.

Back in 1962, the Joint Chiefs recommended to President Kennedy that certain false flag maneuvers be undertaken to justify an invasion of Cuba. It was known as Operation North-woods. Proposed in the plan were terrorist activities in the US that would be blamed on Castro in addition to, among other things, an elaborate plane hijacking that would have included the substitution of a drone aircraft in place of the actual passenger aircraft suppos-edly being hijacked, where the replaced aircraft would land with its passengers. What would then happen to them is not discussed in the retrieved documents that demonstrate the fact of the existence of the proposal.

If one is to suppose that 9/11 included a similar scenario, we must consider what may have happened once those passengers' planes reached the ground. We have all seen enough harrowing products of television and moviemaker's imaginations to conjure at least parts of this dark picture. Lines of passengers herded off a plane into secure rooms at some air force base? Directions given at gun point to frightened husbands or wives to read from some script into their cellphones? Words spoken, many true, bound up in un-certainty for their next hours or days? Could those passengers sim-ply have been coerced, at gunpoint or by some other compelling device, to make the calls that were impossible at 30,000 feet with cellphones that worked just fine in some hangar someplace on the ground?

Is there some reason to give these possibilities serious consideration? Other than our imaginations on which they can be comfortably balanced, there is actually some evidence to point to, but the first I will mention is a long way from plain, and requires a certain, not insignificant amount of suggestion. By writing what I do here, I will befoul any subsequent attempts by readers interested in forming their own opinion, so for those people, investigate CeeCee Lyles's phone message to her husband and skip over the next paragraph. You might even want to have the next page or so read to you so that your eyes don't capture the words in question by mistake.

To find this intriguing nugget requires a very close and determined listening to the tape of a phone message left on an answering machine by a flight attendant named CeeCee Lyles. She is leaving the message for her husband. She appears to be using her cellphone. She gives him the information that there has been a hijacking, and expresses her love and her uncertainty for what will happen next. The message appears to end, but then there is a kind of static that might come from the manipulation of a headset, or the scraping of the surface of a microphone. Then, something appears to be spoken, maybe in a whisper. The more I listen, the clearer it is that the words she speaks are "it's a frame." But that is the problem with suggestion. Once the idea is implanted, it is irradicable, and from that moment on, everything else serves merely to strengthen the conclusion.

The Todd Beamer call, to which reference was made previously, is also supportive of the duress hypothesis. In particular, an analysis of the chronology of the event as set out in the 9/11 Commission Report when compared to the substance of the conversation Beamer has with the GTE operator, Lisa Jefferson, where he ultimately says, "let's roll," makes no sense. According to government documents, Flight 93 was hijacked at 9:28 AM. That is the time when the hijackers took control of the plane. According to the GTE phone logs, however, Beamer is describing three men in red bandannas who have taken command of the passenger compartment of the aircraft, but who have not yet stormed the cockpit to get control of the plane. The problem arises with the time of Beamer's call which begins at 9:43 AM, and which lasts for 7 minutes before the cockpit assault by the hijackers. Such discrepancies are consistent with an attempt to craft a fake scenario using the passengers as tools. The producers of the false story who held the guns, wrote the scripts, and gave the orders either didn't consider the problem of the chronology, or didn't care that the inconsistency would be discovered. Finally, Ms. Jefferson is very clear that the phone line never went dead, but rather stayed simply silent for over an hour, a seeming impossibility if the the call took place on an airplane that was buried in a small mound of dirt in Shanksville, Pennsylvania. There simply seems to be no end to the problems and questions, every one of which should be chased to conclusion.

8

Back to Farmer

But that is what good investigators do. Which brings us back at long last to John Farmer. I have suggested that it may be possible for even a highly-trained, accomplished, and experienced lawyer and investigator to be so bound by their own politics, worldview and philosophy that they are incapable of processing information that falls outside of those limits. It's theoretically possible, but in this case, why adopt a charitable view? John Farmer, to have produced such a work, would have had to consciously turn off his reasoning capacity and thus be complicit, enabling, in fact on a very real level, orchestrating, the cover-up.

The Commission to which he was senior counsel was created because of innumerable questions raised by women known as the "Jersey Girls", wives of victims of the attacks on the World Trade Center. Their efforts focused on the many failures of the nation's defenses and the apparent refusal of the government to address these simple questions honestly. Why weren't the fighters scrambled in time? That question itself led to all kinds of falsehoods and misdirection by the military, many of which are revealed in Farmer's book. These are, in the multiple cases where oaths were taken, instances of perjury for which the country has not one prosecution to show.

If he took his duty seriously, he would not sleep until all of the questions were answered. Why in the world, if there are reasonable explanations, wouldn't an investigator with a large budget and enormous power simply keep asking questions and demanding answers until there was clarity? The problems are not hard to articulate or the information hard to locate. Google may not have been a grandfather yet, but it took about two clicks before all of the issues were staring you straight in the face. At the very least it was incumbent upon Farmer to devote some law clerk hours to a survey of the case in opposition. Close to ten books were on the shelves even at the early stages of his investigation, one of which would have been David Ray Griffin's book, *"The New Pearl Harbor"*. Can anyone read that book cover to cover and be without reasonable question concerning governmental complicity? One of the first things you learn is that steel frame buildings have never before in the history of construction collapsed because of fire. Yet three such structures supposedly collapsed because of fire in the same place and on the same day. And one can find no comfort in the fact that enormous infernos have enveloped other imposing steel-framed buildings, in the last decade, fires that dwarf those connected to the destruction in Manhattan on 9/11, yet those buildings stand to this day. It must be recalled that when the planes hit the Towers, the buildings did not budge. And that is as you would expect. As explained by Richard Gage and his fellow Architects and Engineers for 9/11 Truth, and also the actual architect responsible for their creation, those buildings were designed with the possibility that at some point in their lifetimes, a large plane would fly into them, and that impact would have to be withstood.

I maintain that there are two statements that no honest investigator could become aware of without demanding resolution. The first, three buildings collapse because of fire when it has never happened before, ever, and second, the Pentagon was successfully attacked, and no one was fired. At the time the 9/11 Commission investigation began, as John Farmer was beginning his work, both of those statements had been made. Only intentional efforts to cover up the truth, or willful ignorance amounting to criminal complicity can explain the failure to resolve the questions raised by those statements.

I have omitted libraries worth of information. The scholarship that has been spawned by this atrocity has been prodigious and is a tribute to the human instinct that demands justice. A great many people in this country and around the world have learned from history to understand that whatever exceptionalism to which the citizens of this country would like to lay claim, it does not include immunity from the attraction of evil persons to power and the ability of those powerful people, with enormous amounts of money, to subvert our democratic process with devastating effect.

There is a daunting mass of additional circumstantial evidence that is consistent with the theory that persons at the highest levels of government were responsible for what took place on September 11, 2001. The official story includes multiple acts of incomprehensible and unusual negligence all serving the same function, to allow the attacks to be successful. At some point, an observer must conclude that such coincidental negligence, in fact, isn't coincidental.

I was actually thinking about closing the book on this book without making mention of the following pieces of evidence. I'm not entirely sure why, but it was probably fear of some variety or other, at least in part. You, the reader, will be able to gather its hue. The story goes like this. As the two towers in lower Manhattan were being crashed into by airplanes flying at improbable speeds and in improbable ways, raising questions about whether they were actually at that time being operated by human beings inside the planes, or machines and human beings some place else, it seems there were paid watchers on the ground. In Hoboken.

A woman who lived near Liberty State Park, where five young men were carrying out their surveillance, which included videotaping capability, was struck by their excited high-fives of celebration as the buildings were hit and later when they were nothing but rubble. Calls to 911 led to the arrest of the five in a white van belonging to a moving company called Urban Moving Systems whose owner, Dominick Suter, left town in such a hurry that some furniture never made it beyond the confines of a storage facility. The five spent 71 days in a New Jersey jail before their deportation.

That's right; there were no charges; they were simply deported. Where to? Israel,...the native country of Mr. Suter as well....where a couple of them appeared on a tv talk show to deny that they were happy on the morning of the attack and to say, "[T]he fact of the matter is we are coming from a country that experiences terror daily. Our purpose was to document the event." Turns out they worked for the Mossad.

We will all make of this what we will, but it is surely a fact that you can't pretend to have a good picture of this moment in history if it does not include a recounting of the "Dancing Israelis" as they are known in the ether. A couple more clicks and other startling facts will appear that may be real and may not be. You won't find them in these pages because of the uncertainty. Since these questions were left to our emotionally and psychologically handicapped servants of truth in the media and prosecutors' offices across the land, we will likely never know.

The following three paragraphs should be conceived of as the end of a speech. They were written that way, but the speech has yet to be given.

Some of those who hear me now may be unable to accept what an analysis of the physical evidence in this case demands because of a need to avoid the conclusion that it is a tyranny under which we live, and nothing can be done to change that fact. It is to these people I seek to offer hope. Once we grasp the nature of our condition, and at the same time recognize that there is action that can be taken to improve it, the veil is lifted from our eyes, and the overwhelming and disheartening truth can be seen.

It is my opinion that we do indeed live in a time of increasing tyranny, where the most powerful nation in the world has relinquished its hold, or maybe the pretense of it, on republican government. The forces in power rule with complete control over virtually every aspect of our existence. It has now become time for the citizens of this country to treat their predicament as other patriots at other times, in this and other countries treated theirs, with courage and complete and undeniable determination.

If we as a people must stand before tanks, it is our children who will reap the benefits and our memory that will provide strength for whatever struggles they may encounter. I do not seek martyrdom or anything like it. It is my belief that once we come together and our unity has been demonstrated, the democratic process that has served us for so long will reassert itself, and those currently in power will be cast out, and we will be a better and stronger nation for it.

9

The Beginnings of the Struggle

I am going to leave my friends and family out of this book pretty much. Some have been torches of brilliant insight and encouragement; some have been discouraging, some are friends no more. That is a sad, sad thing to think about, and it has made me all the more thorough in my analysis. If there is a way that I could extract myself from this intellectual and social bog, I would like to do it. There are a few friends who have confronted me head-on with attempts at answers to my questions and arguments. These have rendered a service of inestimable worth. I can withstand a lot, but there is a limit, and had any of these stalwarts approached my tipping point of certainty, I would have caved in and gone home long ago.

It is a fact of great importance that the human mind is capable of only so much. No one would seriously attempt to talk another out of their religious beliefs. It isn't their mind that is at work there, it is their heart. This is the phenomenon that stands in my way. American exceptionalism has become, for a great number of Americans, a religious belief. What is taught in school has only the vaguest resemblance to historical fact in a multitude of important instances, and the idea that ours is a great and good nation incapable of significant evil is simply taken for granted. That is a substantial part of the problem that has caused the field of journalism to fail so totally when it comes to 9/11. It was intriguing and disappointing to learn how wide and deep and all-encompassing that failure was...and continues to be.

Within the first two years after 9/11, while reading the indomitable and brilliant Greg Palast and appreciating his insights and his however-obtained, inside knowledge, I was forced to consider the possibility that the Bush Administration had a hand in the attacks. Even as he raised the issue, Palast assured his readers that he had uncovered no such thing. His report that the connections between Bush and the Saudis were vast and suggestive and deserved scrutiny, not to mention that there were specific orders to the FBI to steer clear, were suspicious to say the least. One would have thought that official directives to not investigate, in the hands of an investigative reporter, would have been an intoxicating catnip that would have driven Palast wild. That he would not have rested until final, fulfilling, unmistakable truth had been dug up and exposed, but I have seen no evidence of interest on the part of Palast, in spite of personal efforts to provoke him at a book-signing in San Francisco in 2006 or so, and other email attempts in following years, interest in discovering this particular truth, that is, if truth it was.

And truth it was. But it was still years away for me. Even after running into an Inside Job rally on the streets of San Francisco which prompted me to search the Internet, a search that produced impassioned declarations that no 757 had hit the Pentagon. I laughed out loud. Three and a half years after the attacks, in March, 2005, I stopped by a colleague's office and sat down to discuss the question of whether or not Bush had cheated in the presidential debates by wearing a wire by which he could be fed someone else's, Karl Rove's presumably, responses to John Kerry's insights or questions. My colleague was not much interested in those manipulations, and he asked, "have you seen this?" as the book literally slid across the desk and into my lap. It was entitled the "New Pearl Harbor", and it was by David Ray Griffin. I moaned paternalistically as I caught from the cover the point of the book. Since then, I have devoured what for me would be considered a library, handicapped by an inability to read faster than I can talk, not to mention a regular job to finish and retire from, a few other odd cases to handle, a family to tend to and enjoy, some furniture to build, and a golf game that needed serious work. The truth announced itself, haltingly at first, but with increasing strength as the official mouthpieces were destroyed singly or in bulk by Professor Griffin. The truth is devastating, but only if one allows oneself access to it. I was attracted to the struggle, and there learned the first of quite a few startling revelations: Not everyone else thought as I did, felt as I did, reacted as I did.

Most everybody else wanted nothing to do with the subject, a fact I learned probably the hardest way for all concerned. I shipped off books to friends and family, expecting thanks and interest. The kindest learned, as one said, "to compartmentalize." I was treated in a way that involved simply no mention of the subject that for me was vital, and took almost all of my time. A few close friends just soldiered on, and learned to live with it. They provided, occasionally, some of the most important insights, and confirmation that the terrain I was trying to traverse was solid and undeniable. No, that was never a problem, the absence of evidence. Having someone sit still to hear it and make themselves available and getting a response, that was and continues to be, the problem.

10

His Name Is Norman Mineta

The most formidable tool of the perpetrators, and their enablers whose job it is to write our history, was and continues to be the ability to ignore critics and evidence. It's almost funny to consider the people who have ignored my efforts and those of the 9/11 Truth Movement. It is perplexing, in fact astounding, that intelligent people can look the other way. Take the example of Norman Mineta.

As a trial lawyer, if one has a choice of witnesses, it's best to pick the one with the airport named after him. If he can be a winner of the Presidential Medal of Freedom and a cabinet secretary too, so much the better. The Norman Mineta International Airport in San Jose, California is named after Norman Mineta, the only Democrat in the Bush cabinet. On 9/11 he was the Secretary of Transportation, and given the fact that it was decided that all aircraft in the

American skies, some 4000 planes, had to be landed immediately, and his department performed this feat flawlessly, he was destined to play an important role. His importance as a witness cannot be over-emphasized. When we learn of the conversation he saw and heard in the Presidential Emergency Operations Center between Cheney and his aide, we are transfixed, unlike the 9/11 Commission, which pretended it didn't occur.

"The plane is 50 miles out," the young man said. Sometimes our brains race ahead, and we are wrong. Sometimes they race ahead and are dead on the money. The plane heading for the Pentagon? Cheney is in a position to do something about the plane heading for the Pentagon? In fact, Secretary Mineta made it quite clear what plane it was. It was American Airlines Flight 77. The one that the official story has flying into the nation's military headquarters. "The plane is 30 miles out," the young man said the second time he opened the door speaking to Cheney. What in the name of all that is sacred? There is actually testimony of the perpetrators committing the crime? "The plane is 10 miles out, sir; do the orders still stand?" And we are going to learn about discussions among the participants concerning the clarity of the orders, the certainty of the directors?? Yes, yes. But we will not know the name of the young man standing at the door no matter how much interest anyone might have about this pivotal moment in the history of the world.

Mineta told the panel, that Vice President Cheney, hearing these words by the young man at the door, "whipped his neck around," and then said, "of course they still stand, have you heard anything to the contrary?" So, Cheney, if not by the words of the United States Constitution, by executive order of the President, was directing the defense of the nation in the midst of attack, and he had the...whatever it takes... to dress down a subordinate in the climax of crisis. A few minutes later, word came of the destruction at the Pentagon.

Why isn't every single person of sound mind brought up short, staggered, by testimony like that? What orders? To shoot the plane down? To let it go? What orders? How can we do without the answers to those questions? Startlingly, as I said above, the 9/11 Commission chose not to mention Secretary Mineta's testimony at all. Think about that for a minute. Later some would refer to the testimony as an account of the actions and words of the prime suspect in the crime at the time of the crime, and absolutely indisputably, concerning the crime, specifically an Instrumentality of the crime, by an eye-witness who, by the way, happened to be a cabinet secretary, who also had an airport named after him, and won the Presidential Medal of Freedom. It is impossible for me to fathom how any person of integrity and responsibility could decide that was of no importance.

Cheney apparently even denied that he was in the room at the time. Does this make it more important that a person of Mineta's rank disagreed, or less important? Where do members of the Commission put this information in their minds? How does one live, much less sleep with such knowledge? Norman Mineta, and whatever he had witnessed or had to say, was written out of history, not included in the best-selling book concerning the day, or in the other work that included highlights in the testimony of important witnesses before the 9/11 Commission, called *The 9/11 Investigations: Staff Reports of the 9/11 Commission : Excerpts from the House-Senate Joint Inquiry Report on 9/11 : Testimony from fourteen Key Witnesses, Including* (PublicAffairs Reports). Norman Mineta does not qualify as a key witness. Author Steven Strasser, could you please have a seat here. We have a few questions. No, that is false and misleading. We have several days of interrogation to subject you to in an effort to learn how you might have honestly arrived at the conclusion that the world had no need of the knowledge of what a former secretary of transportation had to say about Vice President Cheney's actions on this disastrous day.

Even though it is true that I have arrived at a conclusion as to ground truth with regard to those moments in the PEOC, in gross terms, I do not suggest that everyone must stand in the same place. I have invested far more time and energy to the comprehension of these events than could be justly expected of anyone but a serious combatant in the fight. The question for this instant is how can the battle be honestly waged when the Record has been manipulated, or expunged, with the arrogance and disdain on view in such a work as Mr. Strasser's?

And all of that is not to say that some upholders of the government line, Popular Mechanics Magazine, for example, have not made some effort to escort Secretary Mineta not so politely from the stage. Those efforts, broadly, adopt the idea that the poor old gentleman was mistaken. He mistook a very real conversation in the PEOC between Cheney and his aide sometime after 10 AM that actually referred to United Flight 93 for one involving American 77. Of course, the numbers that the aide relayed describing the distance traveled by the airplane, 50, 30, and 10, somehow became 80 and 50, in one telling. And, of course, none of the alternative explanation lives easily with Mineta's account, aided by clarifying questions from Chairman Hamilton as to which plane was under discussion, that has the Pentagon exploding shortly after the final recited mileage. But, most importantly, those interested in truth have to ask one particular question of the non-existent witness called before the People's tribunal to explain how the Official Story stands up to scrutiny.

And that question is, what target was 80 or 50 miles away from Shanksville, Pennsylvania, or some other point on a map even farther away from Washington, D.C.? After all, we are trying to identify which airplane Mineta could have been talking about.

The flight distance from Shanksville to Washington is...127 miles. Khalid Sheik Mohammed, confessed mastermind of the attacks, after 183 waterboarding, otherwise known as torture, sessions, claimed that the debate was between the White House and the Capitol as target for Flight 93. Therefore, this alternative version simply makes no sense. No one would be documenting the progress of an enemy aircraft to nowhere. Only to a target. Washington, D.C. was the target. Therefore, the only airplane meshing with the distances is Flight 77 or the one approaching the Pentagon, not Flight 93 that was flying around Pennsylvania. Mineta's rendition is consistent with reason and all the known facts. The alternative is...not. Is everyone with me here?

How much explanation is too much? Given how comfortably the world has averted its eyes for all this time, maybe I will be forgiven my excessive efforts to have the reader "get it". I discuss more reasons for rejecting any Cheney account in later chapters, but I insist that this be clear. Mineta's detractors make their attack in the dark without night-vision goggles, from a promontory looking out in the wrong direction, and with weapons categorically unequal to the task. And I maintain that those so-far-victorious efforts, in spite of their logical failure, deserve an inference of guilt. In other words, when you go as far as the opposition has gone, Farmer, Strasser, the 9/11 Commission, all of them, one is entitled to conclude that there is, not incompetence, but a cover-up afoot, and it is up to those in-it-up-to-their-eyeballs individuals to prove their innocence.

11

The New York Times Investigates?

Jim Dwyer seems a nice enough fellow. He's a reporter for the New York Times, a Pulitzer Prize-winning reporter, and the author of two books concerning the World Trade Center, one about the bombing in 1993, and the other about 9/11. He was down among the dust and debris interviewing witnesses and survivors. An article of his led me to pick up the phone in the spring of 2006, and he was polite and responsive to my questions. A series of mostly email exchanges began about why I saw things my way and he saw things his way. The exchange is contained in Appendix G.

That exchange had a profound effect on my attitude toward the quest for justice. In the beginning I viewed the events as a political problem that would need a political solution before any judicial action was possible. The books were there. The American people simply needed to read them, demand justice, prodded by a late-arriving but usually reliable cadre of journalists. What could be easier, call them up, ask questions, demand answers. I set it out in essay form, on the Internet, specifically at vealetruth.com. There I discussed the case and the personalities I had encountered and tried to present an analysis that reasonable people could accept. Dwyer and Professor David Ray Griffin got a lot of space.

Griffin, whose book I referred to previously, is a well-respected, now (2010 or so) 74-year-old, retired Theology professor from a school of note who looks that part, and when you see him at the podium, sounds and acts that part. Now no one, of course, should end a consideration of matters as heart-stopping as whether or not the highest officials of US government sacrificed three thousand of its own citizens for power-political reasons with what he looks or sounds like, or even with his credentials, but it seems now, and seemed then reasonable to begin a study based on his recommendation.

Griffin has his look and manner going for him, and he is a recognized scholar, but there is a bit more to be considered before we take the first steps on this journey. For example, he has managed to get twelve books published on this subject, not to mention the publishing he has done as a theologian, another twenty-four books to his credit. Therefore, his history probably does not include disabling mental instability. Since the 9/11 Truth Movement is sometimes accused of lunacy, this characteristic of one of its prophets appears relevant. There is Griffin's own careful circumspection in the first pages of *"The New Pearl Harbor"* in which he plants himself among the majority of American citizens who begin the inquiry disposed toward disbelief. Certainly, this is entirely appropriate given the horror of the accusation.

The book itself is both powerful and disquieting. It contains facts that are disregarded by some for personal reasons or political predisposition and accepted without question by others out of similar impulse. The evidence set out in Griffin's book falls into two categories: first, the matters of science and physics; second, the acts of human beings that contributed to the success of the attacks. ?Everyone has a different understanding of, or tolerance for, proofs that depend on physical evidence. Since many consider physical evidence, the physical world and its properties, the concrete boundary of the possible, I consider this, maybe the most important part of the case. The Truth Movement asserts, relying upon photograph after photograph and video after video, all mercilessly proclaiming to unpoisoned senses, what simply cannot be said in polite company, that the Towers of the World Trade Center collapsed because they were blown up and not because of fire started by crashing airplanes. But senses, poisoned or otherwise, to the side, we are able to know that now-unassailable fact because of that molten steel and nano thermite, to which I referred previously, found in the rubble of all three buildings destroyed that day.

Recalling the reason molten metal has such probative force, because jet fuel fires do not burn hot enough to melt steel and thereby produce molten metal, let us revert to the analogy of the murder case. If the remains of the building (the corpse) contain molten metal (a bullet), some cause OTHER THAN JET FUEL FIRE (murder by gunfire) must be considered. What are the other possible explanations for the existence of molten metal in the rubble?

It is certainly true that external conditions can affect the temperatures achieved by jet fuel fires, even to the point of melting steel, but the amount of oxygen being applied to the blaze must be substantially increased. In the absence of any sort of claim that unusually strong winds enabled the fires to burn much hotter than would be expected, that particular explanation may be put aside.

Griffin and the physicists upon whom he relies say that the existence of molten metal proves the use of explosives like thermite which can cut through steel instantaneously. A series of simple questions require answers: 1. Are Griffin and others right when they state that steel melts at temperatures higher than those attendant a jet fuel fire? 2. Is there some other explanation for the existence of molten metal in the rubble? 3. Was there, in fact, molten metal in the rubble? There are several other "physics" arguments that appear in Griffin's work, that can be subjected to a similar analysis, but the molten metal and the existence of nano thermite are the most compelling.

On the other hand, the instances of human actions that contributed to the success of the attacks are so many that they draw our rapt attention by their numbers if nothing else. In fact, the unbelievable coincidence of so many occasions of supposed human negligence, to some, is the most powerful argument for conspiracy. Along these lines of coincidence, it is well-known that the U.S. has a procedure it employs when airplanes do what is unexpected in or around its airspace. Jet fighters are scrambled; the errant aircraft is located; and choices are made. These choices take into consideration the safety of the pilot, the passengers, and inhabitants of potential crash sites. In the nine months from September 2000 to June 2001 military jets were scrambled 67 times, mostly without real need, but rather out of caution. Air traffic controllers have the responsibility to take the necessary steps to ensure aircraft safety. If called on, military forces must intercept the threat and deal with it.

The number of times that someone failed in their appointed duty on September 11th is quite stunning according to Griffin. The number is so stunning, in fact, that, as suggested above, some people don't need to hear any more. For those individuals, it is simply ludicrous to imagine so many failures by highly skilled, highly trained operatives all on the same occasion and, most importantly, all serving the same purpose. Some say, "you mean to tell me that all of those people just happened to be negligent at the very same time, in some instances the very same way, and their negligence just happened to be required in order for the attacks to achieve the success they did? Come on."

Not to be dismissed is the contending alternative, some suggest, equally-or-harder-to-believe insinuation, that all of these failures were planned as part and parcel of the conspiracy yet all these years later we have no whistleblowers confessing their complicity. I am one that believes confessing to being part of a traitorous, mass murderous conspiracy is not going to come easy to anyone. It is made hard mostly by the fear of reprisal from one's fellow conspirators. Where ideological agreement is insufficient to achieve cohesion within the ranks, there is a quantity of money to buy silence, but it is all backed up by the threat of violence. And no party to what took place would have the slightest question concerning the reality of any threat conveyed. Knowing what these forces are capable of, based upon one's own participation, how could they?

12

Astounding Facts at the Pentagon

A similar tone of disbelief to the one attending the idea of so many convenient pieces of negligence promoting the same end, as well as, for those who adopt it, the idea of conspirators staying silent, surrounds the crash at the Pentagon. Hani Hanjour, the supposed hijacker of American Airlines Flight 77, which the government claims flew into the Pentagon;

1.had trouble flying a Cessna, 2. changed the course of the aircraft in the last two and a half minutes of the flight, 3. from one headed at Donald Rumsfeld's office or the roof above, which 4. would have provided the largest possible target and grandest possible devastation 5. to one, after a 330 degree turn and dive from some 7000-8000 feet, that would hit the part of the building 6. providing the smallest possible target 7. that had been recently reinforced to withstand attack 8. with the fewest occupants assuring the smallest possible loss of military life while 9. flying a 100-ton aircraft virtually parallel to the ground and just a few feet above it at 530 miles per hour, a feat many experienced pilots consider a ridiculous proposition... Really?

The maneuver prompted air traffic controllers to assume it was a military plane. At this point one must carefully consider the startling concurrence of three phenomena. First there is the wildly improbable nature of Hani Hanjour's activities set out in the previous paragraph. Second, there is the assumed massive negligence involved in the failure to adequately protect the headquarters of the American military. Thirdly, there are the actions of Vice President Dick Cheney down there in the bunker at the White House as witnessed by Norman Mineta. Can all of those matters reside together in anyone's mind for any appreciable period without causing a creeping gnaw in the stomach?

Provoked to further inquiry, one finds the government could shed light on the crash at the Pentagon. Seems there was video of the crash. Video? Videos, actually, from 80 different sources near the building that were seized by the FBI shortly after the explosion, and never made public. It is not as if the Pentagon is uninterested. When one author claimed there was no flying object involved in the destruction at the Pentagon, a few frames from a camera at one of the gates to the Pentagon were released apparently showing that a flying object was involved, but almost nothing whatever about what sort of flying object it might have been. In the spring of 2007, as part of a lawsuit filed by Judicial Watch, a conservative legal organization, a few more frames from essentially the same spot were released. Some further releases of video even beyond that have been similarly unhelpful because of camera angle or the number of frames per second. If the Pentagon or the FBI had the slightest interest in satisfying public concerns about what some 80 different videotapes demonstrate about what happened, or in exonerating its officials, assuming a release of pictures would do that, why in the world doesn't it? In other words, if our unjustly accused govern-mental officials' innocence is there for the world to visually compre-hend, why are we not permitted to take a look?

With just this small sampling of disturbing pieces of evidence, some sort of rebuttal seemed to be in order. One would have ex-pected that the 9/11 Commission, appointed to provide the truth to the American people, would have provided that rebuttal. A reason-able person would think so, but a reasonable person can find noth-ing in the report that mentions any of the one hundred and fifteen questions that Griffin has raised.

But a rebuttal certainly was in order, and the editors of Pop-ular Mechanics magazine knew it. Engaging upon the task, the magazine took a sampling of some of the more bizarre and easily refutable claims found on the internet and soundly demolishes them. Left unmentioned are molten metal, the free-fall speed of the collapse of the buildings in New York, the antics of Hani Han-jour, thirty years of US government collaboration with the likes of Osama Bin Laden, and the mountain of instances of government agent negligence all perplexedly serving precisely the same pur-pose. All of these items remain unchallenged by the arbiters of rea-son at Popular Mechanics.

General Mahmoud Ahmad deserves his own paragraph. He was arguably the most powerful man in Pakistan in 2001 as head of that country's CIA, referred to as the ISI. It has been estab-lished that General Ahmad was in Washington, D.C. on September 11th meeting with officials from the CIA and DOD. It has also been established through reporting done by the Times of India that he had sent, through Al Qaeda operative Ramzi Binalshibh, at least $100,000 to Mohammed Atta, the official story's leader of the nine-teen hijackers in the days and weeks leading up to 9/11. It is simply beyond plain that these are matters that should be the subject of of-ficial scrutiny. The most stunning omission by the 9/11 Commission Report is its failure even to mention the transfer of money or the General's presence in Washington, DC that day. There should be no mystery to the persistence of the 9/11 conspiracy theories when the government's effort to quell them does not include mention of one of the most damning pieces of evidence that anyone could imagine.

13

Really, Jim?

Is this all that a reasonable person with a bit of time on his or her hands can do? No one would suggest that the "conspiratorial" thesis has, as of February, 2014, been seriously addressed at, say, the New York Times. A fair amount of space in the back sections with the word "buffs" in the headline established that a number of outside-the-mainstream-looking people gathered in Chicago to discuss the problem in 2005, but none of their evidence was examined. Jim Dwyer wrote in August 2005 about the statements that firefighters had given immediately after 9/11. Some of these, unmentioned by Dwyer, spoke of hearing explosions before, or as, the Towers collapsed.

Reached by phone in the winter of 2006, Dwyer was gracious, gentle and professorial in his denunciations of conspiracy talk. Occam's Razor was invoked, that ancient admonition against employing multiple assumptions if one is sufficient. Up against a deadline, the simple rebuttal to the idea that Occam's Razor supported the government position, that the government's conspiracy theory assumes not just one criminal combination but many intricately-timed necessary instances of gross negligence as well, had to be left unsaid.

Several months later, Dwyer's voice was at the other end of the line again, inquiring why he should spend time chasing down what some professor said about some part of an engine, belonging, according to some independent researchers, to a JT3B fighter aircraft and not a Boeing 757, that was found in the wreckage at the Pentagon. Efforts to convince Dwyer that members of academia don't cast their reputations to the wind willy-nilly were unavailing. Which isn't, of course, to say members of the academy deserve belief, willy-nilly. Just serious investigation. No investigative work in that regard was undertaken that the New York Times reported, or Dwyer later wrote about.

In August 2006 some further accumulation of energy led to an email to Dwyer, asking him to contact Professor Steven Jones who had claimed, during the course of a symposium broadcast on CSPAN, holding in his hand a small piece of metal, that he had tested this tendered sample of steel from Ground Zero and found it to contain thermate, an explosive that is used in controlled demolitions to sever steel. Dwyer replied that he was done talking about the subject, having concluded that the Towers were the victims of suicidal hijackers and nothing more.

In spite of his efforts to put the matter to rest, I wrote back suggesting that he contact the company, Controlled Demolition, which was responsible for hauling part of the rubble to Hangar 17 at JFK. I also alluded to reports that the WTC was closed down prior to 9/11. I asked him to consider the skeptics' scholarship and said I believed there could be a Pulitzer in it for him.

His reply denied that the Towers were closed down and referred me to a National Institute of Standards and Technology website designed to answer some of the questions I had raised, particularly concerning the quantity of explosives required, and therefore the enormity of the task of blowing the Towers up. At the bottom of the email, Dwyer implied that he was not, after all, quite finished with the subject. He asked why the airplane explanation didn't work for me. He also referred to my years of trial lawyering, thinking that they should have taught me something about evidence and proof.

I tried to respond thoughtfully, but there was a sense of urgency and improbability in what was taking place. After all, the New York Times had asked me a question. My reply referred to a witness who said that there had been a power-down at the WTC the weekend before 9/11 and a lot of maintenance people around. With regard to his question, why I could not accept airplanes as the cause, I sent out twenty-seven points of evidence or areas of inquiry that I called my short form. The first eight dealt with the Pentagon and the next two the crash in Pennsylvania. Dwyer responded, "I'm not going to tackle the Pentagon. Or 7 WTC. Just 1 and 2, scenes of the greatest crimes. All must be true for any of it."

This last phrase is the most troubling that occurred during our exchange. There were at least four crimes that were part of the attacks of 9/11. I asked Dwyer what about the search for 9/11 truth allowed one to disregard the Pentagon, Shanksville, and the fact that 7 WTC collapsed without being hit by an airplane—still no answer to that question from him.

One of the ways to cope with evil on such a scale is to construct in the mind a mechanism that delegates to irrelevancy matters not otherwise considered so. This mechanism focuses on a single aspect of the event and sees it as a linchpin for the whole. If an analysis of that focal point leads to a conclusion that conspiracy is impossible, then there is no need to consider the remainder.

Is this a reasonable approach to understanding the attacks of 9/11? Dwyer has determined it's impossible that the Towers were blown up---the main accusation of the Truth Movement. If that is impossible, then, since it is part of an impossible assertion, any issues surrounding the Pentagon or Shanksville needn't be addressed. However, the attack on the Pentagon has its own issues that have nothing to do with physics, or impossibility. We must consider what would be in the mind of a suicide hijacker—would he want to spare as many lives as possible?

The anomalous, according to the "official story," facts that surround the crash site in Pennsylvania, for example, the very large, and very heavy, piece of engine that is said to have bounced to its resting place somewhere near a mile from the strange-looking hole of a crash site near Shanksville requires consideration no matter what brought down the Towers. Dwyer's refusal to tackle the Pentagon or WTC 7 obviously stopped any thorough consideration of 9/11 in its tracks. And whatever he was thinking allowed him to claim that there can be no "mix and match, no hybrid;" No other consideration—either 9/11 was the government, or it was Islamic terrorists; it can't be both. Still Dwyer himself refers to his own book, "Two Seconds Under the World, Terror Comes To America-The Conspiracy to Bomb the World Trade Center" which establishes many occasions of government agents working with terrorists, or at least appearing to.

So here we have a Pulitzer Prize-winning reporter for the nation's premier newspaper engaging in mental gymnastics that relieved him of the necessity of scrutinizing the story as a whole. Or even considering the many disturbing problems that a reasonably open-minded person would want answers to. I suggested it might be difficult for someone in his position to consider the idea of governmental complicity, considering the "strictures of thought" in the newsroom. He didn't deny it, and this may be one of the reasons for his failure as a reporter.

In the beginning I suggested he speak with Steven Jones of Brigham Young University. A professor of physics, Jones wrote a paper on which proponents of governmental complicity have relied. Considering at what temperature steel melts, and the potential heat from a jet fuel fire, for example, Jones concluded that the existence of molten steel in the rubble at Ground Zero meant that there had to be some other source of heat to cause the collapses of the buildings. He asserted that controlled demolition using explosives creates the kind of heat that can in fact melt steel. An inquiring mind might well want to know if something more could be done to determine if explosives were used to blow up the Towers. The answer is "yes," and Jones was the person to ask.

According to Jones's statement on CSPAN, at least one woman, a victim's family member, had access to some of the remains of the building, presumably at Hangar 17 at JFK, and requisitioned a sample of the debris in the interests of truth and science. She sent the piece of steel to Jones for scientific testing. That NIST did not test the steel for thermite-related compounds--- nano thermite, in particular--- the substance apparently used in the demolition, is perplexing considering the existence of the possibility of controlled demolition a long time before the NIST report was published. Dwyer, confronted with NIST's failure, passed the buck to the NIST website, as if he considered his curiosity and his journalistic duties finished.

NIST was asked pointblank about the possibility of testing for explosives. To this day they have refused to conduct any such tests. Why wouldn't concerned citizens turn to independent scientists for answers? Jones announced on CSPAN that his tests confirmed the presence of thermate on the sample. (This was before his identification of nano thermite as the actual chemical compound involved.) He announced that he had actually found thermate on three separate samples from three separate sources, making the possibility of happenstance a long-shot of immeasurable proportion. Since none of this has appeared in the New York Times, I requested Dwyer investigate these matters. Now Dwyer can say he looked into the situation and reported on it. The manner, scope, and lack of energy with which he investigated is a small indication of the harnesses that chain the brains of the best of our news writers.

It seems incredible that he did not fly to Utah to meet Jones, the person with the most serious and important things to say. On the simplest level, if Jones is correct, doesn't some person or agency have a lot of explaining to do? I don't know if Dwyer made the travel request and was denied, but his answers suggest he had no interest in going to see Jones.

That said, it seems plain that the point of contacting Jones at all would be to learn what his claims are; to what extent he is able to back them up; in what ways he employed scientific techniques that are reproducible; who were the sources of whatever substance he tested; the precise kinds of tests that he performed and under what conditions; and whether or not there are fellow scientists who have replicated his work or confirmed his findings.

An investigator would also be interested in knowing what sort of person Jones is, what his credentials are, if he is biased, and what his reputation is amongst academics. These last questions found plenty of space in Dwyer's emails to me. One wonders if the point of Dwyer's work was not simply to discredit Jones. Dwyer found out from the Physics Department at BYU that Jones's work surrounding 9/11 had been disavowed by his colleagues. Jones was a government researcher into cold fusion, though the work he did was not associated with the work of Pons and Fleischman that drew so much well-deserved criticism in the late eighties. Jones's research into muon-cold fusion has turned out to be scientifically valid.

After detailing this in emails, Dwyer asked, "Why is Jones more credible than all his colleagues at BYU?" This question shows a flawed analysis, not to mention careless investigative technique.

Jones stated that he performed tests and found thermate; his colleagues at BYU make no such claim and offer no specific denial of it.

Jones has written a paper which uses scientific principles to demonstrate certain facts; the structural engineering professors at BYU, according to the Department Chair, Woodruff Miller, among other procedural criticisms, have stated that they "do not think there is accuracy and validity to these (Jones's) claims," but have published nothing by way of scientific rebuttal.

Miller further states that the university is aware that Jones's "hypotheses and interpretations of evidence are being questioned by a number of scholars and practitioners " In addition, Miller states that college administrators are not convinced that Jones's work has been submitted to the proper scientific venues of peer review. While each one of these ideas could be troubling in a general sense, and specifically damaging to anything that Jones puts forth as scientifically demonstrated, they do not establish that Jones was wrong in what he says he found or how he says he found it.

The rejection of a hypothesis is a long way from disputing scientific practice.

The conclusion that Dwyer was trying to discredit Steven Jones is supported by a certain point in our email exchange. Dwyer said that he couldn't remember if he asked Jones "pointblank" if he found thermate, much less how, from where, in what concentrations, etc. Reviewing his notes, he said he had asked Jones to comment on the NIST website's Q and A's, which included that NIST did not test for thermate.

Jones's replied: "We, OTOH, are testing for the residue of thermite-reaction compounds (alumino-thermics) both in the toxic

WTC dust and in the solidified metal. And we are finding an abundance of fluorine, zinc and other elements that are commonly used in alumino-thermics, but not in building materials in the concentrations found. We are investigating the possibility of thermite-based arson and demolition."

Yes, but did you find thermate? Is the testing you referred to different from what you discussed on CSPAN? Are you suggesting that the toxic dust tests corroborate the solidified metal tests? Where did you get the solidified metal? Is it possible that what you got did not come from Ground Zero? Were there any inconsistencies in your testing? Who observed your testing? Do you have any doubts about your findings?

In the time since my exchange with Dwyer, these issues have taken on another hue. Most importantly, the substance found by Jones in the samples of dust and debris from Ground Zero, he has determined, is nano thermite. He and Professor Neils Harrit of the University of Copenhagen have published a paper on their findings in the peer-reviewed Open Journal of Chemical Physics.

I hope I will be permitted another short digression, as the question of peer review takes on some considerable importance in this whole affair. In the early days of the Truth Movement, say, its first three or four years, when Steven Jones first wrote his original article, "Why Indeed Did the Towers Collapse?", it was not subjected to peer review in the way in which that term is meant in the scientific community. It was not submitted to a detached, uninvolved group of scientists hired by an accredited scientific journal whose job it was to determine its compliance with the scientific method. To the extent that it was reviewed by other professionals in the field, those professionals were not uninvolved or detached in the way that what is known as the peer review process implies. That milestone of having Jones and Harrit's findings published in a peer-reviewed journal would not occur until 2009 when their article was accepted by the Open Journal of Chemical Physics.

Along the journey of this case, it is impossible not to run into all manner of curiosities. Anthony Summers and his wife, Robbyn Swan, set about to tell the "Full Story of 9/11 and Osama Bin Laden" in 2011 with their book, The Eleventh Day. It would be wrong to say their treatment of the claims and assertions of the Truth Movement does them no credit whatever. They do mention some of the evidence upon which I and others rely. But when the really important matter of nano thermite came up....well, that's actually the core of the problem. The word nano thermite, in any of the ways that it might be spelled, does not appear in the book. Does not appear in the book. Thermite appears, but mostly as an abused and obstinate apparition of no enduring importance. In addition, there are dismissive references to Jones' earliest paper on the subject, with particular emphasis given to the fact of its not being peer reviewed, a criticism that cannot be made of the paper announcing the subsequent finding of nano thermite, the effective DNA in the case.

Can this sort of work be done honestly? That is the question that simply will not go away. Because, it is not, demonstrably NOT, that Summers and Swan didn't find the article that announced to the world, in peer reviewed scientific parlance, for God's sake, that certain very important questions had now been answered. They CITED it. In a footnote, #114 on page 476. But even there they could not bring themselves to include the word "nano thermite." Nano thermite, we are to deduce--- but only in the event we take the time to find the article and read it--- according to Summers and Swan, is Jones's latest "take" on thermite. The point of the reference to the journal article in the footnote is to fire an intentionally destructive salvo at Jones and Harrit's work based on the statement by the journal's editor that she believed the periodical itself, with which she disassociated herself, was "sheer nonsense." Now there will be those, reading these lines, who will see in those words a "Welcome" sign at the end of an arduous drive that it was thought might end even with danger. Some engaged in this pursuit will be in search of just about anything that might undercut what this book has been saying and the conclusion towards which it has been fervently driving since the first page. And if you don't find this peculiar, you are playing a different golf course than the one I'm on. You mean to say that the editor of the journal has dismissed the journal as "sheer nonsense?" Yup, apparently.

Apparently, the article had been published when she wasn't looking. And peer reviewed without her knowledge as well, one assumes. Parenthetically, how, by definition, can anything peer-reviewed and published in something with the words, "Chemical Physics" in its title, be sheer nonsense? Are there that many fraudulent poseur-jokesters in the scientific community? Was she always of this opinion? Just looking for another line on her resume, assuming it would never really matter to anyone? So, Summers and Swan, given this really wonderful opportunity, did their best to denigrate the importance of Jones and Harrit's work, using the very powerful and surprising words of the journal's editor. All's fair in love, war, and the pursuit of history? What has not been done, by anyone, is to publish a peer-reviewed article calling into question the peer-reviewed conclusions of Jones and Harrit. That is to say, no one has produced at the same level, even in a journal whose editor is unhappy with their own product, a peer reviewed disagreement with Jones and Harrit. And for very good reason, as we shall see a bit later on.

I dutifully emailed Summers and Swan with my concerns about the absence of the word nano thermite and a request to discuss the matter. After three email exchanges with Ms. Swan (see

Appendix), the absence of the word or any explanation for that absence has yet to be referred to.

Returning to Dwyer then, with Jones and Harrit's findings, it is possible, as I mentioned above, to consider nano thermite the functional equivalent of DNA in the case. If these scientific findings were introduced as evidence in a court of law, the guilt of the Government (using this as shorthand for the complicity of high-level United States officials) will have been established beyond a reasonable doubt, as they say in the business.

This conclusion is reasonably straight-forward. Nano thermite is a metastable intermolecular composite, actually a kind of advanced weapons system, developed by USG military laboratories. When formed as an explosive or pyrotechnic, it creates temperatures as high as 5000 degrees Fahrenheit, and cuts through steel instantaneously. All of the circumstantial evidence in the case of 9/11, described so meticulously by Jones, and Gage of Architects and Engineers for 9/11 Truth, is explained, bowing politely and deeply to Dwyer's beloved Occam's Razor. Another way of putting this is to say that there is one, and only one, explanation for everything that the Official Story and the known facts contain, and that is the single, simple, though wretchingly unpalatable thesis of a high government conspiracy.

The Towers and WTC 7 were destroyed by agents, (rogue agents?) of our own government using an explosive its military developed for war. It could be none other than government, not just because any successful attack on the Pentagon must have had help on the inside, but because with the demolition of WTC 7 at 5:20 PM that day, a number of government offices were destroyed. Access to buildings such as WTC 7, that housed the CIA, the DEA, the SEC, and the FBI, is tightly controlled. Slathering its innards with nano thermite would have taken a lot of time and effort.

This would require the complete subversion of the building's security system.

What is important here is that Jim Dwyer, from his silence, not only does not agree, but feels the findings of Jones and the efforts and conclusions of over now-3000 architects and engineers are simply worthless—unworthy of even an inch in the New York Times. When was the last time a group of that many architects and engineers united to do anything but teach or congratulate themselves for their achievements? Every now and then in this quest, the plainness, the clarity of the issues, the blatant nature of the efforts to avert one's gaze, lead me to wonder if we are really all the same species.

Reporters have families; they have to pay rent. They may consider themselves too insignificant to make a difference, but there are some jobs that carry with them an ethical responsibility. For lawyers, it's codified. If a law firm demands that some associate lie, cheat, or steal, the duty of the associate is to resign. I don't know if news people have similar standards; everybody bloody well knows their job is to find the truth and tell it. Can Jim Dwyer honestly look himself in the mirror and claim he has done all he could to find the truth about this sick, sorry moment in American history?

None of the questions set out above, that might have been, and should have been, asked of Professor Jones, were asked. We can guess that the reason for their being left unasked is that the underlying premise, the falsity of the official story, was never given the room to breathe in Jim Dwyer's mind. Now, thinking in the most charitable way of the Dwyer-Jones interview, if a few email requests for comment can be so termed, if Dwyer was unaware of his predisposition to dismissal, or if he was aware of it and made no mental effort to compensate, the results in journalism-speak were sure to be a hit piece, properly deserved or not. And that was the product purveyed by our masters at the New York Times.

But since we are awash in thoughts of conspiracy, there is another, further, far more ominous, possibility: that Dwyer understood his role as spear-carrier for the forces of stability and supremacy, and set out, quite mindfully, upon the task of discrediting critics of the regime and its official version. Thanks largely to the work of Watergate-famed reporter Carl Bernstein, we now know that US history is filled with countless instances of compromised and corrupted reporters, whose, at least secondary, master was United States government directive. There is no substantial reason to think Mr. Dwyer is a government operative. But a government operative would act pretty much as he has, and it is sad beyond words that it isn't unreasonable to consider the possibility.

A few more highlights of the email conversation with Mr. Dwyer are worth mentioning. Much space was devoted to describing some of the people who worked at, and were responsible for, the World Trade Center. Dwyer bristled at the inferred suggestion that any of those people would have allowed their building to be blown up without uttering a word. Apart from never having implied such a thing, it seems simply bizarre to me to even entertain such a notion. It is not decent, conscientious people who were responsible for what happened if the government was complicit. Those people had to be kept unaware so that a cabal with its cadres of covert operatives could perform its devastating work without detection. That any time at all was spent by Mr. Dwyer considering how the heroes of the World Trade Center could have allowed such a thing to happen is hard to understand, and he has done nothing to make it easier for me.

Dwyer spent an enormous amount of time and energy studying the World Trade Center attack, including creating databases to track witnesses' stories. It's most peculiar then that he is unwilling, or unable, to acknowledge the numerous firefighters and others who refer to explosions inside the Towers before and during the collapses.

Some of the firefighters' statements are ambiguous, and in some cases, it may be that the explosions referred to are the collapse of one of the Towers, but in virtually every case one likely interpretation includes explosions that caused the collapse of the Towers. Those who obtained the statements were either not interested, or not qualified to clear up these mysteries. In many instances the statements provide no ambiguity at all about what was being said.

It is, however, honestly impossible to say, as Dwyer claims, that there is nothing---- "ZERO"---- to use his word, in the accounts of witnesses to support the theory of demolition. One wonders if Dwyer is making an effort to convince himself. A scholar named Graeme MacQueen did a study of the 503 firefighter and EMT statements that were taken in the months following the attacks. His purpose was to calculate the number of times certain words were used by the witnesses as they told their stories. He was not trying to prove that the Towers were brought down by demolition, but simply counting words.

He found that the words, "bomb," "blast," "explosion," and "explosives" were used 182 times by 118 different individuals. When I informed Dwyer of the study, his immediate reply via email was one word, "preposterous." In the next half hour or so, a further email sought to debunk MacQueen's study as insufficient to the task of establishing that controlled demolition was involved, precisely what MacQueen had not set out to do. Dwyer never, and to this day has not, offered a word to dispute MacQueen's mathematics.

What's going on here? It was Dwyer who spent four years suing NYFD successfully to get these statements. Did he read them? Of course he did. What went on in his mind as his eyes focused on the word "bomb" or "blast" or "explosion?" What sort of mental faculty renders those words meaningless as they enter the brain? And it was not just firefighters who provided substantiation to the Truth Movement's claims.

To take one non-NYFD instance, Mike Pecoraro is an engineer who was working in the sixth subbasement of the North Tower when it was hit. An hour before the Tower collapsed, he went up to the third subbasement and found the machine shop and a fifty-ton press reduced to rubble. Dwyer has not said if he has interviewed Pecoraro to write about his story or determine his credibility.

There is a fundamental obstacle in the search for truth by anyone other than a governmental agency with subpoena power. There is one instance and one instance only, in a democratic society with a bill of rights, in which a citizen is by law required to respond to a question, even if it is only to take the Fifth Amendment, and that is when bidden to testify through the power of subpoena.

Jim Dwyer was in no way required to answer my questions, and didn't answer many of them. He was in no way required to ask Professor Jones any of the questions that seem obvious. He could conduct his business by simply asking for a comment. There are reasons why journalists employ this technique. The foremost may be the desire not to offend, but they are also worried about continued access to highly placed governmental officials.

Whatever the considerations, it is clear that journalists who ask for comments, rather than answers to pointed questions, are afraid for their reputations, or afraid of the loss of their job, and are therefore, not up to the task of saving this country. Independent researchers may advance the cause and in the case of the attacks of 9/11 are due every praise the language contains, but without the law and subpoena power, academics and historians and the apparatchiks of Big Media will not be shamed into writing the history as truth demands, and as their obligations should have dictated.

As a final reflection on my intriguing, and fascinating conversation with such a distinguished representative of mainstream media, it must be acknowledged that Dwyer, in his defense of the official story, has, with the aid of a mountain of speculation, described what would be an amazing undertaking, demolishing the Towers by means of explosives without anyone knowing about it. He also implies that surely someone involved would have grabbed for the brass ring of fame and told all. None of Dwyer's arguments can or should be disregarded.

Set down next to what a tenured professor in physics describes as a physical impossibility, however, a reasonable person would be provoked to find how an organization with the expertise at blowing up buildings might go about doing it in secret. A reporter for the New York Times has all that it takes to get responses to such questions. Have they been asked? Should they be asked? Is it reasonable to think they should be asked, and answered? Jim Dwyer was one of a few journalists who even responded to my inquiries.

On final thought, my seething, raging anger which has no place to go but to this paper, cannot leave the subject of Mr. Dwyer without some sort of exclamation point. Because the character of the betrayal of duty grows starker and more jarring with time. It is the plumber who decided against his wrench; the carpenter who eschewed his saw; the laboratory scientist, his microscope. Those witnesses whose words tell the forbidden tale are the bread and butter of journalism, as well as the brick and mortar of the courtroom. They are veins of gold buried in the rock, but the wealth they may provide is unknowable without determined, hard work. The detective, the journalist must bring their skill to bear and prod and test and examine to be able to know how rich and reliable the information they provide truly is. There may be those whose statements evaporate with barely a hard look, though it seems most unlikely given who these people were. There may be those who have far more important things to say than can now be imagined, but it has now been 19 years with all manner of human experience interposed between the moments of sensation that produced the words of which we have knowledge, and whatever information that might be given now.

Jim Dwyer's DUTY was to understand all of the complexity of these narratives, to relate them to the world for the use of the citizens and their law enforcement representatives, and preserve them for history. Mr. Dwyer, have you no shame?

14

Messrs. Washington Post and Rolling Stone

The biggest name to permit me an interview was Walter Pincus, the national security reporter for the Washington Post, a true grandfather of establishment journalism. He didn't know nor care what I wanted to talk about. He's been quoted as saying he would talk to anyone. I took him up on it, and we spent a very pleasant hour and a half while he ate his oatmeal across the street from the Washington *Post* offices on 15th Street. When it became clear that I was asking him questions because I had learned of evidence suggesting there was complicity of high officials in the attacks of 9/11, he was direct and unambiguous. He could not conceive of such a thing, and hadn't ever conceived of such a thing.

For just a moment or two, he made a stab at explaining one of the pieces of evidence I brought to his attention: a tape-recording of a meeting in an office across the street from the Towers, that captures an explosion 9 seconds before the impact of Flight 11, the plane that hit the North Tower at 8:46 AM. The tape appears to establish TWO loud, explosive events at the time the North Tower is first hit by an aircraft, where the first explosion precedes the airplane's disappearance into the side of the building. His explanation had to do with different parts of the plane hitting the building at 9-second intervals, a valiant effort. I found I did not want to offend him. In another setting, in front of a board of inquiry or in a courtroom, I would not have hesitated to ask about every single piece of evidence. But over oatmeal, I, the supplicant, my questions and his kindness?

Our discussion ranged wide, him scoffing at people who thought Oswald might have had help killing Kennedy, and declaring that Iran-Contra was a minor, unimportant lapse of judgment and certainly not any significant conspiracy. That, despite the several indictments and convictions of high government officials. Walter Pincus and I occupy the same planet, and he has written a lot of the history of the last several decades, a fair amount of which I've read. What is it that allows us both to feel such comfort and certainty that we are right?

Walter Pincus has every right to think his view of the world is the correct view. He has been applauded by the powerful, thanked by his employers and his readers, and exalted by even some progressive forces as a top investigative reporter. What reason does he have to question his assumptions or his understanding of history? He has probably never been in the position of being cross-examined about his techniques. Nobody is; that's not how we do things in this country.

Not everyone knows Matt Taibbi, but as a writer for Rolling Stone and author of books and guest on John Stewart and Rachel Maddow and Imus, he's a serious and scholarly voice on the Left, and, an inveterate smartass. He has a number of books; one, "Griftopia," should be read by everyone with an interest in how this nation's economy does or doesn't function. Another effort of his "The Great Derangement", included some ridicule directed at people like me, members of the 9/11 Truth Movement. When he appeared on one of the talk shows, Jon Stewart, I think, and took his disdainful criticisms into the ether, I considered it an invitation to engage in debate. The entirety of the email exchange can be found in Appendix H. As far as I am concerned, he deserves a smidgen of credit for answering my email at all, though the substance of the questions and answers underscores the deficiencies of any forum that does not require that responsive answers be given. Thank goodness we have courts, I might have said, and probably did say, in my infancy. What he did, in his initial response, was dispense with the niceties and get right to the matter of making fun of me, references to tin-foil hat included. What he did not do was answer the questions. He excused himself saying he had dealt with these issues in debate with Dr. Griffin, and I would be able to read it online at some point.

But anyone who took the time to look at the exchange between Taibbi and Griffin had the choice of their own conclusions because there was no mutual exchange, no cross-examination. Is it your position that there was no molten metal at Ground Zero? Was Norman Mineta hallucinating, in your opinion, or lying? Is Professor Jones mistaken?

Cross-examination, as practiced by the pros, is a series of assertions of fact, followed by a question mark. For example:

You agree that evil men have been attracted to power throughout history??

You agree that humanity has been capable of all manner of atrocity throughout history including acts more horrifying than 9/11? The massacres attendant the unification of China, the Holocaust, the near extermination of the Native American population in the United States, Stalin's massacres before and throughout World

War II, the war crimes of the former Yugoslavia, Idi Amin's Ugan-
dan disgrace, Rwanda, ...

You agree that Americans have engaged in such acts in her history, and even if you don't, you wouldn't claim that citizenship deprives one of the capacities to be and do evil?

You recognize that members of the Bush Administration, as part
of the Project for a New American Century, suggested that greater
steps should be taken to project American power around the world,
but that those steps would not be possible without a "New Pearl
Harbor"?

You agree that 9/11 enabled the Bush Administration to accom-
plish that projection of power, in addition to enacting the Patriot
Act, and allowing its cronies to benefit financially from its enhanced
Defense strategies?

You agree that the tactic of the "false flag" has been employed by
governments throughout history, and the American government in
particular?

You agree that there was no technological impediment to the
high government conspiracy that you (and many others) have
branded insanity?

You are not in a position to dispute the finding of nano thermite
in four, separate, independently collected samples of dust and debris
from Ground Zero, and the peer-reviewed article establishing the
fact?

You have made no effort to examine, much less rebut, by whatever means, the conclusions of over 3000 architects and engineers
that all three buildings in New York were destroyed by controlled
demolition?

You did know that there was a third building, WTC 7, that was
also destroyed that day, that upon its collapse drew virtually identical commentary from Rather, Brokaw, and Jennings: "it's just like

we have all seen on television where buildings are demolished with preplaced explosives"?

You have made no effort to explain, in fact have made no reference whatever to, the eye and ear-witness evidence of explosions in the Towers and WTC7 before and during the collapses?

Do you even know who Barry Jennings was? Do you dispute that he survived explosions within WTC 7 before either tower collapsed? That he told of his survival to a television interviewer on the streets of New York shortly after his escape from the building. That he told about his experience subsequently to the producers of Loose Change, to the BBC, and then to investigators from NIST, but that none of what he said appeared in the NIST report on the destruction of WTC 7, isn't that true? And he died mysteriously just before that report was published?

The pictures of the front of the Pentagon shortly after the attack there show no sign of the crash of an airliner?

An E-4B, the Doomsday Plane, or Flying Pentagon was flying above the White House at the time of the attack on the Pentagon?

The radar tracks documenting that flight have been scrubbed, thus erasing the E-4B out of existence?

There are discrepancies in the flight paths of Flight 77 that allegedly hit the Pentagon as detailed by the NTSB and the 9/11 Commission?

April Gallop walked out of the Pentagon after the attack, with a head injury, when her desk, where she was sitting immediately before the explosion, was in the way of the plane supposedly traveling 530 miles per hour when it hit the building. You have never questioned her location at the time of the devastation at the Pentagon nor the fact of her survival?

Finally, would you not expect a successful attack on this nation's military headquarters predicated on the absolute failure of its defenses to lead to investigations and severe consequences, neither of which occurred with regard to the attacks of 9/11?

The existence of a conspiracy or the identities of its participants will remain hidden without the courage and determination of some members of law enforcement or some practitioners of the trade of journalism possessed of an open mind. That is a fact utterly beyond dispute, is it not?

Taibbi was given plenty of opportunities to answer questions such as those set out above. He declined. One of those opportunities came when I showed up on his doorstep. He decided I was too fearful an apparition to even open the door. Do I blame him? Yes, I guess I do. Did he actually have even the slightest reason to be fearful? Absolutely not. I was 64 years old at the time. I am a lawyer. I mean, I may be reasonably fit, I have that golf game that gets a fair amount of attention, but come on. He could see I wasn't packing heat through the peep hole, though I guess I could have had a piece stuffed in my belt, but it was summer time and I was wearing a tee shirt and khakis. In addition, we had exchanged emails. So, I wasn't exactly a stranger.

But am I someone to fear? You betcha. I'm a gunslinger for truth, and I have a boatload of facts hung loosely over both shoulders. And that has to be why Taibbi decided not to open the door. He was afraid of the outcome of the engagement. There is a class of human beings who feels I should be apologetic for tactics such as these, showing up mostly if not entirely unannounced at a person's home to ask questions. Taibbi was outraged. In rising decibels, he was stunned when I re- minded him who I was; "you come to my house?" There was talk of police, and "how did you get my address?" "I am a lawyer, that's what I do. I'm no threat; I was in town; I'd like to have a conversation; can I make an appointment?" He would have none of it. And, he demanded an explanation for my "bizarre" behavior in an email in the days following as if tracking people to their doorstep were not the very essence of his job. What I said in reply is just what I would say to anyone in that class I just referred to:

Mr. Taibbi;

Thank you for giving me this opportunity to discuss my "bizarre" behavior. Your doorman was not in evidence when I walked in the building, but had he been, I would not have liked my chances at getting a conversation. I have been ignored by some of the most famous names in this country, at least among the politically astute, and in at least one disheartening case, by someone at the other end of the phone with their doorman, having had a day to consider the matter with a legal brief in their possession, read or not, I have no idea.

It is a fact of life that nothing difficult happens, or is accomplished, except eye to eye. I came to your door because I could, and because I must do everything I can. By email I offered you, and asked you for, an opportunity to sit down and talk under any conditions that you might dictate. The result of that was silence. What else could I do but hope you might have a change of heart if you saw me in the flesh? I certainly had no intention of being threatening, quite the opposite. I am only a theoretical threat to what I consider to be the enormous lie that has been told. I vow to combat it any way I can.

Is it rude to come to a person's door unannounced with a request for an interview? It wasn't for the first several millennia; if it is now because we live in fear and have doormen to keep us from the intrusion of the world, it is a sad path we travel. I offer my apology for my ancient and subversive ways with the explanation that in matters of such import, politeness must give way. Or may it be viewed from a different perspective? A traveler has come thousands of miles to see you, and you cannot deign to open the door and look them in the eye?

Let me offer this: I sent out a notice of my head being handed to me by a Federal District Court Judge, and you, of all my non-friends who received it, decided to respond. You could have felt well rid of me as I gently left your hallway the other night, yet you sent me an email demanding an explanation for my behavior. I know you are concerned for the life of this country, I have read some of your writings (my 26 year old son is a real fan of yours and steers them to me), my tennis partner is an Imus listener and has a great respect for your brains and your point of view. I allow myself the hope that you are having some trouble with the official story.

Let me ask one final time, please, give me an hour and a half to discuss the matter, at the time and place of your choosing. This poor misused nation needs your help. I will abide by any rules you lay down; I give you my word which I take seriously.

bv

So, I guess I am not very apologetic about my conduct. As just about any investigator worth the name says, as he or she is standing at a potential witness's door, "sorry to bother you, I'm..." That's about the extent of it. What kind of REPORTER would be unable to figure this situation out and respond in a marginally more empathetic manner? But the most important aspect of the interchange with Taibbi, as was true with Dwyer, is his unwillingness to address facts. In the case of the Mineta-Cheney encounter, he was urged more than once. His refuge is the incongruous nature of the proposed plot. As he put it, why would they do that? Why not just...? I don't mean to suggest that these are not legitimate questions.

They refer, however, to matters of human choice. Molten metal, on the other hand, and erased radar tracks are physical phenomena that can be captured and studied and which are subject to the laws of science. Any human behavior may be seen as bizarre depending on one's perspective, but that does not make it impossible.

15

In the Trenches of Disinformation and Deception

Thus, I am provoked to discuss what I have referred to as the curly-cue factor. What do I mean when I say, as I have many times now, that the most important movie of the 21st century was produced in the 20th, and it was called, "Wag the Dog"? That movie dealt with the ability of a government to create the appearance of a reality that can then be used for whatever its purposes might be. It is a matter of movie-making, with director and producer and cinematic technology. These crucial witnesses in the matter of 9/11, whose names and titles are as yet unknown, are the people whose job it was to get the supposed hijacker's passport, somehow undamaged by the inferno that is supposed to have resulted from the collision of the airliners into the Towers, onto the streets of Manhattan, there to be found and thus providing essential evidence for the official story. These are the operatives of misdirection and sleight of hand and...cover-up. These are the people who place the blame elsewhere. They literally place physical objects at the scenes of the crimes to sculpt the narrative of guilt according to the architects' specifications. The props which function as compelling clues are inferno-defeating bandannas in Pennsylvania, inferno-defeating passports there and on the pavement in New York, luggage in cars in Boston, and a Koran, and admonitions to hijackers within that luggage.

These soldiers, as they most assuredly were, had to plant the red bandanna in Shanksville, and be responsible for the contents of luggage in airports in New England. The red bandanna is supposed to be some sort of signature piece of apparel for Middle Eastern terrorists, so, if you know that, its presence at the bizarre crash site in Pennsylvania is self-explanatory. The contents of the luggage are important because they contain what one reporter called the Rosetta Stone of the conspiracy. The official story holds that Mohammed Atta, who, subsequent reporting established, apparently enjoyed lap-dances, cocaine, and alcohol in Venice, Florida, in spite of his supposed Islamist purity, was the fanatical leader of the suicidal nineteen. But that knowledge of his command position comes to us, depending on which version of the FBI recounting is the focus of inquiry at the moment, from his luggage, found unloaded onto Flight 11 in the Boston airport. Parenthetically, there appears no reason for the luggage not to have been loaded, and Atta was the only passenger whose bags did not make it onto the airplane. Be all that as it may, the luggage is said to have contained Atta's will, (why you would carry this important post mortem document on the plane you are supposed to destroy while piloting is not made clear) and papers sufficient to allow "FBI agents to swiftly unravel the mystery of who carried out the suicide attacks and what motivated them," as Michael Dorman of Newsday writes. Those interested are apparently not supposed to be concerned that the luggage was initially found in a rental car, at one point a Nissan driven to Portland, Maine, at another point, a Mitsubishi left at the airport in Boston, and not unloaded onto American Flight 11 at all.

This is a bit of embarrassment, indeed. Or I guess I should say, it should be a bit of embarrassment. Our vaunted, exalted, world's premier investigative service, the FBI, can't get its story straight? The instances have been tripping over each other now for so long that embarrassment should long since have given way to fear of prosecution for filing false 302 reports, or in instances where oaths were taken, the filing of perjury charges. The governmental agency charged with providing truth has demonstrably broken the law in the documentation of its investigation and thereby as well committed the crime of obstruction of justice.

And along similar lines, it is, of course, peculiar that six of those readily, and so quickly, identified nineteen hijackers have been further identified by names and pictures as being quite alive and well and living in Europe or Egypt or Morocco, or wherever. And as guilty as the FBI is of creating and purveying the false history of which I complain, it is not so easy to construct, on the fly, as it were. What is required is a Big Media that is dutifully compliant. And it most certainly was in this instance. Compliant and incurious, incapable of simply, "didn't you say it was a Nissan the other day?" "I thought it was in Portland." "Why did no one else's bag miss the flight?" I propose that the connection between government and Big Media, both so irresistibly wedded to the maintenance of stability above all else, especially truth, is so corrupted and corrupting as to make the existence of a US Department of Propaganda entirely unnecessary.

But I have digressed again. In addition to having legible hijacker passports appear at burning crash sites, these operatives who were responsible for sculpting the necessary false narrative, had to construct the faked phone calls, if that is what they were, from the airplanes that would take center stage in the Hollywood movie, United 93. Or they had to hold the guns while the scripts were read by doomed passengers.

It is not a bit clear, when considering these constructors of history, what is to be made of the fact that cellphones didn't work at 30,000 ft in 2001, or that American Flight 77, the supposed death plane that dove into the Pentagon from which Barbara Olson called her husband, Solicitor General Ted Olson at the Justice Department, did not have operable air-phones, as best we can figure, the backup position of the official historians when it was determined that the cellphones could not have done the job. And it was the FBI that proved in the Moussaoui, the twentieth hijacker, trial that there were in fact no completed cellphone calls from Barbara to Ted based on government records.

These operatives are skillful, indeed, but as we have now seen, they do make mistakes, many of which may have been completely meaningless. Nevertheless, they played enormously important roles that day, and they worked wherever the curly-cue office was housed. In my imagination, they, or their superiors were charged with the job of making the allegations of conspiracy laughable. You mean to tell me....?, as many of my supplicees have said or implied through their tones of voice, followed by a reference to faked phone calls or the murder of all of the passengers of American 77, coldly and with intricate calculation, to provide props for the most unimaginably sinister, unspeakable covert operation ever conceived by an enormous number of living human beings.

United 93, or its blueprint, was conceived by the masters of this plot with one object: to sell a scenario and make any facts that stood in conflict seem ludicrous. Are those guys ever good at what they do! On top of the wild imagination that they made a prerequisite to the understanding of their game, they get to win when, or because, they made mistakes, if they were mistakes, about which I have tremendous doubts. They carefully plan and then forget to restore the "ground clutter" after they erase the radar track of American 77 after it passes over the Pentagon? That probably requires some explanation. The 84th RADES battalion of the US Army is responsible for keeping track of the radar tracks of aircraft flying in the United States. It was an obvious place to go when there was talk of American 77 not actually hitting the Pentagon. The radar track would show what planes flew where, when, and at what speed and altitude.

The Truth Movement includes professionals in every field, especially aviation. Pilots For 9/11 Truth have been responsible for tremendous leaps in understanding over the past ten years. One particular radar/aviation professional made a study of the radar tracks at the time of the crime, in this instance with regard to American 77. The plane, he found, according to the documents and images produced by 84th RADES, apparently did end its journey at the west wall of the Pentagon.

End of that particular facet of the case, correct? Actually, a lot closer to the beginning. Two minutes before the explosions at the Pentagon in the track of the plane, American 77, there is what is known as ground clutter east-northeast of the Pentagon. Ground clutter is the name given to blips on the radarscope that are caused by tall buildings as opposed to airplanes. In this case it would be the office buildings in Rosslyn, Va. and the Washington Monument. What is significant and devastating to the official story is that after the explosion, or supposed impact of the plane at the Pentagon, on the radar tapes, where it clearly was a second before, the ground clutter that was Rosslyn, disappears. Why else would it disappear except as part, or overlooked consequence, of erasing American 77's (if it was American 77 and not a substituted drone), radar track?

I suppose it is possible to craft a seemingly reasonable explanation for the absence of that ground clutter. It could involve the failure of human beings or technology or both. That explanation, should it ever be required of anyone in a position of power, will be garbage, full-fledged and gold-plated. Fool me once; shame on you; fool me several hundred times, shame on all of us.

So here we see an important, but obscure piece of evidence that helps paint the picture of government conspiracy, because the machinery of the government, its records and data, have been corrupted. In the case of such arcane minutiae it is helpful if there is corroborating, or supporting evidence to enhance confidence in one's reading of the facts.

In the matter of the erasure of radar tracks, there is in fact unmistakable corroboration. That office of imaginative soldiers whose job it was to sell the official story and make contrary claims far-fetched and laughable by concocting and creating false evidence, was either taxed to its limits, or it was quite aware of what can and cannot fly in the court of public opinion, and simply didn't give a damn. A CNN cameraman stood among the evacuees from the White House just about the time the Pentagon was exploding. Sometime in 2008 or so, [why then and not many years earlier, you will have to ask him] John King of CNN decided, or some executive decided, to run the story that included the footage taken by that cameraman, pointing his camera up into the air above the White House. Audible in the sequence is the proclamation that the plane in view was the Doomsday Plane.

As detailed in Mark Gaffney's book, *9/11 and the Mystery Plane,* there are four of these specially fitted 747's in the Air Force line-up. They are also known as "Flying Pentagons." One of them follows the President whenever he goes overseas and provides the ability to survive and conduct a nuclear war from the air. It has a special paint job, and the fuselage is slightly different from a standard 747. CNN was not the only one to capture the plane flying over the White House at that moment. A woman named Linda Brookhart took still photos as well.

The importance of these matters is demonstrated when the radar tracks of the 84th RADES Battalion are examined. According to those records, no such plane flew at such a place at such a time. To say it another way, official military records contradict what any of us is able to see by looking at video footage broadcast on CNN or still photographs taken by Linda Brookhart below the plane on the ground. Therefore, a second instance of the erasure of radar tracks confirms the first instance of the ground clutter disappearance. Scrubbing or erasing radar tracks is entirely within the military's capability, and were heavenly justice ever to grant us the opportunity, the method and procedure would be described in detail in court. The government, in such an apparently unlikely event, would be left to denounce all of those witnesses' lying eyes, and television footage to boot.

One of the premier moments at that trial that will never happen would involve questioning an Air Force general, asking him or her what it is they think is depicted in the stills of Ms. Brookhart and the video of CNN set side by side with photos of the Doomsday Plane produced beautifully and very expensively by the public relations office at Boeing. In case anyone is wondering, the Air Force has insisted, in public statements to CNN, that no Doomsday Plane, and no other Air Force aircraft was in the skies over the White House at that time. When it comes to cover-up, there simply is no limit for agents of the United States government. Whatever resources the imagination can conjure, money, manpower, technology, it is available, but this is an idea which Matt Taibbi has yet to come to terms with.

16

Journalistic Mis- or Malfeasance

Barton Gellman, Pulitzer Prize-winning reporter, of the Washington *Post*, wrote *Angler* about the vice presidency of Dick Cheney. The book came out in 2007. Since 9/11 defined all of the characters in power at the time, that moment is the opening scene in the book. Gellman's account is the official story, including no reference whatever to Mineta's testimony before the 9/11 Commission. I had called Gellman after I read his book to ask if he had interviewed Mineta, and he said "I didn't get to it." He was unconcerned that history had been mis served because in presenting his account, he relied on contemporaneous records and notes of the event, and he said he had no reason to doubt their authenticity.

As long as he was unaware of the existence of Mineta's account, Cheney's interview with Tim Russert on Meet the Press on

September 17th, 2001, Cheney's speech to the American Enterprise Institute in 2008, White House photographer David Bohrer's account, or the statements of Richard Clarke and Condoleezza Rice, I suppose that could be true. Of course, there would have to be a serious misunderstanding or ignorance of the procedures of the United States Secret Service in addition, but why should anyone expect that kind of awareness on the part of, did I mention?, a Pulitzer Prize-winning newspaper reporter for the Washington *Post*?

To explain a bit more completely, Gellman describes Cheney in his office with his staff, watching the television just after the first plane hit the North Tower at 8:46 AM. The vice president is puzzled how such a thing could have happened. Then, at 9:03 AM, United 175 plows into the South Tower, and as Gellman writes, everybody knew that a terrorist operation was underway. Gellman details how the Secret Service then learns that a plane is flying toward the White House. Secret Service Agent Jimmy Scott brings his hand down hard on the desk, says "NOW!", and the vice president is lifted away. When does Gellman say that happened? 9:36 AM. Everyone needs to think about that for a minute. The second tower is hit at 9:03, and it takes over a half an hour for the Secret Service to spring into action? Is it just an urban legend that Secret Service agents are stationed everywhere the President and Vice President are? Did the television program, "The West Wing", take a breather from verisimilitude in this particular instance?

No, it didn't, and we have no less a figure than the Vice President himself for proof of the fact. He told Tim Russert, that you aren't really asked in such moments, you are told in no uncertain terms. Cheney describes to Russert, and later to the AEI, that shortly after the 2nd plane hit he was on his way to the "bunker", which would be the Presidential Emergency Operations Center. Is there any way in the world that "shortly", under these extraordinary circumstances, could be 33 minutes? There is only one way that the Secret Service could possibly have acted with such nonchalance, and that is if they were aware of the architecture of the plot and knew that the Vice President was in no danger. But it is a virtual certainty that if they did know what was going to happen, they would have been all the more sure to keep up appearances and act according to the dictates of the handbook, the contents of which, in broad outline, are familiar to most Americans.

The handbook would say, in the midst of a terrorist attack the vice president needs to be protected. As soon as the South Tower is hit, the existence of the attack is beyond question, but its nature and contour are not. Is a small Cessna, like the one that landed on the lawn of the White House during the Clinton Administration, possibly loaded with explosives, flying under the radar on the way to the West Wing? Is there a truck bomb driving up Pennsylvania Avenue? Does somebody have a stinger missile launcher or an RPG in Lafayette Park? All of these uncertainties are the reason the Secret Service would have Cheney by his belt and off his feet within a very few minutes of the South Tower being hit. In addition, of course, it is a fact that some sort of notice of "planes in trouble," to use a shorthand phrase, had been conveyed to all the necessary parties, and presumably the Secret Service by about 8:15 that morning. As opposed to being asleep with routine, everyone should have had their muscles twitching.

And I am not the only one that thinks so. Philip Shenon was nominated, I think, for a Pulitzer for writing The Commission, the Secret History behind the 9/11 Commission. A lot of what he wrote about was probably intended to be secret, and he certainly made a valuable contribution to an understanding of how the Commission could have produced such a disastrously false depiction. But it isn't that Shenon fouled the pitch off, to use a baseball analogy; he was waiting in line to buy a ticket to the wrong ballpark. I am ever so grateful that he was willing to give me a half an hour at a Starbucks near Dupont Circle even though he knew I was a staunch supporter of the Truth Movement. He was a very likable guy, and he said very complimentary things about public defenders, my calling for 32 years. I handed him Gellman's book, and asked if he would read the two pages to which I referred above. Immediately we stood at agreement; Gellman had simply accepted the official version, the Cheney version, and written it in his book. It was clearly not what happened. Hallelujah, I thought I was approaching a moment. But, no. Shenon got my drift in seconds and said that he hadn't written about Mineta either.

Therefore, I must be critical of him as well. I admitted I was, and tried to learn what it was that kept this witness off of the witness stand of history. In the course of explaining, a number of ingredients were introduced: Mineta was an old man confused by the fog of the moment, inarticulate, and possibly delusional. I have the following things to say about that. I have seen Mineta's videotaped testimony which Shenon had not; why, he didn't say. I have seen Mineta interviewed by activists a number of years later where he was as lucid as he had been before the Commission, and I met Mineta in person at his house in 2009 as he arrived home in his chauffeur-driven, big fancy car, after a day at the office of Hill and Knowlton, the public relations behemoth where he is a vice president. He was not willing to be interviewed which was my request, but he had enough curiosity to inquire about the case that is the subject of this book, and to have me describe for him the moments that were of such interest to the Truth Movement.

He had the bearing of a soldier, was dressed impeccably, and had not the slightest difficulty understanding what I was talking about or posing apt questions to enhance his grasp of the situation. He kept to his refusal to sit down with me after he had exhausted his curiosity. I must have evoked images of Columbo of television detective fame, when, part of the way back to my car, I returned with a further effort. "Secretary Mineta, you have the ability to derail my enterprise entirely. Can you just tell me, is there anything in what you told the 9/11 Commission that you have had reason to revisit and wish to revise or change; were you mistaken in any way; did you get anything wrong?" He was immediate and direct, if unimpressed with the power of his answer; he shook his head and said, "no."

You had to appreciate Shenon, though. He actually said that he would be mortified if he had missed the greatest story of...ever? I can't remember what words he used to describe it, but it was clear he was impressed with the magnitude of his potential failure. But though history and the profession of journalism needed a pronounced aggressive and unstinting boring-in at the reason for his missing what was staring him in the face, the moment demanded civility, and he had no further time for me. He had moved on, his recall of the facts was not as good as had once been the case, and his mind was immobile. I wrote him a week later asking him to provide me with his source for the idea that Mineta was unworthy of belief. I have not heard from him. Like the others, he had, and has, the power to ignore.

My interview with Shenon did nothing to quell my interest in talking to Gellman. He had parlayed his reporting into a book and made his way on to the Daily Show, and at that point Cheney's known, or highly suspected, crimes were enough to get anyone's attention. That Cheney was at the same time demonstrating the kind of character that is capable of engineering false flag attacks that kill American citizens seems to have been beyond the conception of mainstream commentators.

And therein lies the trouble. Pincus, Shenon, Gellman, Taibbi, Dwyer and other victims of my efforts, whom I have yet to describe, are such keepers of the American light, such swallowers of the

US-centric, we-are-the-heroes-of-the-world, pabulum, drinkers of
the USG propaganda Kool-Aid, that certain ideas cannot take form
within their conscious minds. It simply has not occurred to them,
no, more, it is anathema to them; there is an unwillingness, a refusal
to think that as a nation we are capable of unspeakable atrocity,
even to our own citizens.

I had written Barton Gellman that I wanted an interview. I received nothing in return. I went to New York and knocked on his
door. I was as polite as I know how to be and requested a conversation whenever he could make himself available. He was offended
that I was at his door; he thought it most inappropriate, wished me
luck, an interesting notion, and asked me to leave. In our conversation, defending against charges of impropriety, I reminded him,
as a journalist, he was certainly aware, that nothing of any significance gets done except face to face, a fact seasoned investigators
must come to terms with in the early days of their careers. It is nothing to put down a phone compared to asking a person to get out of
their house.

The media is very well fortified these days. Getting to see
someone at the New York *Times* requires a phone conversation
from the lobby or a referral to voicemail. James Risen had not responded to my letter, and didn't call me when I was in the lobby
or later on that week or weekend at the number I left. Frank Rich,
ditto. But Frank Rich appears to be a decent guy, writes so cogently of this nation's indiscretions and heartaches, the vicissi-
tudes of its leaders, and has such a great and eloquent instinct for
what ails the country. Him, I would try to track down.

Having gotten no return call, Friday night and Saturday remained before I had to leave. It was raining and blowing, but
the doorman allowed me to sit in the lobby waiting for Rich's arrival. Finally, it was 7 PM, and no sign of him. I asked the doorman,

and after checking he said that Rich had gone out for the evening. I left a copy of the Complaint that we had filed in the Federal Court for the Southern District of New York and wrote a note that I had one more day, could he please talk to me. When tomorrow came, more rain and wind and no message from Frank Rich, I was not optimistic. I presented myself to the same doorman and asked him to call and say that I was in the lobby. The doorman had a consoling look on his face, but harsh reality in his voice with the words that Rich would not see me.

Everyone has the picture now. Similar scripts were read at the various doors of Chris Matthews, Ron Suskind, and Bill Moyers. Copies of the Complaint were left at their doors, and no acknowledgment of their existence or my existence ever materialized. I wrote to Alexander Cockburn writer for the *Nation* and co-Editor of the newsletter and online journal, *Counterpunch,* asking for an explanation for the presence of nano thermite in four, separate, independently collected samples of dust and debris from Ground Zero, and he referred the question to Dr. Manuel Garcia of the Lawrence Livermore National Laboratory. Cockburn had Garcia write a debunking of the Truth Movement's theories concerning the destruction of the Towers in *Counterpunch.* I responded with an essay on vealetruth.com to which anyone with sufficient interest is invited to refer.

17

A Lawsuit? Do you know what you are up against?

It is with a little reluctance that I admit that I once considered politics the only conceivable road out of our national disgrace. A friend and colleague fairly early on suggested that a lawsuit should be filed. I rejected that idea for a number of reasons, but principal among them was the fact that I am not a civil lawyer, and therefore have no experience in that sort of litigation. I would be chewed up by pretty much anybody that the likes of Cheney, Rumsfeld, and Myers would get to represent them. I honestly didn't think that would be the United Sates government when I first thought of it. In addition, I was aware that civil litigation would be expensive, and take years, if not decades.

So, I started writing to senators and going by their offices with letters. Their offices are every bit as impenetrable as is mainstream media. They do have the ability to write form letters saying these matters have already been investigated and questions satisfactorily answered by the 9/11 Commission. But talking to a real human being with juice or even an interest in discussing the matter is completely out of the question. As District Court Judge Denny Chin wrote in his decision dismissing our case calling the assertions frivolous, the idea that the vice president and other high officials would conspire to enable terrorist attacks that would kill thousands of Americans is implausible. In response to that idea and the U.S. Attorneys' reply to our Opening Brief in the Second Circuit Court of Appeals, which did almost nothing but quote Judge Chin's Decision, I wrote an argument. It was not filed. We filed the one my partner Dennis Cunningham wrote. Mine was better suited to oral argument that I was hoping to give in the event the Court allowed argument. Here is what I had to say:

One is tempted to ask, are they [the Government, the Defendants] serious? The accusations are of mass murder and treason. Their response? A Letter Brief; in every significant respect a recapitulation of what appears in the District Court Judge's Decision. Accusations of the scope and kind made by Appellant in her Complaint are the currency of artisans of the darkest of black humor, the whimsically sick, the thought-disordered, or the very serious among us. Respondents choose to convey the sense that Appellant's lawyers are anything but the latter. They offer not one new case, not one new argument. Barely one of the many ideas articulated in Appellant's Opening Brief is even referred to. Apparently none deserve more than implied derision. Are they serious?

Deadly serious. They pursue a strategy from which they will not deviate. Not only has this strategy found success so far; it is the only possible, theoretical road to victory. How could Respondents (the Defendants) treat seriously the arguments they must claim are the product of fantasy and delusion, by implication, made by psychotics and the deranged? The path set out, and to this point unerr-ingly followed, will be accompanied by whistling, as if past a grave yard. That whistling will attach itself to fervent hope that no one, particularly a judge, will take the time to entertain or conceive of the monstrous nature of that which claws at our innards as a coun-try. Respondents' strategy is all of a piece and has been and will be pursued to the bitterest of ends, but only successfully if the innocent continue to allow themselves to be duped, the responsible evade their responsibilities, and those who have taken oaths leave the tat-tered evidence of those prior commitments like a pile of dust swept carelessly into a corner.

In another world the 65 pages of affidavits, setting out in detail the intricacies of the crime, its complexities, its unspeakable charac-teristics, the accompanying arrogance of its perpetrators, and their many apparent gaffe-like miscues that flout what one would assume were vulnerabilities, in another world, would, upon landing on the desk of any but the most sheep-like practitioner with a law de-gree, have provoked scandalous and subversive conduct. Questions of supervisors would be asked; consciences would be tested to the breaking point, letters of resignation penned and threatened and submitted, in another world.

Instead, readers of this impoverished Letter Brief must recall the works of Louis Carroll and Franz Kafka, maybe the likes of Huxley and Orwell, in order to be guided to a perch from which to see, with some chance of understanding, the premises and underlying strat-egy of Respondent's letter. In the final analysis and in its essence, that Letter most audaciously declares that the law and power, or someone's interpretation of the former and abuse of the latter, iden-tifies truth, regardless of any fact, or boatload of them.

Certainly, it is not the US Code or any of the US Supreme Court Reports that are required here. But in Carroll and Kafka the law can declare to be true that which positively isn't, and that declaration will be accepted and respected as if nothing is wrong. There, the truth is absolutely what power declares, and it is of little matter that facts or evidence may disagree.

And so, Respondents dutifully, and with a certain righteousness, proclaim that the District Court was correct in every respect as it made pretense that most of what was written by Appellant in her Complaint simply did not exist. The agony of April Gallop's psychological victimhood and the abundant reasons for her legal action are evaporated by judicial fiat.

When she sat down at her desk at the Pentagon on September 11th, her two-month-old baby son, Elisha, in his basket beside her, she was incapable of conceiving of evil at the highest levels of American Government. When the District Court Judge asked plaintiff's counsel at the pre-motion conference if the lawsuit that is the subject of this appeal was filed in good faith, it was apparently of a similar disposition.

In spite of reading the contents of the Appendix to Plaintiff's Response to the Motion to Dismiss, which set out in horrifying detail the evidence supporting plaintiff's claim, every page and every paragraph of which the court chose to ignore, it was still no closer to what the Harvard law professor, and discouragingly, Obama-intimate, Cass Sunstein has called a "warped epistemology," one which admits of the possibility of starkly immoral conduct by servants of the American Constitution. The Motion to Dismiss was granted because in the court's view, the claims made there were frivolous and based on "cynical delusion and fantasy."

In the days immediately following the attacks of 9/11, April Gallop became increasingly uncomfortable with the idea that an airplane had crashed into the side of the building. She had seen no evidence of a plane as she made her way out of the destruction. Having regained consciousness and found her baby amongst the ruin, she struggled her way onto the lawn outside of the building, there to collapse, but in the passing hours and days, she could find nothing in her memory that reminded her of the remnants of a crashed airplane. Abominable and manipulative treatment at the hands of officials at the Pentagon, some of whom sought to recruit her to an explanation contrary to the facts as she had experienced them, did nothing to erase her discomfort. Each succeeding year provided more and more reason to question the government's official story. She attended the hearings before the 9/ 11 Commission, and firsthand witnessed the sidetracking of the search for answers and the perversion of the search for justice. She was transformed from a mostly quiet and passive victim into a forceful and determined person who asked questions and demanded answers.

It became clear that no official of government and no institution of justice had the slightest interest in the truth of the matter. On December 15, 2008, she filed her lawsuit alleging that Vice President of the United States Dick Cheney, Secretary of Defense Donald Rumsfeld, and Chairman of the Joint Chiefs of Staff, Richard Myers, had conspired to enable and facilitate the attacks which had killed almost 3000 Americans. The U.S. government, through the U. S. Attorney's Office for the Southern District of New York, assumed representation of the three defendants and informed the court that a Motion to Dismiss would be filed. The US District Court set a pre-motion conference that was attended by all counsel for the Plaintiff and an Assistant U.S. Attorney together with a law clerk from that office.

The court, its clerk, a court reporter, and four law clerks assembled in a conference room, and the court inquired of Plaintiff's counsel what this lawsuit was about. Having struggled with the events of 9/11 for 3 years at the time of the conference, Plaintiff's counsel were more than aware of the difficulties that thrust themselves headlong into any conversation on the subject. That the conversation in the court's chambers was dressed in similar attire was surprising, as well as disheartening.

The court wrote in its subsequent decision: "It is simply not plausible that the vice president of the U.S., the Secretary of Defense, and other high-ranking officials conspired to facilitate terrorist attacks that would result in the deaths of thousands of Americans." This lawsuit is, quite simply, the ultimate challenge to the paradigm that encourages those words. The Court made no effort whatsoever in its decision to undergird, with reference to fact or history, its most pronounced affirmation of American exceptionalism. One must conclude that such an effort is simply unnecessary. The notions are beyond understood, so much so that even to suggest that, is to court blasphemy. Since the Court has sanctioned by its own use reference to the pre-motion conference, it might be remarked that the Court was in fact able, for a short time at least, to consider the ideas contained in the Complaint sufficiently to pose a question concerning counsel's beliefs with regard to whether or not Flight 77 actually hit the Pentagon, the source of considerable and sometimes heated debate within the "Truth" movement. In asking that question one is left to guess if the Court was momentarily able to feel the texture of plausibility beneath the tissue of horror.

Plaintiff, as stated in the Complaint, was well aware of the obstacles to comprehension that would need to be overcome in this titanic legal and intellectual battle. Likely the combination of the deaths of thousands of innocents at the hands of governmental officials and the assumed complete emasculation of the establishment of journalism in this country, the idea that we live in a society with a free press that would surely have uncovered such a story if it were true, provided all of the intellectual support needed to maintain the posture of incredulity characterized by the Court's decision.

If Flight 77 did not fly into the Pentagon, as the evidence known at this time most reasonably suggests, what happened to the passengers on that plane? With that question, one enters a deep and labyrinthine cave of speculation. But for sure, many innocent men and women, in some plane some place, were murdered and their bodies broken and charred in the process, coldly and with intricate, if occasionally flawed calculation. And those murders were integral to the overarching plot that required dead bodies to attest to the dark nature of the evil that had come to the door of America and wreaked its havoc there.

Travel into these areas inevitably stumbles upon an inconvenient fact, or many of them, but first of note is the existence of autopsy photographs of dead and burned bodies and DNA samples alleged to have come from an airplane that, itself, did not survive the heat from the explosions that its impact with the walls of the Pentagon created. This lawsuit is at its essence a proclamation in support of Occam's Razor, because there is only *one* sufficient explanation for the absence of a plane, and presence of body parts and their accompanying DNA, in contrast to the ability of the Plaintiff April Gallop to walk out of a building hit by a 757, her desk sitting squarely in the pathway of that supposed 757 traveling at a speed of 530 miles an hour. That *one* explanation consists of a conspiracy so unspeakable, so foreign to, maybe, the typical American mind as to obstruct rational thought.

There is a second fundamental barrier to the accurate understanding of the powers and forces that expressed themselves in the events of 9/11. It is ignorance of the "false flag." Human beings are innately familiar with the need or tendency to shift blame because it is a technique employed first by children. The "false flag" is a more sophisticated embodiment of the same mechanism conceived before, rather than after the event that is likely to lead to accusation. Steps are taken to make it appear that entities or persons other than the perpetrators are responsible for the acts in question.

History is filled with examples. Organized crime has employed patsies throughout its history in order to avoid prosecution for its more public and celebrated crimes. Most historians agree with William Shirer that the Reichstag fire was a Nazi "false flag" operation. If there were an historical prototype for Plaintiff's conception of the 9/11 conspiracy, the Reichstag fire would be it.

The Nazis learned of the patsy's intentions and then set a fire of its own which would more assuredly achieve their consolidation of power. The Gulf of Tonkin incident served a similar purpose. An event was manufactured or, for some, overblown, to give the U.S. a reason to increase its war efforts in Southeast Asia in 1964. There is a substantial list of apparent "false flag" incidents throughout the world such that no scholar would suggest that governments and individuals do not employ surreptitious means to hide their own involvement in matters conceived to be in those individuals' or nations' interests.

For example:

On September 14, 2005 a number of British soldiers were arrested in Basra, Iraq disguised to look like Middle Eastern men. They were in possession of explosives consistent with the tools of terrorism. Their capture was so significant to British forces that a force of British soldiers then attacked the local police station where the soldiers were being held. There is a famous photograph of a British soldier in flames that was taken during the siege of the police station. The conclusion, that the captured soldiers were arrested while in the process of conducting a "false flag," operation is unavoidable.

Two widely reported news stories demonstrate that the Bush Administration was familiar with the tactic of the "false flag." At a meeting on January 21, 2003 that included British Prime Minister Tony Blair, President George Bush suggested that an American U-2 spy plane be painted with the colors of the UN and flown over Iraq hoping that forces under the command of Saddam Hussein would shoot it down, giving the U.S. a reason to begin hostilities. This would have allowed the US to claim that Saddam was the aggressor when the reverse would have been true. In the summer of 2008, according to a report of Seymour Hersh, it was proposed, within the Office of the Vice President, that a number of boats be built to look like Iranian PT boats, that they be filled with Navy SEALS dressed as Iranians, and that they engage in a sea battle with an American ship, thus providing a pretext for war with Iran.

Lastly, the most senior counterterrorist operative in the Bush Administration at the time of 9/11, after Dick Cheney who had been placed in overall charge of counterterrorist operations in May as the warnings of attack rose in pitch, was Richard Clarke. Important is his work of fiction, *The Scorpion's Gate.* On the cover are found the words, "Sometimes you can tell more truth through fiction," and in the story the tactic of the "false flag" is prominently featured. If more of us were familiar with the term, "false flag," and aware of the myriad accusations of its use and a few of the agreed-upon cases, the court would be incapable of writing words which ladled derisive scorn onto the work of dozens of eminent scholars and hundreds of acclaimed thinkers, to say nothing of us, the Plaintiff's lawyers.

There is a final consideration to which this Court should turn before ruling. To be blunt, the investigative agencies of government in this country have been practitioners of distortion and cover-up. The search for truth concerning these events, however, is a long way from over. Independent researchers and scholars continue to study what is already known and to learn more about what has been hidden. Most recently, NIST made public, pursuant to a FOIA request, hours and hours of videotaped footage supposedly used in its determination of the cause of the destruction of the three buildings in New York. The cache is so large that time and resources have been insufficient to do more than conduct a modest survey of what is there. Even so, a videotape of an interview with some firemen who had just escaped one of the Towers contains references to so-called "secondary explosions," entirely corroborative of Appellant's contention that the three buildings were brought down by preset explosive charges. To those with eyes to see, it is apparent that what history will eventually record will have little in common with government proclamations in 2010, much less 2001, 2004, or 2008, and judged ill will be that institution that turned off the spigot of justice before the water of truth was more than lukewarm.

We each arise in the morning carrying a backpack of uncertainties, many or most of which we barely acknowledge or even realize are there. We follow our routines and in large measure, most of us do the best we can while feeling profoundly insignificant. The world is so large, history so long, our theoretical influence on the course of any event mostly miniscule. Members of this court are entitled, through achievement and position, to feel more exalted in stature than the rest of us. Still, even an appellate justice's sense of insignificance in the long reach of history demands that a shorter, closer view be adopted, one where the hope of a helpful ripple in the ocean of existence is what is sought to sustain and give meaning. Once in the lifetime of a handful of people the opportunity and choice presents itself, to do great good or not, to change the course of human events or not, to live the moment of truth or not. It is difficult indeed to imagine larger issues taking shape before a court. It would seem that the majesty of the simple idea of justice would require both sides of the controversy to give the fight every particle of their available resources in the way of intellect and argument. Respondents have chosen a different path. They have pursued a strategy that belittles and demeans while requiring virtually nothing from its legal executors. It may be well to ask, at what cost to the nation?

18

Lawsuit, Why Not?

So, there I was, sometime in the spring of 2008, angry. I had read and read, and written to big names, and talked to my friends, and it was all going nowhere. The scholarship on the part of the Truth Movement was mammoth and arresting and impressive. The response in the mainstream was silence. Steven Jones's paper about finding nano thermite had been accepted by a peer-review journal, the Open Journal of Chemical Physics, but it had not yet been published. NIST, the National Institute of Standards and Technology, had made its ridiculous findings about the Twin Towers that combined the trauma of the plane crashes and the fires in an explanation that avoided virtually all of the contrary facts and claims of the Truth Movement by simply ignoring them and refused to test for thermite even though they were informed that some such substance had in fact been found by tenured professors at major universities.

NIST's findings made the papers everywhere and the critiques of them, filling books, were ignored. I began to consider legal action in spite of my lack of experience in the civil arena. I had been put in touch with April Gallop, and she ex- pressed an interest in doing something. I shopped the idea of a lawsuit to a representative of a large law firm in San Francisco. I tried with the ACLU, the Southern Poverty Law Center, and Public Citizen. Most were more or less polite in turning me down.

When I got married, I fell wonderfully into the sphere of one of America's great and pioneering trial lawyers, Susan Jordan. It is so sad that she died in a plane crash in 2009. Everyone who knew her had their lives changed to the good for that connection and profoundly disrupted by that loss. She was kind enough, and patient enough, to listen to me go over the evidence that I had become acquainted with. She had suggestions; she had criticisms, but most importantly, she had a name. "You should talk to my pal, Dennis Cunningham."

Some people make it hard to get a hold of them. Some people make it hard to talk to them. Dennis is neither of those. He gave me the address and told me to come on over. His office had 70's movement lawyer written all over it, with prominent posters of the 90's case of Judi Bari and Darryl Chierney, the Earth Firsters blown up with the apparent connivance of the FBI in Oakland, who, in the case of Judi, posthumously, got $4 million dollars in a jury verdict from agents of the FBI and members of the Oakland Police for denial of their human and constitutional rights in the aftermath of the bombing, all thanks to the team whose indefatigable leader was Dennis Cunningham.

Tall, thin, balding, white beard, enormous smile, bigger brain, feet up on the desk, relaxed in his 70's, "what brings you to town?" I have been called upon to give the answer to that question, or similar questions with the same answer, on many occasions. I have adopted, as a defense mechanism, a kind of apologetic tone of resignation following a pronounced sigh, "9/11." "Oh," says he, "that's a good case."

Only then did I get around to surveying the walls of his office there to find, quite prominently displayed, if golf courses have signature holes, this would be the signature photograph of the 9/11 Truth Movement. It came from the front of a newspaper, probably the San Francisco *Chronicle,* and was the South Tower of the World Trade Center in mid collapse, or in mid destruction as one should rightly say. That photo itself should spawn graduate school courses in a variety of subjects. One surely would be the ability of the human brain to conform stimuli to preconception. I showed a large color rendition of that picture to a gathering of old friends, and one nearly fell off of his stool as he blurted out that it depicted an explosion as opposed to the effects of gravity.

At any rate, I understood that I was comfortably within the walls of unacceptable thought; Dennis did not need convincing that the government was involved. He had been wondering what could be done about it for quite some time. My plea for help put him over the line, and we had ourselves a partnership in subversion, with nothing less than the impoverishment, and we hoped silently to ourselves, with the eventual help of elements within the very forces we sought to attack, the imprisonment, of a vice president, a secretary of defense, and a chairman of the Joint Chiefs of Staff.

For most of the time forward, I was kibitzing over the shoulder of a legal artist, occasionally looking up things in books I had read. Dennis had spent his life in Federal Court fighting the government in every way he could. He's featured in the Assassination of Fred Hampton, by Jeffrey Haas, a book about the murder of the famous Black Panther leader in Chicago in 1969 by the FBI and members of the Chicago Police Department and the legal efforts to make his killers pay.

Dennis spent a number of years in New York working on the Attica prison cases and then came to San Francisco in the late 70's to continue his efforts at justice for the poor and the disregarded and the politically despised. Susan had steered me well. He did not have to look up the Federal Rules, and his writing style was brilliant. We both have tendencies toward the purple when we write, and were lucky to have some ex officio teammates who could talk us off of whatever precarious linguistic perch we were unaware we were on.

It was in December of 2008 that it came to me to file the Complaint and attempt to serve it on the defendants. As a lawyer, serving anything in a clerk's office carries with it a certain dread. I shall never forget my first occasion at the First District of the California Court of Appeals. I was a brand new zipper of a public defender, and I was bent on showing some complacent, sanctimonious right-wing jackass of a judge that my clients were going to be entitled to a hell of a lot better understanding of the Bill of Rights than his however-many decades in service of the forces of stability had allowed him to feel comfortable with.

That put me in front of, frankly, a similar looking character, well into his sixties, reading glasses down on his nose, stern look, very imposing, yet, I may have noticed as he got up from his desk and grabbed his file stamp, the slightest piece of pleasantness in his eyes. Something told me I should confess my unease, plead youth and ignorance, and hope that what I put in front of him came close enough to measuring up that the problem could be fixed there as opposed to driving back to Martinez, tail between my legs, whimpering that they wouldn't accept it for this reason or that. There was the merest notion of a smile as he took the documents and then began one century of wait as he looked with seeming infinite attention to positively everything on every single page. I can recall the tightness in my chest, I get it just about every time I compete, as he stopped and told me, as if it were a joke just between the two of us, that I would need to sign over the xeroxed signature on page whatever. I can't remember how groveling the "thank you" was as I left, but I am quite certain I was an embarrassment to anyone who had ever practiced law. We, after all, are the lawyers; they are the clerks. I am sure I will come to that attitude and feeling of self-assurance any year now.

In the winter, December 2008, approaching the U.S. District Court for the Southern District of New York across the river from where I stayed in Brooklyn, there was a sense that I was doing something big that I was not up to. And sure enough, the young woman clerk found our papers wanting in some regard. I simply can't remember what it was now, but it involved calls across the country to Dennis and some xeroxing on the machine upstairs from where you actually file the document. By reasonably early afternoon the case of April Gallop and her son Elisha against Dick Cheney, Donald Rumsfeld, and General Richard Myers had been filed, and I had in my hands a Summons to be served on each of the three defendants.

I took the train to Baltimore where I borrowed my sister's car for the drive to the Eastern Shore of Maryland and St. Michael's, the town that holds both Cheney and Rumsfeld for part of the time that they curse our existence. I didn't know which house Cheney owned, but Rumsfeld, I had learned, lived in the house made famous by a fight there that involved Frederick Douglas when he was 18 years old or so. I drove down the short driveway, went to the door, saw through it decorations for Christmas, heard a dog barking, and determined that no one was home.

I went to lunch, returned, found the same conditions and took up a position down the road and around the bend a bit, where I could see any car that might enter the driveway. After an hour and a half or so, a pick-up truck stopped at the mailbox and then drove to the house. A late middle-aged man in a baseball cap got out that could, from the distance, have been the then-former Secretary of Defense. I drove to the house and knocked on the front door. A man who was not Donald Rumsfeld came to the door. I asked if the Secretary was home as I had some documents for him.

I don't remember if the gentleman ever actually acknowledged that Rumsfeld owned the place or lived there, but as I left, he asked for my name, and I gave him my card. The next morning, I received a telephone call from the Pentagon. A very pleasant gentleman referred me to someone in the General Counsel's Office. Within a week or two, a representative of the U.S. Attorney's Office, or the Department of Defense, I can't remember which, was asking why efforts were still being made to serve Secretary Rumsfeld at his retreat in New Mexico. I called back and assured them that our agreement for the U.S. Attorney's Office to accept service for the three defendants was in force; I simply hadn't been able to contact our operatives in New Mexico the evening before when our agreement was made.

Attempting to serve the vice president on the 16th of December with a lawsuit accusing him of mass murder and treason bore fruit eventually, but of most interest was the conversation on the phone with today's version of the trial lawyer's Prince of Darkness, the Vice President's personal lawyer at the Edward Bennett Williams law firm in DC. I don't remember his name, and it wasn't until the 6th of January that he took my call. What I remember most was the grandeur and size of the obviously polished marble pedestal from which he dealt with the rest of the world, me at least. When he could muster enough interest to ask what the lawsuit was about, I told him that it accused the Vice President of complicity in the attacks of 9/11.

What did he say in response? He wanted to know if I had contacted my malpractice insurance carrier. Isn't that touching, he being so helpful as to remind me in one phrase that my license to practice law and my financial well-being might be in need of some tending? He sensed a soft spot and continued to press the question as if he were my mother. I ducked and parried and, in the end, told him I actually would very much like to discuss matters with him, but I wasn't sure to what end.

I never talked to him again. The U.S. Attorney for the Southern District of New York, the prosecutorial arm of government for the jurisdiction of the crime, the worst single criminal act ever committed on American soil, had taken over representation of three of the individuals with the highest ranks within that government and the greatest quantities of evidence demonstrating their complicity in that crime.

I am, as I have suggested before, willing to concede that people of goodwill have some substantial reason, at least superficially, to dismiss the substance of our lawsuit. As I have also said, however, even though our rendition of events may strain credulity, even be, at first blush highly unlikely, the Government's case is abjectly impossible, failing every test of science and history.

What does it take for occupants of the U.S. Attorney's Office to summon the stones to question an assumption or two? Sure, your boss thinks it is a joke; what level of curiosity did you bring to the table when you read the 65 pages of affidavits submitted by the Plaintiff's lawyers filed in response to your assertion that the lawsuit was frivolous? What goes on when you look at that famous picture of the North Tower disintegrating? What questions do you ask when you read of the sworn testimony of a cabinet secretary placing your client at the scene of the crime, at the time of the crime, and confirming orders with regard to a principal instrumentality of the crime?

19

Scientific Scrutiny

There remain a couple more exchanges that shed a bit of light onto the matter. Several years ago, I purchased the expertise of a renowned physicist at the University of California, Berkeley. I asked that Professors Jones's and Harrit's paper be scrutinized. I wanted to see where the vulnerabilities were if there were any. The conclusion reached by this eminent physicist was that Harrit and Jones had performed admirably as scientists; there was nothing that required correction in terms of the method that they had employed, but that the conclusions that they had reached created some hesitancy in the mind of my consultant. It appears that there is more that could be done, and in the mind of this particular scientist, should be done. There was, he asserted, the theoretical possibility that the substance found could be paint. It would be quite expensive, this expert suggested, given the vast expanse of paint possibilities from now back to what may have existed in the 70's when the buildings were built, but it seems they all need to be tested. Why exactly? Because unless you do, you will never know whether or not there is a kind of paint out there that…well, that explodes when you light it. Until that testing is done, absolute certainty of the scientific variety cannot be proclaimed.

The chances that what was found is paint, from my cross-examination of my consultant, don't amount to even barely appreciable, but until every theoretical test has been performed, the demanding scientists among us will be allowed to remain with legs on either side of the fence.

That, of course, is not how the world works. People make decisions about unimportant matters all the time on conditions that don't approach certainty. In court there are a number of standards of proof, from preponderance of the evidence, in essence, the scale is tipped ever so slightly in one direction as opposed to the other, to clear and convincing evidence, which allows children to be taken from their parents, to beyond a reasonable doubt, the highest standard of proof---required for the imposition of incarceration, and the death penalty--- known to man outside of the field of science.

When the former vice president is awaiting the verdict in his trial for mass murder and treason, he will be hoping that the jury can find a reason to doubt that of which he is accused. In the civil case that at one point was sitting on the desks of justices at the 2nd Circuit Court of Appeals, should they have allowed it to proceed on the merits of the case, a determination of what the facts actually tell us, the standard of proof that the jurors would have been called upon to apply is known as "a preponderance of the evidence." If the jurors were to think it more likely than not that Cheney and Rumsfeld and Myers conspired to aid or abet, foster or promote the attacks of 9/11, more likely than not that they were complicit in the terrorist acts, they would have been duty-bound to find for April Gallop and her son Elisha.

None of that makes the reticence of some scientists to sign on to the unspeakable unimportant or irrelevant. It simply establishes a context. Those, like Jones and Harrit, who are at least prepared to see the world for the catastrophe that it mostly is, who have access to more than what we were taught to consider about reality, have done the admirable job of simply stating what is true, what the world can rely upon, where the boundaries of discourse should be, appreciative of, but not hamstrung by, the extremely remote possibility that the nth degree of scientific certainty may have some relevance in this case.

If one employs a scientist to view, as a scientist, a scientific study, and judge its validity in the scientific community, which is what I did, the verdict that is rendered, that the scientific method employed was unimpeachable so far as it went, what was found is perfectly consistent with nano thermite, is not the last judgment with regard to the existence or non-existence of high governmental complicity. That verdict can only be rendered after all of the evidence has been evaluated, or at least an amount sufficient to negate the reasonable possibility of innocence on the part of Cheney and his brethren.

Just to look at the nano thermite question a bit more closely. Jones and Harrit have established beyond a reasonable doubt the presence of nano thermite at Ground Zero. I can say that because the possibility that the WTC Towers were painted with paint whose properties and constituent elements are identical to nano thermite are unquantifiably small in my judgment. That is what Jones and Harrit found after all, a substance thought to be unignited nano thermite that is in fact combustible, that ignites at approximately 430 degrees C; that, as well, it should be mentioned, does not dissolve in Methyl Ethyl Ketone, a paint solvent. But not just for that reason. There are other things that take place with the use of thermite or its derivatives. There is a certain color to the fire produced; there is a certain color smoke that is produced; and there is molten metal produced.

Therefore, it is important to take note of not just one, but all three of those phenomena in videos of the 83rd floor of the South Tower just before the Tower crumbles to the ground in free-fall, as if the 82 floors below it simply had evaporated, which is more or less what took place, with in some cases enormous pieces of the steel frame of the building expelled sideways into adjacent structures there to be photographically captured for all time to the abject embarrassment of any holder to the "Official Story".

So, inhabitants of this world, the world where life goes on and people need to make decisions on a daily basis, the real world as opposed to the scientific world, are not bound by a single piece of evidence and any theoretical scientific possibility that an almost infinite amount of money would be required to eliminate from consideration, but rather must consider all of the things that happened, all at once, all in the same place, all serving the same purpose. Real people must ask themselves how many zeroes are involved in describing the probability that all of those characteristics of controlled demolition occurred, consistent with the findings of Jones and Harrit, but still it was *not* controlled demolition. If you live in the real world, it is far too many zeroes to give the matter the slightest further thought.

With all that in mind and girded as required for another joust with the scientists, the name Thomas Eagar could be ignored no further. He is a professor of something germane, physics, I think, at no lesser university than MIT. He was provoked to write a paper about the destruction of the WTC Towers in the months after it happened. I am not guessing when I say he is a stalwart of the academic and political establishment. Our email communications made that abundantly clear with his derisive hurling of the epithet "conspiracy theorist", included in the event that whatever else he said left a question in anyone's mind.

The gist is that I wrote to ask if he disputed Jones and Harrit's findings in the peer-reviewed *Open Journal of Chemical Physics.* Not only did he dispute their findings, saying what they found was paint, he asserted that the paper they published was not peer-reviewed and would not pass muster in the event it was ever submitted to such a publication. So, leaving the substance of the matter to one side for a moment, in order to climb on board with Professor Eagar, one has to sign on, at least in some sense, to the idea that the USG would give substantial research money, as they clearly did, to a tenured professor at Brigham Young University who is incapable of ascertaining that the journal which published his paper was not peer-reviewed.

We may all rest easy that such is not the case. Professor Eagar is absolutely 100% wrong about the *Open Journal* not being peer-reviewed. In addition to everything that is clearly stated when one accesses the publication, I am personally aware of the importance placed by Jones on having the paper published in a peer-reviewed journal. The idea that he was swindled into having it published in a journal that did not meet the most elemental step to consideration evokes an image of as many zeroes as were involved in the other matter of probability referred to with regard to the presence or absence of nano thermite.

Add to that the breath-taking arrogance of dismissal that guards the wagon train of his conviction. I was accused of being in an argument, when I asked if he might be mistaken about the peer-review matter, that being such a simple question, so easily verified or proven false, an error I thought way out of the reach of a man of such credentials and accomplishment as Steven Jones, not to mention his principal co-author, Neils Harrit of the University of Copenhagen. I thought about diving into an argument with Professor Eagar, but apparently, if my email file is properly labeled, I thought better of it and simply asked for help. What I got was silence, then at least.

This effort at writing a book has required follow-up requests for interviews, out of fairness, to complete the record, but more importantly, as a further mechanism to achieve what this whole enterprise has been about, attempting to engage the establishment and the "Official Story" in debate. My further request for an interview referred to not wanting the reader to have to speculate about the professor's positions. He responded that he did not have a lot of time, maybe questions could be emailed, and what sort of speculations was I referring to? I submitted four or so questions that anyone who has read this far would be able to craft on their own, one of which had to do with the finding of molten molybdenum at Ground Zero, important because it melts at about 5000 degrees Fahrenheit, temperatures requiring explosives and far beyond the capabilities of jet fuel or the contents of the offices inside the Towers.

Those questions, left unaddressed, unanswered, and unreferred-to, brought an email that laughed at my ignorance of science - no argument there- spoke mumbo-jumbo on the question of molybdenum, and called me a conspiracy theorist. I replied:

Professor Eagar: My ignorance of science, which you have managed to uncover, is woeful indeed, but in my business it can prove to be an asset, as I am actually called upon to explain to jurors, sometimes far more ignorant than I, why some part of science has some bearing on a decision they are called upon to make. This allows me to extract from scientists their simplest crucial understandings about important matters.

Therefore, since you and I are both pursuing truth, it is honorable work that we each do, and I shall continue, while waving aside mostly meaningless appellations that do not promote our search. As you are surely aware, 9/11 was never about conspiracy or not, but simply the identities of the conspirators. So, to push on, in the face of the questions I asked, I am not sure what standing by your paper means. You did not mention the presence of molten metal in your paper. I am led to believe, now by many scientists, that its presence is pivotal. If it was there, something other than jet fuel was igniting. So, was it there?

When I ask questions and they are not answered, I have a very elaborate system that speaks to me in myriad ways, telling me in essence, "for God's sake, don't stop, there is something there." I think I could go on for a very long time, but I will ask you just this, in all seriousness and as a proffered mechanism to reach common ground: what goes through your mind when you see Building 7 drop like a stone, or more aptly, like those other controlled demolitions we have all seen so many times on television, as Rather, Brokaw, and Jennings put it, virtually in unison?

Grandiosely, I say, I don't think there is much that is more important than you and I figuring this matter out. I wonder, if your children or grandchildren were to ask you any of the questions I have, if you would simply stand by your paper.

With hope, Veale

I guess the fact that those have been the last words between us means that I won't be getting my questions answered; I won't be getting an interview; and it is Professor Eagar's opinion that whatever I may want or think, matters not in the slightest. I guess that is what that means.

20

Rather's Contribution

Here I have invoked again that famous name of American journalism, Dan Rather. I had a chance to see him up pretty close. It was at Wheeler Auditorium at UC Berkeley on Tuesday, April 25, 2006. I was invited to attend a lecture by a friend, but the world, should it have been reported on at all, was offered a confession of such poignancy and such significance, that it should inspire a generation to revisit all that has been taken for granted in its lifetime. Dan Rather had a conversation with the dean of the UC School of Journalism, Orville Schell. Wheeler Hall is one of the imposing venues on the campus, and the place was packed for, as it turned out, a polite discussion of the highlights of Rather's career. There was, however, one obviously difficult moment in which Rather was able to keep from crying, but from the second row, it appeared to be a monumental battle that he waged.

For his efforts to maintain his dignity, he should not be criticized. For his recognition that tears were entirely appropriate, he deserves no praise. For the crowded world that listened, outrage precedes bereavement. Dan Rather has much to be sorry for; but that he was able to tell us, even at this late date, he more than seventy years old, even as sparsely confessed as the substance turned out to be, is to his credit.

I can't remember at this point if Mr. Rather was technically between jobs at the time of his appearance with Mr. Schell, but his time with CBS had ended over a year before, when during the 2004 election, he reported about George Bush's evasions of his duties in the Texas Air National Guard during the Vietnam War. Thanks to the reporting of Greg Palast we know that Rather was wrong, only significantly, to the extent that his,? Rather's, reporting did not detail the precise nature of Bush's failures and the grandeur of the quid pro quo corruption involved in covering up Bush's war time crime of being AWOL. Though Rather may well have been fooled by some Karl Rove plant, he was most assuredly correct in his premise that Bush had been insufficiently attentive to his duties as National Guard pilot, a position he used his connections to obtain in the first place in lieu of hearing bullets fly in the jungle. So Rather appeared on stage as a victim of Rove's as well as a famous television journalist.

The essence of his confession is that he has been too fearful and timid to do his job. That he must be compared, so decidedly and unquestionably to his disadvantage, to Edward R. Murrow, was obvious to everyone in the room, but none more than Mr. Rather himself, and that was surely the moment that provided the greatest test to his composure. He offered as explanation for his failure, among others, the lack of civic virtue among the population, and it struck a chord of truth for some of us. There was barely a significant minority of the audience who had written their Congressperson in the last month, a parlor trick performed at Rather's instigation. When Dean Schell rose to the moment and inquired if Rather had made efforts to go to the top, as Murrow did with Paley, Rather did not hesitate in his denial. Had he written letters to the head of Viacom? "No".

During the course of describing the decision to do a story, much was made of the question of ratings, and the 18-35-year-old demographic. They agreed that CBS is no longer just CBS, but a subsidiary of Viacom, an enormous conglomerate whose tentacles stretch into every part of our lives and whose interests may be affected by any serious look at the injustices and inequalities of American life, precisely the mandate of Dan Rather for his entire career. In a more perfect world, a media company's corporate charter would have to do with the provision of news or entertainment, and nothing else, and could not be owned by interests defined by a different charter, the manufacture of armaments for sale to the government, or for the government to sell to whomsoever it may choose, for fees and bribes and every other imaginable indicia of corrupt practice, for example.

This nation is a long way from that world; in fact, it might be said, our makeup is the antithesis of that notion. Mr. Rather was given the opportunity to discuss the BBC. He was polite and politic. He meted out praise in conservative doses, but could not be misunderstood to prefer the British model, taking refuge in the smiling retort that they confuse being boring with being serious. What Mr. Rather appears unable to understand, or at least articulate in public, is the symmetry displayed by the government ownership of the BBC in the UK and the government de facto ownership of the media in this country. That was an opportunity devoutly to have wished for. It was an opportunity for Mr. Rather to pay homage to the countless studies that demonstrate the extent to which the mainstream media acts as a propaganda arm of the US government. It was an opportunity to discuss the last century's history of journalists being on the government payroll. It was an opportunity to refer to only the latest scandals of government stipends to supposed independent journalists. It was an opportunity missed by Mr. Rather and Mr. Schell. Can it be that they are unaware of this history? Or do they deem it unimportant? How much time must be taken exploring Mr. Rather's parents' newspaper reading habits, or long ago yesterday's laurel-earning journalism? With a guest like that at one's disposal, mustn't politeness give way to the fact that he on the stage is our representative in the quest for knowledge? None of us will ever have that chance to ask questions.

So, Mr. Rather, what then must we, you, do? What will come with your recognition of failure? You look hale and hearty. The room was full; you have a voice. You were weak and could not understand your duty to resign in the face of corrupt influence. You could not understand the monumental place you could have guaranteed for yourself in the annals of journalism. Was it the money you wouldn't have had? One would have thought you had enough, if not when you were

fifty, surely when you were sixty, or sixty-five. Was it ancient friendships in the world of corporate wealth that you simply could not betray even though your journalistic integrity was at stake? Were you afraid to lose your access, a topic given much time that night, but understood by Mr. Rather to be a problem more of the last ten years than of the structure of our media system as discussed by people like Chomsky twenty years ago?

Is this not the moment to seek redemption? This government lied this country into a murderous and illegal war. As unpardonable as that seems to many, and as clear as that must be to you, it has yet to provoke you to put your spine into play. It was you who embraced the metaphor from the stage, suggesting a spine transplant for those in your position in this society. Is it not time for you to come clean about your life and times? Is it not the moment for you to evaluate what it was that led you to say "Boom" during the Gulf War as one supposed Patriot missile took out another Scud? Is it not time for you to rethink what it is that prevents you from explaining and thereby condemning this country's death squad foreign policy? Is it not time to discern what kept you from informing us of the lies that covered up Gulf War Syndrome? Those of us who cared realized the weak reed upon which we were leaning when George Bush, Sr. scared you off of his criminal complicity in Iran-Contra with a cheap reference to a fit of pique to which you were most probably amply entitled.

Oh, yes, and for those of us who simply cannot put it behind us, is it not time to take an honest look at that day to which you repeatedly referred, 9/11? Is it not time for a look within to divine what allows you to say there are no eyewitness, earwitness accounts, no empirical evidence that suggests, much, much less, demands the conclusion that members of this government were authors and integral participants in the crimes of 9/11? Dear Mr. Rather, the bookshelves are filling up with, and the New York Times has sued to produce, precisely such accounts and precisely such empirical data. Your opinion that a government conspiracy on 9/11 was "bullfeathers" is something to which you are decidedly entitled. The American people, however, are possessed of entitlement as well, as long as icons such as you profess an allegiance to the truth. They are entitled to learn the facts so that they can come to their own conclusions. Based upon your confident pronouncements on that Tuesday evening, a citizen would be entitled to dismiss government conspiracy as unworthy of passing thought, not to say honest consideration. Honesty, however, has to give the scholars and investigators who have written on the subject what is due to them, a recognition that there is an enormous amount of evidence at their disposal. Your "bull feathers" comment demonstrates willful ignorance, or a mindset that is simply inconsistent with the search for truth that knows no preconception.

In addition, that comment requires one to stare quizzically at your refusal to state the bold truth, that the story that ushered you out of the office, probably fooled by Karl Rove or his kind, that George W. Bush had cheated his way out of military service, was, in its essence, right on the money. Your reticence to proclaim an opinion in the instance of your departure from your job, and lack of it in the case of government complicity in 9/11 is ...peculiar. Is a line being toed?

What precisely is it about the history of the last seventy years that makes government complicity in the venality and atrocity of the crimes of 9/11 inconceivable? What was it about the firebombing of Dresden, the eradication of a rural population in Vietnam through "Operation Speedy Express", the machine-gunning of as many as 700 villagers at El Mozote in El Salvador with US Government tacit approval if not active connivance, an important distinction that really only a Dan Rather could have gotten to the bottom of, the running of drugs into this country by our own governmental agents, a story which your brethren at "West 57th Street" courageously took on in the 1980's; what is it about any of these paltry examples that gives the apparatus of governance in this country a pass at the greatest crime ever committed on American soil?

Dan Rather has an opportunity right now to look deep within himself, something he is obviously able to do; close to tears is evidence of that. Dan Rather has an opportunity to become his promise as a journalist by recalling the particulars of his shortcomings, and by looking with a journalist's zeal into all of the evidence concerning September 11, 2001. If he decides not to avail himself, the temptation to believe him just one more in a long and ignominious line of government-co-opted journalists will shortly become overwhelming.

21

Some Other Notable Failures

Rather is obviously not alone in averting his eyes. It is a bit strange that he has been considered by some the face of the "liberal media." Today, there are actually some real, honest-to-God, liberal/progressives on television. Men and women who don't mince their words. Rachel Maddow and Bill Maher and Keith Olbermann, for example, and, of course we have had Bill Moyers for quite some time. But they can't be found when it comes to the question of government complicity in the attacks of 9/11, except perhaps to laugh or deride. Take Maher who had Cornell West and Richard Clarke on his show and asked them, what about these conspiracy theories, do you believe them?, or words to that effect.

Cornell West had an enigmatic response that contained the word "no." Clarke burnished the already well-used retort: First, the government is incompetent (couldn't pull it off), and Second, no one can keep a secret (there would have been a leak).

There is much that can be said in response to these assertions, but Maher was capable of none of them. He might have summoned the facts that, 1. The FAA landed 4500 airplanes in minutes without event, the same morning it is supposed to have clumsily forgotten how to perform its most basic of Standard Operating Procedures, i.e. alert the military to scramble jets in case of emergency; 2. The US military managed to invade and occupy two countries in three years without much in the way of casualties. Clearly the government's incompetence is not entirely reliable.

Or, Maher might have done enough study to know there are in fact dozens of leakers and whistleblowers, private citizens, government informants, FBI agents, and most recently, a first responder who happened to overhear the countdown to the demolition of WTC 7, by mistake, then to be told by the Red Cross official who happened to take his hand away from the earpiece of the walkie-talkie at the wrong moment, to keep his mouth shut.

Maher and Olbermann and Moyers, and a host of less visible journalists, apparently don't have the time or the stones to read some of what is available to anyone interested. Which should prevent them from relying on another favorite argument: the government couldn't have done it because the risk of discovery would have been too great; they would be afraid of getting caught. Why prevented? Because, even with the issue so prominent as to be the subject of a national TV show (Maher's), no person of real significance, or importance, or national stature, or substantial voice has bothered to learn enough to address the questions. There is, now, an exception that should be acknowledged. Geraldo Rivera of the Fox network, hosted a program that included interviews of Tony Szamboti, an engineer with Architects and Engineers for 9/11 Truth, and Bob

McIlvaine, the father of a man who died when the South Tower collapsed. At the end of the show, Rivera acknowledged that his previous conclusion that his guests must be crazy was all wrong and that further study was most certainly warranted.

Maher, however, as a prime example, did not know enough, or care enough to try to confront Richard Clarke with his own story that contradicts the 9/11 Commission Report's finding that Cheney was not in the Presidential Emergency Operations Center at the time Norman Mineta describes him giving orders which were either, 1. obeyed, allowing Flight 77, or some other aircraft, to hit the Pentagon, or 2. disobeyed, which failure has led to no disciplinary action against any person whatsoever, and no mention in the US mainstream media. A person in Maher's position might feel awkward not knowing about the finding of nano thermite residue in the rubble at Ground Zero, or, knowing about it, not inquiring about it of supposedly knowledgeable insiders, or better yet, having one of the 9/11 Truth scientists on the show. Or, he could choose to debate a trial lawyer possessed of some familiarity with the case.

22

CIA Executive Director

I have left for last, probably a matter of small importance, but you never know. You really can't read too much about 9/11 without coming across one strange set of facts that needs some discussion. It seems someone knew that the attacks were going to take place. Apparently, someone tried to make some money off of it. In the week leading up to 9/11 unusual quantities of shares of stock in at least two airline companies were traded such that the investor would make money if the companies' stock price declined. They sold the stocks short, in other words. Why would you do such a thing? Well, if you knew that the companies were going to be cast in a disparaging light because of an event of which you had foreknowledge, you would be in a position to make money when the stock price fell after the event.

And so it transpired. Stock in United Airlines and American Airlines took a serious jolt when their planes rammed into three buildings, or two buildings and whatever happened at the Pentagon, and crashed in the field in Pennsylvania ---leaving virtually none of the usual signs of an airplane crash, such as large pieces of tail or wing. One hopes the digression into argument by exposition of fact will be pardoned. It has become impossible to discuss any aspect of this case without arranging before the audience another couple of paragraphs of important information.

It is an apt moment to describe the saga of United 93 in some greater detail. According to the government, it is supposed to have dived into the ground because its passengers stormed the cockpit causing it to fall in one piece, or maybe several pieces, from the sky. Some of its contents, however, were found 8 miles away, and a large piece of the engine was found over a mile from the designated crash sight, all of which suggests that it was shot down as has been relayed to family members by at least one Air Force officer in a position to know. Of course, the crime scene doesn't pass any sentient being's straight face test. The trees and shrubbery are falling in the wrong direction according to the government's version of the flight path, and the color of the smoke is all wrong.

Furthermore, it is an unfortunate fact of aviation that a number of plane crashes have been videotaped. You take a look at the deep black oily smoke that erupts from one of those scenes, and you will find no tendency to equate it with the much lighter gray smoke arising above the field in Shanksville. There is in addition an eyewitness to a missile in the vicinity just before the crash, a woman driving in her car whose story has been straitjacket-immobile over the many years since it was first told, but why does the world need to worry about such matters?

For those unmoved, actually for everyone, a final devastating bit of bother for the official account: an analysis was conducted by the Pennsylvania Department of Environmental Protection of the soil in the area of the supposed crash. The state was attempting to determine if there was environmental contamination to the area as a result of the crash. They dug their wells and employed their sensors, but they found no contamination whatever. Seems there were 37,500 gallons of jet fuel remaining in the tanks and unaccounted for at the crash site. According to that agency, the jet fuel was not on the ground, and it did not contaminate the waters under the ground. One look at the uncharred, grass-fringed margins of the rather diminutive hole which is supposed to contain the plane and all its passengers makes it clear that the fuel did not burn up in the vicinity. Is this when you say, "I'm just sayin'"?

To return to the matter at hand, somebody was poised to make some money because United and American fared poorly that day and their stock prices reflected the fact. The subsequent sales were made after 9/11, but for some reason, nobody has had whatever it takes to pick up the cash. No one knows a fraction of what we should know about these trades that appears to prove foreknowledge by someone. What is known is that the firm that made the trades was Deutsche Bank Alex Brown. The efforts to find further facts, undertaken by independent researchers, uncovered a familiar name.

A.B. "Buzzy" Krongard was the head of Alex Brown, an investment bank in Baltimore in 1999, when it was taken over by Bankers Trust who subsequently sold it to Deutsche Bank. In 2001, on September 11th, Buzzy Krongard was the Executive Director, generally thought of as third in command at the U.S. Central Intelligence Agency.

Those facts have led to the wildest sort of speculation and conjecture that concludes that Mr. Krongard should be seen as some sort of suspect. I am not a bit sure precisely how I would have conducted myself in 2001 or since had I been in Mr. Krongard's shoes. As far as I have been able to learn, no journalist has seen fit to publish any efforts they have made to learn precisely how he actually did conduct himself. We have learned that he currently has a relationship with Blackwater or whatever it is called now, and that he might be thought of as something of a cowboy when it comes to U.S. interests in foreign lands, and that he once punched a shark on a bet, and has bidden an interviewer to punch him, so confident of his martial arts/physical fitness prowess is he. But, what he knows about 9/11 and his reactions to the event are not the subject of anyone's interest, that has access to him, and the desire to publish anyway.

Therefore, I found myself in an interesting position, staring at the no trespassing signs nailed to the trees bounding the back entrance to his property. The front driveway prominently displayed signs about guard dogs. Naahhh, I thought to myself; write a letter, presume civility and see what it gets you.

October 24, 2010,

Dear Mr. Krongard; I see no reason to be anything other than blunt; this letter is an effort to inspire action, written by someone probably insufficiently talented to accomplish the goal. ..... I have thought about dropping by your house to see if you would talk to me.

I have abandoned the haunts of my childhood, except for the occasional visit back to see family, and have been living and practicing law in California for the past 35 years. About six years ago, a very bright colleague put a book in front of me, and my life has not been the same since. The book had to do with 9/11, and now I represent a woman who as a soldier was hurt during the attack on the Pentagon.

Given the library I have consumed in pursuit of an understanding of the events of that day, I have come upon your name, a person at one time of enormous stature in the CIA and at another, at Alex Brown; a place of such familiarity to me, if only from a distance......The references to you in the literature are primarily opaque and suggestive and cradled in circumstance, from which platform one may see nothing or everything as one is predisposed. I have not much use for the possibilities, which are too many and too varied. I would like to have the opportunity to make a more astute and valuable assessment based upon what you are prepared to tell me, or write.

As I see it, the possibilities may be set out as follows: 1. You are one of the 7 people who run the world and will not open your mouth about the horrible events of 9/11, ever. 2. You were a participant in the conspiracy whose existence I am prepared to prove in court, should I ever be given the opportunity, which remains in the hands of the 2nd Circuit at the moment. Ergo, your silence. 3. You are so much a part of the Establishment and such a committed member of the apparatus, and so thoroughly indoctrinated in its premises, that you have spent almost no time considering the possibility that your brethren have done something evil, and at any rate consider that possibility inconceivable. 4. Though not a conspirator, you know what happened, and you have information of priceless value to any investigation of the event.

I am unaware of any journalism that seeks to establish which, or what, of the foregoing is true. I have done enough to know that your silence means neither complicity nor ignorance. I would like to know as much as you might be prepared to tell me. If that means you use me to obfuscate, I am prepared to take the risk. If it means you become Deep Throat, I am prepared to act in whatever manner you require. If it means something else, you need to simply tell me what to do.

I will pledge at this moment to keep our communications confidential for a month or until we make other arrangements, whichever comes first. Let me assure you that I write this letter because I feel I must, because I am most certainly "on a mission", and because I was brought up to obey "no trespassing" signs. I have no illusions about the ease with which I can be ignored; it has been nearly universal. If your impulse and your judgment is to do just that, but something in you wants something to happen, because what happened was as wrong as anything can be, pointing a journalist in my direction might be a way to go.

I hope to hear from you, but most of my hopes about this matter and the possibility of justice have gone unfulfilled. As I said, I write this because I can, and my duty tells me I must.

Sincerely, B.V.

October 31, 2010

Dear Mr. Veale; I have carefully read your letter and, in reply, categorically state to you that I am unaware of any information which would support your premise of a conspiracy in connection with the attack on our Country on 9/11. I can further assure you that if I had such information, long ago I would have provided it to the appropriate authorities.

Personally, I have been defamed by bloggers who claim that I sold airline stocks short on 9/10 and profited thereby. Such an accusation is preposterous and no shred of evidence has ever been produced. This bizarre accusation seems to rest on the theory that I worked at Alex. Brown, which was sold to Bankers Trust, which was sold to Deutsche Bank, which may have executed some such transaction. The fact that years passed between these events, I was at the CIA and, therefore, any securities transaction I was part of was reported and monitored seems to be ignored. Therefore, perhaps I am a bit sensitive to your surmisal.

A.B.Krongard

Mr. Krongard,

I could not possibly have hoped for more than your straight-forward response to my letter. I have many questions. Would you meet with me to discuss them?

V.

November 22, 2010

Dear Mr. Krongard,

As you may have had the misfortune of learning through a bizarre email, my email was hacked, and I have lost a week and a half of communications. I hadn't heard from you before it happened, but I want to make sure I didn't miss something. I am in Baltimore till next Wednesday, if there is any chance you would be interested in meeting with me.

V.

November 22, 2010

***

Dear Mr. Veale

As I told you, I see no reason to meet with you since I have no knowledge of anything which would be relevant to what you are interested in researching.

A.B.K

Mr. Krongard, I must have missed an email. Thank you for responding anyway. I appreciate your view that nothing that you know has any relevance to my inquiry. For clarity, I will write out a few questions to give you a sense of my precise interest. Should you feel of a mind to answer them, I would appreciate any help you can give me.

How did you become aware that your name had been in some way associated with the "9/11 conspiracy theory", if I can use that as shorthand for the idea that high government officials were in some way complicit in the attacks?

Did you ever get a call or a visit or a letter from anyone investigating 9/11 or your alleged connection with the conspiracy theory?

Did you ever take any steps to learn what the precise basis for your claimed association with the conspiracy was?

As far as you know, is it true that Deutsche Bank had something to do with trades in American Airlines, United Airlines, and Morgan Stanley stock(I may be wrong about which brokerage house's stock was involved, that info is not at my fingertips at the moment) prior to 9/11 which trades earned a lot of money after the attacks for the entities making them?

What steps, if any, did you take to get to the bottom of the matter?

What were the results of your efforts? 7. If you took none, why not?

There are many other questions which any investigator would want to ask you because of the place that you held in government at the time, having to do with your whole story vis-a-vis the attacks: where were you, who were you with, when did you first hear of any conspiracy theory, what were your reactions and those of the people you were around at the time?

Bill Veale

November 23, 2010

Veale,

I have never received any interest orindicationof interest in my participating in any conspiracy involving 9/11 from any government agency

That addresses questions 3,5 and 7. 1 and 7. Because the only place this insanity shows up is on blogs written by people who have no basis for making outrageous accusations, I have ignored

this stuff. I became aware when told of some of these accusations by others.

4.I have never met, or to the best of my knowledge, even seen anyone from Deutsche Bank other than former Alex. Brown people who may now work for it. I left Bankers Trust in January of 1998 and had no part in the transaction between DB and BT.

A.B.K

November 23, 2010

Mr. Krongard,

You have been more than indulgent. I find myself wanting to say, "I don't want to argue with you," but that would be patently false. I can't imagine a more fascinating enterprise, more perfectly suited to my nature. I will continue this communication because what you have told me has been invaluable. You are, of course, free to ignore my questions, but I am hoping that some of what made you so successful will challenge you to want to engage.

You agree that evil men have been attracted to power throughout history?

You agree that humanity has been capable of all manner of atrocity throughout history including acts more horrifying than 9/11?

You agree that Americans have engaged in such acts in her history, and even if you don't, you wouldn't claim that citizenship deprives one of the capacities to be and do evil?

You recognize that members of the Bush Administration, as part of the Project for a New American Century, suggested that greater steps should be taken to project American power around the world, but that those steps would not be possible without a "New Pearl Harbor"?

You agree that 9/11 enabled the Bush Administration to accomplish that projection of power, in addition to enacting the Patriot Act, and allowing its colleagues to benefit financially from its enhanced Defense strategies?

You agree that the tactic of the "false flag" has been employed by governments throughout history, and the American government in particular?

You agree that there was no technological impediment to the high government conspiracy that you and many more have labeled insanity?

Did you know about the finding of nano thermite in four separate, independently collected samples of dust and debris from Ground Zero, and the peer-reviewed article establishing the fact?

Are you aware of the conclusions of over 1200 architects and engineers that all three buildings in New York were destroyed by controlled demolition?

Did you know that there was a third building, WTC 7, that was also destroyed that day?

Are you aware of all of the eye and ear-witness evidence of explosions in the Towers and WTC7 before and during the collapses?

Do you know the story of Barry Jennings?

Have you seen the pictures of the front of the Pentagon shortly after the attack there?

Are you aware that an E-4B was flying above the White House at the time of the attack on the Pentagon?

Did you know that the radar tracks documenting that flight have been scrubbed, thus erasing the E-4B out of existence?

Are you aware of the discrepancies in the flight paths of Flight 77 that allegedly hit the Pentagon as detailed by the NTSB and the 9/11 Commission?

Did you know that my client, April Gallop, walked out of the Pentagon after the attack, with severe head trauma, when her desk where she was sitting immediately before the explosion was in the way of the plane?

How did you react to the news that our headquarters had been successfully attacked?

There is much more, but I would simply love to know your answers to these questions. I obviously, even more, would be un-endingly grateful for the opportunity to discuss them with you in person.

Bill Veale

***

November 24, 2010

Veale,

May I suggest a sanity test for you. As a lawyer, you should be familiar with the concept of "summary judgement." Assume that everything you allege is true and this giant conspiracy actually took place. Think of how many people would have had to have been involved. The idea that all of those who conspired have remained silent and that those investigating this absurd theory have either failed to find a conspirator or, themselves, been co-opted into the conspiracy boggles the mind. Such secrets just don't stay secret.

Please do not respond to this since this is the end of our correspondence. Thank you.

A.B.K

***

And so there you have it. If you go back to my original letter, all four possibilities to which I referred, 1. That he is one of the magnificent seven world dominators, 2. That he is an active member of the conspiracy, 3. That, due to his long-term marination in the assumptions of empire, he is psychologically incapable of conceiving of our premise, or 4. That he knows a lot, if not all, though personally innocent of wrongdoing, each seems still theoretically in play. I see no good reason, however, to reject Option 3 having to do with being so completely a part of the establishment as to never have given the potential of high governmental complicity a second thought. For my money as a human being, that is quite unsatisfying.

How many of the premises in my last email does he accept and how many does he reject and if he rejects them, why does he, and how does he articulate that rejection? Here I might refer people to my previous discussion about a forum that demands answers to questions. Email between people who have never met simply does not do the job. Those who wish to read his failure to address questions as indicative of something are on their own. A. B. Krongard is a man of amazing accomplishment, and from what I know, charming to boot. He is apparently the physical stuff of legend, and entitled to every impulse toward arrogance that he may or may not possess. People close to him will know better than I.

What I can say is that he is a member of a subset of human beings who, as a class, have a tendency to spend very little time questioning their assumptions about the world. They are richly endowed with talent, have used it wisely and accomplished much, earning great wealth in the process. You can say that the individuals in this subset have served to promote the interests of the financially successful, power-endowed, socially prominent among us; were it to be referred to as the ruling class, few of them would take offense. Their skills were useful to the dominators of our culture, and with success, they could become dominators as well.

And once you are a dominator, what cause do you have to question assumptions or paths taken, choices made, associations cultivated, relationships allowed to lapse, parties attended, conversations cut short, more important conversations pursued, all that which contributes to what we are, the sum of our actions and our words? Why question them when a quick look around demonstrates the absolute correctness of each selection along the way?

There is such a thing as disabling arrogance. That is when one's assumptions about the world and feeling of entitlement to its bounty become tenets of belief akin to religious faith. With this condition comes the dysfunction of a part of the master circuitry where actual facts are translated into an unknown language and become meaningless. It may be that Krongard and Matthews and Moyers and Maddow have had a part of their brains corrupted through service to the ruling masters.

If the world is the way I say it is and not the way they say it is, what would their positions be then? How would they view the persons who hired them? What would they think about all of the things they have so confidently asserted these past 10 years? When it is your job to get the story right, and you got it wrong, and by the way, it was the biggest story of all time, how exactly would you face the day? And with a glimpse in that direction, understanding those consequences, your every cell knows to construct that edifice, that fortress of denial, vast in scope and scale, fortified indeed, and impregnable. And it all happens buried so deep within our subconscious that we didn't know the door was opened or that the construction crews had entered and had silently set about their business of building our haven of preconception, keeping us safe from the world as it really is.

Where do we turn for hope? I believe there is a power in truth itself. People like me, following the examples of our heroes in the civil rights movement, once we have the piece of wood in our mouths, are not going to let go. The ideas that drive us become more unassailable every day; the bookshelves are full to overflowing. And with each year, more participants who know important pieces of information come closer to their deaths and closer to the meaning of their lives. Susan Lindauer was a CIA asset who began working with the Iraqis in the late 90's as what she calls a back channel to the regime. Her CIA handler made it clear to her that he knew the attacks of 9/11 were on their way so much so that he warned her not to go to New York in the weeks before 9/11.

At some point, Mr. Fuizz, her CIA handler, will have to make the decision of his life and tell what he knows. Ms. Lindauer's broken silence may be the sort of catalyst that Mr. Fuizz and some rogue reporter will be unable to resist. It will be someone previously possessed of disabling arrogance, someone who has found the way to question the assumptions that have served them impeccably throughout their lives, that hold the keys to truth. It will be some private redemption that knocks the board onto the floor for some chaos-creator, having found a strength of Titanic dimension, a moment of clarity, a moment of religion, a moment of transcending courage. The rest of us do what we have been doing and wait.

23

Inside a Courtroom

While waiting, a strange thing happened. Dennis Cunningham had written with precision of the abject failure of the legal analysis of U.S. District Court Judge Denny Chin. Our papers on appeal from his ruling dismissing our case had been filed. The Defendants by their lawyer, the U.S. Attorney, had filed their Letter in response, and we, our reply to their Letter. We thought we would wait for a very long time before hearing that the appeal had been denied with a short and perfunctory Per Curiam decision.

When notice came, initially by email from our local counsel, Mustapha Ndanusa, that we had been granted argument in the case, on April 5th, 2011, there was a substantial moment of shocked jubilation. They are going to allow me to stand up and say these things *in court?* Not long thereafter, the full and resplendent nature of our predicament was made apparent. We were to have 5 minutes of argument...in New Haven, Connecticut. Apparently, whatever words there were, would be few, and they certainly wouldn't be uttered anywhere near headquarters on Pearl

Street in Manhattan. Did you think we had lost our collective mind? Or control?

Dennis referred to it as a mockery; he wouldn't buy a plane ticket for that kind of time. A lawyer close to the 2nd Circuit said that it was extremely unusual for an argument to be 5 minutes in length, but even more so for it to take place in New Haven. Why bother to schedule argument? There is no legal requirement in the 2nd Circuit. These and other questions would divert me as I sought to conjure what those five minutes would be like, and how I should spend them. After 10 or 12 versions certain phrases and ideas recurred sufficiently to be granted space in the final product:

Oral Argument to the Court, April 1, 2011

April Gallop's desk was situated so that she was in the way of the left wing of that Boeing 757 that supposedly disappeared into the side of the Pentagon at 530 miles an hour leaving not a trace, yet she was able to walk out where the plane flew in, in a matter of minutes, according to the government.

And so the Court found on a Motion to Dismiss

No court has ever been so bereft of authority or so wrong in conclusion.

Does the government disagree that the District Court omitted any reference to the words and actions and locations of the three defendants at the time of the crime, and most jarringly, any reference to their lies, with regard to those matters?

And with respect to Defendant Cheney, concerning an instrumentality of the crime? That airplane, whatever it did when it got to the Pentagon?

And in his case, testified to, by Norman Mineta, a cabinet secretary and recipient of the Presidential Medal of Freedom, a man with an airport named after him. ?Trial lawyers will wait their lives to claim a witness with those credentials.

It was the Pentagon-- The headquarters of the mightiest military force ever created by man. Where was its protection? Where were the interceptors that could have prevented the destruction?

Do we actually need more than the words of Secretary Mineta to defeat the Government's challenge?? We have more:

Where were the Courts Martial when the failures became apparent?

Why were the occupants of the building not warned, an issue that escaped the District Court's decision entirely?

What was the E4-B doing flying over the White House at the time of the attacks? An essential means of coordination of this crime.

What is nano thermite doing in the dust at Ground Zero?

Can any human being with a brain and a pulse look at the destruction of Building 7 and not think controlled demolition as Rather, Brokaw, and Jennings remarked virtually in unison at the time?

The warnings that produced no actions, how many instances of incompetence, all serving precisely the same purpose, can anyone have stuffed down their throat without choking?

It would take me an hour to demonstrate all of the factual assertions in the Complaint that do far more than suggest a mere possibility that the defendants are liable.

But the Court below said our claims are implausible, the product of cynical delusion and fantasy, therefore he needn't address any facts.

Does anyone seriously want to debate this question with me? We don't want it to be true, so it isn't?

Where is the scholarship in that? How many libraries of history books must be forgotten in order to arrive at that conclusion?

No court has ever been more wrong. We are here because of the nature of the human species. The holders of power, the wielders of power, power itself, in this world cannot abide the truth of this matter, and humankind has great difficulty stomaching it. That aversion provides to the good, and to the deliberate, the capacity to reject unpleasant truths.

There is simply no other rational explanation for the District Court's opinion, what it says and what it doesn't say, in fact what it leaves out entirely.

The District Court chose not to consider dozens of concrete allegations set out in our Complaint or the myriad others contained in the appendix filed in response to the motion to dismiss, but is there some other more powerful response to the charge of frivolousness than, "How can it be frivolous when it is true?"

Did he not notice that every one of the facts included in our appendix could have been included in an amended complaint? Is this not further indication of a judicial mind temporarily incapacitated; certainly, one untethered from the dictates of the Iqbal decision?

What possible offense to justice can come from allowing this case to go forward, with sanctions standing there ominously in the wings in the event our effrontery falls on its face.

No one wants evil to exist in the world, but it does, and it is attracted to power, and it has no regard for citizenship.

As long as we rely simply on the essential variability of the human soul and its physical, scientific, and technological capabilities, we must be allowed to proceed with our proof.

No court has ever been more wrong.

That speech would never be given, parts, yes, but there was much more water yet to flow over this dam.

It is the usual practice of the 2nd Circuit to publish the assignment of the three judges to the cases to be heard on a certain date five days ahead of time. At 12 noon on March 31, 2011, it was known to all who cared. The panel in Gallop v. Cheney would consist of Chief Judge David Winter, Yale BA, Yale JD, Judge Jose Cabranes, Columbia, BA, Yale JD, and Judge John M. Walker, Yale, BA, University of Michigan, JD. Everybody was over 70. Everybody was conservative. Everybody was a Yalee of some stripe or kind, but none of that was enough to raise an eyebrow. What stopped everything, in a powerful affront to impartiality, was the fact that Judge John M. Walker is the first cousin once removed of former President George W. Bush.

What is the proper way to set all of this down? Fiction writers might be left with some sort of block or other in their efforts to portray the navigation through these iceberg-laden waters of intrigue. What had *they* done? Why had they done it? Standing before the court, figuratively speaking, accused of mass murder and treason were three men, all appointees of the former president.

Who empowered them to act as they did? George W. Bush. Who was, as John F. Kennedy said after the failure of the Bay of Pigs, the responsible officer of government for the failure of 9/11, or the success of 9/11, were one to adopt the position argued in the Complaint that I was to stand in front of this panel of the 2nd Circuit to defend? George W. Bush.

Whose brother and cousin, Marvin Bush and Wirt D. Walker, respectively, and of necessity family members of Judge John M. Walker, were referred to in Paragraph 70 of the Affidavit of William Veale attached to the Plaintiff's Response to the Defendants' Motion to Dismiss as directors or CEO's of Stratesec and Securacom, two of the companies responsible for security at the World Trade Center from 1998-2002, whose operatives were in a position to enable or prevent the lacing of the Towers and Building 7 with explosives including nano thermite found so provocatively in the dust and debris at Ground Zero? George W. Bush.

Whose family name would be besmeared with the most unspeakable accusations ever conceived in any democracy should the lawsuit be allowed to advance to the discovery stage where the actual facts could be examined? Judge John M. Walker. I live for the unmasking, that moment when no one but the deranged will be able to avoid our conclusion. Did the mask just slip, visibly?

Aboard United Flight God-knows-what on the Sunday before the Tuesday of argument, 500 or so miles an hour toward JFK, I wrote a Motion to Disqualify Judge John M. Walker. Thinking about it later, I should have moved to disqualify the entire panel. Conflicts of interest are not a strange occurrence in the law or on the bench. It doesn't happen to any one judge much, and may never, but it happens all of the time in courtrooms all over the country. Whether recusal (disqualification) is legally required almost never comes up, because as soon as the judge becomes aware that his associate or family member is involved in the matter before him or her, they recuse themselves to avoid a distasteful appearance or an uncomfortable moment. The case is assigned to another, unconnected judge and, any caseload imbalance is rectified in the subsequent days or months.

It is quite difficult to imagine the scene there in New Haven. Somehow, by some route or machination, the case of Gallop v. Cheney found its way to Winter, Cabranes, and Walker, and then to a series of law clerks, one presumes. Who put it there? With how much of an understanding of its nature was that done? How much thought was involved? How many conversations with how many people, and what people, took place before the file came to rest on these several desks? Do the American people have a right to know the substances of those conversations?

For most people, I think, something bad happened. An interested party was assigned to decide a case of the greatest magnitude, a case of historical significance. What prevented the person most seriously affected from simply sending it back where it came from, as happens probably on a daily basis in the country? But the other judges and the law clerks cannot escape scrutiny for their failures to act. The judges have a duty to justice and to the institution of which they are an enormously powerful and important component, to protect it from that which would erode its credibility. For Jesus's bloody sake, what of the sanctity of the law?

The law clerks. Their duties are to their judges and their oaths as lawyers, but most importantly it is to themselves. They were tested at early stages of their careers, and they were found wanting. Or maybe not. Maybe there were threats of resignation and counter threats of great damage to careers. Maybe truth was spoken to power, and searing drama played out in some door-shut chambers, quietly, nervously, stayed-up-all-night angsting, and now feverishly sweating and leg-jiggling scared. "You have come to lecture me on the sanctity of this court, young lady?"

This case does not create small dramas, only go-to-jail, lose-your-license, we're-finished, how-about-divorce dramas. And in some cases, only a few of which we will probably ever know about, face-down-dead drama.

24

Barry Jennings

Speaking of which, what is the story of Barry Jennings? I, and the interested parts of the world only know small bits of it. What we know largely comes from the young filmmaker, Dylan Avery, responsible for the millions-of-hits internet documentary, "Loose Change," in its several iterations. Barry Jennings was an official of the New York City Housing Authority. When he heard of the plane impacts, he headed for his headquarters that were located in WTC 7, the building that came down looking for all the world like a controlled demolition at 5:20 PM on 9/11/01.

As he told it, when he got to the 23rd Floor, he found it empty, with cups of hot coffee sitting on desks. He made the obvious calls and was told to get out of there as soon as possible. He found he was not alone; a lawyer for the city, Michael Hess was in a similar predicament. They went to the staircase to get out of the building. It was around 10 or so in the morning. The elevator no longer worked so they took the stairs. At about the eighth floor, there were explosions in the building damaging the stairwell and leaving the two men hanging on to the bannister for dear life. Jennings got onto the landing, helped Hess do the same, and began screaming for help. Jennings was sure all of this happened before the South Tower came down because the Tower's collapse interrupted efforts by the police to rescue them.

They heard more explosions in the building, waited some time for their rescuers, and finally were led down some stairs to safety through the lobby, which was in ruins and filled with smoke. Nothing is simple or easy or uncomplicated, especially in this case. There is controversy concerning the next parts of Jennings' story. When he was first asked by Dylan Avery to describe his descent into the lobby, Jennings said he felt like he was stepping over or among dead bodies. In a later conversation with Avery, while affirming all of the other circumstances surrounding his ordeal, Jennings denied seeing any dead bodies.

In fact, Jennings had been interviewed by some media outlet at noon on the streets of lower Manhattan and told of the explosions before the Towers came down, a statement that certainly should have alerted the investigating press to a very serious and troubling problem with the official story. But it didn't. Except for the account in *Loose Change* Barry Jennings remained unknown to the world. And the timing of his notoriety was to become a bit of a "situation" for NIST, who in 2009 was finally coming out with its declarations of "All is Well" in the case of the destruction of Building 7. Significantly, though he said he was interviewed during their investigation, the final report contained no reference to his account.

Mr. Hess, a friend of Mayor Giuliani, had managed to right the ship by denying the important points of Jennings' tale, particularly the explosions and their existence before any Tower's demise. Dylan Avery was not about to let any of this sit when the news arrived:

Barry Jennings was dead. This just as the NIST report was issued in August, 2009. There may well be more important eyewitnesses to the attacks of 9/ 11, but probably not significantly more important. This was a devastating blow to the efforts at truth. How did he die, wondered Avery?

NYPD seemed opaque and impenetrable on the question. Avery hired a highly acclaimed private investigator to pursue the matter, handing her his credit card. In a matter of days, according to Avery, the PI gave him a refund and asked never to be contacted again. In an extremely competitive business where acclaim and reputation are all, this is a striking gesture.

It is a business, where, simply, courage plays a part, sometimes a profound part. When the story is told that an investigator bowed out and slunk away, that is profoundly revealing. The reaction one would expect would see the car immediately in a lower gear with the pedal buried, such is the power of denial of access to information to the goods and greats of that profession.

So, there it is, another question carved into the granite of this case, glaring there amongst the noise and obfuscation, begging for the right brand of intrepid to look and ask and not slink away.

25

The Argument

Walking into the courtroom in the Federal Courthouse in New Haven an hour and a half before the case was due to be called, a pleasant clerk turned the sign-in sheet in my direction. I asked how unusual a five-minute argument was. Not particularly, he said. Really, says I. How many have there been in the last month? Well, they mostly come with pro se cases, cases where the appellants, the party appealing, has no lawyer. I see, says I. Can you think of any non-pro se cases where there was a 5-minute argument? Maybe, I think he said, but I understood the ground upon which I was walking. I was to be treated as if I wasn't a lawyer, and so I shouldn't have been surprised to hear Chief Judge Winter inquire if I was licensed to practice before the 2nd Circuit, a question I am sure he asks all who come to argue before him. Okay, so not that I heard as I waited for the case to be called and listened to other litigants battle for their clients.

The more I sat and considered the Bush cousin before me, the more I saw the perfect combination of Presidents 41 and 43, shape of face, bearing, smirk. There had never been much in the way of optimism concerning our chances. Any appraisal of Judge Chin's decision makes it very clear that our words and facts and analyses can be quite inaccessible even to very large legal brains. That, of course, assuming honesty and integrity on the part of the judge. Though my beliefs are sorely tested on a regular basis, before I learned of Walker's presence on the panel, I was accepting of the notion that the great chasm that gaped between the facts as I know them and the facts as assumed by the government and Judge Chin was the result of a sharp divergence in world-views and had nothing to do with character.

The more I looked at him and the more I considered the decision not to recuse himself, and the decision by the other judges not to take the case away from him, the more I thought my nephew's idea, of walking into the courtroom with my golf bag over my shoulder, instead of leaving it at his place to be picked up later in the day, might have struck just the right attitude: you don't take me seriously; I don't take you seriously.

The case was called; I rose and went to the wrong table. Asked to approach the podium to begin argument, I oh-so-gently reminded the court that there was a motion pending. "that motion is denied," declared Chief Judge Winter. "I move for a continuance to seek appellate review of that ruling," I say. "That motion is denied," says Winter. And so, I begin. Fifteen or so minutes later, I sat down. I had been asked if I was licensed to practice before them. I had been asked if I had filed other lawsuits for other clients alleging these facts. I might well have been asked that twice, or maybe it was whether I had filed other lawsuits for April Gallop. I still don't understand the relevance of those questions, the answers to all of which were "no", but Judge Walker assured me it was substantial indeed.

I managed to say most of what I set out to say; I think I said no judge (Chin) had ever been so bereft of authority or so wrong in conclusion. I showed sufficient amazement that April Gallop had managed to walk out where the supposed plane flew in, leaving not a trace, vaporized by the heat, and she sitting no more than forty feet from the point of impact, if there was one, which there probably was, but not with a Boeing 757.

I extolled the credentials of Norman Mineta, cabinet secretary and all, recipient of the Presidential Medal of Freedom and all, man with an airport named after him, and all. That provoked Judge Winter who wanted to know what airport that was. Santa Clara County, California, I think I said, demonstrating how the mouth doesn't always work as one might wish. It is in Santa Clara County, but it was the San Jose International Airport.

And that was not the only failure of mouth or brain. I found myself suggesting that statements in other Complaints filed on behalf of April Gallop, against the airlines or airport security, by other lawyers, which said that Flight 77 had in fact crashed into the Pentagon, should not be considered an admission by her, which it most certainly must. To which I in time conceded, but forgot to make the larger point that, whereas such an admission may or may not be influential at a trial, that it exists is of no consequence at this stage of the proceedings where a judge must consider factual assertions to be true.

There were moments of some fun, as when I asked if anyone really wanted to debate the implausibility of vice presidents doing horrible things. Judge Cabranes chimed in that Judge Chin wished to debate the question. I remember saying, in essence, no, I mean debate!, you know, in the same room, talking at the same time. I'm not sure how much of it came out that way, but I do recall a mild feeling of satisfaction.

At some point Judge Winter asked about my co-counsel, Mustapha Ndanusa, who was in the courtroom and admitted to practice in the 2nd Circuit, and Dennis Cunningham who was not present. I'm sure there was a good reason why any time was taken up with the status of lawyers not then doing anything before the court. These were efforts to demean me and my colleagues that created a very real feeling of self-righteous indignation, which probably didn't hurt at the time.

When I got around to asking "what possible offense to justice could come from allowing the suit to go forward, with sanctions waiting ominously in the wings in the event our effrontery falls on its face?", it may well have been the last thing I said, which is fine, since it was the most important thing I said. My reference to the existence of evil in the world, its attraction to power, and its disregard for citizenship was interrupted by Walker with some kind of inanity. At one point I said, "the holders of power, the wielders of power, Power itself in this world, simply cannot abide the truth of this matter." Walker had something to say about that too, but I think whatever it was reflected the difficulty he was having reading the heading of the Complaint.

When I took my seat, a young African-American Assistant U.S. Attorney, named Alicia Simmons rose for the Defendants and proclaimed that she had nothing to say, unless, of course, the judges had a question. Winter did. He wanted to know if the Defendants had pursued sanctions. The Complaint having been dismissed as frivolous, this is precisely the situation where the government and the courts should take steps to make sure their valuable time is not wasted with absurd, unthinkable, unspeakable, implausible, and unprovable claims.

No, allowed Ms. Simmons. And the Defendants had no position with regard to sanctions. There may have been hesitancy in seeking sanctions because of the manifest injustice of such a thing. And, of course, in order for sanctions to be imposed, a court has to make a finding after the proposed sanctionee has had an opportunity to defend against the claim of frivolousness. Would any opponent want to give us another opportunity to tell the world why we were not delusional?

26

A Speech to the Choir

Sometimes and again, it feels like what I have to say should be delivered from a podium, and so the following should best be thought of as a speech since it, or a very close relative, was given to a group of partisans at Valley Forge, Pennsylvania a number of years ago:

When Dick Cheney and Donald Rumsfeld and Condoleezza Rice offered their wisdom to the world as the fires were still burning at Ground Zero, they made reference to the opportunities that often arrive with disaster.

People like us may be forgiven for thinking along similar lines, but the opportunities about which we dream do not have to do with the unchecked projection of American power; they do not have to do with legislative obscenities like the Patriot Act; they do not have to do with reaping financial rewards around the world by dispensing no bid contracts to our friends and associates; they do not have to do with abolishing habeas corpus or the detestable ability to torture those we feel might be useful as we carry forth our designs.

The opportunities that occupy our dreams have to do with the reclaiming of the democratic process, as our founding fathers, or some of them at least, might have conceived on their best day. That is the view we can carry into the future, because what those sick sonsofbitches did when they decided to engage in their treasonous conduct was provide us with the opportunity to unmask the American oligarchy as it is now constituted.

They have given us the opportunity to see not only the structure of our oppression, but the means of its exercise. Thanks to the fabulous array of scholars and investigators beside whom we are so fortunate to march, we have learned of their ability to manipulate our military defenses, to co-opt our civilian investigative agencies, to subvert the fact-finding missions of reputable scientists, and probably most important of all, their ability to cow, intimidate and silence what once could have been called the establishment of journalism, but has for eleven years now given up whatever claim there may have been to the title.

Those of us in this room have a tendency to be hard on the mainstream media. I am the worst offender. But in my better, more charitable moments, I understand their plight and that of the scientists of NIST, and all of the others similarly situated. They have families to feed and jobs that carry enormous prestige. Just imagine what a life that must be, to have millions of people interested in what you have to say.

In the beginning of my personal struggle I had no understanding of what was preventing these journalists from looking at the truth, much less speaking it, but now with more experience, I am able to empathize. So, I have a proposal, that a request be made to each of them, not that they become like us, not that they utter even one word, yet. Let us ask them, in the privacy of their own living rooms, just between the two of them at a bar after work, on the sidelines of the little league or soccer game, ask them to speak in secrecy to others of them who are friends, whom they trust, who travel the same perilous avenues, ask them to begin a consideration of the topic, in bits and pieces, swearing each other to secrecy after each meeting.

Then let us ask that the secret meetings grow larger, that the step be taken to broaden the inquiry, and then, when there is sufficient mass, then, when there is the comfort of numbers and amalgamated power in the room, then, please, for the sake of our nation and its democracy, ask them to speak the truth.

There is a particular moment of truth that is screaming for attention, and has been now for a very long time. Its actual time is a matter of dispute, but the place is quite certain. It is the Presidential Emergency Operations Center, and we should not know exactly where underground it is or exactly how far from the West Wing, but it is that place, referred to by some as the "bunker," to which Cheney was taken, as he said, shortly after the second plane hit the South Tower, grabbed as he was by Secret Service agents with a clear mission to prevent destruction of the structure of government.

This will be a moment in history of rare importance, for an understanding of which we must turn to the journalism profession and the writers of our history. For this analysis, I must single out one particular practitioner, with apologies. Glory, fame, and prestige, and an appearance on Jon Stewart, have, occasionally their price tags. Barton Gellman was a reporter for the Washington *Post.* He wrote a book called *Angler* about the vice president. In it he told the story of the morning of 9/11 as seen by those at the center of power. The story he tells is well told and compelling and minute in its detail and, regrettably, false.

In my view it is the job of historians to bring their views to bear, to be skeptical of the existence of impartiality. As I have said repeatedly to juries for 35 years, there is no such thing as an unbiased witness. Whatever a human being observes leaves an imprint on their psyche, and it is not to be erased by an oath or any solemn wish to be fair.

So, when Barton Gellman tells his story of the vice president, it is perfectly appropriate for him to arrive at whatever conclusions his intellect has dictated. What cannot be forgiven is to deny the reader information that might lead him or her to a different revelation.

Norman Mineta was a witness to history because he was in the PEOC at 9:15 or 9:20 that morning directed there by the Chief of Counterterrorism, Richard Clarke. Each of you knows this story. Norman Mineta was a witness to the giving of orders by the vice president, orders that had to do with a plane heading for the Pentagon, orders that immediately preceded explosions at the Pentagon and the devastation there that each of us is all too familiar with.

The 9/11 Commission found that the vice president was not in the room so as to be able to give or affirm those orders. I suppose the 9/11 Commission is entitled to its opinion about that fact, just as Barton Gellman is, but what is unpardonable is not to mention Secretary Mineta's sworn testimony about those crucial moments, testimony that he gave to that very Commission, who then decided as well that it should not even be mentioned at all in their bestselling book.

That is sad, so sad because there is another book to which we pseudo-scholars have turned entitled the *9/11 Investigation* which contains excerpts of testimony by *key* witnesses. How in the world the editor of that work, Steven Strasser, could decide that the testimony of the Secretary of Transportation disputing the important time line of the 9/11 experience, was undeserving of inclusion or mention in any way, used to beat the livin' bejesus out of me, but I have grown up in recent years.

Barton Gellman deceived history by denying those interested the ability to make their own selection as to whom to believe. To be fair, Gellman, when asked by me if he had interviewed Mineta, he said he "didn't get to it", and the reason for his comfort in excluding the Secretary's part from the tale was the existence of multiple other sources of information all of which corroborated what the vice president apparently, although not consistently, claims. He said he had "no reason" to believe the records were not authentic.

I have five reasons :1. The person you have chosen to believe is the prime suspect in the case; 2. That person has been inconsistent in his telling of the tale, on at least two occasions, one only about a year ago, when he said he went to the bunker shortly after the second tower was hit. In the context of this terrorist attack, 33 minutes cannot be considered "shortly. 3. That very 33-minutes. Gellman chronicles that there was a 33-minute interlude between the plane's impact with the second tower and the secret service agent's hand coming down hard on the table saying "NOW" In Watergate there was an 18 minute gap, here it's 33. 4. Would anyone seriously contend that the government does not have the resources, the capacity, the ability, or the many-times-displayed disposition to fabricate evidence? That is a large part of the business of the CIA and the Joint Special Operations Command. Conducting violent covert snatches and executions while hiding the hand of the USG, and directing blame elsewhere, except when taking credit is virtually the point of the whole exercise as in the case of the operation to end the career of Osama Bin Laden. The manipulation of evidence is the essence of the "False Flag." The reason there is anyone in those chairs before me, is because of an awareness that this crime is the very endstage of an avalanche of fabrication. 5. Norman Mineta said so. Having spent several minutes in his presence, talking to him, the idea that anyone, Washington Post reporter, Editor, or Chairman of the 9/11 Commission could wipe that man's testimony off of the tabletop of history without so much as a passing reference to its existence, is shameful.

There is an old saying in my business: If you have a choice of witnesses, you probably want to take the one with an Airport named after him. Those three entities, Gellman, Strasser, and the 9/11 Commission, and all of American mainstream journalism have denied Norman Mineta his word. It must be up to us to give it back to him.

27

Ink of Our Own Invention

On April 7, 2011, the day after the argument in New Haven we succeeded in having a press release printed in the Sacramento Bee and on the websites of CNBC and Reuters, and in the Times of India. It read:

Extraordinary Conflict of Interest: Bush Cousin Presides Over Federal Court Case?Against Former Bush Administration Officials

Confounding lawyers and legal scholars all over the world, Judge John Walker, first cousin of former President George W. Bush, was one of three judges of the 2nd Circuit Court of Appeals to hear argument Tuesday in Gallop v. Cheney, Rumsfeld and Myers.

The lawsuit was brought by a soldier injured during the attack on the Pentagon and accuses former vice president Dick Cheney, former Secretary of Defense Donald Rumsfeld, and former Chairman of the Joint Chiefs of Staff, Richard Myers, of conspiring to facilitate the terrorist attacks of 9/11.

The attacks killed 3000 Americans, plus many who have died from the toxic clean-up conditions at Ground Zero.

Attorney William Veale, acting for April Gallop, learned of the assignment the usual 5 days before the argument, and filed a motion to disqualify Judge Walker.

There was no prior decision regarding the motion, and when Veale asked about it in court the motion was denied by Judge Winter. Veale then requested a continuance to seek appellate review of the court's ruling but that was denied as well.

Argument followed but Walker, and fellow judges Cabranes and Winter diverted attention to whether Veale, former Chief Assistant Public Defender, and lecturer in Criminal Trial Practice at the University of California, Boalt Hall, was properly licensed to practice before the court.

The Tuesday appeal followed a ruling by then District Court Judge Denny Chin, dismissing Ms. Gallop's lawsuit with prejudice, writing that the allegations are "implausible" and the product of "cynical delusion and fantasy." The judges were apparently unaware of growing world doubts about the official story of 9/11, including a recent poll by Germany's prestigious Emnid Institute, reporting 89.5% of Germans in doubt.

Gallop's appeal brief stated that Judge Chin's summary misrepresented important allegations in the case, and failed to consider virtually half of the factual assertions contained in the Complaint. Chin also failed to mention the words, actions, and locations of the three defendants at the time of the crime.

Veale, amidst frequent interruptions from the three judges, managed to point out Cheney's direct involvement in tracking and dealing with the airplane that was heading for the Pentagon, as reported to the 9/11 Commission by then Secretary of Transportation Norman Mineta, a winner of the Presidential Medal of Freedom.

Judge Cabranes gave no sign of being familiar with the allegations in the Complaint concerning conflicts about the flight path of AA 77 (which allegedly hit the Pentagon) between the National Transportation Safety Board and the 9/11 Com- mission.

Nor did he show any sign of being aware of the scrubbing of the radar tracks in the area at the time of the attacks, nor of the counter-intuitive strategy of the suicidal hijacker who chose not to kill 20,000 occupants of the Pentagon, including Secretary Rumsfeld, by flying into the roof of the Pentagon.

Instead this novice pilot allegedly executed a spiraling descent, beyond the capacity of the plane and certainly the capability of the pilot, to accomplish an incredible horizontal ground level entry into a sparsely occupied and recently reinforced section of the building, causing 125 deaths.

Veale asked what offense to justice could come from allowing the case to go forward, when the possibility of sanctions awaits purveyors of frivolous accusations. Gallop's lawyer's final lament acknowledged the existence of evil in the world, its attraction to power and its disregard for citizenship, but Walker interrupted that sentence before it could be completed as well.

So, we waited. Waited for their eminences to rule, sometime between then and never. Waited to petition the entire 2nd Circuit in the event Walker, Winter, and Cabranes ruled against us. Waited for an angel to appear with sufficient funds to attack this public relations problem as required in this open but intensely controlled society. Waited for the private act of redemption; waited for Power to agree to be interviewed.

28

The Court Rules

And then...

Well, it really didn't take that long for all bloody hell to break loose, or at least within the context of my existence. On April 27th, 2011, the three-judge panel affirmed the decision of then-District Court Judge, now Circuit Court Judge Denny Chin. They found the case similarly frivolous and based upon delusion of some kind or other. None of that was particularly surprising. After all there were nothing but ominous portends as I stood up to argue.

First, there was Cousin John Walker, who had not seen fit to recuse himself from the case. Maybe you have to be a trial lawyer to know just how strange and troubling that is. I contend that if you have been in the business even a year, you have heard of a judge recusing themselves because of some connection to the case. Maybe they had been drinking with the defendant the night before, one of the first that I witnessed, or had represented a party when they were in private practice. No one in the court bats an eye; it happens all the time. The file is simply sent to another judge unpossessed of the offending conflict.

It is essential to understand that it is rare indeed that the conflict is actually a danger to justice. In all of the cases the efforts to put the matter into such a psychological posture that the judge can deliver the proper decision based on the law and not whatever interests may theoretically provoke some emotion or non-judicial concern, are minimal. Judges derail their abhorrence of rapists all the time as they judge whether to let them go because of insufficient proof. The reason that they recuse themselves is to avoid even the appearance of a conflict of interest. Simply put, it doesn't look right for the president's first cousin once removed to judge the propriety of the actions of that president's appointees, for which he is the responsible officer of government. One might well inquire, "why does history need to be saddled with such a blight?"

These are questions which, as far as the public record is concerned, were never addressed, not only by Judge Walker, but by the other two senior judges on the panel, Cabranes and Winter, and all of the ten or so law clerks that chatted amiably in the jury box before and between when the cases were called for argument.

Maybe there was a moment of moral courage as a law clerk, deep breathe having been taken, composure summoned, tapped in the usual manner on the door of one of these judges. Maybe they entered nonchalantly and took their accustomed chair, sitting quietly as the judge finished his phone conversation or bit of reading and looked up, absolutely and unequivocally in charge of just about everything he sees, knows, or thinks about. Or so it seems. Maybe the mind of the young clerk changed a time or two in that period of wait, or maybe this was a clerk of clear understanding and substantial spine, for whom it was a pretty easy call, having to bring the matter to their judge's attention.

If such a moment transpired, when the discouraging words, "conflict of interest", were spoken, those interested will have to wait for that person to achieve something really significant in their life, where then this small moment will take its place next to the others, more elevated, but maybe not as important, that formed their character and led them to the heights of renown that we will be lucky enough to hear or read about twenty years from now.

Judge Walker had no business hearing our case, and it is a scar on the court's reputation that something wasn't done about it. And all of that analysis could be performed before a word was spoken in New Haven. So, there was no reason for optimism as we read the April 27 decision. But the last part, I did not expect. *Sanctions.* We had 30 days to respond to an Order to Show Cause why we should not be sanctioned for filing a frivolous appeal. Sanctions, you say? For what precisely? Because our claims are implausible, the product of delusion, impossible to be believe, could not be true.

I will have to admit I laughed when I read the words. I queried my friends and colleagues, was this Kafka, Carroll, Orwell, or Huxley? You are sanctioning me? The irony that on the very day of the attacks, by their operatives' own admissions, there were enough failures, mishaps, miscalculations, mis maneuvers, missed warnings, and slow responses to fill several training manuals, and yet NOT ONE government official has been SANCTIONED for their failures of performance which led to the deaths of 3000 people, is cruel and poignant and ...infuriating.

And that was surely the source of some of our subsequent problems. Neither Dennis Cunningham nor I are imbued with the Zen calm we wish we had when perched before computer. In our souls we knew precisely what was going on. This was the stark-naked brandishing of power by the world's regulators' judicial operatives. There was a spot of bother over there in the Second

Circuit. A rather gaudy, crass, and tasteless piece of the petticoat of crime was showing and steps beyond the usual needed to be taken. There is no need to be concerned that anyone "of weight" will ever know. All of the organs had been very strictly informed that there was a refusal-to-be-interviewed policy in effect. So, there was no need to worry about CNN and its sisters straying off course. But down there on the ground, there was a case that needed to be dealt with in a certain way.

None of these words need to have been spoken, though they may have been. If you wind up on the higher reaches of the Federal bench, you are a strange cat indeed, if you haven't figured what your duties are in moments of extreme...concern. The structure of state is the preeminent consideration, and that is bloody-well that.

So, in judicial matters of extreme concern, sometimes the delicate, nuanced, barely noticeable mal-use of precedent just isn't going to do the job. The ham-hand must appear, and the bull must rage in the china shop of statute and common law, and, well, the damage...hopefully that will be someone else's problem. And so the extremity of the perceived danger is manifest in the extremity of the means employed to stomp the livin' be-Jesus out of it.

First, abandoned, shredded, and discarded alongside a rusted stove and a '53 Stude stuck halfway down a ravine is the precept of law, taught very close to the first day of indoctrination, that factual assertions in a complaint, at the first instance, are presumed true. You can't really find much of an earlier stage in a lawsuit than before the defendants have denied the allegations set out in the complaint, which is where we are even now.

The Government, on behalf of the defendants, moved to dismiss our complaint before answering it for failure to state a claim for which relief can be granted, claiming in its essence, so what? In other words, they said we hadn't set out an actionable claim;

we hadn't made allegations that amounted to a wrongful or negligent act, or, we hadn't hit the defendants with our arrows. No matter how it is put, when judging the strength of a complaint, the ruling judge MUST accept any factual assertion as true.

Now, there is an obvious exception to this rule, about factual assertions being presumed true. The exception is that the assertions must be plausible. Whatever is claimed must be within the realm of the theoretically real. For example, one could not survive a motion to dismiss in a civil action for police brutality, if the plaintiff claimed the police had entered the plaintiff's locked bedroom by dematerializing outside of the room and then rematerializing within the locked, confined space, there to do violence to the plaintiff. Every judge would be acting lawfully if that complaint was dismissed because the claims are not plausible, because they offend the laws of physics as we know them. If what a plaintiff is claiming is other-world based, they won't succeed and shouldn't succeed. So, except for that obvious exception, factual assertions must be considered true.

Unless you run the world, or help run it, and you know no one will have the courage to irreverently make reference to any sort of judicial impropriety. The Second Circuit panel, including Bush's cousin, did precisely what Denny Chin had done. It found facts. It had a trial without the giving of testimony, without the taking of depositions, without the defendants answering the complaint. They decided that when April Gallop said that there was no sign of a crashed airliner in the ruins of that building through which she crawled to safety, that she was unworthy of belief. This is as abject a betrayal of the judicial principle that forbids a court from invading the province of the jury as a reader of legal opinions is likely to find.

And upon what basis did the court so find? Since the decision didn't really say, it must be supposed that it relied on the mainstream media reports, or the 9/11 Commission Report, or accepted wisdom, or the official story, or their own finely-sculpted world-view, not one piece of which had found its way into a courtroom, by testimony or inscribed upon a single piece of paper. The Panel tried the case of Gallop v. Cheney, in their own perceived reality, be-tween their ears, and if there was a lawyer for the plaintiff available to argue during the course of whatever conversation so silently oc-curred, I am relatively certain the Court was distracted by the over-awing presence of power at that moment.

That is a simple statement of Count One of the Indictment against the court's opinion and OSC Re: Sanctions. Count Two is equally capable of taking one's breath away. They simply failed to acknowledge, by one count, some ninety assertions of fact every one of which was entitled to be presumed true. See how wicked is the stratagem here. The world knows its law by reading judicial opinions. That is entirely reasonable. Why in the world should we not rely on the purveyors of justice to fairly set out the facts upon which they are relying to fashion legal principle? Gallop v. Cheney would be one reason. If all one did was read the opinion of the court, there would be no reason to think, except for the monstrosity referred to in the previous paragraphs, that there was this imposing foundation of facts upon which the Complaint was built.

Just to take the most glaring example. The deci-sion doesn't mention what Cheney said or did, or where he was when, that morning. It doesn't mention that his words applied to a plane heading toward the Pentagon, that they concerned a principal instrumentality of the crime, and, as most comfortably understood, consisted of a standing down of American defenses of its own head-quarters just as the attack took place. The black humor of the public defender conjures the image of the critical review of a report of a liquor store hold-up where there is no mention that the suspect was seen walking into the store with a gun.

It is as if most of our Complaint had been redacted for security reasons, but the members of the panel lacked the proper clearance. Or there was a language problem; they read a different dialect of English in New Haven. It is that stark, that mystifying, that bold. They simply pretend that vast acres of factual assertions don't exist. Then, when the opinion is crafted, there is no need to refer to the forgotten, overlooked, uncomprehended, strategically ignored contents of the Complaint. If everyone on the Panel is of a like mind, the world will go ignorant of what actually took place. When was the last time a skeptical journalist read a complaint in a case or the briefs on appeal? I am prepared to surmise that the underpinnings of our vaunted democracy were not called into question in whatever case that might have been.

Now if there is dissension amongst the judges, you have a whole other matter entirely. Dissenting judges get to...dissent. They get to write down their disagreements and the reasons for them. If the majority whose beliefs won the day performed poorly as they wrote their decision, the dissenter(s) can say so.

And if the majority opinion overlooks vast swathes of facts, every one of them will appear in the dissent to the great embarrassment of the majority. The majority, knowing this, operates accordingly and only bends precedent or overlooks facts in the most unimportant, or, paradoxically, in the most crucial instances where there was no other way, and the costs were worth the benefits.

Bush v. Gore is a good example. The 2000 election was won by Gore in every way it could be won except the one that counted: before the United States Supreme Court. To say that the justices cheated, acted outside of the law and virtually all precedent to render a purely political decision is almost an understatement. And there were harsh words in dissent.

The Supreme Court took a hit, as some have said, but the stakes were high enough, and the benefits so enormous that the five

who took leave of their oaths decided they could weather the storm.
And weather it they have. April Gallop will be the worse for it. That
whole episode is just another piece of evidence that we don't have a
working democracy in this country. We don't have representatives
who are beholden solely and completely to the commonwealth. We
have paid and owned executors of the policy preferences of the seriously rich.

As we stared down the highway of this case, we knew that
there was, even at that particular moment, an En Banc Petition
pending. We had asked the whole court to consider the case. For
those, right then in search of a glimmer, the smallest particle of
hope in the case, that was it. It is always the prerogative of the
judges who might have wished the case to be heard by the whole
court to dissent from any decision not to grant the En Banc Petition.
So, when such a petition is filed, one honorable soul, judicial class
honorable soul, has the ability to unmask utterly the scoffers and
miscreants he or she regularly sits next to. If nine out of ten of
the active judges available to vote (Chin was ineligible since it was
an appeal from his decision) decided it should not be heard by the
whole court, and write not one word in explanation, that lonely dis-
senter could still have gone on for pages and explained exactly how
this game is played and why they didn't care to join in.

Now it is a fact that very few of these sorts of refusals of En
Banc Petitions get any notice at all. After all, if it is an important
matter, the whole court would certainly want to get involved...wouldn't it? Nevertheless, the words will be sent out
around the world, and it will not be a "lawyer for the plaintiff" who
wrote them, but an active member of the bench of the second highest court in the United States of America. Anticipating the decision
on the En Banc Petition, we knew we would learn how powerful
indeed, these forces are. Are they capable of silencing, and conform-
ing the conduct of every last judge? Is each being told separately

and in the most solemn way at this very moment, that there is certainty of making the short list for the next vacancy on the Supreme Court?

There is a third count in the Indictment against the three-judge panel, which applies equally to Denny Chin in the District Court decision. It is reasonably esoteric legal stuff, but it is a clear leaving-behind-of-the-law by judges who marinate it and sauté it and flip it at the highest levels for a living. The controlling case is *Iqbal.* It says quite clearly that courts are only required to presume that factual assertions are true in a complaint, not what are referred to as conclusory statements.

You can't win with, "he committed a battery on me." But you do win if you say, "he hit me in the mouth." You don't win with, "they conspired," but if you can show that their actions and words served a joint criminal conspiratorial purpose, you have passed the *Iqbal* test. The requirement for a court under the dictates of *Iqbal* is to identify which statements are found to be conclusory, and therefore warrant deletion from the analysis as to the sufficiency of the complaint.

That is what has yet to happen by any of the two courts that have written decisions in the case. They were required to identify what it is that we say about Dick Cheney, and then explain how it is not a factual assertion. That he was in the PEOC at 9:15 is a factual assertion. That he said, "have you heard anything to the contrary?" is a factual assertion. When the Court refused to address the dozens of assertions in the Complaint and state whether they were factual or conclusory, it was acting outside of the law, ignoring precedent, and breaking the oaths that each seated member of the court had taken.

This was all bold and naked and plain, what the court was doing, and it was not lost on Dennis Cunningham or me, and I am afraid we took it kind of personal, if one is to know what I mean. We had been called, at bottom, just plain crazy, as Dennis said in some brief or other, by Denny Chin. That is what delusion is, crazy. Then, I had been asked if I was licensed to practice before them. Then, they had affirmed every dastardly thing Denny Chin had done, and issued the OSC for Sanctions, *on their own motion* to boot; that means the opposing party, generally speaking the enemy in such situations, the court normally being the umpire, had nothing to do with the Sanctions. The word "frivolous" can be paraded before the world only so many times before anger begins to grab ahold of one's typing fingers.

29

Sanctionable Contempt

We made a motion to recuse the Panel from any further actions in the case. It has been called "over the top", "contumacious", "a very bad decision", and a lot of very nice things too. The dilemma upon which we sat was a prickly sort that asked what are we doing, really. Are we trying to provoke the beast? Are we speaking truth to power? Are we trying to play the game, even though it is clear they aren't going to let us win, even though they have already left their oaths shredded in a pile on the floor? Should we simply say what is true and let the country's power structure declare by its actions the negation of those wonderful words, "we are a nation of laws and not of men?"

None of what we said was mild, but that anyone might have thought of it as sanctionable was a complete surprise to me. A problem with the procuring of justice had made itself known to us. The court had failed in three major ways and there were only two explanations that we could imagine. Either power was being wielded in an unwholesome and deleterious way to our disadvantage, without regard for the law, or the judges were in good faith doing as their consciences dictated, but their consciences had become disabled, we suggested in our papers, by the victimhood that wrought such destruction all over New York. It is mostly impossible for people to conceive that their distress is the consequence of the actions of their own government, actions as depraved and inhuman as were the attacks of 9/11.

In other words, we said these judges' cranial circuitry, with regard to this issue, had been compromised, and the resultant damage, likely combined with well-set, lifetime-cured-and-seasoned world views, rendered them incapable of processing certain ideas in the way required by the law. This is known as bias. It is inconsistent with justice. It was pretty much the nicest thing we could say and still make a motion that would give our client a chance at success. We included the stunning presence of John Walker on the panel in our complaint that the recusal of the panel sought to remedy.

We filed our motion and the Petition for Rehearing and the Petition for Rehearing En Banc on June twenty-something. On July 7, I was notified that the three-judge panel had ruled. Our Petition for Rehearing was denied. Our Motion to Recuse was denied. So what; totally expected. How about a second OSC RE: Sanctions? You ready for that, kid? You ready to read your name in an opinion of the second highest court in the land? How about next to the words "bad faith" and "malicious." How does it feel to be accused of making a motion for no other purpose than to "harass and disparage the court?"

I don't know that I have arrived at a real understanding of this event in my life. For starters. I have never been accused, to my face, of being malicious in my life, ever. To my knowledge, I have never been associated with the idea of bad faith. Well, surely there remains a prosecutor or two who are, and were, not at all happy with some turn of phrase or line of argument which had the effect of conveying my apparent belief in the innocence of my mostly unfortunate client while, importantly, never actually saying so. They are free to think of that, and their failure to sufficiently or successfully point out the perceived disingenuity to the jury, as some kind of bad faith on my part, but it most assuredly wasn't. Their complaint should be with the designers of the adversarial system or, as I suggested, with themselves at the crucial moment. I was doing as I was taught and as I swore to do, for my client.

I am sure I have made disparaging remarks about just about everything. I am particularly outspoken about what has happened to the Baltimore Orioles since their capture by Peter Angelos. I am outspoken about my politics. You might hear some rancorous invective about Republicans and a large number of Democrats for whom, it seems, the whole point seems to be to achieve and maintain power, and if there is an unimaginable quantity of money involved, corrupting and sullying and debasing us and them in the process, okay, if not good.

So I don't spare my enemies as I identify them, and I certainly didn't care if the panel members who had "disparaged" my efforts with references to delusion and fantasy took umbrage at my motions or preferred not to have it suggested that they were coming up short in an important way, as judging goes, but the idea that I would make a motion that had no honest, good faith purpose is all wrong, ridiculously all wrong. So all wrong, that part of me exalted in being so falsely accused. How far had they, apparently, had to travel to deliver any sort of meaningful blow against whom, what? Their enemy? Had I achieved something I had never thought of, or dreamed of? Become an enemy of the umpire? Are we judged by the power and majesty and ferocity of our opponents? Are we actually getting somewhere, on some obscure level?

Though a smile would find its way to my face in the midst of all this, occasionally, and Dennis and I would enjoy our sense, which is clearly all it was, of achievement at having provided the smallest amount of discomfiture to the beast, I was not happy, having been told I had done wrong. I spent my entire youth and certainly the bulk of my adult life trying to do good. Always seeking the approval of my parents, with satisfactory results. Always being the goodie-two-shoes straight arrow of adolescence. Always being impressed with the decency and majesty of my teachers whose similar approval I was most clearly in need of, but also adept at acquiring. My award from my high school of private privilege upon graduation said something about "cheerful" and "calls to duty." I was a first-rate suck-up, but will still claim guileless and incapable of manipulation. I just wanted to please and be like my teachers, who remain, in my estimation maybe the finest group of human beings I have ever known, second, if second, to all of those public defenders with whom I laughed and raged and struggled and celebrated for all those years. One doesn't appreciate being called bad or malicious, even if it is by instruments of...you know...evil.

So, I got a lawyer. We hadn't done that, against some sincere advice, in the matter of the first OSC for Sanctions. The idea that our appeal or case was frivolous was the most outrageous bit of horseshit. In some ways, I wanted to be the sacrificial martyr to that claim. When the story is eventually told by someone with sufficient clout or spine, we will do very well indeed by the telling. I thought to myself, heroically but fleetingly, at the time, I will gladly strap on the handcuffs for failure to pay the $15,000 on the first OSC because right is right, and that is precisely what I have done. They are wrong; they have cheated; their reward will be wherever, not mine. I tried to tell a truth in the way that lawyers do, according to their rules. Every once in a while, someone must suffer unjustly.

At least my family will be proud of my efforts; so I thought to myself.

But the second OSC didn't mention a specific figure or amount of the sanction, but rather ordered that for a period of a year I inform any federal court in the 2nd Circuit before which I appeared that I had been sanctioned. Some suggested that a great deal of money could be involved even though that might violate some notice requirements of due process. And, we were criticized by some of our friends for going "over the top." One simply doesn't say such things to a federal appeals court panel, even if it is the nicest possible way to say something that must, in order to make a proper record and to avail one's client of every possible avenue to a fair hearing, be said. At any rate, one doesn't say such things. They own the hall; they own the cards; you play or not at their discretion. And I get to be thought of as stupid by my wiser friends because I did not act according to all wise men's understanding of the rules.

Just as there are wise and smart and astute human beings who are unable to conceive that high officials of their government did what I am able to prove in court that they did, there are people who can't conceive of taking a political step for whatever reason, principled or otherwise. These people are not activists, as I obviously am. Their lots are to succeed according to the rules laid down. Any efforts in defiance of those rules, the ones I have engaged in, for example, are certainly unwise, clearly poorly regarded, quite possibly stupid, and most-assuredly embarrassing, unfortunately, I am afraid, for them. I have become an embarrassment; and if, in the end, I am sanctioned and cause some greater stir through resistance to that, I will be an even greater one. Therefore, you have no choice but to apologize to the court.

Fact is, I would not mind apologizing to the court. I have some trouble imagining how anyone could see sincerity in it, no matter the elegance of the craft of the lawyer who writes it. Any discerning being would understand its meaning, as my daughter did immediately when she read the OSC. "What, you made them feel bad?" I am sorry that I used the harsh words and tone of voice that I did when I made my motion. I am sorry that I suggested that you were in some way less than perfect, how else was I supposed to protect my client?

One is taught as a trial lawyer to make a record. There is always a higher court that will consider one's cause. Not necessarily. The Second Circuit Panel was seeking to make the cost of application to the full court or the Supreme Court, unaffordable. And, since there is really no reason why I would do what I was accused of doing, making the motion with the sole purpose of disparaging the court, the reason why they would make such a ridiculous accusation is to teach other potential miscreants like me a lesson. Don't fuck with us, mother-fucker; you are in way over your head. Truer words were never spake.

30

Hope, or Just the ACLU?

I was still reeling from the second OSC on day two and I ran into a magnificent quart of cream of the San Francisco legal establishment. I said I needed him, except in the Second Circuit. Could he find me a name? I said I had considered an overture to the ACLU, the American Civil Liberties Union, proud protector of freedoms and speech for a century or so. He was sorry after several days, that he could find no one in New York willing to handle the matter with such short notice. The decision had said specifically that there would be no continuances granted. That is when you know the court is PISSED.

He had, however, made inquiries for me with the ACLU, and they were discussing it with the New York CLU where the decision would be made. I waited, made a call or two, unreturned. Another call; yes, we are trying to track down your case. Two days later, sorry, haven't found anything. I said thanks for your kind attention to this matter, maybe a little sarcastically, called the wonderful lawyer that I had been referred to in New York, who had said he would do it, represent me, because what the court did was wrong, even though it would not be a good idea professionally for him to take the case, and I said, I am very sorry, but saddle up.

Not ten minutes later, I received a message that the ACLU in New York had located my case, and it was being considered. I was to call the legal director. I received a call from the San Francisco ACLU that told me to call New York. They were getting back to me after, a week? So I called the legal director in New York and was informed that he was going to discuss my case with his associates tomorrow, and would call me with a decision. I asked for the opportunity to make a pitch, and he was deft at deflecting the request, but suggested there would surely be an opportunity to make such a pitch at some point.

Friday morning, he called and informed me that the ACLU would not be representing me in this matter, but the question of their filing an Amicus brief was left open. That's a brief that an uninvolved organization files with a court, as a friend of the court, because that entity wants to weigh in on some issue raised by the litigation in question. There it was, the ACLU was considering lending its weight to my struggle, on behalf of me. Monday or Tuesday, I would have a chance to make my pitch. So I was informed.

It was well into Saturday before it was clear to me that an opportunity was presenting itself that, under any circumstances, given the matters involved and the stakes on the table, I would have paid dearly for at any point in the last six years. The most prestigious organization of lawyers ever assembled was going to give me time to tell them why they should get involved in some way in my case. As a lawyer with more ammunition than I had any idea what to do with, I really could not possibly have asked for more.

The facts are so powerful; I simply had to set them out in a marginally coherent fashion. But, it occurred to me; I should be there to do it in person. I had an instinct that I had to grab for as much...I don't know, control? as possible. So, I hopped on several planes, quite a considerable number now as I think back on it, last minute prices being what they are, and went to New York, bracing for the 103-degree heat that the broadcasters of Baltimore Orioles baseball games were complaining about, that had enveloped the eastern seaboard.

I got lucky; the weather broke and a cooling, very, very gentle rain greeted me most politely. Had the ACLU been slightly so kind. I called and left messages for two days without one return before hearing at 5 PM on the second day that the legal director had too much on his plate this week. He would call me next week when he had the time. The hours were running down relentlessly for my response. My lawyer was on the case, but here was the ACLU putting off the decision to weigh in or not to weigh in till a week before my deadline, and, if I remember the rules for an Amicus brief, two weeks before theirs.

All of that time I had spent war-gaming with myself; what if it is a large room full of people? What if some lowly assistant? What if three high muckety-mucks, as I was given to believe would be the case over the phone, albeit over the phone? Conference call? I unable you read a face or a reaction; unable to smile unthreateningly; unable to show a picture. Show a picture of an OSC RE: Sanctions? What precisely was I seeking to have the ACLU do? Wade into the waters of 9/11 conspiracy theory? Not simply say that speech was being abridged by an embroiled court? Aye, there's a matter of some importance, indeed. It remains my belief that the ACLU has a couple of reasons to get involved here. One, as you can imagine, important but...small. And one, so enormous as to defy description. Maybe it would be a good thing if courts could keep their shirts on when a litigant raises the possibility of their imperfection to their face. Maybe, the ACLU, in addition to defending the rights of Nazis to say whatever the bloody hell they want, should make a statement in support of the mildly untethered aggressive advocate, however wrong, the poor soul.

But how about the aggressive advocate who has spoken the pure and righteous truth? What says the ACLU to that person's civil liberties, to the civil liberty of citizens of the nation to be free from the violent assault of representatives of their own government? Is this a civil liberty worth some political capital, some moral courage?

How would that meeting have gone, had it ever taken place? Am I wrong to deduce from the unavailability of the principals to a traveler of great distance and expense that whatever interest may ever have existed on the part of the ACLU was tepid and halting, and most probably ill-, from the point of view of the organization's political realities, thought-out? What did they suppose I was going to be asking of them? Was I to avoid the guts of my case? Make no mention of the rather much larger quadruped in the room? How could any lawyer make the case for intervention and leave out reference to the stunning and, at this point, frankly undeniable fact that all of the evidence pointed to treason and nothing had been done about it?

I don't know what drives the people who run such organizations as the ACLU. Are they talented egghead lawyers? Politicians? Academics? Patriots? Activists? Bureaucrats? Fundraisers? I don't know. There is likely some of all of that in the mix. I hate for this 9/11 problem to be the litmus test of all society, and it clearly shouldn't be for a great many powerful people, but how about if you are the ACLU? I doubt that I will take the time to read their charter; I guess I don't care enough.

But I would certainly dearly love to know how the first thoughts of inside job got digested by those lawyers and what forms any discussions took and whether some summer intern was ever asked to take a look at the literature, or prepare a paper or organize a debate or show a DVD or do something to satisfy the organization that something horrible hadn't happened, the correction of which might have been the business of that very organization. I'd like to know all of that, and maybe, if there ever actually is a call from the higher ups at New York center, I will inquire, was my thinking at the time.

I have been told by someone with a far greater feel for these matters that the ACLU is never going to get involved in this "mess" because the political downsides are much too inescapably visible. No mainstream organization is going to take the risks of infection. So maybe I will have an opportunity to mouth off to the comfortably powerful, albeit at long distance and over the phone, but that is about it.

According to a then-fresh email, it appeared the Petition for Rehearing En Banc had been denied without a mumbling word by any judge, there being no dissent to the belief that this whole quixotic exploration of a terrifying moment in American history was just a frivolous bit of delusion, unworthy of a footnote anywhere. Unworthy of a footnote...anywhere.

31

Afterword

Depleted and defeated. Strangely, not the least embarrassed. Quite proud actually, now that it is final. Sanctions, that is, in two instances, one for the frivolity of the legal action, and the other for harsh words spoken to our betters. The first has the $15,000 price tag, which was sent off to the Justice Department in December, 2011. The second I will wear as a badge of honor till I expire. I am ordered to tell any Federal Court in the 2nd Circuit in which I may appear in the next year that I have been sanctioned. My days of lawyering now pretty much spent, and my days in federal court in any Circuit, non-existent, Gallop v. Cheney to the contrary notwithstanding, the penalty imposed by those miserable, duplicitous bastards will have no effect whatsoever on me.

But I was not the reason any sanctions were imposed. Sanctions were imposed because their eminences saw what we did as a threat. And therein, inchoate and abstract and theoretical as it is, is maybe a bit of sparkle to be seen in the dishonor strewn all around. It is possible to get to these people in a way that makes them uncomfortable. When the high horse of sanctimony and privilege has been ridden for as long and as comfortably as it has by Walker, Winter, and Cabranes-- how many Yale dinners and toasts and ad hoc lectures have extolled the grandeur of the law and their duties and the difficulty of certain decisions?-- it must be truly unnerving to have it all read back to them to the point of choking.

It would be grand and beautiful and wondrous to know how the conversations went between them. But I don't guess they are talking. If there could be some organizer in the crowd to produce a constant stream of inquiries of the panel, such that the mainstream could no longer ignore. Ignore. The masters probably now feel, given the prodigious string of victories which is the history of the world for the last eighty years or so, that they are capable of redirecting, co-opting, diffusing all manner of political maelstrom. In spite of brilliant scholarship and reporting by Robert Stinnet in *Day of Deceit,* there persists doubt that FDR knew all he needed to, to save 2300 soldiers during the attack on Pearl Harbor. The New York *Times,* when last I noticed, was still embarrassing itself with the proposition that Oswald acted alone, in spite of revelations far too numerous to mention, but most recently by Phillip Nelson in *LBJ, Mastermind in the Assassination of JFK.* The overwhelming probability, --no...there isn't the slightest question anymore-- that Bobby Kennedy and Martin Luther King went the same or a similar way, yet the Establishment refuses to acknowledge the facts, toasts the efficiency of the apparatus of information as it deserves to be toasted, for its directors and its practitioners are without parallel in their accomplishments.

And 9/11 is their finest moment. It was then that the greatest possible impulse to evil found expression and accomplished every last one of its goals, stated and implied. With spectacular impunity. There is nothing new under the sun. As ever, it is for the people to rise, the people to speak, and the Titan to quake at their thunder.

32

After-Afterword

This story may not be over yet, or so I thought at the time. Dennis and I had surely been stomped upon, but the way that was accomplished all kind of a sudden opened doors that beckoned us on. When we were sanctioned the second time, it was really just me, William Veale is ORDERED, etc. That is because it was I who signed the Affidavit which apparently suggested such contumacious things about the three gentlemen of the 2nd Circuit. After all, it was I who argued the case and who had taken the steps to be licensed to practice before that particular Court of Appeal.

But it was Dennis Cunningham who had done almost all of the writing. Those were fundamentally his ideas that gave the panel such a fit. And, mensch that he is, he was not about to let his co-contemnor take all the heat by himself. So, Dennis informed the court of his principal responsibility, and they promptly informed him that he would be required to respond to a second sanctions order as well. So, in terms of time, Dennis and I were on two different tracks. I received notice, in spite of my lawyer's superb efforts, that my defense to the sanctions was of insufficient merit, according to the Court.? As had been true in the other decisions, none of the factual assertions upon which all of our efforts relied were mentioned by the court. That hypothetical critique of the liquor store hold-up indictment still finds no room for the defendant with the pistol as he enters the premises.

Dennis would have to wait for his similar ruling for another couple of months. And that is when it started to get a little more interesting. When the Court affirmed its proposed sanctions of Dennis, it revisited an issue that had not been addressed from the first decision ordering sanctions which we felt quite confident in doing, and the US Attorney's Office made no effort to correct the situation, due to the ambiguity of the Order given the misplacement of a comma. We had been ordered to pay "double costs", and the Court apparently meant them to be in addition to the $15k as opposed to the whole bill adding up to $15k.

So, in the Order affirming the Sanctions against Dennis they straightened out the ambiguity and established a Master, a District Court judge, and a time schedule to determine precisely what the costs were that we were again, now they said, ordering us to pay. What is odd about this? As Dennis so eloquently put it when I read him the decision, " Th'ain't no fuckin' costs in this case!" Which anyone with any judicial experience and the slightest familiarity with the case would have realized after about two minutes of thought. Costs are things like copying documents and transporting witnesses and hiring stenographers, the normal expenses incurred by lawyers if they have been allowed to litigate. Which is precisely what we had not been allowed to do. And when we had our required phone hearing with the District Judge, the Assistant US Attorney acknowledged that there were no costs in the case. The 2nd Circuit's resurrection of the first sanction order and clarification of the ambiguity found within it, was going to have no effect whatever upon us miscreants, a fact which they must, or surely should, have understood. Yet, its meaninglessness did not prevent them from getting another dig in. Why? To underscore their disdain? To make it clear they meant business?

I took it as a sign. Whereas I had foregone the opportunity to seek En Banc review of the sanctions when I first got the ruling, or to appeal them at all; now I felt like there was no good reason not to revisit that decision. I decided that the worst that could be done to me had been done, and, after all, I was right.

I started writing. Firing from the pinnacle of righteousness, I left absolutely nothing in the bag of eloquence, as far as I was concerned, and shipped it off to my lawyer for his opinion. He was blunt. "This will avail you nothing." Before I could feel the sting of deflation, the next sentence registered. He offered to write a Petition for Certiorari to the Supreme Court of the United States of America, free of charge. Thank Godamighty. And so he did. And here we are, mid-August of 2012, the Petition having been filed in the first days of May, and we have yet to hear a thing.

Stay tuned?

Come on; you didn't really think there was going to be a happy ending to this tale, did you? Petition for Certiorari Denied, without dissent, October 3, 2012.

33

Final Epilogue, I
Promise

Apparently, I must write some more. You see, it is now 2018. When I submitted what I considered to be the finished manuscript to the publisher who had been encouraging me, and Dennis, for four-plus years, it was February of 2014. There were a few requests to add this or that and a discussion of the cover of the final product, and then: "We are sorry but we will not be able to publish your book." My anger and disappointment did not prevent me from inquiring as to why, but other than some reference to a "contracting network" in the original notification, I received nothing by way of explanation. So we can all wonder, if we are bent in that direction, if this is the Deep State in action. I doubt it, but how would I know?

So, I closed up the computer and, but for a couple of efforts at other publishing houses which proved fruitless, said to hell with it. Now, four years later, I have decided to make the work available to the world one way or another. But time has passed, and there has been a thing or two to report with regard to the struggle over justice for 9/11. In some way, this is an effort to contribute to the history of 9/11, generally, at least from my point of view. It wouldn't make a lot of sense to leave out the part where Osama bin Laden gets killed. That was in 2011. President Barack Obama took a lot of credit. The story has been told quite a few times, but I was particularly taken with the movie made about it. It was called *Zero Dark Thirty.*

There is no denying its place as propaganda for the US military and the CIA. Its rendition of events can and should be questioned especially in terms of the supposed positive role torture is alleged to have played in tracking down OBL. Nevertheless, I loved it as a movie. Here is the review I wrote in 2013:

There is a great, really great, story out there. Is it the one we are being told at our local movie theatre in ZERO DARK THIRTY, great as that one is? When the event being depicted is as seminal, as landscape-changing, as the gunning down of the entire globe's most infamous terrorist, and reputed orchestrator of the earth-defining attacks of 9/11, is it acceptable that serious, and entirely reasonable scholars and observers of world events cannot agree about, or at least express sincere uncertainty concerning, the facts?

And I am not talking about the question of whether Osama Bin Laden could or should have been captured alive. I am not talking about the doubtfully helpful role that torture played in his demise, or the movie's depiction of that conundrum. I am not talking about whether he was armed when he was gunned down, had used a woman, a wife, as a shield, whether there was a weapon within reach or how baggy his clothes were. The question, strangely enough, that is still in dispute is, was that Osama Bin Laden.

Let's get the obvious rejoinders out of the way. Clearly some very important people, almost certainly the soldiers firing in the dark, thought it was OBL. The prickly, and probably in real life, captivating female CIA officer who did the hardest work of coming to the pivotal conclusion that it was he, she surely believed it was OBL. And in retrospect it seems almost silly to question the premise. Why in the world would anyone live in a house with a 12-16 foot high concrete wall around it, and be able to look forward to only a shaded walk in a very small circle in the back yard once a day, every day, if you weren't hiding from the world's most formidable weapon-toting information apparatus, and hiding for very good reason?

So, what is the point of this exercise? Is there any reason at all to think that was not OBL lying there supposedly with a hole through his eye, body later slid mostly unceremoniously into some sea or other, no independent authority having made what is the cornerstone of any homicide prosecution anywhere in the world, a positive identification? Other than the troubling notions contained in the preceding sentence, yes, as a matter of fact there are a number of reasons, and a simple list should suffice.

According to the Observer newspaper in Pakistan, he died around December 13th, 2001 in Tora Bora and was buried the next day in an unmarked grave, attended by 30 or so Al Qaeda fighters. He looked calm and relaxed in repose.

He suffered from kidney failure, this according to CNN's Dr. Sanjay Gupta and a Bush Administration official citing "American Intelligence," requiring dialysis, which would be hard to survive in a cave at the top of a mountain range. It has been shown that he was visited in a hospital in Dubai in the summer of 2001 by a CIA case officer, confirming the illness and also his relationship to American intelligence, he carrying the name Tim Osman in the 1970's as a CIA asset. What's more, there has been no reference to finding a dialysis machine in Abbottabad, nor to any of that which attends the medical treatment for kidney disease. President Pervez Musharraf of Pakistan actually said OBL had died in 2002 of kidney failure.

In the years following, President George Bush, having once said OBL was wanted "Dead or Alive," expressed no interest in his whereabouts or in any efforts to capture or kill him, actually saying at one point that he didn't know if he was alive or dead.

General Richard Myers said the mission in Afghanistan had never been to get OBL, a surprising statement given all that had been said previously and the presumed suppositions of the American people. His acknowledged death too soon would have undercut the reasons for war, one guesses.

There is a "confession" videotape, "found" by US forces in some raid in Jalalabad in December of 2001, dated November 9, 2001, which purports to be OBL but doesn't look all that much like him and might be fake for a number of reasons, among them:

He appears too fat;

There are those who say the nose is wrong; some say the cheek bones are wrong; it would take a pro to make an accurate determination

He is seen writing with the wrong hand;

He is wearing what appears to be a gold ring, which is unIslamic.

His language contains none of his normal religious usages, and there are arguably illogical statements contained in it.

Up until this tape, he had denied any responsibility for the 9/11 attacks.

There are other audio and videotapes which some well-informed observers say are fakes, at least one of which was proclaimed fraudulent by Bruce Lawrence, head of the Religious Studies Department at Duke, and foremost expert on OBL and his utterances.

An audiotape from November 2002 was proclaimed a probable fake by a forensic lab in Switzerland, the Dalle Molle Institute for Perceptual Artificial Intelligence.

A number of CIA/military intelligence types have opined that he is dead, one of whom is former CIA case officer Robert Baer who proclaims death emphatically and refers to a polling of his former colleagues in coming to his conclusion. Another is Angelo Codevilla, now a professor at Boston University. Another is Oliver North. When you use Oliver North in an effort to prove a point other than his own depravity, you have probably gone as far as you should under any circumstances, but I don't know why he would say such a thing with the damage it could do to his ideological confreres then in residence at the White House, if he weren't speaking what he believed to be the truth.

The appearance of one of the declared-fake tapes played an arguably pivotal role as an October Surprise in the 2004 election that beat John Kerry with the help of other electoral manipulations on the part of the Republican apparatus.

One could go on; Professor David Ray Griffin wrote a book on the subject in 2009. What is found above are some of the significant highlights. As other far more astute observers than I have documented, Russ Baker at WhoWhatWhy.com for example, there are in addition to these elements which existed before the killing in Abbottabad, some troublesome questions that have arisen since. The story of what happened was mangled by USG spokespersons as soon as there was anything to report, and most importantly, with regard to the absence of a positive identification, Baker reports that the body was disposed of before there was adequate time to determine if there was a DNA match. As a result, American authorities may think they know now whether that was in fact OBL sinking beneath the waves, but they certainly didn't know it as the splash subsided. So, what is one to think? Maybe there is an explanation for the known anomalies. One very plausible one deals with the "too fat" question, but leaves the right hand use and ring issue alone. There are just a troublesome number of unanswered questions.

Maybe Bruce Lawrence and Dr. Gupta and the Swiss lab are wrong, but when something very significant is used by a morally bankrupt group of politicians in October of an election year, and they had something to do with its production, AND non-politicians question its provenance, it pays to be very, very skeptical. Waving off the fakeness of the tapes requires a leap of faith beyond my capability.

Why would there be fake tapes if OBL could denounce them to Al Jazeera and disrobe White House efforts to manipulate the electorate, for example? The editor of Politique Internationale, Amir Taheri, declaring OBL dead in July, 2002 made a similar point referring to OBL's Everest-sized ego. One suggestion is that the fake tapes are efforts by the CIA to smoke OBL out, they being, at that moment, quite hot on his trail. The reason he hasn't put the lie to the subterfuge is that he realized some of his fundamental protective strategies had been compromised, and he went deep into the hole not to come out again except in a bag; so the theory goes.

The lengths that must have been traveled to achieve the fake version of events that include the on-the-screen assassination of some sort of double, if the suppositions of fakery are correct, are really quite staggering. Al Qaeda appears to have accepted his recent death. The assaulting force in Abbottabad is said to have found at least a son, at least a daughter and a wife or two. In addition, Gareth Porter has written a long article for Truthout that lays waste to almost all that the USG has said about OBL's death, except for the identity of the dead man, who Porter agrees is OBL, though the question of his identity is never addressed in the article. The article is based on reporting done in Pakistan with a named Pakistani general as a source.

Is it possible that the wives and Pakistani sources for Porter were all unknowing or knowing participants in an incredible charade? Seems very unlikely, but I am not making up any of the facts to which I refer above. How do they and an only-recently-killed OBL live together in the same universe? What are the explanations for this bizarre cohabitation? It is hard to conceive of a factually accurate ZERO DARK THIRTY that does not involve some deceptive manipulations of public perception by some dark forces at some point along the way, possibly ones impelled by some marginally honorable motives.

Isn't that even a better story, the myriad ways that the USG used OBL, or tried to fake him out, that for a decade were unsuccessful, including notices of his funeral in 2002, and changing the tone of public statements after that? Provocatively, are we to give the Bush White House a pass for jiggering with the democratic process in 2004, if they did, because the activity had as a primary motive the capture or death of our national nemesis? Such moral complexity is the soul of great cinema.

So I ask, doesn't this nation have the right to know, and agree upon, the facts of the matter in a moment of such enormous importance? This is an invitation to the filmmakers, Ms. Bigelow and Mr. Boal, to divulge all they know about the smattering of factual assertions contained in this essay, or explain how and why they were unaware of them.

The other matters that have driven me back to the computer I will put in three categories. The first will have to do with some excellent citizen sleuthing concerning the handling and analysis of some of the physical remains of the devastation at Ground

Zero. The second will involve a discussion of the famous 28 pages that the Bush Administration classified following the work of the 2002 Joint Inquiry of Congress that was chaired by then-Senator Bob Graham of Florida. It was the first governmental investigation into the attacks of 9/11. The last part of this last part will concern more work by the inestimable David Griffin, and the citizens whose work he has reported on, that shore up conclusions that were never in danger of collapse, in fact whose integrity, if you really think about it, should never have been in question. The question here is the pivotal one, where was Dick Cheney, and what was he doing at the time of the crime?

34

Pieces of Metal

From the very beginning, when I was laughing at the idea of an inside job, rolling my eyes with the best of them, others were reacting differently, sometimes to their credit for great wisdom and knowledge of history, sometimes to their disrepute for their overzealous and untethered proclivity always to believe the worst of their government, or the more powerful generally. Those people were suspicious, and their scholarly investigative inclinations led them to...investigate. Some of them possessed no accredited skills; in some cases, maybe many cases, they had no particularly relevant educational experience. They just had curiosity and worthy human brains.

One such, with a particularly noteworthy human brain, is David Cole. He lives somewhere and made it into and, in fairly short order out of, college with nothing for his wall. At some point, driven by a profound love of country and some of those suspicions to which I have referred, he looked where others hadn't and came into contact with the work of Professor Abulhassan Astaneh-Asl, Ph.D., P.E. of the University of California, Berkeley where he is a member of the Civil and Environmental Engineering Department.

Professor Astaneh sought and obtained a grant from the National Science Foundation to study the remains of the buildings at Ground Zero since the structural safety of buildings is his life's work. He arrived in lower Manhattan within a week or two and set about inspecting and photographing those pieces of metal that he could, either on their way away from the scene or in New Jersey where they were deposited before being sold to China for scrap. One of the most important pieces he studied and photographed was designated C-89. The professor can be seen in a video declaring the significance of this large piece of traumatized metal, "[W]hat you see here is actually very critical. Very, very important. Perhaps this is the most important piece I have seen so far. This piece comes from, most likely, Tower Two, where the plane went in and exploded." He is pointing to C-89.

David Cole managed to get ahold of the records of Professor Astaneh's work, despite what can fairly be described as persistent and dedicated efforts by the University of California not to be forthcoming. He reviewed them as only the truly gifted and determined can. Found deep within the digital cardboard box, otherwise known as a Compact Disc, that finally arrived in his mailbox compliments of UCBerkeley, without index or organizational explanation, are documents that are well-known to builders. Among other things, he found spreadsheet charts which list the piece in question, C 89, and then set out the numbers identifying it, which give the information that was used when the tower was initially constructed. In the simplest of terms, the contractor did not want to build the building with a flange or spandrel that belonged on the third floor somehow bolted into the sixteenth. So there are letters and numerals which denote which floor and where on that floor each column or brace or beam is to be assembled. Strangely, there is a misprint in the document which renders it close to meaningless, but if you have sufficient understanding of the scheme, it isn't hard to know what the letters and numbers actually denote. The numbers and letters are L3 144 146 50 B215 15 12. In this instance, the significant numbers are "15 12." They should have been written down as "12 15," which is consistent with the scheme, as opposed to "15 12" which is not. The important, truth-defining point is that those numbers mean that the piece ran from the 12th to the 15th floors. They mean that the piece ran from the 12th to the 15th floors. THEY MEAN THAT THE PIECE...you get the point; it was nowhere near the 80th floor. If it had been from around the 80th floor, pretty much any scientific investigator would be justified in thinking that explosive force from the collision of a speeding airplane had caused the discoloration and disfigurement. Which is to say, Professor Astaneh could be "understood" in the error that he made, because he probably was not then familiar with the markings designating placement in the building found on the beam. Since the piece ultimately was determined to have come from a floor about 65 or so removed from what he postulated, we know we have strong, not to say irrefutable, evidence of explosives that had nothing to do with an airplane. And Professor Astaneh? Can he not be aware of the mistake now? What of his failure to correct the pronounced conclusion that he rendered as he inspected the beam? Well, he simply climbs aboard the same windowless boxcar already enclosing the likes of Jim Dwyer and Walter Pincus and Matt Taibbi and Barton Gellman and Rachel Maddow and ....

So, let us recap what we have here. Professor Astaneh of UCBerkeley, such an expert that he managed to secure a grant to study the matter, opined because of the existence of evidence of explosion on a piece of steel from the South Tower that he had found where the plane entered the building. He, in our dreams, will come to court and swear that that is a video of him saying what I quoted him as saying a paragraph or so ago. He will acknowledge that he used the word "exploded." He will agree that he used it because there was no other explanation for the pattern of destruction and the evidence of extreme heat that he saw in the spot at which he was pointing. At some point, however, he will have to face the fact that no plane came anywhere near the spot at which he was pointing, and he will have to agree that there was some other cause for the explosive destruction, and he will be asked if nano thermite and explosives might be an explanation. He will say....

Brother Cole was not finished. There is after all, K-16, for example. Here we have NIST staring down at a photograph depicting a piece of severely malformed and eroded steel, called slag, resulting from exposure to extreme heat. It appears as a kind of bulging, discolored imperfection the size of a fist on an otherwise apparently unaffected steel beam. Rather than taking samples and studying and searching the world and the literature for a possible explanation for the occurrence of this slag, considering for example the obvious possibility of some sort of pyrotechnic explosive; rather than that, they cut a coupon, which is to say a small section about the size of the slag itself, from a spot nearby the slag on K-16. They then blithely determined that there is nothing of importance with regard to any of it that might upset the required conclusion. That conclusion is that the culprit in the devastation of the building was fire, not pure and simple, but...you know...pure and simple.

I do not understand how these people sleep at night.

35

29 Pages

In the year 2016, July 15th, to be clear, what, till then, and still is as far as I know, was referred to as the "28 pages" were released of almost all of their classifiedness. Of very little importance is the fact that the last page is numbered "29." There is very little of any significance on that last, 29th page.

The Joint Inquiry was a Congressional Investigation into 9/11 performed in 2002. The members of that panel did not come close to getting to the bottom of things as this book, for example, has done. And I will forever cling to the notion that, had any of its members chosen to go rogue and divulge to the world what the Bush Administration had determined should be classified, (those 29 pages), this sad chapter of our Nation's history would read in a much different way than it does now.

The 29 pages were declassified as a result of a kind of public outcry. You see, there is a lawsuit pending even now that claims the government of Saudi Arabia and its operatives were responsible for 9/11. This, apparently, is a claim that is not beyond the pale, and sufficient loud voices said it enough that political pressure was placed in sufficient amounts and with sufficient force to lead Congress to vote to declassify most, but not all, of the 29 pages. Those are the pages of the Report of the Joint Inquiry that seem to support the idea that the Saudis were responsible. When you learn what is in the 29 pages, you will be particularly curious about those parts which have yet to be declassified.

So, what is in them, the 29 pages, and how was that information treated by the news media? Not to fiddle around, they demonstrate, with only the mildest bit of inference required, that Saudi government agents acted as handlers of two of the 19 hijackers, Khalid al-Mihdhar and Nawaf al-Hazmi. The handlers' names were Omar al-Bayoumi and Osama Bassnan.

"... Al-Bayoumi provided substantial assistance to hijackers Khalid al-Mihdhar and Nawaf al-Hazmi after they arrived in San Diego in February 2000. Al-Bayoumi met the hijackers at a public place shortly after his meeting with an individual at the Saudi consulate and there are indications in the files that his encounter with the hijackers may not have been accidental. During this same time frame, al-Bayoumi had extensive contact with Saudi Government establishments in the United States and received financial support from a Saudi company affiliated with the Saudi Ministry of Defense,"

to quote from the 29 pages. For example, they helped arrange living situations for the two hijackers including putting them up for a number of days, introduced them at the local mosque, provided them with a translator, helped get driver's licenses, and introduced them to a flight instructor. Osama Bassnan actually bragged to an FBI informant that he had done more for the hijackers than Al-Bayoumi.

The crucial information contained in the 29 pages is that these two "handlers" received in the neighborhood of $130,000 from Princess Haifa Brint Sultan. Who is Princess Haifa? The 29 pages modestly describe her as the wife of Prince Bandar, the Saudi Ambassador to the United States. There are, however, other ways to describe her and him, particularly him. He has recently been the director general of the Saudi Intelligence Agency, and a member of the Saudi National Security Council. But it was from 1983 until 2005 that he was the Saudi Ambassador to Washington. During that twenty-two-year time period, there were three US Republican Administrations and one Democratic one, all of which had extremely close ties to Saudi Arabia, and for about fourteen of those years, there was someone named George Bush either as President or Vice President. And here is the fact that you will not find in any discussion of the 28 or 29 pages that occurred in the mainstream media: Bandar's nickname was Bandar Bush.

Many pages ago I suggested that Bill Maher pick on somebody his own size when it came to 9/11, he having had fun at some heckler's expense on air. If he had been paying much attention at all in the last decade since enjoying his derogation of people like me, he would have rethought his attitude, and he would have used his considerable voice to urge justice; or one would have thought. The fact is that all of the scholarship in the last decade has amassed to support our contentions, and nothing has been produced to refute them. But I assume that Maher and people like him have simply willed their minds in another direction and successfully ignored the facts upon facts that undergird our claims. For certain is that he has not changed his mind in the slightest about high government complicity in the attacks. That possibility is worthy of ridicule and derision and no more of his time.

And then came the 28 pages, and Maher just could not keep himself out of the arena. He invited Lawrence Wright, celebrated journalist of the *New Yorker* and author of *The Looming Tower*, about the historical antecedents to 9/11, which recently became a hit miniseries on Hulu, to come on his show. This was before the 29 pages were declassified, but when everybody who had any interest already knew the essentials of what is contained in the preceding paragraphs. I suggest that Maher and Wright knew it all, because these are two really brilliant minds in my opinion who have staffs, Maher at least, if nothing else, whose job it is to keep them informed. How much of the previous paragraphs did Maher's audience learn about? I don't think it learned Bandar's name—his real name, that is—but I could be wrong about that. What they absolutely did not learn was the nickname—Bandar Bush. And they weren't provided the slightest suggestion of any enduring connection between Bandar and the Bush clan.

Andrew Cockburn is one of the celebrated Cockburn family of journalists; Alexander, his brother, now deceased, was the publisher of *Counterpunch*, a left-wing radical magazine inspired by I.F. Stone of the mid-twentieth century. Andrew has done great work, authoring a book about Donald Rumsfeld which thoroughly demonstrated how deeply a part of the Deep State Rumsfeld was and is and what a profound jackass in some circumstances. But that book, published in 2007, never came close to the facts set out in this work and so maybe what happened in 2018 should not surprise. He wrote a seven-page article in *Harper's* that dealt with the question of whether the Saudis would ever see justice for their involvement in 9/11. It will be recalled that there is that lawsuit pending which is meandering vaguely in the direction of justice. In that article Cockburn refers to previous investigations, including the Congressional Joint Inquiry, that I mentioned above. While there discussing this pertinent and important history, it would have been difficult indeed to avoid mention of the 28 pages, and he doesn't, avoid it, that is. What he avoids is the same thing that Maher and Wright avoid: the Saudi Ambassador in Washington's nickname was Bandar Bush, i.e. he was considered part of the family.

Messrs. Cockburn, Maher, Wright; raise your right hands to be sworn. Did any of you not know Bandar's nickname? What in the Good Christ, to use Wilfred Brimley's magnificent phrase from *Absence of Malice*, went on within your brains that prevented you from informing your readers and listeners of that damning piece of information? Would you, along with all other sentient beings, have been unable not to connect that dot with the fact of the Bush Administration's deep and disturbing enmeshment in so many of the 9/11 attacks' disturbing features detailed, for example, in the pages of this book?

It is hard to know just how much of this needs spelling out. Most of us have nicknames but very few if any of the readers of these words are, or ever have been, ambassadors to the most powerful country in the world, or members of the family that occupies, or occupied at one time, the White House. I certainly agree that it would be of some importance to know how many ambassadors had nicknames. But even if it was quite a few, it is clearly incumbent upon those potentially maligned Bushes to argue that it was not any sort of indication of significant social closeness or affection. When one looks at the picture of Bandar lounging on the arm of an overstuffed chair in what looks like President George W.'s Crawford, Texas home, the possibility of close familiarity between the two is not instantly banished from one's mind.

What really are the odds of Saudi Arabia being deeply involved in the attacks—fourteen of the nineteen hijackers were Saudi nationals you will recall— against an ostensibly extremely close ally—hands-clasped dancing and all—billions of dollars in armaments and all—oil deals with the kingdom since beloved FDR and all, without the okay from Cheney and Company? Most fundamentally, what would be the point of it? Saudi involvement, that is? Ordinarily, the sources of such attacks are investigated and found out. Maybe it takes a decade or two, but as we are seeing with the pending lawsuit, "the truth will out," if only small parts at a time. What enormous benefit accrued to the Saudi regime as a result of 9/11? Wasn't it pretty much the status quo between the two nations? Yes, the American military bases from the Gulf War were removed from Saudi soil in the ensuing years, but didn't they simply have to ask in order to accomplish that?

On the other hand, the benefits to Bush and Cheney and the Saudis, by virtue of the enduring alliance in the region, are several, substantial, and articulable, and appear early on in this book—fear in the population, two wars, the Patriot Act, unending military contracts and enhanced defense spending, i.e. opportunities to make money in quantities it is hard to fathom, and the ability forever to project American power around the world, assuring access to oil and other natural resources and influence, if not hegemony, in every corner of the earth.

Maybe this is a last and timely opportunity to discuss the matter of presumptions. This book has shown that the false flag attack is a fact of history. That does not mean, however, that it should be the first thing to come to mind when mass disasters take place. As a general rule, presumptively, as a matter of common sense, people do not attack their own. That is a general rule that serves us well as we live our lives. The idea of false flag, a government or other entity employing force against its own citizens or associates with blame arranged in another direction, should only arise because accumulated evidence requires it.

These fundamentals are the reason why Bandar's nickname is so important. It suggests, presumptively, as a matter of common sense, that there is a close relationship between the Bushes, the ultimate beneficiaries of the false flag attacks of 9/11, and Bandar. Presumptively, Bandar would not be involved in attacks on the Bushes. Presumptively, then, Bandar is not a suspect in 9/11. But,... when sufficient evidence accumulates in the form of large quantities of money to the handlers of the hijackers out of Bandar's wife's pocket book, then, presumptions of his innocence disappear. As an aside, for those looking to dodge the inference with some sort of "that's the wife, not the husband," formulation, only on its best day a weak and bending reed, it is a fact that drivers' licenses for women are only at this moment becoming an element of life in the Kingdom. As a member of the ruling elite, though, the Princess's status would be different from the average Saudi woman. Yeah, maybe, but does he, Bandar, get a pass even from investigation as a result of the theoretical possibility that she, the Princess, was acting on her own? I am happy to assert that she has been given a pass as well. Why?

Now that Bandar is tainted, or at least should be, are all presumptions instantly abolished? Absolutely not. They are peeled away like the layers of an onion, but only by evidence. So the presumption that you don't attack your own house or your own associates comes into play again, in the following way: We thought Bandar wouldn't attack Bush, yet there is evidence that he did. Where do our presumptions take us then? Well, what is more likely, that Bandar attacked Bush with a malicious intent toward Bush, or that he attacked Bush with Bush's acquiescence? Common sense suggests that, as between those two scenarios, the latter is more probable. Friends collude; they do not murder each other. Now, of course, betrayal by friends is obviously not unheard of; it is part of human history as much as the false flag. It is, simply, a lesser probability. It is not banished from consideration, but it is definitely in the back seat. Maher and Company turn the entire matter on its head. They refuse to allow the common sense presumption a place in the automobile.

Now, does any of this mean that the case is closed? May we conclude, because Bandar supported the hijackers, through the handlers, that Bush and Cheney are guilty? I'd say that is a personal judgment of significant complexity if all we were talking about were contained in the previous sentence. That, however, is surely not the case. Though much of the world would prefer to ignore the previous 200 pages...

36

Where Was Cheney?

The final matter to which this work will address itself is the important discovery of additional information bearing on the location of Vice President Dick Cheney in the morning on September 11th, 2001. It may be recalled that where he was and what he was doing were central to the claims of Gallop v. Cheney. The testimony of Norman Mineta concerning Cheney's presence in the PEOC and his giving or confirming orders about Flight 77 before it hit, or flew over, the Pentagon was the part of the story that the District Court and the 2nd Circuit could not bring themselves to mention in any of the several opinions they felt it necessary to write. That is how powerful the information was deemed to be by, among others, the second highest court in the country. It is powerful, to reiterate, because if he was in the room when Mineta says he was, then there is no reason to believe he wasn't doing what Mineta says he was doing: Giving or confirming orders concerning a principal instrumentality of the crime, or metaphorically, walking into the liquor store with a gun drawn.

I was as convinced by what Mineta and, to review, Photographer Bohrer, Counterterrorism Czar Richard Clarke, and Cheney himself said,-- that Cheney was in the PEOC before Flight 77 did whatever it did,-- as I needed to be to put my name to a legal document asserting the fact. And that is a very high standard indeed. But that doesn't mean everyone will see it the same way.

When the United States government makes a proclamation, as the 9/11 Commission did, generally, about who was responsible for the attacks and specifically, about when Cheney arrived in the PEOC, about 10 AM, it carries some serious weight of credibility. As it should. We rely on our government's pronouncements daily, routinely, thoughtlessly. As we should. The effort to sell a lie on a massive scale is an enormous undertaking, and it makes very little sense to live one's life without believing what the government is telling us. Unless it comes to one's attention that things are amiss in some respect.

That is what the Truth Movement has done. It has brought certain matters to our attention, and one of them is the trouble with the time set out by the 9/11 Commission for when Cheney arrived in the PEOC. So, it is important for the case to be examined thoroughly and intently, bringing all relevant information into the light, so that if a determination is to be made, that, maliciously or negligently, the 9/11 Commission erred in this particular regard, it can be made with confidence.

David Ray Griffin has come to our aid again with his recent *Bush and Cheney, How They Ruined America and the World.* On page 239, he gives credit to another citizen investigator, Aidan Monaghan, for using the Freedom of Information Act to retrieve the government documents that pertain to the very question before us at this moment. One such document is a memorandum from the Technical Services Division of the Secret Service. Titled "Actions of TSD Related to Terrorist Incident," it states that when Danny Spriggs, the Secret Service assistant division chief entered the PEOC at 9:30, Cheney and Condoleezza Rice and ten other "Presidential and Vice-Presidential staff" were already there. Flight 77 is alleged to have hit the Pentagon at 9:38 or (it will be recalled) 9:32. So here we have an official document produced by a division of the Secret Service which establishes the presence of Cheney in the PEOC before the Pentagon was hit, confirming my long-held conclusion and shredding one of the principal deceits of the 9/11 Commission Report. Cheney had indeed lied about the time of his arrival in the PEOC.

We are not finished. Investigators from the 9/11 Commission interviewed members of the Secret Service, one of whom was Carl Truscott, the Special Agent In Charge. According to one report marked "Commission Sensitive," Truscott escorted Condoleezza Rice down to the PEOC just before 9:30. The report states, "[U]pon arrival at the shelter the VP and Mrs were present; VP on the phone." In addition to being another formidable blow to the Commission's lies, out of the darkness comes the glorious complicity of the charming Ms. Rice whom I confronted at the President's Cup in 2012 or so, offering her a small postcard of 9/11 facts and the French words, "J'accuse" of Emile Zola fame. She declined to receive the document, and I was led away for a brief detention by a very polite sergeant of the SFPD. Some of Ms. Rice's lies are among the more notable in the history of 9/11. She falsely managed to distance herself from Pakistani General Mahmoud Ahmed when he was in Washington, DC on 9/11, or at least that week. It was he, it will be remembered, that provided about $100k to Mohammad Attah in the weeks leading up to the attacks. She is also famous for the searingly outrageous notion of the mushroom cloud that threatened us all and drove the country to war against Saddam Hussein based on the lie that he possessed weapons of mass destruction. For those interested, aiding and abetting the crime of aggression, which is the prosecution of war without justification, is a war crime, and it is punishable by death.

More still? Oh, yes. Another declassified report provides a similarly damning timeline set out by Special Agent In Charge, Anthony Zotto, the man specifically in charge of Cheney's personal safety. Griffin concludes that, "Cheney was in the PEOC at least eight minutes prior to the attack on the Pentagon." A trial lawyer's mind wanders when considering evidence like this. At some point in these pages, I have highlighted and denigrated "planted" evidence; the hijacker's passport found on the street that survived the fiery explosion as United Flight 11 hit the North Tower, for example. The passport and red bandanna found at the Shanksville site would be some more, in addition to the various cellphone calls from high-flying jetliners for which the technology did not exist in 2001 and Mohammad Atta's supposed will from the Mitsubishi, or was it a Nissan, (the FBI appears confused as to which) that was declared to be the Rosetta Stone of 9/11?

Prize-winning journalists who are relied upon by sanctioned thought to provide us with the history of these events have pointed to the Secret Service logs to recount when Cheney and his retinue entered the PEOC. Is it wrong to consider them as potentially "planted" evidence?

It has become necessary to insert here reference to one more piece of evidence, fairly recently brought to my attention. It is a series of photographs of Vice President Cheney. They become important, to the extent they are important, because of the question of when they were taken. They have been scrutinized carefully by a committed truther who has declared that the clock whose face is barely visible at an angle reads 9:25 in one picture and 9:35 in another. If we assume that the pictures were taken on 9/11--who knows; it seems silly to put anything beyond these people at this point--there are two possible conclusions: 1. Cheney was in his office at 9:35 AM and 2. The photographs are the result of staging or doctoring. Anyone reading this will have no trouble guessing which conclusion I adopt. Are they that devious? Yes, Sir, Madam, they are. Further reasons for my view appear in subsequent paragraphs.

Mr. Gellman, can you tell us what this appears to be (handing him a copy of the Truscott statement of a couple of paragraphs ago)? You agree that it appears in direct contradiction to the logs upon which you relied when you were writing your book about Vice President Cheney in 2006? Those logs were provided to you at that time by agents of the defendant Cheney, were they not? This Truscott report which states that the vice president was already in the shelter just before 9:30, on the other hand, was not made available to the public until 2012, and only then because of the threat of a lawsuit, correct? What would your book have said if you had had that Truscott report in your hand? For that matter, what would your book have said if you had "gotten" to interviewing the Secretary of Transportation, Norman Mineta? The Truscott report would have been a reason not to believe the logs, wouldn't it, and that is why you said you didn't get to Mineta, wasn't it, because you had no reason not to believe the logs? Objection, Compound, Sustained. Mr. Gellman, Counsel's objection is well-taken. Why don't you pick whichever question you would like first, answer it, and we will proceed with the others in an order of your choosing. One can get very snippy in the trenches.

Before you go, Mr. Gellman, do you know who Eric Edelman is? In 2001 he was deputy to Scooter Libby who was Cheney's Chief of Staff as well as Cheney's National Security Advisor. He is a career foreign service officer, accomplished public servant, and presumably a patriot. He gave an interview to Evan Thomas of Newsweek on October 25th, 2001; were you aware of that fact or the contents of that interview? Mr. Edelman waxes rhapsodic about Cheney's performance that morning, wouldn't you say? He provides a lot of praise for Cheney's cool under pressure and his insights? So, it is probably doubtful that Mr. Edelman would intentionally give information that would be damaging to the vice president, you agree? On page 5 of that transcribed interview we find the following words, do we not: "I was already down in the PEOC with the Vice President when we got word that there had been an explosion at the Pentagon?"

Mr. Gellman, how do you reconcile those words with the scenario portrayed in your book, *Angler?* I would expect a sort of long pause at that question, but on the other hand, these guys are very smart, and they can figure out where you are going with a line of questioning. I now expect, upon reconsideration, that whatever garbage he was going to come up with would be there for his expectoration pretty much as soon as the question mark had been arrived at.

Mr. Edelman's interview is useful for more than just the Cheney-was-in-the-PEOC-before-the-Pentagon-was-hit piece. He is also a big problem for co-defendant Rumsfeld. He, it will be recalled, was not "situationally aware," according to him, until 10 AM or so. How that could be true of the TOP OF THE CHAIN OF COMMAND during a major terrorist attack on the country is way beyond my ability to comprehend, but nevertheless, Mr. Edelman makes it quite clear that it wasn't true, and he does so in his interview with Evan Thomas. "And at one point -- and again, I can't tell you exactly when this took place -- but we established a video conference with Secretary Rumsfeld at one point," he says on page 7 of the transcript. Now I am going to admit that it is possible to read the interview in such a way that the video conference was not set up until 10 AM, or at least that that is a possibility. I am simply not going to adopt that interpretation when the interpretation that I am attached to happens to be not only reasonable, but at least has the Secretary of Defense at his duty station where he should be, and where absolutely everyone with the slightest grounding in the affairs of government would expect him to be.

Lastly, for Mr. Edelman, he provides us with some intriguing tidbits about Principal Defendant Cheney. Edelman manages to begin the sculpting of the American people's "official story" as he recounts the hours spent with Cheney that morning, particularly in two regards. First, Edelman discusses the destruction of the Twin Towers thus:

Some of us, when the Trade Center came down, and then the second one came down, some of us I think were a bit stunned by how, the way it came down. As you recall from seeing the tapes, it almost looked like (inaudible) charges on each floor to bring it to the ground. Some of us were speculating that maybe, you know, there was some kind of charge on the ground or in the building.

He says this in the context of his admiration for Cheney and his grasp of all things worldly, including specifically Cheney's having been a "CEO of a large company that does a lot of construction stuff." Cheney, that morning in the presence of Edelman, sets the record straight and explains what happened with one of the Towers: "it just pancaked and (inaudible), top (inaudible) came down; just pancaked the rest of the building. His sense of all this was pretty impressive, I have to say -- not just because I work for him."

Those of us of the Truther stripe can point to Mr, Edelman as we underscore all that our architects have been telling the world for a decade and some. He was right on the money when he thought there were "charges", i.e. explosives, in the Towers. Edelman was talked out of his own sense of what happened by the voice of authority, and it is the denial of just that "sense" that NIST would spew out in service of their masters with their embarrassing report that in instance after instance cannot withstand scrutiny and amounts to scientific fraud.

The other time in which Cheney, through Edelman, begins his work on the "Official Story" is when Cheney predicts the tales of heroism to emanate from the wreckage and disappearance of Flight 93 in the environs of Shanksville, Pennsylvania. As set out previously, a movie was required to really sell the story, passengers charging the cockpit, "Let's roll," etc. and sure enough, it is hinted at by the vice president during the time Mr. Edelman, his very impressed subordinate, spends with him that day. As they hear of the demise of Flight 93, Edelman recounts,

I think when they finally figured out that it was down in southern Pennsylvania, and we had eliminated every other explanation for why it went down, I remember him saying -- at that point he said, I think an act of heroism just took place on that plane. He was ahead of a lot of the rest of us. I think he had figured that out.

Lord. Y. Be. Them's some fine beans there for the cross-examination of Mr. Cheney. Fine beans, indeed.

And lastly, and finally, we as a Nation are the recipients of such sweet grace in the form of the recollections of one Ashley Estes. She was President George W. Bush's secretary. You would expect that someone would be interested in what she recalled. Strangely, or not, given all we now know, it wasn't an obvious arm of the National Security State that was interested in taking a statement from this percipient witness, which is one who actually saw or heard something first hand. Which is to say, the interview of which we are aware was not the FBI's work product, and there is no mention of her having been interviewed by them in what we have. No, this is *60 Minutes II*, though we have it by way of the White House Office of the Press Secretary, an internal Transcript from August 29, 2002. White House staff was making a record of what Ms. Estes said to *60 Minutes.*

And there is great beauty here in that Ms. Estes is almost precisely what one might expect under the circumstances. She is very proud to have been a Bush team player, and makes no effort to hide the fact. And it is to their credit that the conspirators felt no need to corrupt her by shaping her testimony. Okay, so it isn't much credit. They knew all they needed to do was sit on whatever she said for a decade or so, employing all the while the mechanisms that the present work has set out to explore in a small way. The mainstream predictably took up their picks and shovels for empire, for the Deep State, and poor beset-upon truth never had a prayer.

But now at least we have what she said, and it is EXACTLY what I, and you by now, should have expected. She says she was watching as the second plane hit the South Tower,

And then I guess the thing that — I heard a noise, like a — kind of like a body bumping a door, or something. And at that point, I kind of looked out into a hallway and saw the Vice President with Secret Service, that are always around him, but Secret Service this time was - had kind of lifted him up, underneath his arms, and running with him. I was like, this is not normal, and why am I still sitting here?

Did I already mention that two years ago I took a garden tour of the White House? I decided— why not? — to ask a question of one of the Secret Service agents who were making sure this group of citizens didn't go sideways on them. "On 9/11, after the second plane hit, how long would it have been before Cheney was on his way out of his office?" I asked of the short-blond-haired, six-foot tall, 30-year-old male officer. "Seconds," says he.

You see how this business works? Your brain and your common sense, your instincts, are just fine if they are allowed to be used. They have just been immobilized by a full court press of propaganda orchestrated by the conspirators to cover-up their deeds. Ashley Estes didn't leave out 33 minutes of action right next to the vice president's office. She was a living witness to history, and an enormously important one, because she exposes Richard Cheney for the evil, villainous, lying psychopath that the 9/11 Commission could not bear to conceive of. Under the circumstances the Commission's work was the vile corruption that should have been expected.

...That was to be the end...in 2018. Now we have taken a fair chunk out of 2019, and, Thank God Almighty, I have been apprised of material that simply cannot be left out of this book. It comes to me because of a principled stand taken by a, now formerly, professor at Sussex University in the UK. His name is Kees van der Pijl. He published a tweet in essence saying that the Israelis had blown up the World Trade Center on 9/11. Sussex University took serious offense and told him to delete, retract and apologize. Professor van der Pijl said no, no, and I quit, writing 39 pages in explanation.

Now, given what is contained in the present work with the story of the "Dancing Israelis" in Hoboken, what's contained in his tweet is a long way from ridiculous, but I was unaware of the principal pieces of evidence upon which he rests his claim. It comes largely from the work of a woman named Rebekah Roth, a former flight attendant who has now written four books about 9/11. She has written them in the form of novels, but a few inquiring emails from me have established what should actually be thought of as the product of imagination and what the reader can rely upon. By "rely," I mean it in the sense that there is a witness or a document providing support.

And that material which I will summarize here is...well, see what you think.

You will recall or understand, if you have given the attacks of 9/11 some directed attention, that a large unknown has always been, what happened to the four airplanes and their passengers if they didn't crash into the buildings? Flight 77 has always presented this problem for me because, although certainty about it has not been possible, I was pretty sure, given April Gallop's experience, that an airliner didn't hit the Pentagon.

Flight 93 certainly didn't end up in that divot in Shanksville. It, or a substituted plane, was probably shot down by USAF pilots. If it was a substitute, the location of Flight 93 is a mystery. With regard to United 11 and American 175, there has been the claim that they were flying too fast to do what has been attributed to them. If that is true, in order to have a fuller picture of the event, those two planes need to be accounted for, it being assumed that other planes or missiles did the damage to the Towers.

Ms. Roth, with help from other airline veterans, analyzing FOIA-released radar tracks, making computations of speed and altitude, and carefully reading maps of airport locations with sufficiently long runways, determined that the four planes were landed, probably, though not necessarily, by pilot-overriding remote control, at Westover Air Force Base in western Massachusetts. Her conclusions were then supported by eyewitness accounts of the morning of 9/11 by people who live very near the base.

Next, she managed to get in touch with two witnesses who provide evidence against the idea that Flight 77 hit the Pentagon. One military officer was on the scene tending to the wounded and dead and saw no airplane. Three days later he was in Afghanistan with Osama bin Laden in his sights but was never given the order to shoot him. The same thing happened again at Tora Bora where OBL was allowed to escape once more.

Another witness was near the Pentagon in the morning of the attack and gave the mistaken impression to someone that he had seen what had actually hit the building. He was tracked down by government agents and shown a video of a missile hitting the side of the Pentagon. He was asked, "is this what you saw?" When he corrected them referring to his lack of a view, they folded up their laptop and left, never to be heard from again.

And then there is the matter of the "Israeli artists," some of whom I had been aware of for a long time, and a few of whom were complete news to me. It seems the Israeli government decided to run an intelligence operation in the US beginning in 2000 that involved sending young artists into federal installations housed in office buildings to sell art for the walls. It was the DEA that came to the conclusion that this was unusual. The 200 or so "art students" were questioned and sent back to Israel. All of them were determined to have military experience, and some were platoon leaders with demolitions training.

Around the same time, a group of Israeli "artists" posing as Austrians moved into a space on the 91st floor of the North Tower of the World Trade Center. Their game was a piece of performance art that involved taking out a window and being photographed in a one-person wooden balcony hung from the opening by someone in a passing helicopter. The group called themselves Gelatin and the stunt was recorded in a book titled "The B Thing."

It is plenty peculiar at this point, but gets extremely interesting when photographs in the book show the inside of the space out of which Gelatin was working. The wallboard has been removed from the walls exposing the beams. A young man has a harness on by which he might hang from a wall,... or an elevator shaft. And the space is lined with unfolded cardboard boxes marked

"BB 18." Ms. Roth provides us with the information that boxes marked "BB 18" are used by the Littelfuse Company to contain fuse holders such as might be required in a controlled demolition. She also prints a copy of the World Trade Center Temporary Construction ID that Gelatin member Alexander Janka had, permitting access to the Towers seven days a week until May 1st, 2000.

Ms. Roth gives us much more than I have set out here in her four novels, "Methodical Illusion," "Methodical Deception", "Methodical Conclusion," and "Methodical Exposure," but this is what I was most struck by. She was interviewed on the radio, and people who had something to say but had kept it hidden decided to contact her. According to her, one individual learned through contact with high-ranking military officers back in the 1980's that a terrorist attack on the Twin Towers was being considered by elements within the US Military as early as 1983.

The world should be enormously grateful to Rebekah Roth and to those, even all these years later, who have unburdened themselves of truth.

And it might have ended there. But now it is July, 2020. We are in the middle of the coronavirus pandemic with 130,000 dead in this country and counting. We have hope that our suffering at the hands of the sociopathic 12-year-old narcissist named Trump will end with an election in November. I have not been possessed of whatever it takes to have this work put into print. That's the way I am I guess, but Dick Cheney still haunts my dreams. And I mean that literally. Few months go by without his malignant presence captivating some space in my sleeping mind.

So here I will try to put it to rest and to paper, but there is a last bit of business to be included before it will feel done. Several bits of business actually. First, there is the Hulsey Report. No one who has read this far will find its conclusions newsworthy. Professor Hulsey of the University of Alaska has finished a multi-year study which establishes to a scientific certainty that WTC Building 7 was destroyed by controlled demolition just as Danny Jowenko, the expert demolitionist, said it was. And, unsurprisingly, no one will be reading about the Hulsey Report in the New York Times.

The second matter before the close is to inject a measure of skepticism into the claims of Rebekkah Roth which I set out briefly a year or more ago. It is a fact that Ms. Roth has left us to believe her about her sources, or not. She has written novels with made-up names, and created imaginary scenarios that are a product of conjecture. I didn't include any of that as I referred to her "important work" a couple of pages ago. But I did refer to two witnesses that she said are actually sources for actual events that go a long way to proving that Flight 77 did not fly into the Pentagon, but that some sort of missile was responsible for the damage. This, of course, is the enduring enigma of 9/11. I was glad to read in Ms. Roth's work, that my suspicions that it had been a missile, as Rumsfeld had stated in a press conference, were true. Now, I am not so sure, and here's why.

Maybe a touch more background. In 2016, I was asked to speak at a 9/11 conference in New York City for the 15th anniversary. It was put on by Richard Gage and Architects and Engineers for 9/11 Truth and something called the Lawyers' Committee for 9/11 Inquiry. It was held at the Cooper Union Theological Seminary, the site of Abraham Lincoln's address in 1860 that propelled him to the Republican nomination for president. It is a source of some pride to think I stood at the same podium as...Abraham Lincoln. I used the occasion to confess that Dennis and I had made a decisive mistake when we filed our complaint against Cheney. We made the decision not to incorporate the events in Manhattan into our Statement of Facts, but rather to rely on what took place at the Pentagon, the site of our client's injury. We did this for political/legal reasons thinking that we would amend our Complaint at a later time to include all of the destruction and consequent evidentiary material in New York. We thought it would be marginally easier for a New York judge to handle our claims if they only involved the Pentagon, at least initially. Our mistake was to allow for the possibility that the merest ounce of judicial integrity would be brought to bear by the likes of Denny Chin. Had we properly evaluated the chances of honor playing a role, we would have included New York in the first instance, only because it would have been extraordinarily difficult for Chin, or anyone else, to have disregarded the legion of factual assertions which we included in our later papers, as he ignored what we included in very clear English about then-Vice President Cheney, still unmentioned by any employee of government.

After my speech, I was invited to present my arguments to the Lawyers' Committee as to why a new lawsuit should be filed, one that included everything. I did that in a phone call conference a few weeks after the speech. What struck me the hardest in the moment of the call, and in the days following, was the silence. We lawyers are not a bashful bunch, as a rule. We, trial lawyers especially, say what is on our mind, luxuriating in the challenge of arguments and ideas. There was not a word or phrase of opposition to my proposal. There was no reason advanced for some perceived weakness of strategy or misunderstanding of the fight. One way of looking at it is that the attendees didn't want to embarrass me with the truth of what they would have been required to say, had they been required to respond. Since they were not, they chose silence. I don't think that is what was going on. They didn't want to proceed as I advocated, but they didn't want to say why.

At any rate, in the years since, the Lawyers' Committee has produced a good document or two moving the US Attorney for the Southern District of New York to do what their legal duty demanded of them with regard to a Grand Jury. But that duty is really no different than the one Gallup v. Cheney should have provoked, or that was summoned as soon as the first loud noises began to fade away on the morning of 9/11: investigate the crime and prosecute the perpetrators.

The work surrounding the Lawyers' Committee brought an inquiry to me from some of our most accomplished citizen researchers, David Cole among them. They familiarized me with work that had been done by a group of other researchers concerning the question of what hit the Pentagon. I had a long Skype session with David Chandler who has done excellent work for the Truth Movement where he came very close to convincing me that Flight 77 hit the Pentagon. Even as I write these words, I am unable to decisively assign a degree of certainty to any of the various possibilities. For a decade or more, I have known that it could not matter less what caused the devastation at the Pentagon. We are unable to know for certain if it was Flight 77, a similar airliner, a missile, or some combination of these because the Government has covered up the crime, leaving large gaps where a just inquiry should have provided answers. Nevertheless, some things are probably true. April Gallup probably made a mistake when she said she climbed out of the building along the path of destruction. Statements by other witnesses suggest her exit was through a window some distance removed from the alleged impact point of the plane or missile and the wall of the building. Those witness statements were procured through research and FOIA petitions in the years since the end of Gallup v. Cheney. They would have been the product of discovery had that lawsuit been allowed to proceed. They may have led us to amend our Complaint to conform to our latest understandings of the facts. The trial that never took place would have posited those final, discovery-informed conclusions, and it would have been those that the government would have been required to defend against. Whatever relatively small details, or even large new understandings, that came to light, had we been allowed to proceed, would not have changed the fundamental claim, that Cheney, and Rumsfeld, and Myers, and others unnamed, knew precisely what was happening that morning, knew precisely what they were doing that morning, and in all of the mornings and days and nights since, when they covered up their crimes that killed 2977 human beings that day and countless others in the years following as the dust filled the lungs of heroes.

Other matters have come to light as well. Some of them have to do with a troubling figure in the whole story of the Truth investigation, some of whose work we included in our Complaint and subsequent papers. She is Barbara Honegger. She was an early proponent of the theory of government complicity, and a journalist who worked for the military in some capacity. She published interviews with service members involved in the investigation, and appeared to have access to witnesses with important information. At this point it is not important for me to critique her every utterance. Many, if not most, may be accurate and based on honestly held beliefs. I certainly hope so since I relied on them many years ago.

David Cole, however, and his fellow researcher Simon Faulkner, made me aware of recent actions on the part of Honegger that made me believe she is not an entirely credible investigator or reporter. In the first instance, she has given a speech where she presents a graphic depiction of the side of the Pentagon being impacted by a Boeing 757. The point of the picture is to establish the fact that the airliner is much too large to have created the holes that resulted from the impact. The problem with the picture is that the size of the plane is misrepresented to be much larger than a 757 actually is. The facts are that Flight 77 could have, and may well have, caused the precise scars to the building found in the photographs the government has provided, often at the threat of a lawsuit. I am unable to conclude, based upon exchanges that have taken place between Ms. Honegger and other researchers, that the images she uses in her speech were not there to deceive. I asked her to respond to this and other criticisms. She referred me to work that does not address the question of the improper scale in the graphic depiction of the airliner. I think I am to infer that this particular question will be addressed "when I [she] have [has] time." That was over three months ago.

I don't think I will hear from her further because I found it necessary to bring my concern about her judgment to the Lawyers' Committee concerning a presentation she made in San Diego in March of 2020. An important part of her presentation included her reference to a supposed eyewitness/participant to a supposed meeting with Prince Bandar of Saudi Arabia in California in the late 1990's. The claims that the witness makes in an Affidavit referred to by Ms. Honegger are absurd. They are so preposterous that, in a case of this importance, the FIRST AND MOST PROBABLE explanation for their existence is that the teller of the tale is struggling for the limelight. It is a well-known phenomenon in criminal investigation. This particular fabulist, in his account, plays a central and compelling role, including physical bravery and prowess, at critical junctures. I expressed to the Lawyers' Committee my view that it was a disastrous decision to promote this witness without an enormous amount of documentary corroborating evidence in the way of police reports, phone records, medical reports, and all of the other business records which are part and parcel of proof in a criminal case. I complained that the Committee, which includes Ms. Honegger as a member, would lose any claim to credibility if steps were not taken to separate the Lawyers' Committee from Ms. Honegger.

This small bit of recent history leads me to some thoughts about the struggle for truth, the nature of humanity, the forces of darkness...stuff like that. The forces of darkness have most assuredly contributed to the quagmire of immobility which is the history of

9/11 Truth for going on twenty years now. It is impossible, without an inside source, to know all of the lengths to which they have gone to make sure the "truth hasn't out." How much wiretapping-- that was the subject of a running line of jokes within my household-- was really going on? Was every email read and evaluated? I remember at least one phone call that was designed to make me appear the fool. Someone called claiming to have been part of the operation to lace the World Trade Center with explosives. They laughed when I took them seriously for a minute or so. Then there was the thirty-something 6 ft 3in, white, smoking, scruffy-looking, shortish brown hair, with shirttail out, fellow who stayed parked in a red American unpretentious car two doors down from my house for some unremembered period of time in the late 2000's. I was unable to attach significance to him until, maybe years, later.

Not long into my association with the Truth Movement, I guessed that if you hadn't been referred to as a government agent, you probably weren't contributing at all. But the rancor that pervaded the atmosphere that coexisted with deep humanity in such a noble pursuit was, or should have been, an indication of two things--the righteousness of the fight and the disfunction of man. Egos, except for mine, were constantly erecting barricades. The smallest disagreements provoked unholy attacks, and some of them were warranted. The claims to which some continue to cling have a vastness to them which leaves some of us, possessed of deep wisdom and judgment, with our heads in our hands. But, this little lightness to the side, the government, I have absolutely no doubt, employed some of their best minds to ensure that there were adequate outlandish theories in the works so that those with hard evidence at their command could never speak a sentence without having to defend or distance themselves from possibly well-meaning members of the Movement and the arguments they were wielding without success. Were there mini-nukes used on the Towers? I spent a considerable sum of money consulting with members of UCBerkeley's atomic science community because strontium 90 was found in the dust at Ground Zero. I was assured that nuclear weapons could not have been used because some other element, I can't remember which, was not present as well. But there was no actual explanation for the presence of strontium 90, and the words, "we are not aware of any such ability on the part of anyone" left me with the question, "has some sector of life on earth exceeded the accomplishments of our finest known brains?" I have read about a man named Randy Cramer who claims to have spent twenty years fighting alien beings on Mars for the US Marines, then to be given back those twenty years, regressed, in his body, when his hitch was up. He is googleable. Is he delusional, another fabulist, or is there something very significant that our government isn't telling us?

There are strange ideas out there in the world, and it is hard not to come into contact with them if you are claiming the most powerful men on the planet conspired to commit mass murder and treason. The trick to staying in the game, even if, metaphorically, you never get the bat on the ball, is to ask, "what's the evidence of that?" This book and this life experience are the product of an examination of evidence, the way I learned it reading police reports and cross-examining cops and civilians and "experts" for 40 years.

APPENDICES

A.LETTERS

DWYER EMAILS

?C.FLIGHT 93?

D.PETITION FOR CERTIORARI TO UNITED STATES
SUPREME COURT

PLAINTIFF GALLOP'S COMPLAINT

COURT DECISIONS

TAIBBI EMAILS

SUMMERS AND SWAN EMAILS

OIG Complaint

APPENDIX A: LETTERS

Alphabetical with description of each.

I wrote to the following people: Professor Perry Anderson,
UCLA and New Left Review; Senator Barbara Boxer, Wes
Boyd, MoveOn.Org; the late Alexander Cockburn, Co-editor of
Counterpunch and columnist for The Nation magazine; Congress-
man John Conyers; David Corn, Mother Jones; Dean John Farmer,
Rutgers University Law School; Senator Dianne Feinstein; Senator
Al Franken; Barton Gellman, Washington Post; Judge Richard
Goldstone, former justice South African Supreme Court, now pro-
fessor at University of Virginia Law School, Amy Goodman,
Democracy Now; Christopher Hayes, The Nation and

MSNBC; Christopher Hedges, former New York Times corre-
spondent and now Truthdig; Hendrik Hertsberg, The New Yorker;
Mark Hertsgard, The Nation; the late Christopjer Hitchens, Vanity
Fair; the late Molly Ivins; syndicated columnist and author; Robert
F. Kennedy Jr., environmental lawyer and radio host; David Kor-

ten, former professor Harvard Business School and founder of YES! magazine; Former Congressman Dennis Kucinich; Rachel Maddow, MSNBC; Chris Matthews, MSNBC; former Congresswoman Cynthia McKinney; Phil Mole, Skeptic Magazine; Bill Moyers, formerly of PBS, now Bill Moyers and Company;; Ralph Nader, consumer advocate, Green Party presidential candidate, President Barack Obama; Keith Olbermann, formerly of MSNBC and Current TV's Countdown; Greg Palast, freelance nvestigative journalist for BBC's Dispatches and best-selling author; Walter Pincus, Washington Post; Randi Rhodes;, progressive radio show host; Frank Rich, formerly New York Times columnist, now New York Magazine; Charlie Rose, PBS's The Week; Phil Shenon, former New York Times writer and author; Secretary Kathleen Sibelius, Department of Health and Human Services; David Sirota, columnist and author; Normon Solomon, Fairness and Accuracy in Reporting; Aaron Sorkin, West Wing and Newsroom; Jon Stewart, the Daily Show; Ron Suskind, author and former writer for the Wall Street Journal; Professor Jonathan Turley, George Washington University Law School; Kathleen vanden Heuvel, editor of The Nation magazine; Garry Wills, author.

A representative sample follows.

CHRIS MATTHEWS

Dear Mr. Matthews:

.....I write, most immediately, because of pages 114-115 of Barton Gellman's Angler. He says 33 minutes elapsed between the time that the South Tower was struck on September 11th and the time that the secret service agent insisted that V.P. Cheney come with him, "Now!"

I find this impossible to believe for a number of reasons. First, I think there would be a more immediate sense of urgency when it is recognized by all involved that the country is under attack. Second, I see no reason why the secret service would only be concerned about an airplane attack; truck bombs and stinger missiles are only two of the theoretical threats to the White House by suicidal attackers. Third, Norman Mineta was directed to the PEOC well before 9:36; why would that be so, if no threat to the White House had yet been perceived? Fourth, V.P. Cheney has stated that he was moved with dispatch shortly after the second tower was hit, which doesn't comport with 33 minutes. Fifth, Norman Mineta testified that Cheney was already in the PEOC when Mineta got there between 9:15 and 9:20 a.m.

Lastly, Mineta's testimony concerning the orders that Cheney confirmed to the young man, which he says preceded the explosion at the Pentagon, are far too elaborate a recollection to be considered some sort of mistake. It is, to say the least, disconcerting that there is no reference to

Mineta's account in Gellman's book or the fact that it was the subject of actual testimony to the 9/11 Commission.

***

CONGRESSMAN JOHN CONYERS

?Dear Congressman Conyers;?.....On December 15th, 2008, I, and veteran civil rights lawyer Dennis Cunningham, filed a lawsuit in the Southern District of New York against Donald Rumsfeld,

Dick Cheney, and General Richard Myers alleging that they conspired to aid and abet the attacks that injured my client, a soldier working at the Pentagon named April Gallop. The docket number is 08 CV 10881.

The defendants have until the 24th of March to respond to the Complaint. We assume there will be a motion to dismiss that we will be litigating for the next considerable period of time. We could use help with our fight. In fact it is wrong that it is left to us to seek justice for the worst single crime ever committed on American soil.

I have sought help every place I have been able to imagine and found only silence and derision, and an almost complete unwillingness to address the issues that the evidence raises. I am sorry to say that it is my assumption that most elected officials in this country know that the attacks were, on some level, an inside job, but do not have the courage to take the necessary steps to establish the fact to the American people. I acknowledge that my assumption may be incorrect because of the enormous power of denial and the unspeakable nature of the accusations that I make.

Right or wrong in my assumption and regardless of your particular views, I want the opportunity to prove to a member of Congress that which I have the confidence I can prove in a federal court as I demonstrated with the filing of the lawsuit. May I say that I have difficulty imagining that you are unaware of the truth, given all of the wonderful work you are doing and have done, and the intelligence with which you have approached every issue. Your silence, if I am right about that, is a frightening testament to the powers that so emphatically need opposition at this desperate time.

As can be seen in the Complaint, available at centerfor911justice.org, there is no mention of the destruction of the buildings in New York, through the use of thermate and other explosives, forensic physical evidence of which we have now in abundance. That was a strategic decision which will be amended as the suit progresses.

I am available to travel to Washington at any time your office suggests. I will take whatever time you are prepared to give me, but it would be extremely difficult to do justice to the complexity of the case and the quantity of evidence in less than an hour. ?I know I ask a lot. I am sorry that the situation demands it.

***

MARK HERTSGAARD

Dear Mr.Hertsgaard ,

I extracted from you a promise to give me 30 minutes of reading;
I was a bit diminished by your injunction that it be something
you haven't read before. God knows how I would comply with that.
I give this my all and my best, hoping that you will understand that
the case, the cause, and the nation deserve several hundred pages of
brief.

You will forgive me if I begin simply, but I believe it essential.

The Pentagon was successfully attacked; no one has been disciplined for that failure. Norman Mineta testified to the 9/ 11 Commission that at 9:15 or so, Cheney was in the PEOC when Mineta
arrived there pursuant to command. Cheney was giving orders. A
young man entered the room several times reporting the position
of the plane that was flying toward the Pentagon.
When he told Cheney that the plane was 10 miles out, the young
man asked if the orders still stood. Cheney whipped his head around
and said, "Yes, they still stand; have you heard something to the contrary?" Moments later the Pentagon erupted in flames with various
military witnesses saying they smelled cordite.
Mineta said that he had assumed that the order was to shoot down
the plane, which he thought had not happened due to some failure.
Virtually no questions were asked of Mineta at the time of his testimony, a failure as bold as the lie that "the core of the Twin Towers
was a hollow shaft," 9/11 Commission Report, p. 541, a falsehood
patently obvious to anyone who has seen the photographs of the
Towers in mid construction.

The litany of failures that had to have taken
place in order for the attacks to have succeeded, is described in
many books and would take up much too much of my 1/2 hour,
were I complete. As a summary, the FAA is said by the 9/11 Commission to have been lax in a myriad of ways, not taking seriously
reports of airplanes straying from flight paths or being hijacked,

not passing along such information to the military in a timely fashion, with each failure repeated for each subsequent hijacking, all this on the day that agency landed 4500 airplanes on unintended landing fields within minutes without incident. The tiresome retort that our government is too incompetent to have pulled off such an operation simply sates the need to feel superior, and serves as an excuse to ignore the evidence.

My first witness, were this nation allowed the luxury of a trial, would be then Lieutenant, now Captain, William Walsh of FDNY, who was on a gas leak call on Canal St. after 8:30. He heard an explosion, looked up, and THEN saw United Flight 11 fly into the North Tower. This is according to his statement to the FDNY in the months after 9/11, when an effort was made to collect a history. Walsh's statement is corroborated by a wealth of other evidence.

Walsh and others went to the North tower and found substantial damage to the lobby, including broken windows, marble panels knocked off the walls, and, most significantly, an elevator door blown off its track.

This point is important because the elevator in question went from the 6th subbasement to the 30th floor. It did not go up to the 92nd floor where the shaft could have been a receptacle for jet fuel that could then flow to the basement and explode.

None of the content of this testimony is alluded to in the 9/11 Commission Report.

My next witness would be William Rodriquez, who had been a janitor in the Towers for twenty years, and who became a hero that day, rescuing many people and becoming the last man to leave the North Tower before it collapsed. He felt an explosion BELOW him, and then seconds later, another WAY ABOVE him. He was then confronted by a co- worker in the sub-basement who was horribly burned from an explosion that had taken place almost 100 floors below where the first plane hit, but at almost precisely that time.

Again, there is no mention of these facts in the 9/11 Commission Report, nor of the following two witnesses.

Next I would call Philip Morelli, who was knocked to the ground twice by two explosions in the sub-basement. As he escaped he saw that one of the lower parking areas had been destroyed.

Mike Pecoraro has a similar tale to tell as a machinist working on one of the sub-basement floors. He felt an explosion and went to his machine shop, but when he got there, the shop, a three hundred pound door, and a fifty ton press had been reduced to rubble. All of these
"basement of the tower" witnesses are relating events that occurred right around the time Flight 11 hit the North Tower at the 92nd floor.

Craig Furlong and Gordon Ross did a study of the seismic data from Columbia Seismology Center and determined that there was a recorded event, consistent with some sort of explosion, between 9 and 15 seconds before each tower was hit. This is a controversial matter that would be subject to contrary interpretations, but their scholarship is precise and persuasive.

There is an audiotape made by Ginny Carr, at a meeting she was taping that morning, that establishes two explosions nine seconds apart. There is controversy here, because there are two versions of the tape, about which of these explosions is Flight 11 hitting the building. In either event there is an explosion which corroborates the eyewitness testimony and
which must be explained. A review of the video shows that the eruption of the jet fuel is virtually inseparable with the moment of impact, and therefore, could not have been what was recorded on the tape.

There are multiple scientific studies establishing that there was molten metal in the rubble of Ground Zero. There are multiple eye-witness accounts, including those by observers from Johns Hopkins

University, as well as photographs of orange to yellow to almost white hot metal in

the rubble, weeks after 9/11, which further establish its presence. This fact, by itself, disproves the conclusions reached by the official agencies of government.

The existence of molten metal in the rubble has led scientists to query how the metal could have gotten that hot. If the original source of the fire was jet fuel, the maximum temperature would not exceed 1,850 degrees Fahrenheit. The photos, the statements of observers, and satellite images all establish much higher temperatures weeks later, all of which is physically impossible if the only

source of heat were the jet fuel fires.?10. Among other scientists, Professor Steven Jones, astounded by video of the destruction of WTC 7, a forty-seven story building, on fire, but never hit by any airplane, decided to study the events. The collapse of WTC 7 mirrored that of many controlled demolitions that he was aware of, with their symmetrical, free-fall speed descents, their ejection of large pieces of steel below the level of collapse, the enormous clouds of dust, and the fact that the antenna, and in the case of WTC 7, the penthouse, drop first.

Scientists were able to obtain a photo of the jagged edge of a cut and corroded steel beam which they believed had been subjected to extremelyhigh temperaturesconsistent with explosives.

Civilians connected to the tragedy provided Jones with two samples of material from Ground Zero: dust from an apartment whose front window was blown out when the towers collapsed, and a piece of metal intended to be used by Clarkson College in the construction of a monument to four

students who died on 9/11. Jones analyzed both of these in- dependently collected samples - one dust, one metal - and found identical levels of zinc, manganese, barium, copper, and sulfur which cannot be explained by the contents of the buildings, whether fire damaged or impacted by airplanes. They are, however, completely consistent with a reaction to thermate, a substance used to cut steel in controlled demolitions.

It is hard to deny that the fingerprints and the DNA of 9/ 11 have in this last amalgam of evidence been found and identified.

The Pentagon was the subject of a successful attack, but its contours are difficult to discern. It appears that the building was either hit by a missile, as Rumsfeld said (undoubtedly by mistake) in the days after the attack, or by demolition by previously placed explosives, for which a supposed suicide aircraft hijacking provided cover. Kelly Knowles actually saw two aircraft in the midst of the attack. But these are speculations based upon the following decisively proven facts:

There were five light poles found knocked over in the aftermath of the explosion. The light poles describe a flight path of an airplane which is completely consistent with the shape of the damage done to the inside of the building, in essence a forty-five degree angle moving from right to left as one faces the building.

The 9/11 Commission adopted the flight path de- scribed by the light poles and the damage to the building, and published a computer simulation setting out the course that American Flight 77 is supposed to have taken.

The NTSB, claiming to have the black box belonging to Flight 77, found in the wreckage of the Pentagon, published the data supposedly found there, and a computer- simulated flight path that inexplicably ends just before the plane reaches the Pentagon.

The 9/11 Commission flight path and the NTSB

flight path DO NOT AGREE in a number of critical ways:

First: The NTSB flight path follows a path that runs north of the Navy Annex and the Citgo Gas Station, which would make it impossible for the plane to have hit the light poles.

Second: The NTSB computer simulation has the plane at an altitude of 480 feet at the termination of the simulation, which is far too high for the plane to have hit any 40+ foot tall light pole. The actual altimeter reading as displayed in the simulation says 180, which, assuming accuracy, would not coincide with the video of something flying at ground level into the Pentagon, which was released by the military pursuant to a FOIA lawsuit brought by Judicial Watch. A group of experienced pilots, having analyzed the data, have demonstrated that the 180 is inaccurate, because the reading was 300 at the time just before takeoff, and the altimeter was not reset, as is SOP when the aircraft passed back through the 18,000 foot level.

Third: Two civilian witnesses, Edward Paik and Robert Turcios, have given statements confirming the NTSB flight path. Both witnessed the plane, whatever its actual identity, flying overhead and heading toward the Pentagon.

Fourth: Two Pentagon police officers, Sergeants Brooks and Lagassie, though demonstrably anxious to destroy any theory that did not involve American Flight 77 flying into the building, have given statements expressing the utmost certainty that the flight path of the plane that they claim to be Flight 77 was, without question, to the North of the citgo station, and thus completely incompatible with the downed light

poles and the damage done to the inside of the building. These two police officers. seeking to be the most important witnesses in support of the official story, have unwittingly destroyed it.

To summarize, the towers and WTC 7, NY headquarters of the SEC, FBI, and CIA, were destroyed by explosives, according to video, photographic, audio, scientific, and seismic evidence, and, according to civilian and FDNY eyewitness statements, some in the weeks and months after the at- tacks, and others recorded that morning as the explosions were taking place.

The Pentagon was the subject of an attack that was sculpted to conform to a predetermined cover story. The plan involved a hijacker who was refused rental of a Cessna due to incompetence. In addition, it involved a 2 1/2 minute maneuver, turning 330 degrees and diving 8000 feet, described by an air traffic controller as that of a military aircraft, enabling the plane to hit the smallest possible target, which was occupied primarily by construction workers because it was under- going a retrofit to better withstand attack, thus assuring the smallest possible loss of military life.

Assuming, for the purposes of argument, that Flight 77 hit the Pentagon, and assuming further that the hijacker was in control of the airplane, had he simply flown straight and nosed the aircraft down, he could have had the benefit of the largest possible target, the entire top of the building, but, more importantly, he could have killed many thousands of people, including the Secretary of Defense, who was, at the time, predicting that the terrorists were not likely to be satisfied with what took place in New York.

All of this, of course, took place at a time when the world knew there was danger in the skies, and when jets, only minutes away, were flying out over the Atlantic, a course of action for which no military personnel has ever been disciplined.

In a famous interview, Dwight Eisenhower explains that he had no idea how any soldier was going to manage to scale the cliffs of Normandy; he simply put brave men at the bot- tom of those cliffs and assumed that they would do the job. I am no Eisenhower, but this may be a moment akin to D-Day, and you have shown your decency, and probably your bravery, if I understand your career properly.

DENNIS KUCINICH
?Dear Congressman Kucinich,
***

I offer the following as arguments in support of an official investigation into the events known simply as 9/11:

There are many eye and ear witnesses to explosions at the towers, but I will cite just a few here. Lt. William Walsh, FDNY, was on a gas leak call on Canal Street. He heard a loud explosion, thought it was Con ED, looked up and saw the first airliner fly into the North Tower. He went there, found burned, dying bodies in the lobby, saw the huge marble panels blown off the walls,

and found the doors to the elevator shaft that goes from the 6th subbasement to the 30th floor, and no higher, blown off their hinges. This is clear evidence that there was an explosion involving the elevator shaft at some point lower than the 30th floor.

William Rodriquez, a janitor in the building for twenty years, was in the 1st subbasement when he felt an explosion below him and then, a few seconds later, an explosion far above him. The second proved to be the first plane crashing into the North Tower.

Philip Morelli, a construction worker, was on one of the subbasement floors when he was

knocked off of his feet twice, by two explosions, seconds apart, one of which destroyed walls in the parking garage.

Mike Pecoraro, a machinist, was on the 6th subbasement floor when he heard and felt an explosion. He went up to his machine shop on the 3rd subbasement, and found the shop, a fifty-ton press, and a three hundred pound door reduced to rubble. This was all an hour or more before the building came down.

The seismograph at Columbia University records an incident nine seconds before the first plane hits the North Tower and another at the time of impact according to the NTSB. A third incident is recorded twelve seconds before the second plane hits the South Tower, and a fourth at the

time of that impact.

Jenny Carr taped a meeting that morning at 1 Liberty Plaza. Very clear on the tape is a first explosion that has one participant at the meeting asking what that was, and a second explosion, nine seconds later, that is the first plane hitting the North Tower.

6. Jannette Mackinley had an apartment near ground zero whose front window was broken by the collapse of one of the buildings. For some reason, an artistic impulse, she collected some of the dust. When she learned that there was a physicist doing a study, she gave him the dust. The physicist, Dr. Steven Jones, conducted tests and found concentrations of zinc, manganese, and sulfur that were consistent with the use of an explosive, thermate, and inconsistent with any other theoretical explanation.

An aunt of a dead student from a small college in up- state New York went to a memorial that was going to be constructed out of rubble from ground zero. There was a pile of scrap from which she removed a handful. She gave it to Dr. Jones who found similar levels of the same residue that he found in the dust.

There is a photograph of the end of a steel beam with an extremely jagged edge that is consistent with the results of a thermate explosion.

There are pictures of yellow-to-orange hot, molten metal in the rubble consistent with the extreme temperatures that accompany the use of explosives and inconsistent with a jet fuel fire.

Multiple experts have now written papers establishing that the buildings, all three, came down as a result of con- trolled demolition. They cite the pouring molten metal easily visible on videos, the squibs blown out below the level of the fire, the speed and symmetry of the collapse, the movement of the antennae, and penthouse in the case of WTC 7, at the initiation of the collapse, the quantity and size of the dust particles, and numerous other factors.

Debris from the plane found in Shanksville was found over an eight square mile area, impossible unless the plane was shot down.

The Pentagon, presumably defended by sophisticated weapons systems, was hit,

according to the government, by a jetliner flown by an incompetent pilot, Hani Han- jour, who decided to change course in the last two and a half minutes of flight from a path that would have allowed him to hit the top of the building, which would have provided the largest possible target and the greatest possible devastation, or Donald Rumsfeld's office, to a path, after a 270 degree turn and dive from 7000 feet, an acrobatic maneuver for such a plane, that allowed him to fly into the side of the building, the smallest possible target, that was under construction hav- ing been recently reinforced to withstand attack, insuring the smallest possible loss of military life, while flying parallel to the ground.

Norman Mineta was called to the PEOC at the White House where he found V.P. Cheney in

charge. A young man entered the room shortly after Mineta arrived and told Cheney that the plane was fifty miles out. The man reappeared several times, announcing the distance had decreased to 30, 20, and finally 10 miles. With this last information, the man asked Cheney if the orders still stood. Cheney turned abruptly and said "yes, the orders still stand, did you hear something to the contrary?" Mineta testified to the 9/11 Commission that he thought the orders were to shoot down the plane. When it hit the Pentagon, Mineta assumed that the intercept had failed. No questions were asked about the Pentagon's defenses.

World Trade Center 7, the 47 story building housing offices of the SEC, CIA, and FBI collapsed at 5 pm on September 11, 2001, having suffered significant, but survivable damage from the collapses of the towers, in addition to several

small fires. The penthouse, near which no fires burned, is visibly the first part of the building to go. The collapse is a precise replica of a controlled demolition, a fact noted by Dan Rather and Peter Jennings on national television.

Though after five years the government has no explanation for the building's demise, many scientists and structural engineers, including Drs. Bachmann and Schneider from the Swiss Federal Institute of Technology in Zurich, have concluded that its collapse was the result of controlled demolition. The statement by Mr. Silverstein, the leaseholder, that the decision was made to "pull it," (the building), does nothing to end the debate. There is no mention of the collapse of WTC7 in the 9/11 Commission Report.

If the three buildings met their ends as the government suggests, they were the first three steel-framed buildings in the history of mankind to collapse as a result of fire.

Thank you very much for any time you give to a consideration of this matter.

***

B.V.

Dear Congressman Kucinich;?.....My studies have taken me places I never would have foreseen, and have established conclusively that the government was complicit in the attacks. I am prepared to prove that fact in court, but I am more than aware of the obstacles in the path of justice.

The defendants against whom I would file a lawsuit have resources that are difficult to imagine much less oppose. The jurisdiction for the lawsuit I envision, as prescribed by statute, is the Southern District of New York, where Judge Hellerstein has made unprecedented rulings in an effort to avoid the setting of a trial date and the taking of depositions in other cases involving the terrorist attacks.

The most reasonable interpretation for the status of the various cases in his courtroom involves the worst possible view of judicial performance and the most involved and intricate manner of governmental malfeasance, all of which interpretations are confirmed the more that is known about the details of the 9/11 attacks.

I do not believe that I suffer from any sort of delusional or paranoid ideation when I assert that I believe the only security that any of us who are involved in this struggle for justice can rely on is the existence of a mass movement of the kind that only presidential candidates are capable of creating. I believe it was your duty as a representative of government to learn the evidence upon which I and those with my convictions have come to rely. But it must certainly be the duty of anyone seeking the power of the presidency to understand the extent to which that power has been used for corrupt and horrifying purpose in the very recent past.

It is true that the damage that is currently being done by US foreign policy throughout the world is similarly egregious to the acts of 9/11. The important distinction in the case of 9/ 11 is that the conduct can be proven beyond a reasonable doubt, and, there is no theoretical defense. I would like an opportunity to discuss these matters with you in pursuit of a specific statement that I propose you make in the course of your campaign.

Although I think it would be completely reasonable to expect you to have an investigation conducted concerning the scholarship that has been produced demonstrating govern- mental complicity in the attacks, by yourself, or persons that you might designate for that purpose, the demands of politics may prevent what I think is reasonable at this time. An abbreviated look into the matter should allow you to say the following:

It is time for a presidential candidate to address the question of whether or not representatives of our own government were complicit in the attacks of 9/11, a moment in our history which has served as justification for two wars, countless deaths, and a concerted assault on the civil liberties of our citizens. I am not at this moment prepared to accuse any member of any administration of conspiracy to commit mass murder and treason.

I am not prepared at this moment to declare that such accusations are the inevitable, or even likely, consequence of the investigation that I here call for. But I am prepared to say, right now, that the report prepared by the so-called 9/11 Commission, is a document completely unworthy of the reputations of the men and women that served on that body. It is a demonstrably false account in many areas addressed and serves only to make clear the need for an international body of renowned jurists, untied to the strictures of party, politics, business concerns, or governmental philosophy that will conduct an adequately-funded and time-unlimited, deliberate investigation to determine if there was criminal activity that would fall within the jurisdiction of the World Court.

Because no governmental authority within this country has seen fit to call for the kind of investigation that the stark horror of the crimes demands, I here stand with those who call for the citizens of this nation and of the world to mobilize to insist that their representatives carry out their will to see that justice is pursued and achieved. I will march with those citizens on the 26th of April, 2008 in Washington, D.C., and I will ask all of my opponents in this presidential race to speak out on this issue which calls into question every part of this nation's allegiance to its own founding document.

***

BILL MOYERS
?Dear Mr. Moyers,
....I am writing this letter because I saw your show on the run-up to the Iraq War. What would a different conclusion about 9/11

have meant to such reporting? I gave a speech to an arrangement of upper-crust Republicans two weeks ago and showed them some pictures produced by the group, Architects and Engineers for 911 Truth. I rather doubt that many of those to whom I gave the presentation will have the strength to think about the matter again, but their reactions suggested that a person with your voice and moral authority could indeed, "change everything" but in a much different way and for the much greater good.

B.V.

Mr. Moyers;

In the spirit of Margaret Flowers, I went to your home when I was in New York a week and a half ago. I did not want to discuss healthcare, however. I am a partisan of the 9/ 11 Truth Movement. I am one of the better-prepared members of that movement in that I am a veteran criminal trial lawyer. I overcome my humility to say that I am ready and eager to debate anybody concerning the facts of the case, advancing the idea that the USG was complicit in the attacks. Specifically, I accused Cheney, Rumsfeld, and Myers, in a lawsuit filed in the Southern District of New York, of conspiring to enable what took place.

We ran into a bit of misfortune last week when Judge Denny Chin dismissed our lawsuit with prejudice because it was based in "cynical fantasy and delusion." If you have studied the case at all, it is hard not to be cynical, but I reject the idea that I live in a world of fantasy or delusion. I admit that I entertain the notion of a deep and corrosive power being at the heart of many of this nation's misfortunes, much as you set out years ago in Secret Government, if I remember the title correctly. That had to do with Iran-Contra. Those actors, and their mission, have not gone away.

I do not adhere to my beliefs about 9/11 because Bill Moyers planted the seeds 20 years ago. The evidence upon which I rely is far beyond overwhelming at this point, and subscribed to by a legion of learned, patriotic people, from around the world, including at least one Nobel Prize winner and many current and former government officials. See PatriotsQuestion911.com. Driving me to my substantial despair is the idea that Judge Chin could first, be unable to entertain the idea of governmental complicity, and second, be able to engage in the deceptive practice of failing to address many, if not most, of the factual assertions that our Complaint contains. See centerfor911justice.org. I would give a lot to know if Judge Chin is simply a victim of a very limited world-view that disallows the conception of US governmental transgression, or if he has become a player. He literally had to ignore a tremendous amount of information as he wrote his decision. What did he tell his law clerks?

If the power of denial, that accepts as a given our government's goodness and the impossibility of the existence of evil within it, is so powerful as to overcome the oath of a soon-to-be Second Circuit Court of Appeals justice, is it, as well, powerful enough to make the likes of Bill Moyers forget what he taught the American people a couple of decades ago? Or is it not denial operating here?

What I ask of you is this: that you sit down with me, in strict secrecy, until whenever you say, or forever, and tell me why I am wrong. One question should be confronted in deciding how to respond. Do you know what you know because of more than the work of mainstream journalism, or would an encounter with a proponent of the most disturbing ideas about 9/11, who happens to be a criminal lawyer, be a first?

RALPH NADER

May 16, 2005?.......Having paid no attention to 9/11 conspiracy theories for 3 years, I have now read David Ray Griffin's two books, the *New Pearl Harbor,* and *9/11 Commission Report, Omissions and Distortions.* The conclusions with which one must, upon reading, reluctantly agree are unspeakable.

The smartass in me might ask, "what exactly are you planning on doing about this?" But that is a side of me that I try to suppress. I can't imagine a person more knowledgeable or sensitive to the machinations of Washington, D.C. Nor can I think of anyone whose life has demonstrated a more steadfast commitment to the ideas to which I have tried to cling throughout my life as a public defender and as a father and citizen. I don't have anywhere near the stuff of which you are obviously made, but I believe I recognize greatness when I see it. I also think I recognize true calamity when it is going on around me.

I have been paying reasonably close attention in the last thirty years, and have been appalled and active when con- fronted by our atrocities throughout the world. Our support for the death squads in Latin America, coupled with the Phoenix Program and the Indonesian massacres, and East Timor, etc., etc. prepared me to believe there is abject evil in the world, and that our government was often responsible for it. Nevertheless, the idea that we could have been complicit in the attacks of 9/11 was beyond my ability to conceive; so I scoffed at the idea until one of my brightest associates put the books in front of me.

What I want more than anything is an opportunity to discuss the issues with you. I am actually thinking I can no longer stay on the sidelines, which means that I am considering being a candidate. I would benefit enormously from your counsel. Are you available for a phone call? Or some time in D.C. at your convenience?

I have assuaged my psyche by convincing myself that I have been fighting the forces of reaction, as would say, in my job for all of my working life, but that is small potatoes indeed compared to what I am compelled to acknowledge took place on 9/11.

BV

September 14, 2007 Dear Mr. Nader;

Residue of explosives, precisely thermate, has been found in at least three separate samples of dust and debris from Ground Zero, originating from three independent sources. That is, for all intents and purposes, the same as saying we have DNA proving governmental complicity in the attacks of 9/11.

At this point, I have done almost all that I can think to do. I have written to you on a couple of occasions. I tried to get some time with you on the Nation Cruise. I sent you the letter below while we were on the boat. Since returning, I have called your office seeking some time in the third week of October when I will be in Baltimore. I have yet to hear a word from you in response.

I appreciate that the subject is as horrifying as any of which we might conceive. I also understand that the conclusion may call into question the essential and long-term efficacy of your entire life's work. (People capable of this atrocity will not likely be deterred by legal mandate, or any sort of legislative activity of the kind you have been promoting for forty years.) None of that means you are not compelled by circumstance and your duty as a leader to stand up to those powers you have so bravely identified and fought for that same period of time.

There are those, perhaps the substantial majority, including who are simply unable to allow themselves to conceive of what I could prove, were I given a courtroom and the opportunity. They are a different sort of person from what I am. I am simply constructed differently, and by virtue of that fact, feel an obligation not to let my convictions lay dormant. Your history demonstrates you are similarly incapable of inaction.

Were this 1776, I cannot imagine you doing anything other than writing the Declaration of Independence, an act requiring the greatest courage while not immediately in range of a bullet. Am I wrong to find the parallels to which I refer? Since the question may be the power of the evidence, I will attach a letter I sent to a journalist at his behest. Though I know, based upon subsequent correspondence, that he is seriously considering the matter, he has yet to take action.

By virtue of your position in this society, I see it your duty to either take up the banner of our cause, or provide answers to the myriad questions which serious and scholarly men and women have raised. My years of experience investigating and trying criminal cases convince me that there are no satisfactory answers, but as one more frail and flawed human being, I can be wrong.

I hope to hear from you; I will be in town from the 15th of October to the 20th, but I will extend my stay if that is what is required.

?On *Nation* Cruse Dear Mr. Nader;

....The idea of becoming a politician is foreign to me. At the same time, it seems, in some way, to be the next part of my duty as a citizen. I really have no idea how I would go about trying to lead, but my understanding of what has taken place in the world would be the reason I take the steps as well as the centerpiece of any campaign.

I came on this cruise because I thought there might be an outside chance of discussing the attacks of 9/11 with you. I want to know why you are silent. Our brief exchange yesterday, when I handed you my invitation, suggests that the requisite amount of evidence has not yet been presented to you. That fact, in and of itself, provokes all kinds of questions about what takes place in the mind of the man who knows more than pretty much anyone else, about the way the world operates.

The evidence at this point is overwhelming in scope and persuasive power, and that is said by a person who laughed at the idea of government complicity for 3 1/2 years.

I have been doing as you have been exhorting, in terms of writing to leaders, and more. I now write to America's greatest leader and ask what can I do to get your help?

January 20, 2008 Dear Mr. Nader,

.....Here I make my final plea for an opportunity to meet with you to discuss the many questions which you and virtually every other leader in this country have refused to acknowledge. I write today out of the despair generated by the thought of another Clinton White House. I have adopted the Korten paradigm and am convinced our children will not survive in a meaningful way if we do not turn from the path of Empire to the path of the Earth Community.

I persist in the conviction that the crime of 9/11 was important; that its nature can be proven; and that having been proven, the effect on the population will be revolutionary. Though it is possible that I could be wrong about the last, I doubt it. All that keeps the people from being up-in-arms is the permission given to them by their leaders to deny the truth, or simply look the other way. The only real question, in my opinion, is that of proof, and I maintain that I have it. Further, I maintain that it is not close. I am sorry that your surrogates were unmoved by what they saw on the cruise. Not even enough to repeat just one provocative claim? This issue should not dissolve because of the failures of the impoverished messenger, if that be the case.

I ask you to consider the probabilities that a professional with a lot of experience would, 1. risk being wrong, and, 2. likely be wrong, about a case that he claims is not close. Lawyers analyze facts all of the time. Of the thousands of cases I have come into contact with, there have been many where knowing the truth was a difficult proposition. There have been many more where the amount and quality of proof were simply too substantial to allow serious doubt. It is in the neighborhood of the second category that the 9/11 case re- sides. For an impressive list of knowledgeable citizens, including a retired Major General, who call for a new investigation, see www.patriotsquestion911.com.

Is that not enough to spur you to inquiry?
***

?Dear Mr. Nader,

I appreciate the comments you left as voicemail. The surrebuttal, etc. is contained in the enclosed writings, in shorter form, and in the book, in the long and exhaustive form. I believe Griffin has left nothing out, and that his logic is foolproof and unassailable. But I bought the product some time ago.

I am looking to the 26th of April for the march on Washington. What do you say?

March 29, 2010?

Dear Mr. Nader;

One might assume, given your apparent lack of interest beyond a phone message left a couple of years ago, that further efforts were pointless. Maybe. I can't believe you would disagree with

any of the following: 1. If the lawsuit I filed against Cheney and Rumsfeld is based in truth, there should never be an end to the efforts to pursue it. 2. There is nothing in history to which one can point that makes the claims in the lawsuit implausible. You implied as much when you cautioned to me on the cruise in 2007, that "plausibility is not evidence." 3. There is a substantial mass of evidence that calls into question the findings of the 9/11 Commission, see Kean and Hamilton's book, Shenon's Commission, and Farmer's Ground Truth, each of which acknowledge falsification and irregularity in the conduct of the investigation. 4. If an investigation is carried out with deception, at least one of the reasons can be the desire to cover up guilt on the part of actors with great power.

I proceed as I do here because I seek common ground. If you are disabled from action because of an inability to conceive of the truth of my allegations, I ask you to agree that that fundamental impediment exists. Your plausibility quote may have simply been an off-hand parry of an unwanted intrusion on a cruise ship. If, while acknowledging the in- surmountable obstacles in your own mind, you, nevertheless, agree with the four points set out above, it may be possible for you to agree that someone, at least, should be pursuing the question. I write to ask for some time to discuss who that should be and how they should be approached.

Our suit was dismissed with prejudice two weeks ago. We will be appealing to the 2nd Circuit, but Judge Chin did not spare himself in his decision. He said, after 6 « months under submission, that the claims we made were based in cynical fantasy and delusion. As evidence of his inability to handle the truth, or as evidence of his lack of desire to con- front the issue honestly, I point to the fact that his decision refers to about half of our factual assertions, and most notably, avoids the question of where Cheney was at what time, and what he said and did that morning, much of which I believe we know from the sworn testimony of Norman Mineta to the 9/ 11 Commission, set out in depth in our Complaint. Judge Chin pretends those matters do not exist.

If I am the wrong messenger to make this appeal, I give you leave to say so, and I will set about to find a better one. I am as committed to the pursuit of this struggle as I believe it is possible to be, but that does not mean I am qualified to accomplish the task. I recall your comment that whoever saw

my presentation on the cruise was unimpressed. That kind of review will keep a trial lawyer awake at night, but essential ego strength has no trouble finding an explanation. If I were sent to scout an issue for Ralph Nader, that carried with it the enormous social stigma that this one does, it would take serious strength to give these claims any credence at all.

***

ALEXANDER COCKBURN

Dear Mr. Cockburn;

I have written to you before about various issues; I am sad to say, except for once many years ago, there has been no response. Responding to mail may be a luxury you can no longer afford, or the ideas may have been unworthy. Regard- less, I write now because I believe a bit of persistence is called for....... I will refer to as the September eleventh, two thousand and one matter. Strange what a person will do in an effort to keep from being disregarded. I have now spent many too many hours trying to figure what is solid and what is garbage in what has been written about that day. My conclusion, however, is that there is enough that is solid to overwhelm any opponent in any courtroom where a hearing on the question was allowed to proceed.

I cannot imagine you have no interest in the subject. You have been chronicling the crimes of American governments for three decades or so at this point. You, of all people, know what they are capable of. What can be the source of your resistance?

As I consider that question, I must speculate about a journalist in your position. This is not a story like Watergate where Woodward had Felt. Buildings falling down when they shouldn't, pilots like Hani Hanjour doing things with air- planes that he and it couldn't, and holes in the Pentagon that are inexplicable from a simple physical and scientific point of view are the essence that has driven me to write to you. I want to know what it is that has prevented you from speaking out. In my estimation it cannot be a lack of courage.

The problem may be the quantity of garbage through which one must navigate in order to extract the truth. There are a lot of people being very wrong about quite a lot in the consideration of this question. But they are primarily wrong for going too far, wanting to provide too many answers. If the analysis focuses on the lies and simple physics, government complicity is established. The question of what happened to a plane one-third full of people, an extremely perplexing question for anyone, will have to wait for regime change, and subpoena power.

It would be mind-blowing if some insider couldn't live with their deeds anymore and decided to tell you, but the number of threats of which I am aware makes that unlikely. I just don't know how you can bear standing on the sidelines of this debate about the precise nature of that beast that you have been studying for all of your adult life.

Your voice could provide the impulse for more physicists and engineers to make the case even more solid than it is already, with tremendous benefit in my opinion. It is our opportunity to prove the rotten essence that you have decried. It is an opportunity to inspire organization. It is organization which has inspired your congratulations over the years.

I have been emailing physicists and mechanical engineers in an effort to direct their attention to the problem with only one interesting phone call to show for it. How people have managed to avert their eyes so successfully would be of interest if there was any interest at all on the part of the me- dia. Printing a released photo of the crash at the Pentagon, front page of the *San Francisco Chronicle* above the fold, which clears up exactly nothing with no story at all, much less one mentioning all of the other videos that are, to this day, unreleased, is something of an indication of the news world's lack of interest, lack of insight, craven thirst for an- other dollar, or fear.

A number of us current and former public defenders are in the process of forming an association because we are convinced of the government's complicity, and we cannot do nothing. This letter is part of not doing nothing. We are not idiots. We have been wading in the pools of government lies for our working lives, but none of us was predisposed to believing what we now know. There was, in fact, an amazing resistance to the idea for each of us that has been overcome by study and nothing more.

If you have made it this far, I appreciate your patience. I also appreciate whatever in the way of thought you give to my request for some of your time to discuss the matter or, ideally, to submit to an interview. As a last idea, I can imagine that expressing an interest at this point may be difficult for you because of what you have said and written on prior occasions. I believe that redemption is there for all of our taking, an appealing aspect of the human condition.

B.V.

Dear Mr. Cockburn;

Thrilled to have you in the debate; in my worst moments, I will probably be taking credit, however ill-deserved it is. Mr.Garcia's remarks could prove quite helpful though a long way from dispositive at this point. The government has spent a lot of money so far and none of its product seems to travel down the road he set out.

I wrote the enclosed letter to the *Nation* with very little hope of its finding space. My seeing my name in print is really not the point, however. I would ask you to consider the matters I set out in the letter. I would also ask that you share it with Mr. Garcia along with the following:

My analogy for the WTC is an autopsy in a homicide case. If a bullet is found in the body, it needs to be explained. According to a number of physicists, there is molten steel in the rubble of the WTC which is inconsistent with a jet fuel fire. I say it must be explained, something that has yet to happen in all that I have read, which doesn't mean everything, but does mean a lot.

Does Mr. Garcia agree that molten metal is inconsistent with a jet fuel fire? Does he have an innocent explanation?

Similarly, what of the existence of thermate?

ROBERT F. KENNEDY, JR. August 10, 2006?

Dear Mr. Kennedy,

It has been said that General Eisenhower had no idea how his troops would get up those cliffs on the beaches of Normandy; he simply put them in position and hoped and expected that there would be heroic men there to accomplish the job. I am no Eisenhower, but you have demonstrated some

heroism recently in espousing the cause of the stolen 2004 election. I liken the obstacles facing this nation to the cliffs that stood in the path of Allied forces sixty-some years ago.

This letter seeks to enlist aid in maybe the most important work that can be done in this country today. It is my conclusion that there is little of note left of our democracy, and the most profound indication of that fact is the atrocity of 9/ 11. I believe that "it" was an inside job, enabled and fostered and abetted by our government at its highest levels.

My opinion is not an unschooled opinion. I recently retired as Chief Assistant Public Defender in Contra Costa County, California. I was at it for thirty-one years, trying hundreds of cases, all of the worst, fighting as best I could to give those with nothing at least a chance at the illusion of justice. I have been conducting investigations and arguing to juries and judges and prosecutors for all of my career with every bit of passion and commitment that I could find within me. I never left much in the bag, and I think I got everything I could out of the experience. Which is to say that I am pretty sure I know how to analyze evidence.

I scoffed derisively at the idea that the government was in on 9/ 11 for three and a half years, so I come to this question as almost everyone else has, with the proponents of the inside job theory bearing an enormous burden. After about fifteen books and scholarly articles, the burden has been borne, and there is not the slightest doubt in my mind that the most unspeakable is true.

Since my life will never be the same, I have spent my spare time writing to officeholders and opinion leaders, with virtually no response. But I can't let it go. I don't seem to have a passive bone in my body. I am asking for you to look into the matter. What I would really like is an hour of your time to make my case, anytime you say.....

BV

January 30, 2007?

BARACK OBAMA

Dear Senator Obama

......A couple of years ago I thought I knew a fair amount about the nature of our democracy.

Then a bright colleague of mine introduced me to the question of 9/11. A small library later, I will never be the same. There isn't the slightest doubt

that elements of our own government aided and abetted and fostered the attacks if they weren't simply the instigators from the outset. I will summarize a few of the relevant pieces of evidence at the end of this letter, but now I want to address what comes from an understanding of the facts.

"What then must we do?" In terms of self-preservation, a sensible course of action would be to do nothing. If these people are capable of the atrocity of 9/11, can there be much else away from which they would shy? I understand you have a wife and kids as do I, but this is a time of tyranny, and some of us must be patriots. You have chosen to lead. From what, toward what, upon what, will you lead us? Will you lead within the strict confines of that which our stewards permit? Or will you lead us to justice based upon truth?

Martin Luther King sought truth, found it, and died for it. I don't happen to believe that such a tragic end is necessary or inevitable. What is required, however, is for the citizens to be given permission to think. That comes from a person in whom they believe, not the likes of a retired public defender of whom they know nothing. If I thought it would have the desired effect, there is little I would not do to shake this nation out of its denial. It takes far more, however, than marshaling facts and arguments. What is required is an established voice and presence within our society. You have that. Let me propose what you say.

My fellow Americans, I seek to address you at this hour upon a subject as difficult and disturbing as any citizen can imagine, as monumental as any politician might conceive. After a long period of frank denial, I have been brought to study the

horrible attacks of September 11th, 2001. With the conclusion of that study, it is with the deepest dismay that I say to you that the absolute worst fears and nightmares and imaginings of any of us have now been proved to be true. Those attacks were the willful intention of leaders of our own government.

Let me just pause for a moment and allow those words, that accusation, to make its way into your conscious minds. For the last seven years this nation has been led by men and women who now deserve the term mass murderers. There is simply no reason to attempt to say that in a more polite way.

For what pittance it is worth I am able to imagine that the people who made that sick, sorrowful decision thought that the long-term good of the country required it. They may make their pleas for a just sentence when that day comes, but for right

this minute, the most important thing is for each of

you to take as much time as you can to learn as much as you can, so that you will be as outraged and provoked as are those, now many thousands of people around the world who arrived at this conclusion before I did, and who have made it possible for the rest of us to get there as well.

I believe that this is a moment in this country's history, every bit as significant as the struggle for civil rights, in fact every bit as profound as the moments of the birth of this nation. If we fail to

act when the need to act is so plain, the tyranny into which our country has fallen will envelope us and our means of governance, and as a democratic society, we will not survive.

I intend to act in conformance with the conviction I have here expressed. I will speak of little else, as little else matters. I will march in every city and town that I can. I will proclaim the facts in every forum to which I am invited, and I will demand admittance to every hall where parts of this population have assembled, and I will not rest until every one of our citizens has been made to face the desperate cruelty that our own leaders visited upon our land.

The case for treason in brief:?1. There are many eye and ear witnesses to the explosions that brought down the World Trade Center Towers. I will mention just a few. Lt.William Walsh, FDNY, was on a gas leak call on Canal Street. He heard a loud

explosion, thought it was Con Ed, looked up and then, saw the first air- liner fly into the North Tower. He went there, found burned, dying bodies in the lobby, saw the huge marble panels blown off the walls, and found the doors to the elevator shaft that goes from the 6th subbasement to the 30th floor, and no higher, blown off their hinges. This is clear evidence that there was an explosion involving the elevator shaft at the core of the building at some point lower than the 30th floor.

William Rodriquez, a janitor in the building for twenty years, was in the 1st subbasement when he felt an explosion below him and then, a few seconds later, an explosion far above him. The second proved to be the first plane crashing into the North Tower.

Philip Morelli, a construction worker, was on one of the subbasement floors when he was knockedoff ofhis feet twice, by two explosions, seconds apart, one of which destroyed walls in the parking garage. This was just as the first plane hit.

Mike Pecoraro, amachinist, was on the 6th subbasement floor when he heard and felt an explosion. He went up to his machine shop on the 3rd subbasement, and found the shop, a fifty-ton press, and athree hundred pound door reduced to rubble. This was all an hour or more before the building came down.

The seismograph at Columbia University recorded an incident nine seconds before the first plane hits the North Tower and another at the time of impact according to the NTSB. A third incident is recorded twelve seconds before the

second plane hits the South Tower, and a fourth at

the time of that impact.

JennyCarrtaped a meeting that morning at 1 Liberty Plaza. Very clear on the tape is a first explosion that has one participant at the meeting asking what that was, and a second explosion, nine seconds later, that is the first plane hitting the North Tower.

JannetteMackinleyhad an apartment near ground zero whose front window was broken by the collapse of one of the buildings. For some reason, possibly an artistic impulse, she collected

some of the dust. When she learned that there was a physicist doing a study, she gave him the dust. The physicist, Dr. Steven Jones, conducted tests and found concentrations of zinc, manganese, and sulfur that were consistent with the use of an explosive, thermate, and inconsistent with any other theoretical explanation.

An aunt of a dead student from a small college in up- state New York went to a memorial that was going to be constructed out of rubble from ground zero. There was a pile of scrap from which she removed a handful. She gave it to Dr. Jones who found similar levels of the same residue that he found in the dust.

There is a photograph of the end of a steel beam with an extremely jagged edge that is consistent with the results of a thermate explosion.

There are pictures of yellow-to-orange hot, molten metal in the rubble consistent with the

extreme temperatures that accompany the use of explosives and inconsistent with a jet fuel fire.

Multiple experts have nowwrittenpapers establishing that the buildings, all three, came down as a result of con- trolled demolition. They cite the pouring molten metal easily visible on videos, the squibs blown out below the level of the fire, the speed and symmetry of the collapse, the movement of the antennae, and penthouse in the case of WTC 7, at the initiation of the collapse, the quantity and size of the dust particles, and numerous other factors.

Debris from the plane found in Shanksville was found over an eight square mile area, impossible

unless the plane was shot out of the sky.

The Pentagon, presumably defended by sophisticated weapons systems, was hit, according to the government, by a jetliner flown by an incompetent pilot, HaniHanjour, who decided to change course in the last two and a half minutes of flight from a path that would have allowed him to hit the top of the building, which would have provided the largest possible target and the greatest possible devastation, or Donald Rumsfeld's office, to a path, after a 270 degree turn and dive from 7000 feet, an acrobatic maneuver for such a plane, that allowed him to fly into the side of the building, the smallest possible target, that was under constructionhav- ing been recently reinforced to withstand attack, insuring the smallest possible loss of military life, while flying parallel to the ground.?

According to his testimony to the 9/11 Commission, Norman Mineta was called to the PEOC at the White House where he found V.P.

Cheney in charge. A young man entered the room shortly after Mineta arrived and told Cheney that the plane was fifty miles out. The man reappeared several times, announcing the distance had decreased to 30, 20, and finally 10 miles. With this last information, the man asked Cheney if the orders still stood. Cheney turned abruptly and said "of course, they still stand, have you heard anything to the contrary?" Mineta told the Commission that he thought the orders were to shoot down the plane. When it hit the Pentagon, Mineta assumed that the intercept had failed. No questions were asked about the Pentagon's defenses.

World Trade Center 7, the 47 story building housing offices of the SEC, CIA, and FBI collapsed at 5:20 pm on September 11, 2001, having suffered significant, but survivable damage from the collapses of the towers, in addition to several small fires. The penthouse, near which no fires burned, is visibly the first part of the building to go. The collapse is a precise replica of a controlled demolition, a fact noted by DanRather andPeter Jennings on national television. Though after five years the government has no final explanation for the building's demise, many scientists and structural engineers, including Drs. Bachmann and Schneider from the Swiss Federal Institute of Technology in Zurich, have concluded that its collapse was the result of controlled demolition. The statement by Mr. Silverstein, the leaseholder, that the decision was made to "pull

it," (the building), does nothing to end the debate. There is no mention of the collapse of WTC7 in the 9/11 Commission Report.

If the three buildings met their ends as the government suggests, they were the first three steel-framed buildings in the history ofmankindto collapse as a result of fire.

Senator Obama, I have no idea if, in your position, I would have the strength and courage to do and say what propose. I simply know that I would hope I would.

?B.V

BARACK OBAMA   July 22, 2008?

?Dear Senator Obama;

I am writing out of an abundance of caution, and with an eye toward preparing you for what is to come. I am a trial lawyer with three decades of experience, having retired as Chief Assistant Public Defender in Contra Costa County, California two years ago.

I am a partisan of 911 Truth. For our purposes, that means I believe at least Cheney and Rumsfeld were complicit in the attacks that took place that day. My associate, a veteran civil rights lawyer, and I intend to file a complaint against Cheney and Rumsfeld some time in September, alleging on behalf of my client, a soldier injured in the Pentagon, a conspiracy to commit murder.

The complaint will set out a large measure of the evidence upon which we intend to rely. I have run this by some veteran political operatives whose candidate you are, and received assurances that my actions will have no negative bearing on your candidacy. Since I want that to be true, and because there is so much room for varying opinions in politics, I decided to write you directly.

GREG PALAST   July 10, 2006

Dear Mr. Palast,

......I read your last book, am reading your newest, get emails from you on a regular basis, and have enormous regard for what you have accomplished. I have a number of questions, and would do close to anything to be able to ask them in person. I am going to try to make my next career that of a politician or a writer, beginning with the latter in the hopes it might meld to the former.

Some of us take the things you have written about our government seriously. I have written to politicians and opinion leaders a lot over the years and, for the most part, am ignored. I don't think my letters are demonstrably those of a raving lunatic, but the subjects about which I inquire are rarely comfortable for the recipient, though uniformly polite.

Since I have been speaking in public for a living for my working life, and because I have been thinking about policy for all of that time, and because I have watched CSPAN and know I can do at least that well, I don't see why I should not answer the call which has been sounding in my brain for I don't know how long now. But that is a distant dream, which I begin to pursue by writing about the issues that provoke me. One of them is 9/11 and the fact, now clear in this trial lawyer's mind after more reading than my family can understand, that the government was complicit.

I would like to ask you how you have been satisfied by the conclusions rendered by the 9/11 Commission. I would like to ask you what the explanation is for buildings collapsing that never should have; what the apparent explosions at the World Trade Center were if they weren't explosions; how were temperatures that melt steel achieved by jet fuel that can't; etc., etc.. I would like to ask you how you think Hani Hanjour did what they say he did. I would like to ask if you don't think there is a logical and physical inconsistency in most of an airplane becoming confetti upon hitting the side of the Pentagon, including thousands of pounds of two engines that did nothing to that part of the building with which they should have collided, while another part of it managed to penetrate three rings of the headquarters of the most powerful military establishment in history, leaving a hole seven feet in diameter in the wall, but doing not very much in the way of damage to posts in its apparent path within the building.

I see Bin Laden's words that you quote in your newest book as entirely consistent with his plan being hijacked, or piggy-backed-on-to, by the likes of you-know-who. After all, how could a star civil engineer have been so wrong in his most optimistic appraisal of likely damage?

So, you see, I have questions. I would deeply appreciate an opportunity to ask them in person, with dueling microcassettes. The more I write, the more I think I would like you to give me a job. Would you consider any of these suggestions?

B.V.

***?APPENDIX B: DWYER EMAILS

(The email conversation began as follows)

8/6/06?Dear Mr. Dwyer,

I am the now-retired public defender from California who remembers an enlightening chat with you in February or so where we jousted over the applicability of Occam's Razor to the collapse of the WTC.

I referred you to Professor Fetzer about two months ago over the rotor found at the Pentagon. I don't know what you did about that, but I understand it is not at all clear whether that rotor is consistent with a 757 or a JT3B or both. Understanding that I may well be writing to no end whatever, I now ask that you investigate Professor Steven Jones's claim that he has samples of metal from ground zero that contain thermate, the explosive that is used to cut steel in controlled demolitions.

I saw this on CSPAN. I can't imagine an explanation for the presence of such a substance in the wreckage of the towers that does not include the most condemnatory conclusions about our government, but I think the people who put it there should be entitled to offer whatever they can come up with. Do you have sufficient interest in the worst single crime ever committed on American soil to ask the obvious questions of Professor Jones, BYU, and others?

I apologize for the snide tone, but I suppose you can understand it at this point.

Bill Veale

8/?/06 Dear Bill,

***

To answer your challenge, I have enormous interest in the worst crimes committed on American soil. I don't believe that the towers were blown up by demolition. Two planes flew into them and killed them.

No one can explain to me how demolition experts could 1. carry hundreds of pounds of explosives into the building, getting past the security and loading the material into the elevators; 2. bring it to individual floors, make it past the security operated by each of the corporations on those floors, sometimes, in multiple layers because there are multiple ten- ants. 3. open the interior skin of the building to a sufficient depth to locate the structural columns; 4. insinuate the explosives and

fuses into the interior body of the building. 5. re- peat four times, for all four corners of the building; 6 repeat steps 1 through 5 on at least 20 floors, probably 30;. 7 run fusing material through 20 or 30 floors at timing intervals such that a progressive collapse explosion actually took place; 8: do all of the first seven steps to identical specifications in a second tower; and finally, 9. do all eight steps (actually, 16 steps, since two buildings are involved). without getting caught by anyone, without anyone ever remembering it, without a single credible eyewitness mentioning an iota of such work.

For those reasons—each and every one a necessary condition —I think demolition by controlled explosion did not happen and death by suicide hijacked airplanes did.

I'm not going to waste time calling anyone to ask why some substance was purportedly found in the Ground Zero debris. Being on CSPAN doesn't prove anything.

I enjoyed speaking with you last winter. I have spent the last 13 years considering how and why someone would kill the World Trade Center. I have written two books about it. No one has seriously challenged the reporting in either book. I'm done talking about the subject.

Jim,

8/?/06

You have exposed yourself as a reasonable human being. I appreciate your tone and your time. A smartass likes nothing so much as another.

Conan Doyle said when you have eliminated the impossible, whatever remains, however improbable, is the truth. It is impossible to create molten steel from a jet fuel fire of the duration we know about on 9/11. No matter the physics of it, it is pretty much impossible to imagine attaching thermate to three separate pieces of steel obtained from three separate human sources all from the wreckage at ground zero without the use of explosives. That leaves your string of improbabilities, if they are indeed so improbable, which I doubt.

I am not a bit sure you need hundreds of pounds of thermate, even if you would need that much of the 1993 fertilizer mix. Were I in your shoes I would want to have a conversation with the operation that hauled all of the evidence away, except what is in hangar 17 at JFK, that is. That company was, it's hard to make this stuff up, "Controlled Demolition," but I hope that isn't news to you; or maybe I hope it is.

I have read that the WTC was in fact closed down for some period of time in the weeks or months preceding 9/11. Is that true? If it is, the rest of your improbable occurrences lose their power.

I know you said 'I'm done talking about the subject," but what's the worst you can do? Your reaction to the supposed rotor at the Pentagon-"first I've ever heard about it" suggests that you have not made the skeptics' scholarship a priority. Maybe you should.

I think there is a Pulitzer in this for you, or at least a best seller when you resign because they pulled you off of the story. What can I do to help you win it?

Bill Veale
8/?/06 Dear Bill:
***

The WTC never closed down. There were people in there every day. On weekdays, there were between 16,000 and 25,000. No one—not one—ever saw anyone opening up the interior of the building to reach the structural steel columns. ?According to NIST, which today issued a communique on these issues (entirely coincidental to our exchange), not hundreds of pounds of thermate but thousands were needed. Here's a link to what they call a fact sheet. It was developed to answer questions about other explanations (ie, demolition) of the WTC.
http://wtc.nist.gov/pubs/factsheets/faqs_8_2006.htm
I am thinking of writing about this. Why doesn't the airplane work for you? You must have tried scores of criminal cases and understand evidence and proof.....
Jim,
Bless you, sir, it's actually hundreds, and I guess I think I know a thing or two about evidence. So here we are, a couple of seasoned veterans who view a bunch of facts differently. One of us is wrong; I have already admitted as much on a couple of occasions concerning this case. Are we looking at the same facts?
Scott Forbes says there was a power-down the weekend before 9/11 and a lot of maintenance men. One of my people, those with an interest but neither subpoena power nor press credentials, understands that there was a maintenance con- tract for suspicious places in the Towers, but don't you think if the government wanted to do such a thing, it could, with spy techniques or intimidation or both? If you really want my unabridged lawyer's case, say so and I will provide it to you. It will take a couple of weeks. Short form is as follows:?1. They hit the Pentagon. How much more really needs to be said??2. They say it was an incompetent pilot who performed

a very difficult maneuver for a 757, to hit an uninhabited part of the building so that the least possible damage would be done when flying straight into the top(the plane's initial heading) would have provided a much easier target, a staggering death toll, and the possibility of Donald Rumsfeld himself.

They smelled cordite at the Pentagon and felt shock waves, and there was a secondary explosion.?4. They have the ability to nail a lot of it down by releasing videotapes from a number of cameras around the Pentagon and they haven't.

There was an airplane,maybe oneof the fancy big ones, in the sky above the Pentagon when the rest of flying America was on the ground.

The exit hole in the inner ring looks a lot like it was blown out from the inside, an explosivewall-breaching in essence.

The columns in the Pentagon were damaged in such a way as to make one skeptical that a flying 757 was responsible. For example, tests performed at Sandia show jetfighters dis- integrating on impact with reinforced walls. The absence of any significantly-sized debris at the scene suggests that the plane did indeed become confetti. That is inconsistent with busting through

all those columns and making it through the back wall. Either it is mass A, or it is mass B.

Some analyses of the released frames from the Pentagon cameras conclude that what is found there is not big enough for a 757, but Idon'tneed this for my conclusion that it was an inside job.

Cell phonesdon'twork above 6 thousand feet or so.?10. I can't explain what the wreckage of a crashed plane is doing spanning a mile or more of the Pennsylvania land- scape. A shot-down plane is another matter.?11. Dan Rather said that WTC7 looked like a controlled demolition. I agree with him. Larry Silverstein said as much on TV.?12. All three WTC buildings contained molten metal weeks after 9/11. That is consistent with extremely high temperatures(explosives) and not a jet fuel fire that lasted a very short time.?13. Steel framed buildings had never collapsed due to fire and several have had the opportunity-Philadelphia and Madrid, for example. That three would on the same day, hours apart, one of which was never hit by an airplane, actually makes me amazed at what it is possible to get away with.?14. Your reporting established many eye/earwitnesses to explosions at the critical moment.?15. The first thing to go in WTC7 is the penthouse, but there is no fire anywhere around.?16. There were 47 enormous steel core columns that ended up in 30-50 ft lengths. There is no way that the short-burning fires of that day could have severed the steel columns in such a manner.?17. It seems far more likely, had the theoretically weakened steel of the perimeter collapsed due to heat, that the core columns would remain standing or fall over whole since the fires were no where near long enough to get them hot enough to collapse. Steel conducts heat away from the source. That's an awful lot of steel.

If the hottest parts of the core columns got hot enough to be plastic, they would bend and fall over. They would not break up into30-50 footlengths(conveniently sized to fit the trucks that hauled them away, owned by Controlled Demolition, but I think I already mentioned that).

As you watch one of the Towerscollapse, you see the top, above impact, telescope down appreciably. If it is a weakening at the point of impact due to fire, there is no reason for the top to compress; nothing beyond what usually does, is weighing it down.

There are unmistakablesquibs(in some cases large pieces of steel) ejected from the sides of the building up to two hundred feet away, well below where the fire is burning at the time of collapse.

The concrete in the building waspulverized.?22. Physicist Jim Hoffman studied the quantity of dust created by the collapse and found it to be ten times what you would expect from the potential energy in a collapsingburing building of the size of the towers.

?23. The second one hit fell first.

?24. A reputable tenured professor at an accredited university, with post doctoral work at Cornell and Stanford has publicly claimed to have tested a piece of steel from Ground Zero and found it to contain Thermate, an explosive. He has actually tested three from three different sources all containing the same substance.

The NIST report is a sham. See the foot note on page 80, I think, which admits that theydidn'tstudy what happened after the conditions for collapse had been achieved. Would you ever conclude a homicide investigation without studying the corpse or the place where it was found?

The mountain of human direct and circumstantial evidence that playsreally wellwith juries but that is hard to evaluate on the printed page. In sum, Ahmed's War on Freedom, Ruppert's Crossing the Rubicon, Griffin's New Pearl Harbor, Marrs' can't remember the name, Hufschmid's Painful Questions, Hoffman's various scholarly articles, Steven Jones' scholarly articles, Fetzer's article. There are flaws in each of these but none that warrant dismissal. Peter Lance and Jane Davis, along with several others that don't come to mind at the moment, have contributed a lot.

The number of instances of supposed negligence, well into the hundreds if you go back a number of years, all around the same focal point, all contributing to the same end, as if they had the same purpose, at some point must no longer be called negligence. It is an in-one's-tracks-stopping notion to think that our trained professional intelligence and military operativescan'tdo anything right when their untrained, or ill-trained, martyrdom-seeking zealots can do nothing wrong. Add to that the elements of cover-up and unwillingness to do an investigation, and the fact that the 9/11 Commission refused to even address, much less answer the questions I set out above, and I hope I haven't cracked under the pressure. The thought that a *New York Times* reporter might be listening, and that this might be the nation's only chance, is kind of hard on my constitution.

Aug 31, 2006

***

Bill:?

How did you get started on this? How persuaded are you??I'm not going to tackle the Pentagon. Or 7 WTC. Just 1 and 2, scenes of the greatest crimes. All must be true for any of it. See my notes on your annotations.

First, in re: quantity of stuff, this is from Jones's papers. And I don't see that Jones tells us he found thermite, but he conjectures it's there:

"Thus, we find substantial evidence supporting the current conjecture that some variation of thermite (e.g., solid aluminum powder plus $Fe2O3$, with possible addition of sul- fur) was used on the steel columns of the WTC Tower to weaken the huge steel supports, not long before explosives finished the demolition job. Roughly 2,000 pounds of RDX- grade linear-shaped charges (which could have been pre- positioned by just a few men) would then suffice in each Tower and WTC 7 to cut the supports at key points so that gravity would bring the buildings straight down. The estimate is based on the amount of explosives used in controlled demolitions in the past and the size of the buildings. Radio- initiated firing of the charges is implicated here, perhaps using Joule heating or superthermite matches. Using computer- controlled radio signals, it would be an easy matter to begin the explosive demolition near the point of entry of the planes in the Towers (to make it appear that the planes somehow initiated the collapse; cutter-charges could have been pre- placed at numerous spots in the building, since one would not know exactly where the planes would enter.)

***

8/31/06 annotation responses to my email:

Veale commentary: With regard to Scott Forbes and others who saw maintenance people or knew of a maintenance contract, Dwyer says nothing. As to whether he thought the government could have done the demolition job, he responds:

No. Maybe in a limited area, but not over 25 or 30 floors, in two buildings occupied by thousands of people, day, night and weekends.?

B.V.

A 1,500 pound bomb didn't put a serious dent in the place in 1993. Each face of the tower had to take enormous, enormous wind loads every day -- far greater than a 1,500 pound bomb. So you would have had to put tons of explosives around to get the job done. Read Wikipedia on thermite. It's not easy to handle. Who uses it for demolition?

Moreover, you couldn't open all those walls without people finding out. In 1978, the Citicorp Tower on 53rd Street was built with a structural flaw -- its main columns had been bolted, rather than welded together. An engineer doing wind studies figured out it would blow over in the wind.

They had to go in and open the walls on 30 or 40 floors, apply welds to the columns that had been bolted together. Everyone in the building knew. There was a newspaper strike on at the time, and even I -- a junior in college -- knew.

Further Veale commentary: He chooses not to respond to the comment about the Pentagon's apparent vulnerability, but rather wants to know who, it is believed, were the perpetrators? Points 2-10 in the email to which Dwyer is responding engender nothing by way of response. The comment about the owner/lessor of the building, Larry Silverstein, in point #11 provokes this:

I believe Silverstein was talking about pulling the fire- fighters out of an empty burning building. (And why would he be in on it?) Fire Chief Pete Hayden, who commanded the operation after the first two towers fell, said precisely that (in his oral history).

Veale commentary: The problem of the molten steel, serious enough to provoke more than one physicist to generate a purportedly scholarly paper, evokes the following perplexing answer:

I covered a dump in Jersey City that was burning for 25 years in 1980. They could never put it out. Why is an explosive - literally a fraction of a second - more likely to create molten steel? Wouldn't temperature have cooled weeks later?

Veale commentary: Point #13 having to do with the lack of prior history of steel-framed buildings collapsing because of fire and the strange coincidence of three such collapses, etc., etc. yields nothing in response. What precisely one is to make of such silence is hard to know. The witnesses to explosions within the WTC prompts the following:

Jones cited the FDNY oral histories to argue that the explosions began in the basement. I have read all the histories of the 50 fire-fighters who were in the buildings. (I sued four years to get them.) No one credible says that. It is preposterous. There were people in the base of the building. They walked out -- civilians, firefighters, and so forth.

Veale commentary: The implosion of the penthouse of WTC7 is apparently unworthy of mention, but the 30-50 ft lengths of the severed steel columns elicited this:

During construction, the columns were field assembled from 20-40 foot lengths. So it's not surprising that they ended up in such lengths.

Veale commentary: Point#17, having to do with the length and the heat of the fires being insufficient to severe the steel and more likely to make them fall over whole, finds this in response:

How can you say the perimeter is theoretically weakened? It was hit by an airplane! Dozens of those exterior pinstripe columns were destroyed, across 8-10 floors.

Anyway, NIST says the core columns -- damaged by impact, weakened by fire -- sagged first, pulling the floors inward, which pulled the compromised perimeter columns in, seen as bowing on the videos.

Veale commentary: And then this to the related Point#18:

I think the columns sag.?But wait: you're not saying Controlled Demolition set up the demolition, and had it worked out so it fell in truck sized pieces?

Veale commentary: Point #19 referring to the telescoping of the tops of the towers in mid collapse occasions no response beyond a question:

Does that mean there is agreement as to the assumed fact? If the core goes first, wouldn't we see the TV antenna at the top start to sink into the middle?

Veale commentary: Point#20 concerning the ejected pieces of steel finds no rebuttal. Point #21 about pulverization elicits this:

Some of it was pulverized. I walked on top of it. Some of it was in hunks. Only the floors were concrete. The point of the trade center's design was to keep it very lightweight, to re- duce the amount of steel needed. The walls were all drywall. That was pulverized.

Veale commentary: Point#22 concerning the work of physicist Jim Hoffman evokes nothing. Point#23 about the second tower falling first prompts this:

It was breached across two faces, as the plane went from south to northeast, and according to NIST, significantly more core columns were damaged,

Veale commentary: Point#24's reference to an academic finding thermate on steel from ground zero finds this response:

Do you mean Jones? I can't find that.

Veale commentary: Point #25 that refers to the National Institute of Standards and Technology's report as a sham and queries whether a homicide investigation conducted in a similar fashion would be acceptable leads Dwyer to say the following:

I disagree. I think viable evidence expires at that point.

Veale commentary: Point#26's mention of the many authors who have studied the issue led to this response:

I haven't read all of these. Jones's article is filled with conjecture, and he uses that term himself. It is supposition that thermite is consistent with his scenarios, not direct evidence.

9/?/06

***

You're not cracking.

Best,?Jim

Jim, ?I have never been a part of a more fascinating conversation. The implosion world stuff is very powerful, and it will probably have to be up to the physicists on my staff to properly rebut it. I clearly rely on the existence of molten steel and thermate. Blanchard kind of suggests that the photographs in Jones' paper were doctored. It sure looks yellow and dripping to me. There's an extremely weird story if true. Jones stated on the panel discussion on CSPAN that he had tested a piece of steel and found thermate. My source tells me Jones has tested three samples from separate sources, none of which is included in the paper I read.

Blanchard takes refuge in the chain of custody problem with Jones' tests. That's fine technically, but figuring out how and why thermate got on the steel in some other way detracts from the safety of the refuge, to torture the metaphor a bit. Blanchard does not suggest what is essential to put this matter to rest. Four different scientists with no prior pronouncements on the issue should be allowed into Hangar 17, to take as much steel as they want, to then publicly and transparently test it for thermate and then render their conclusions.

What's the matter with the Pentagon and WTC7? It is a fact that this case has a cumulative effect on the truth-seeker. The tentative conclusions with regard to one aspect lend weight to impressions with regard to another. The "they"? What I have been saying for a year or more is--give me subpoena power and I will find out.

There are two very significant problems with not dealing with WTC7 and the Pentagon. They are the ancillary crime problem and the character evidence problem. So many of my clients avoided major disasters as they were commit- ting the murder, but got sloppy when they were trying to fence the stuff.

It is often the secondary that gets them. WTC7 should be viewed as the ancillary crime. When somebody explains why the penthouse is the first thing to go, which Blanchard doesn't do, very significantly, people like me may begin to quiet down. Silence under these circumstances comes close to being an adoptive admission-admissible in court because an innocent person would have spoken up. The Commission's failure to mention WTC7 is explosive.

The Pentagon will never go away because of the broad outlines of the crime, as discussed previously. That is character evidence. These people are capable of everything. To dis- regard the criminal's prior or subsequent crimes is to close investigative eyes. As an aside, 9/11 is what seals the question of whether the 2000 and 2004 elections were stolen, which RFK,Jr.and I are ready to debate whenever called upon.

You make excellent and perplexing points about the enormity of the task of blowing up the buildings that Jones addresses to some extent. I admit I really don't even get there because no one has sufficiently addressed the satellite photos and the molten steel questions. First you eliminate the impossible. Since it is far from physically impossible to blow up the building, we are in that instance dealing with the concededly improbable. Blanchard seems to agree that the presence of molten steel would defeat the fire hypothesis, doesn't he?

Underlying a consideration of how hard it would be to plant the explosives is the voluminous history of government intimidation of witnesses, not to mention firing and silencing whistle-blowers. If the best rebuttal is "there would be witnesses," I think of that history.

At base, my belief requires the understanding that very powerful people did something horribly wrong because they had convinced themselves they were right. They were the heroes awakening a sleeping nation in the only way they knew how. 1993 and Bojinka were obviously insufficient. They then let their servants(only the absolute minimum, the rest are duped) in on the true value of their vision and let patriotism and threat of prosecution or worse take it from there.

I like the business about the dump, but at what temperature was it burning and what does that say about the nature and temperature of the initial fire? The last thing I am is a physicist, and I have the same question with regard to cooling down, but I rely on Hoffman and Jones for the notion that explosives create tremendous temperatures which create molten metal. It is not from the airplanes as has been suggested- 1. too heavy, and 2. it was found in WTC7 which wasn't hit by one. Molten metal, therefore, disposes of the jet fuel hypothesis. Do we have dueling physicists on these issues?

I must say I get a little anxious when witnesses are referred to as not credible without being cross-examined; it is so easy to dispose of inconvenient discrepancies that way. May I amend to say theoretically heat-weakened steel of the perimeter? Everyone agrees, however, that the planes did not cause the collapse except insofar as they started the fires, right? So, the crash-destroyed perimeter is not particularly relevant. The building was entirely stable after impact, no??I would need subpoena power before I asserted that Controlled Demolition had anything to do with blowing up the building, but whoever did blow up the building would have done more or less what was done.

The most stunning notion to which I have been introduced in this exchange is that of the expiration of viable evidence. If I understand you correctly, you just relegated to irrelevance an entire branch of criminology(criminalistics) as well as forensic pathology. I can't imagine you meant to do that, but then again, that is what NIST did, establishing forever their lack of credibility and providing the kooks like me in the audience with yet one more reason to believe.

If we have thousands of photographs of the steel, I'm told it is a simple matter to look at it and determine if it was cut by explosives or not. But the body of the building, that NIST had no interest in, would also have contained, or not contained, thermate. I can't tell you how many of my clients are in jail due to forensic science, evidence that was, according to those infallible juries, quite viable enough, thank you.

To my credit, or not, I laughed at the skeptics for 3 1/2 years. Then an extremely bright colleague, so smart he does nothing but fancy appellate work, threw Griffin's book across the desk at me. My life will never be the same. How's that for drama?

As to how persuaded I am, I shot past beyond a reasonable doubt when the Commission didn't even deal with Griffin's issues, and Lance's testimony was given no space. But it is a fact that I am constantly reevaluating my level of certainty. I think we would have to say morally certain at the moment, made stronger by the unwillingness or inability of smart guys with power like you to deal with the Pentagon and WTC7.

Having now read the story in Saturday's paper, did you ask Jones if he found thermate? Is he backing off of his pronouncements on CSPAN? What does the presence of zinc and fluorine mean? Does the fact that Kevin Ryan is actually a whistleblowing former NIST scientist give you pause? I noticed that fact didn't make it into your story. My recently-graduated-from-law-school son wanted me to object to "Conspiracy Theories" in the headline, saying every theory about 9/11 is a conspiracy theory. I told him you didn't write the headlines and shouldn't be chastised for "playing the game" as he put it.

9/?/06 19:41:25 -0400

Bill

***

Bill:? I watched the NIST investigation because I was writing a book at the time; they had to suspend the investigation of 7 WTC because they were so in the woods on the analysis of 1 and 2 WTC. Now they say they will be finished the 7 WTC inquiry next year and will include something about a demolition thesis.

Either the whole thing -- the WTC, Pentagon, Shanksville -- was Islamic fundamentalists in planes, or it was all done by people in the US. There's no hybrid., no mix and match?So I'm sticking with the WTC because I've studied the thing. I'm not sure Blanchard concedes that it's molten steel or its fire.

I wrote a book about what happened inside the towers after the planes hit. By chance, one of the people who is in- side the north building and rescues a whole bunch of people is named Frank De-Martini, the construction supervisor for the WTC. (Doors on the 88th, 89th, 86th, 84th floor were jammed shut by the impact; De-Martini and another man, Pablo Ortiz, found a tool and pried them open.) Then around 915, a half hour into the crisis, DeMartini, who has a radio, calls a colleague on the ground. He is on the 78th floor sky lobby and sees structural damage to the building core. He wants a structural engineer to come up because he doesn't like what he sees. On the ground, though, the engineer can't get past the police cordon because of the dangers on the street.

What does this mean? This means the very core of the building was wounded, and DeMartini saw it.

That damage could only have been caused by the airplane.

Why would DeMartini, who oversaw every piece of construction in the building for compliance with code, who had two young kids and whose wife was visiting him that morning (he sent her down the stairs, promising to be along shortly), permit people to plant demolition charges all over the building he knew like the back of his hand? Why would he stay in the building if he had the slightest idea? I mean, here's your character evidence: brilliant, dynamic construction manager of the WTC somehow doesn't notice people planting bombs in the structure of his building? And it's not just DeMartini -- there are dozens of people like him who work in the trade center, many of whom did not get killed.

How could this demolition project go forward without their consent and five years of silence?

Who was deemed not credible? There are people who are in this argument whose crediblity is nil. But I don't think I dismissed anything on those grounds alone, did I?

I think NIST says it was the destruction of structure and weakening of the surviving pieces by fire that led to the collapse.

I guess what they mean is they lose track of viable dynamic photographic evidence (ie, cameras can't see what's happening as the buildings start to fall), because video and still photography underlie their analysis up to the point where the collapses begins. They certainly did examine quite a bit of steel -- after the fact, though not for thermates or thermites, but for meeting the code requirements. The code said fire-test 17 foot lengths and those passed the test. But the actual lengths were 34 feet, and those didn't pass the test. (as the structural member gets longer, it becomes more frail; think of dry spaghetti, a stub versus a full length piece. The longer the piece, the less vertical strength it has.)

Here's something to consume a few hours: http://www.debunking911.com/index.html?The 7 WTC thing about "pulling it" is a chimera. It misconstrues what was going on. ?I thought Ryan was a former Underwriter Lab guy. And Jones is a cold fusion man. (He is also the author of a paper, "Behold My Hands: Evidence for Christ's Visit in Ancient America") Jones wrote to me about possible thermite dust collected from an apartment near Ground Zero. According to Jones, zinc and flourine mean...maybe there were thermates or what have you down there.

As for the headlines, right, not my job; I didn't call anyone a conspiracy theorist or alternative theorist, or anything. Jim

***

9/5/06

Jim,? Last and least important first, Ryan was a site manager of Environmental Health Laboratories, a division of UL. A headline in an article refers to him as a NIST scientist; appropriate description or not, it was the whistleblower part that I considered important that was not included in your article.

I thought I had escaped witnesses I had to apologize for in my last career. That Jones is a cold fusion guy, I have been frightened of for some time; that he has some interesting religious beliefs, ...you are the bearer of that news.

Point 1. It is not my impression that Jones is not well-qualified as a physicist; he was actually doing work for the government in the cold-fusion instance.

Point 2. It is also my impression that the area in which he is working (9/11) is not...rocket science. In other words, temperature at which steel melts, how long a fire stays hot, how long however hot a fire would have to burn to create plasticity, etc. are not PHD thesis material.

Point 3. As funny as we may look at him for his religious ideas, what do they have to do with his ability to analyze physics problems?

Point 4. Can't the NYT prevail upon some well-known uninvolved physicist to answer some of these questions so that we don't have to rely on others with baggage? Was Jones one of the arguers whose credibility is nil? How do you like Jim Hoffman? Have you talked to him? I don't think you answered the question whether you point blank asked Jones if he had found thermate? It is after all what he said on TV.

Why didn't NIST test for thermate? The demolition thesis was out there long before any report was written? Have you asked them?

DiMartino clearly had character, and that is an extremely important story. That strong character, however, does not add to, or detract from, the weak and flawed character of the perpetrators demonstrated by everything else that happened to which I have previously referred. As to how, I imagine that the night security staff was compromised. All of the DiMartino's in the world can't speak if they are ignorant. The actual executors of the demolition are obviously government operatives who will be dead as soon as they open their mouths, and they know it...if they aren't dead already.

Or, how about this? Any building that big has to have a self-de-struct capability to minimize damage in the event it started to fall over, but the calculus is so horrible, only a few know, and they are sworn to secrecy. How's that for an overheated imagination?

The NUB- no hybrid? I will say I am a bit shocked by that asser-tion for the following reasons:

As Zbig Brezinski has detailed, we began working with and sup-porting and fostering Islamic extremists in 1976. He says it brought down the Soviet Union and was worth it. Bin Laden and Abdel Rahman have been working for us and recruiting fighters for 20-30 years. It takes nothing for me to imagine the USG finding out about the 9/11 attacks from one of our agents, and then using it and them as patsies for our purposes. What about the six or so of the 19 who are still alive and living in Europe? I'm sure you are aware of the pi-lots who say the planes were remote controlled. I have no idea, but it is easily within USG capability. Nafeez Mossadeq Ahmed's book, War on Freedom, exhaustively documents, about every third page, another instance of USG and UK dealings with Islamic terrorists.

Is the idea that it couldn't be a hybrid an accepted notion at the NYT? I would have every bit as much difficulty with the ideas I have espoused if they had to fit into that particular paradigm. That I haven't felt so constricted I will now begin to attribute to my vast knowledge of twentieth century history and the field of intelligence, but honestly, as outrageously full of myself as I am, I thought the ba-sic notion of our past collaboration was common knowledge.

In fact, however, there needn't have been that much in the way of collaboration. If we simply learned of the particulars from an in-side source, as we had from the Egyptian Army officer, Emad Salem, in the 1993 bombing, we would have been in a position to take over airplanes as necessary, and then do whatever USG sick minds con-ceived of.

***

9/?/06

Bill,?

Whatever about his religious beliefs: more relevant is that the structural engineering faculty at BYU has disavowed Jones en masse.

I can't remember if I asked him point blank about thermate. NIST had, I think, 100 outside advisors, some of them quite contrarian on their views. None of them took up the demolition banner.

It's not just DeMartini -- it's the whole community of people who worked in the buildings, who were fanatical about their character as the tallest, the fastest elevators, all that stuff. None of them noticed anything. They loved those buildings. They jealously defended them. They were proud of working in them.

Not to quote myself incessantly, but CIA blowback was one of the themes of my book on the first WTC bombing (lots about Emad Salem in there). The opening scene involves one of the Afghani mujahdeen, our own trained warrior, watching across Park Row as he waited for the towers to come down from the truck bomb.

It's not that I have any lack of faith in the perfidious possibilities of our government (or any other one); it's my lack of faith in its competence.

In re: thermate, I will put my thoughts on that below. I've actually now truly reached the end of my imaginative and intellectual rope with the WTC. I have lived in those buildings and thought about their assassins for 13 years. For the more recent book, I spoke to hundreds of people who were inside the towers and sued the government in three states and five courts at multiple levels of appellate review to get the first hand documentary record, which is in the tens of thousands of pages, and dozens of hours of tapes. With help from other people, I built databases to find patterns, to piece together where people were, what they saw, who they saw, what they said.

Nothing -- zero -- in there supports the demolition thesis. It wasn't that I knew what was going to be in there, or that I was resistant to the notion. It's just that none of the evidence in there supports it. Perhaps some factual wisps exist that people of goodwill feel point to demolition as the real cause; I don't have the freedom to entertain those thoughts, having absorbed so much substantial information from which any corroboration of such a notion is utterly lacking.

The reality of the thing -- the cold, concrete provable factuality of it -- has occupied the rapidly diminishing space in my middle-aged brain. I actually don't have the physical or mental strength to imagine scenarios where the nightguards all live in terror of being killed by the government. If they exist, others can find them. I can't.

As for thermate - here's what NIST said on their web- site:

Did the NIST investigation look for evidence of the WTC towers being brought down by controlled demolition? Was the steel tested for explosives or thermite residues? The combination of thermite and sulfur (called thermate) "slices through steel like a hot knife through butter."

NIST did not test for the residue of these compounds in the steel.

The responses to questions number 2, 4, 5 and 11 demonstrate why NIST concluded that there were no explosives or controlled demolition involved in the collapses of the WTC towers.

Furthermore, a very large quantity of thermite (a mixture of powdered or granular aluminum metal and powdered iron oxide that burns at extremely high temperatures when ignited) or another incendiary compound would have had to be placed on at least the number of columns damaged by the aircraft impact and weakened by the subsequent fires to bring down a tower. Thermite burns slowly relative to explosive materials and can require several minutes in contact with a massive steel section to heat it to a temperature that would result in substantial weakening.

Separate from the WTC towers investigation, NIST researchers estimated that at least 0.13 pounds of thermite would be required to heat each pound of a steel section to approximately 700 degrees Celsius (the temperature at which steel weakens substantially). Therefore, while a thermite re- action can cut through large steel columns, many thousands of pounds of thermite would need to have been placed inconspicuously ahead of time, remotely ignited, and somehow held in direct contact with the surface of hundreds of massive structural components to weaken the building. This makes it an unlikely substance for achieving a controlled demolition.

Analysis of the WTC steel for the elements in thermite/ thermate would not necessarily have been conclusive. The metal compounds also would have been present in the construction materials making up the WTC towers, and sulfur is present in the gypsum wallboard that was prevalent in the interior partitions.

Veale commentary: My response attempted to duplicate his method of placing comments or questions in his email;. In toto, it proceeds as follows: (With regard to the denunciation of Steven Jones)This is devastating. How did they do it? Publish a denunciation? Did it include a scientific rebuttal of his paper?

Veale commentary: Responding to Dwyer's inability to remember whether he had asked Jones about the finding of Thermate:

This a little touchy; I apologize. I was able to win a bet with a beautiful reporter once because she had her notes. Before being enormously enlightened in this conversation, but maybe even after, I would have thought that the single most important thing that

Jones could add to this debate is the fact that he found thermate from three different sources from steel in ground zero. The circumstances of that, the testing, etc. would have been the focus of any questioning I did of him. Had I the opportunity, I actually would have set about to test him and his assertion, because that is what I am trained to do, and because I can't stand not getting to the bottom of things, and that is the best way.

It leaves me thinking that your mindset is a radically different one. In as polite a way as I can think to ask, does having written two books on the subject and coming to a certain conclusion about matters arrange your consciousness in such a way that potentially conflicting ideas become off-limits? I prefer to think you aren't simply tidying up after the forces of stability have made a bit of a mess. You are, presumably, far better aware of the newsroom strictures of thought than my reading would have made me, but it would be my theory that it would take something of a revolutionary act to think out-loud that there is reason to believe the whole thing was an inside job. Care to enlighten me about any of that?

Veale commentary: About the failure of the outside NIST experts to take up the demolition banner:

With WTC7 looking so much like a controlled demolition(Dan Rather) that would be astounding but for the "strictures of thought" extant in the world as well as in the newsroom.

Veale commentary: Responding to the DiMartini reference: Amen, but not QED.

Veale commentary: With regard to Dwyer's belief in governmental incompetence:

Bingo, this is almost the beginning and end of it all. Would you agree that at some point, some number, a string of incompetences serving the same end are no longer a coincidence of incompetence? Roosevelt said there is no such thing as coincidence in international relations.

Robert Stinnett proved to me that Roosevelt should know, given what he knew about Pearl Harbor.

I detect in at least one of the collapses a shortening or compressing of the top floors on the way down. Am I wrong about that? Seems a simple matter of measuring with more technological savvy than I possess. I suppose demolitionists can do what they do in a variety of ways depending on the needs. In my hypothesis they had a need to keep people off of the track and to make it look like it was the planes that did the job. By the way, what do you do with the freefall speed problem?

Is Hoffman wrong that, had there been resistance at each floor, it would have taken a much longer time to col- lapse?

Veale commentary: Responding to Dwyer's assertion that nothing in the record supports the demolition thesis:

I have just reread New Pearl Harbor or at least relevant portions. Griffin and Jones both refer to a number of people who heard and saw the effects of explosions, most importantly Mike Pecoraro who saw a crumpled up door etc. after hearing an explosion. I don't understand how you can use words like "zero" and "utterly lacking" in the face of those stories.

I have been proving things for years with a lot less than Mike Pecoraro. You are all wrong about the diminishing space. It just seems that way. My mind has improved enormously in the last 20 years. What is sad is the note of resignation. I had forgotten that the nightguards worked for Marvin.

What does it take to hire ex-covert ops guys to do your security work; they come complete with ideological strait jacket, I understand.

Have you made any effort to find out who it was that kept interrupting Cheney telling him the plane was 50, 30, 20 miles out-the Mineta story. I know it isn't WTC, but it sure is explosive.

Veale commentary: About the presence of thermate not being conclusive of anything:

Conclusive is a bit much to ask. You aren't saying it wouldn't be extremely important to know are you? And then the metallurgists and physicists can battle about how it was attached to what pieces of steel in what proportions consistent with which scenarios. Possible presence of certain compounds is a long way from the end of the story.

Have you contacted an uninvolved physicist yet?

I understand that I am communicating with someone who has made up his mind. I am saying that areas have not been explored, questions have not been sufficiently answered, mine for example. Do you think we have gone as far as we can, and it is worldviews that prevent further progress?

9/?/06?Dwyer replied as follows: (quoting from the BYU faculty statement) "I think without exception, the structural engineering professors in our department are not in agreement with the claims made by Jones in his paper, and they don't think there is accuracy and validity to these claims"

"The university is aware that Professor Steven Jones's hypotheses and interpretations of evidence regarding the collapse of World Trade Center buildings are being questioned by a number of scholars and practitioners, including many of BYU's own faculty members.

Professor Jones's department and college administrators are not convinced that his analyses and hypotheses have been submitted to relevant scientific venues that would ensure rigorous technical peer review." - A. Woodruff Miller, Department Chair, BYU department of Civil and Environmental Engineering http://www.et.byu.edu/ce/people/
people.php?person=1&page =miller/vita.php

"The structural engineering faculty in the Fulton College of Engineering and Technology do not support the hypotheses of Professor Jones." - The College of Engineering and Technology department http://www.et.byu.edu/index.php?m1=faculty&n=2

This is from our[Jones and Dwyer's] exchange -- I had asked him to comment on the Q and A of the Nist statements. His comment follows. As I read it, he found compounds consistent with, but not exclusive to, thermites. (ie, Type O blood, counselor, doesn't your client have type O blood, and wasn't that found on the murder weapon?) It's also consistent with the plastics and metals of thousands of burning desktop computers. (But 70 percent of the population has Type O blood...)

Q: Was the steel tested for explosives or thermite residues? The combination of thermite and sulfur (called ther- mate) "slices through steel like a hot knife through butter." NIST: NIST did not test for the residue of these compounds in the steel.

We, OTOH, are testing for the residue of thermite- reaction compounds (aluminothermics) both in the toxic WTC dust and in the solidified metal. And we are finding an abundance of fluorine, zinc and other elements which are commonly used in aluminothermics, but not in building materials in the concentrations found. We are investigating the possibility of thermite-based arson and demolition

Here's a little more on the thermite problem. It's from debunking911myths.com (in case you wonder what their bias is). They claim 18,000 pounds of thermite would be needed to account for the amount of aluminum drops that were filmed.

How much mass would be required to produce molten iron from thermite equal to the same volume of molten aluminum droplets shown flowing from the south tower window:

A mole of Fe weighs 54 g. For every mole of Fe produced by thermite, one mole of Al and 0.5 mole of Fe2O3 is needed.?2Al + Fe2O3 = Al2O3 + 2Fe

One mole of Al weighs 27 g. 0.5 mole of Fe2O3

weighs 80 g.

Therefore, (27 + 80) g = 107 g of Al and Fe2O3 is needed to produce 54 g of Fe.

That means the mass of the reactants to that of Fe produced is a ratio of 107/54 = 2. The mass of thermite reactants (Al, Fe2O3) is twice that of the molten iron produced.

Comparing the weight of molten aluminum droplets compared with iron:

Iron is 7.9 g/cc. Aluminum is 2.64 g/cc. Fe is denser than Al by a factor of 3. For the same volume of droplets, Fe would have three times the mass as Al.

To produce the iron from thermite requires a reactant mass that is a factor of 2 more than the iron produced. Also, Fe is 3 times as dense as Al.

So, it would take 2*3 = 6 times as much mass to produce the same volume of molten iron droplets from thermite compared with molten aluminum droplets.

Example:

Assume 3000 lbs of aluminum fell from the towers. If it had been molten iron produced by thermite, then 6*3000 = 18,000 lbs of thermite reactants would have been required to produce that same volume of falling mass.

Suppose 10 tons of molten aluminum fell from the south tower, about 1/8th of that available from the airplane. If it had been molten iron produced from thermite, 60 tons of thermite reactants would have to have been stored in Fuji Bank to produce the same volume spilling out of the south tower. The section of floor would have to hold all of that plus the aircraft.

*Amount of aluminum can be ascertained by counting the droplets and measuring their size compared to the known size of the window. It's not easy to get a good number on this. It's based on the number of slugs seen in video stills, their size relative to the window width which was about 22 inches, and the density of aluminum, assuming this was aluminum.?http://www.coolmagnetman.com/magconda.htm

The weight of a gallon of aluminum is about 22.5 pounds. A hundred of these would already be 2250 lbs. A gallon size is not unlike the size of the slugs that were pouring out the window. Look at them relative to the window size.

They look small at first, but when you realize how big the towers were, the slugs were fairly large. It must have been in the thousands of pounds.

Some of the video stills show what look like 50 to 100 slugs in just one frame.

Strictures of thought? Well, probably.?But:? No witnesses where one would expect them; buildings collapse where planes hit them, not at the bases; expert eye (DeMartini) sees serious damage to the core post-impact. If not QED, it's a constellation of realities versus Jones's compounds that are consistent with thermite (and other bldg compounds)

I don't know about the compressing of the floors. The freefall speeds apply, as I understand it, to the unimpeded facade, parts of which hit the ground first (and registered the first seismic vibrations, there being no explosive seismology, yet another non-existent "witness" where one would expect to find one). The collapse continued for about 20 or 30 seconds, much slower than free fall.

Where did the explosions happen? The witnesses who survived in the base of building don't report any; the tapes from 911 don't, either.

When did they put the thermite in there? How? When was the thermite allowed to begin burning? How did that happen? Someone show me how you could knock the building down with thermite before I would entertain that there could be something irregular about those trace elements.

Who's an uninvolved physicist? Not to be touchy, but there are 100 people who don't work for the government -- FDNY, structural engineers, family members, fire engineers -- who sat on the NIST oversight panel for this investigation. There are severe critics of the NIST case, but they have to do with the mechanism -- how the fire spread, did the floor go first -- but not on the central pathway to collapse of damaged structure plus unimpeded fire plus weakened structure.

There isn't a single structural engineer in the world who has written a paper in a peer reviewed structural engineering journal that supports controlled demolition.

Why do I have to get someone? Why is Jones more credible than all his colleagues at BYU?

Veale commentary: Beyond an inquiry about whether he had anything else to add, the last exchange involved the following email to him on the 9th of September or so:

9/9/06 ?Jim,? With whom is poor Prof. Jones eating lunch now?

To take up his cause, the last place I would have expected to find a 9/11 "conspiracy theorist" physicist was BYU, so it is all understandable from a political point of view. The problem, of course, is that they reject his hypothesis but not his science, at least not in what you showed me. Where is he wrong in his application of physical principles? All that said, ugh! I think I asked you before if Jim Hoffman is similarly afflicted.

Re: Jones exchange: Is this the difference between a journalist and a trial lawyer, one asks for a comment, the other asks for an answer? That sort of politesse is bled out of us in the first battle. I think I understand your line of argument, but disagree with your reading. The "in the concentrations found" suggests an inconsistency with building materials. Where does the desk hypothesis come from?

Griffin refers to a guy named Mike Pecoraro, being in the 6th subbasement, seeing explosive damage in the machine shop. Does that not contradict your assertions about survivor witnesses? Has he been debunked as well? And what of the others mentioned in Griffin and referred to in Jones? Are these people you have interviewed and discredited?

There are questions that you have not answered, and it is my sense that you feel that the burden at this point is on the skeptics to prove the mechanism of explosive demolition before you would feel compelled to attempt to deal with the questions you have not answered. I, of course, can't bear that burden. Had I the juice, I would inquire of a government demolitionist, "assuming this is your mission(destroy the towers) how would you accomplish it?" I definitely don't have that juice; maybe you do.

One of the reasons I don't think the conversation should stop with your shifting of the burden, is that I believe a prima facie case has been made of government complicity for all of the pieces of circumstantial evidence that don't make sense to which I have made reference previously- government incompetence too many times, magnificent skill on the part of the terrorists, tactics that make no sense- Hanjour(unlikely candidate in the first instance) hitting the Pentagon in the hardest possible way allowing him to kill the fewest number of people, the Mineta story, Shanksville engines strewn over miles, Mahmood Ahmad having money sent to Atta, and WTC7, where it is patently obvious that the penthouse goes first, equalling controlled demolition.

I am not bound in any way in my consideration of the case. You have said you are sticking with the towers. What part of the search for the truth allows you to disregard an enormous proportion of what my experience tells me is powerful evidence?

Bill

***

Veale commentary: There was no reply to the email immediately above. Three months later, I tried again.

At 05:43 PM 12/6/2006, you wrote:

Jim,? I read a study that concluded 118 firefighters used the word "explosives" or "explosion" in their statements, that you sued to get, where it was clear they were not referring to the collapse of the buildings. How have you managed to do whatever it is you have done with these 118 instances of evidence that do not fit your conclusion? I still have hope, as you can tell.

Veale

***

Response from Jim, in minutes, "Preposterous."

***

Second response within 30 minutes: ?Go this link, and choose item No. 4 and you can read them all for yourself.

Only 50 or 55 of the 500 oral histories are from fire- fighters were inside the buildings. If this link doesn't work, go to www.nytimes.com/sept11, and there is a five year archive of Sept 11 mutlimedia. Click on that and you will end up at a long list of our materials.

We posted those oral histories the day we got them. Then I spent several weeks sifting the histories of those who were inside the towers from those who were not, what they heard and what they knew.

***

Jim,?Thanks for responding. I am afraid I have a

handicap which prevents me from reading all that I would like. I read Brosnan's statement with interest, and determined that his could be read as supportive of the explosion thesis, though his interrogators made no significant effort to nail down precisely what he was saying and where the explosion that he refers to came from.

I was particularly perplexed to find a page or so of his statement redacted. If I have the time, I will endeavor to read more of the 503.

Luckily for me, there are scholars who have studied the matter in more depth. Graeme Mac Queen, for example, the study to which I referred. I don't know how he would respond to your "preposterous," but then I am still wondering what you have to say about Mike Pecoraro and the 50 ton press in the 3rd subbasement of the north tower.

If I can show you multiple statements by firefighters that can reasonably be read as supporting the demolition hypothesis, what will you do? How about we spend an afternoon going over whatever I can come up with?

Veale

Dwyer response, 12/6/06 I scanned MacQueen.

He credits the firefighters when they say they thought it was an explosion and believes they have been re-educated when they later say they realized it was the collapse of Tower 2. He disallows any non-human evidence. That would include seismographs that show there were no explosions before the collapse of either building, which ratify the firefighters synthesizing of their own experience (tremendous forces that they thought were an explosion or explosions) with objective fact (another building fell down at the time they experienced these forces).

I read Brosnan (and others, civilian and FDNY) as describing the collapse of Tower 2 as experienced by people in the lobby and lower floors of Tower 1.?Here are my reasons:

Tower 2 fell down before Tower 1.?No seismographically recorded explosions proceeded the col- lapse of Tower 2.

The explosions people in Tower 1 describe occur right after Tower 2 collapses.

Multiple seismographs record the collapse of Tower 2. The fall of Tower 2 released a tremendous amount of stored energy in the building (approximately equal to one percent of a nuclear bomb, according to *Scientific American.)*

The buildings were 131 feet apart.?People in Tower 1 experienced a tremendous blast of air and dust when Tower 2 fell and initially thought it was an explosion. At the time, virtually no one in Tower 1 realized that Tower 2 had fallen.

Tower 1 did not collapse until 29 minutes after the "explosions" Brosnan believes what he experienced as an explosion was the collapse of Tower 2.

At 06:39 PM 12/7/2006? Jim,

?Wow, I just started reading a seismographic study at *Journal of 9/11 Studies,* concerned with two spikes before the two crashes, that refers to Lt William Walsh's statement that while on another call for a gas leak on Canal Street, he hears an explosion, thinks ConEd has erupted, looks up and then sees the *first* plane hit the North Tower. When he enters the building, the lower elevator doors have been blown off the hinges, not something one would expect from a plane hitting 90 stories up. But, one can say, he was actually mistaken about the timing...he saw the plane first, got confused, associated the crash with an explosion, and all is right with the world.

The point of all of this is not that the truth can be established from 118 people using the word explosion, but rather that any serious investigation would have trained interrogators, shed of all preconception, trying to figure out exactly what each of these people saw, heard and felt. The endeavor is not advanced by attempts to read what we may want into what each of them said.

I can go through Brosnan's story and show you how he may well not have been talking about the other tower going down, his directions and use of phrase are completely ambiguous, begging for diagrams to be drawn and all of the other accoutrement of fact-finding to be employed.

If I were an investigator for the 9/11 Commission, and had Pecoraro and Walsh's statements in my hand, ...ah, yes, I could have been somebody, instead I got a one-way ticket....

Veale

Dwyer's final words on the subject, 12/7/06 "I give up."

***

Appendix C

APPENDIX C: UNITED FLIGHT 93

Because we haven't dealt with it, etc.

United Flight 93 took off from Newark International Airport at approximately 8:42 AM on the morning of September 11th, 2001. It never arrived in San Francisco, its destination. Whether it crashed near Shanksville, Pennsylvania after being hijacked by Arab terrorists, is a matter of extremely serious debate. What is virtually certain at this point is that the questions raised by students of what took place deserve investigation. The only public investigation that has taken place was conducted by the 9/11 Commission that assumed the conclusion that has become the official story set out in the 9/11 Commission Report.

Far from being a simple, non-controversial matter of fact, there is probable cause to believe that something other than what the government has proclaimed took place with regard to the end of United Flight 93. The organization Pilots for 9/11 Truth has created a DVD entitled, "Pandora's Black Box, Chapter Three, Flight of United 93," that sets out some of the glaring incongruities, and should be referred to by anyone interested in the questions presented in this memorandum. This memorandum will refer to a number of facts that should impel further study and investigation.

Crash site

The crash site that the government claims is that of United 93 does not resemble that of any similar airplane crash site. There are virtually no parts of an aircraft to be seen as is expected given other similar events. There is no significant burning of the surrounding area to anywhere near the extent of comparable crash sites. The direction and pattern of damage are different from that expected given what the government claims was the airplane's heading, broken limbs and trees impacted by the aircraft show no signs of having been burnt. There is no jet fuel in tests of the soil in the surrounding area.

Fire on impact

As shown in the "Pilots" DVD, video footage of crashes of similar-sized airplanes show enormous plumes of black jet fuel smoke in addition to fireballs at the time of impact. The one photograph taken by a nearby witness, Val, shows a lighter-colored smoke plume of significantly smaller size than should be expected. As mentioned above, there is no evidence of the kind of fire that would have been occasioned by the thousands of pounds of jet fuel carried aboard United 93, traveling to San Francisco. If it did not ignite, it should have saturated the ground, which tests show it did not.

Witness discrepancies

There are witnesses who agree with the government's designation of the flight path supposedly followed by United 93. Investigations by various organizations and individuals, including the "Pilots," establish that there are glaring incongruities in what they have to say. Most significantly, as shown in the analysis of the NTSB computer simulation and data from the flight data recorder, the witnesses place the plane at places and at altitudes that cannot be reconciled with the information released by the government. In one case a witness says the plane was 2000 feet in the air as opposed to the 6-8000 feet described by the contents of the CDR. In an- other, a witness puts the plane less than a thousand feet, when the government information establishes several thousand.

In addition to the difficulties in accepting what witnesses supportive of the official story claim, there are multiple witnesses who describe a different flight path, a different altitude, a different attitude, and a different size of plane from what the government has claimed.

Rebuttal to government claim

The account accepted and propagated by the government explains some of the anomalies that have to do with the absence of significant wreckage and the small area of impact by referring to a virtual vertical descent of Flight 93 into the ground. The claim concludes that such an unusual and devastating impact at such a high rate of speed, leaves very little physical evidence behind for forensic examination. The analysis conducted by Pilots for 9/11 Truth demonstrates that however unusual the impact may have been, there are examples to which it might be compared, none of which show similar total obliteration of the remains of the aircraft. As mentioned before, similar studied crashes are responsible for enormous eruptions of fireballs producing large plumes of black, jet fuel smoke. But, more significant than these inconsistencies is the fact, demonstrated by the "Pilots" that, ac- cording to the information supplied by the government, the aircraft identified as United Flight 93 did not hit the ground at such a steep angle. According to the data supplied by the NTSB, the airplane hit the ground at a 35 degree angle at the very most. Such a crash should have produced the easily recognized trench containing large pieces of debris and identifiable evidence of an airplane crash with which virtually all citizens of the world are familiar. Nothing of the kind could be found near Shanksville, Pennsylvania on, or after September 11th, 2001.

APPENDIX D
PETITION FOR CERTIORARI TO UNITED STATES SUPREME COURT

QUESTIONS PRESENTED

United States Army Specialist April Gallop and her young son were injured in the 9/11 attack on the Pentagon. Plaintiffs brought a civil action against Vice President Richard Cheney, Secretary of Defense Donald Rumsfeld, General Richard Meyers, U.S.A.F. (Ret.) and John Does 1-X, alleging their complicity in the catastrophe. The district court dismissed the complaint as frivolous even though it included abundant factual allegations that colorably pled at least two causes of action. Plaintiffs appealed. The Second Circuit, after denying a motion to disqualify from the appellate panel Circuit Judge John W. Walker, first cousin once removed of President George W. Bush, affirmed the dismissal and then, *sua sponte*, ordered Petitioners to show cause why they should not be sanctioned $15,000 and double costs for pursuing a frivolous appeal. After Petitioners moved for rehearing and to disqualify both the appellate panel and any other second circuit judge who might be biased, the court denied rehearing and, again *sua sponte*, ordered Petitioners to show cause why they should not be required to tell all judges within the second circuit before whom they appeared for the following year of the sanctions it intended to impose pursuant to its first order to show cause. After rejecting Petitioners' responses to the two orders to show cause, both threatened sanctions were imposed, ostensibly under F.R.A.P. 38, 28 U.S.C. § 1927, and the court's inherent powers.

The question presented in this Petition is whether the Second Circuit Court of Appeals erred as a matter of law and abused its discretion in imposing monetary sanctions and a nonmonetary "scarlett letter" sanction on Petitioners for (1) filing a frivolous appeal, when in fact Petitioners had a reasonable basis for appealing the dismissal of the Complaint which contained factual allegations that colorably pled at least two causes of action, and (2) for including, in a motion to disqualify the panel considering Plaintiffs' motion for a rehearing *en banc*, an incidental request that any members of the court *en banc* who had any bias in light of the nature of the Plaintiffs' Complaint, recuse themselves, when in fact Petitioners had reasons, independent of the adverse decision on their appeal, for questioning the impartiality of the court.

PARTIES TO THE PROCEEDING

The Plaintiffs are April Gallop for herself and her minor child, E.G.

The Defendants are the former Vice President of the United States, Richard Cheney, the former Secretary of Defense, Donald Rumsfeld, and General

Richard Meyers, U.S.A.F. (Ret.), along with unknown others named provisionally as John Does.

Petitioners William W. Veale and Dennis Cunningham are attorneys who represented April Gallop and upon whom monetary and nonmonetary sanctions were imposed by the circuit court in the course of that representation.

TABLE OF CONTENTS

TABLE OF AUTHORITIES

Cases

Compensation and Punishment, 74 Geo. L.J. 1313 (1986) ......
Meehan Rasch, *Not Taking Frivolity Lightly: Circuit
Variance in Determining Frivolous Appeals Under
Federal Rule of Appellate Procedure 38,*
62 Ark. L. Rev. 249 (2009) ....

PETITION FOR A WRIT OF CERTIORARI

Plaintiffs' attorneys, William Veale and Dennis Cunningham, petition for a writ of certiorari to the United States Supreme Court to review and reverse the *sua sponte* orders of the United States Court of Appeals for the Second Circuit imposing on Petitioners two sanctions, to-wit: (1) $15,000 and double costs for filing a frivolous appeal; and (2) a requirement that Petitioners inform all judges within the Second Circuit before whom they appear within the next year of the first sanction, for having moved to disqualify certain judges from ruling upon Plaintiffs' petition for rehearing.

DECISIONS BELOW

Gallop v. Cheney ("Gallop I"), 642 F.3d 364 (2d Cir. 2011); *Gallop v. Cheney ("Gallop II")*, 645 F.3d 519 (2d Cir. 2011); *Gallop v. Cheney ("Gallop III")*, 660 F.3d 580 (2d Cir. 2011); *Gallop v. Cheney ("Gallop IV")*, 667 F.3d 226 (2d Cir. 2012).

STATEMENT OF THE CASE

On December 15, 2008, April Gallop, a specialist in the army who was working in the Pentagon on September 11, 2001 ("9/11") in the company of her infant son, E.G., filed a Complaint in the Southern District of New York. Gallop alleged that certain high-ranking U.S. officials were complicit in the attacks of that day. These persons – named as Defendants – included President George W. Bush's Vice President Richard Cheney, President Bush's Secretary of Defense Donald Rumsfeld, and General Richard Myers, U.S.A.F. (Ret.).

The Complaint suggested various theories of what may in fact have occurred on 9/11, subject to further discovery to flesh out the facts. Certain of these theories unquestionably would be considered fantastical by most persons, whereas others were more plausible. Given the nature of the claims and the paucity of pre-filing discovery, some of the claims were, as well, inconsistent. However, the Complaint made numerous, specific factual allegations in support of Gallop's claim that her injuries and those of her son

(described as "serious head and brain injuries," Complaint at ¶ 57), were caused by Defendants, including, by way of example, the following:

Little or no attention was paid by Defendants and others responsible to an increasingly explicit series of warnings, during 2001, that Al Qaeda was hoping and planning to strike inside the U.S.; and that there were concrete plans – which cadres in U.S. agencies were aware of, and were in fact conducting exercises to prepare for and defeat – which included attempting to crash planes into important buildings. Complaint at ¶ 17.

Responsible intelligence officials were aware that Al Qaeda members were operating inside the U.S., and there were a number of critical investigative leads. Id. at ¶ 18.

Despite the flow of ominous information to various sections of the U.S. counterterrorism apparatus, and the danger

to innocent people – and as a result of the conspiracy among Defendants Cheney and Rumsfeld, and other members of the Government in various positions – the numerous warnings of a coming attack by Al Qaeda forces (as many as forty messages in all, according to the [Report of the 9/11 Commission], from eleven different countries) were studiously ignored. Id. at ¶ 19.

Defendants and others in the highest circles of Government knew more than enough beforehand about the imminent threat and gathering danger of an attack by Al Qaeda in the U.S. to understand that they needed to take strong thoroughgoing measures to increase the country's protections and alertness. Instead, led by Defendants Cheney and Rumsfeld, and because Defendants were callously indifferent to the rights and safety of innocents – including their own people in the Pentagon, Plaintiffs among them – the Government did not respond. *Id.* at ¶ 20.

Then U.S. Secretary of Transportation Norman Mineta testified before the

9/11 commission that when he arrived at the White House after the World Trade Center was struck, he was sent to the Presidential Emergency Operations Center ("PEOC"), and arrived at around 9:20 a.m., to find Cheney there, and in charge. He said he sat at a table with Cheney for the next period of time, during which a young man came in the room, three times, and informed the Vice President that an "unidentified plane" was approaching Washington, D.C., first at 50, then 30, and then 10 "miles out"; and that, when he reported the distance as 10 miles, the young man asked the vice president, "Do the orders still stand?" Secretary Mineta testified that defendant Cheney responded sharply, "Of course the orders still stand. Have you heard anything to the contrary?" Whereupon the young man left the room; and a few minutes later, the hit on the Pentagon was announced. This testimony by the Secretary has never been contested, discredited or explained away by any U.S. official. Plaintiff alleges that the "orders" were orders not to intercept or shoot down the approaching plane. If the orders had been to attack the approaching plane, it would have been shot down before it reached the Pentagon — or at least some attempt to stop it would have been made; and the world would know of it. *Id.* at ¶¶ 29, 30.

No interceptors came to defend the Pentagon, in particular Plaintiffs and other occupants, because of the actions and failures to act by Defendant Rumsfeld, Defendant General Myers and John Doe others in concert with them, even though more than an hour passed between the time the first warning went out to the Military, at or about 8:21 a.m., and the attack on the Pentagon at 9:32; even though the first tower was hit in a suicide crash in New York at least 46 minutes before the Pentagon was hit; and even though 'combat air patrol' jets from any of several bases in the region could have reached the Pentagon – or the path of flight 77 – in a fraction of that time. *Id.* at ¶ 24.

Plaintiffs' injuries could have been avoided had an alarm been sounded. Despite the undoubted knowledge of the Defendant commanders and operators in the system, however, that an unknown aircraft was headed towards Washington, possibly as part of the apparent terrorist suicide attack begun earlier in New York – and in spite of

well-established Pentagon emergency evacuation procedures and training – there was no alarm. *Id.* at ¶ 35.

Defendant Rumsfeld – like the President himself, then-National Security Adviser Condoleeza Rice, Defendant Gen. Richard Myers, and others – testified and said in public repeatedly that no one in the Government security apparatus ever imagined terrorists suicidally crashing planes into buildings. This claim is absolutely false. In point of fact, the CIA, the NSA, the FAA, and NORAD had planned and trained for just such a possibility. *Id.* at ¶ 54.

Gallop based the allegations in her Complaint regarding the Defendants' actions or lack of actions and lack of warnings, prior to and on 9/11, on, *inter alia*, the testimony (before the 9/11 Commission) of then Secretary of Transportation Norman Mineta; Richard Clark, then Director of Counterterrorism, as

recounted in his book "Against All Enemies"; published FAA records; and the 9/11 Commission Report: Final Report of the National Terrorist Attack Upon the United States (2004) (hereafter "9/11 Commission Report"); as well as her own observations and various publically available accounts of the circumstances surrounding the Pentagon and other 9/11 attacks. *Id.* at ¶¶ 16-17, 21-33.

Through their Complaint, Gallop and her son sought compensatory and punitive damages for (1) violations of her rights under the First, Fourth, Fifth, and Ninth Amendments to the United States Constitution pursuant to *Bivens v. Six Unknown Named Agents of Federal Bureau of Narcotics*, 403 U.S. 388 (1971); (2) the common law tort of conspiracy to cause death and great bodily harm; and (3) a violation of the Antiterrorism Act, 18 U.S.C. § 2333(a), which provides civil remedies to U.S. nationals injured by "an act of international terrorism."

On May 6, 2009, defendants moved to dismiss the Complaint on a variety of theories. The district court (Chin, J.) dismissed the Complaint with prejudice

as "factually frivolous" without reaching the other grounds for dismissal. *Gallop v. Cheney,* No. 08 Civ. 10881, 2010 WL 909203, at *3 (S.D.N.Y. Mar. 15, 2010). In performing its analysis pursuant to this Court's decision in *Ashcroft v. Iqbal*, 556 U.S. 662 (2009), the district court found most of Gallop's allegations to be unsupported "speculation and conjecture," *id.* at *5, and thus not entitled to be accepted as true. It found, however that the following allegations were not unsupported, and therefore assumed they were true:

Gallop alleges that government officials missed warnings that Al Qaeda was going to attack and that fighter jets had sufficient time to intercept the hijacked airplanes but failed to do so. I will assume, for purposes of this motion, that these factual allegations are true; after all, four commercial jetliners were hijacked and three of the four attacks succeeded.

Id. at *5. Nevertheless, the district court, finding the Complaint frivolous, stated that Gallop's claims that Defendants conspired to facilitate terrorist attacks

were not plausible, calling them "factually baseless," "because they are fanciful, fantastic and delusional." *Id.*

Gallop appealed the dismissal to the Second Circuit Court of Appeals, arguing, *inter alia*, that the district court, in dismissing the Complaint as frivolous, had misapplied *Iqbal*. Among other things, Gallop pointed out that since the district court found that the allegations that the government missed warnings (in point of fact, Gallop argued that the government "studiously ignored" warnings, Complaint at ¶¶ 17, 19, 20) that Al Qaeda was going to attack and that fighter jets had time to intercept hijacked planes but did not, were sufficiently pled and accepted them as true, it should then have considered, per *Iqbal*, whether those facts gave rise to a plausible claim or claims.

Shortly before the scheduled oral argument, the panel members scheduled to hear the appeal were announced and they included the Honorable John M. Walker, Jr., first cousin to President George H. W. Bush and first cousin, once removed, to President George W. Bush. Gallop, through counsel, immediately moved

– on April 4, 2011 – to disqualify Judge Walker, citing both his familial relationship to both Presidents and also that President George W. Bush would likely be deposed and would otherwise figure prominently in the litigation should it be permitted to proceed (Docs. 78, 79).

At the oral argument on April 5, 2011, Petitioner Veale asked the panel whether it had considered his motion to disqualify Judge Walker. He was told orally that the motion was denied and the denial was thereafter memorialized in an order dated April 26, 2011 (Doc. 89). At another point during oral argument, Judge Cabranes interrupted Mr. Veale's argument to ask him whether he was admitted to practice in the Second Circuit (Doc. 110, n.1).

In a decision dated April 27, 2011 (*"Gallop I"*), the panel affirmed the dismissal of the Complaint, finding that the Complaint's assertions consisted principally of "speculation" and "conjecture" and failed to "plausibly

allege the existence of a conspiracy." 642 F.3d at 368-69. Principally, the court held:

After a *de novo* review, we have no hesitation in concluding that the District Court correctly determined that the few conceivably "well-pleaded" facts in Gallop's complaint are frivolous. While, as a general matter, Gallop or any other plaintiff certainly may allege that the most senior members of the United States government conspired to commit acts of terrorism against the Untied States, the courts have no obligation to entertain pure speculation and conjecture. Indeed, in attempting to marshal a series of unsubstantiated and inconsistent allegations in order to explain why American Airlines Flight 77 did not crash into the Pentagon, the complaint fails to set forth a consistent, much less plausible, theory for what actually happened that morning in Arlington, Virginia. *See, e.g.,* Complaint ¶ 3 (alleging that defendants may have caused "high explosive charges to be detonated inside the Pentagon"); ¶ 21 (alleging that defendants "may have employed Muslim extremists to carry out suicide attacks; or ... may have used Muslim extremists as dupes or patsies"); *id.* (alleging that "four planes" were in fact hijacked on the morning of September 11); ¶ 33 (alleging that "[i]f Flight 77, or a substitute, did swoop low over the [Pentagon], to create the false impression of a suicide attack, it was then flown away by its pilot, or remote control, and apparently crashed somewhere else"); ¶ 40(d)(3) (alleging that apart from Flight 77 "a different, additional, flying object ... hit the Pentagon"); ¶ 43 (alleging that there "may have been a missile strike, perhaps

penetrating through to the back wall, which helped collapse the section that fell in, possibly augmented by explosives placed inside").

Gallop I, 642 F.3d at 368-69.

Having affirmed the dismissal of the Complaint, the court then considered, *sua sponte*, whether sanctions should be imposed under "Federal Rule of Appellate Procedure 38, 28 U.S.C. § 1927, and the inherent authority of the court to consider sanctions on parties who pursue patently frivolous appeals and force this Court to consider – and the government to defend – vexatious litigation." 642 F.3d at 370. The court stated that the appeal, "was brought without the slightest chance of success and therefore should not have been brought at all," and was an unnecessary imposition on the government and taxpayers. *Id.* (internal quotations and citations omitted). The court ordered "Gallop and her counsel" to "show cause in writing within thirty days from the date of entry of this order why they should not pay double costs and

damages in the amount of $15,000, for which they would be jointly and severally liable...." *Id.*

On June 13, 2011, Gallop, through her counsel, filed a petition for rehearing (Doc. 108) arguing, principally, that the panel "did not fairly assess the facts alleged in the complaint," or apply Fed. R. Civ. P. 8 and this Court's decision in *Ashcroft v. Iqbal*, 556 U.S. 662 (2009).

Shortly thereafter, on June 16, 2011, Gallop, through Petitioner Veale, moved to disqualify the three panel members collectively for bias that Petitioner Veale believed was evident from the court's April 27, 2011 opinion; Judge Walker individually for his relationship to the Bush family; and "any other members of the bench of this Circuit who share their feelings." (Doc. 110).

Mr. Veale stated that this case was an exception to the rule "that a judge can't be disqualified from a case for an action or ruling in that very case" (Doc. 110 at 4), because (1) the three panel members who decided the case had reacted based on emotion to the very idea of a 9/11 conspiracy and therefore failed to

give serious analysis to the legal sufficiency of the Complaint (*id.* at 1-9, 15-16); (2) the same panel had failed to disqualify Judge Walker from the panel deciding the appeal, evidencing a "biased frame of mind," (*id.* at 17-19); and (3) that there was a possibility that what Mr. Veale perceived as the reflexive bias of the three-member panel to the notion of a 9/11 conspiracy would also apply to members of the court *en banc*, because of the emotion associated with 9/11, particularly in New York (*id.* at 10-11, 15).

On July 7, 2011 the Second Circuit issued its ruling in "*Gallop II,*" denying the motion to disqualify the panel as well as the petition for rehearing. The court denied the motion to disqualify the panel, stating, "the only evidence Gallop proffers establishes no more than that the panel ruled against her … [and] that alone is insufficient to establish the sort of extreme antagonism required for disqualification." 645 F.3d at 520-21. It also denied the petition for panel rehearing. 645 F.3d at 521. The panel then focused on that part of Mr. Veale's

motion that "'demand[s]'" not only that the panel, but 'any other members of the bench of this Circuit who share their feelings[,] be recused.'" *Id.* Stating, "We know of no precedent for recusing *unnamed* judges based on a prejudice, the only evidence of which is manifested in a decision adverse to an attorney's (or a party's) interests," and concluding, "rather than pursuing his client's interests, Veale's actions appear to be malicious – intended, in bad faith, to use his position as an attorney of record to harass and disparage the Court." *Id.* The court then issued a second order to show cause, as follows:

Accordingly – wholly apart from the order to show cause required pursuant to our decision in *Gallop*, 642 F.3d at 370-71, for which briefs are now due on July 11, 2011 (for Gallop and her counsel) and July 14, 2011 (for the government) – William Veale is hereby ordered to show cause in writing within thirty days from the date of entry of this order why this Court should not impose additional sanctions pursuant to Federal Rule of Appellate Procedure 38, 28 U.S.C. § 1927, and the inherent authority of the Court, requiring him to provide appropriate notice to any federal court before which he appears of any sanctions that may be imposed against him by this Court.

Gallop II, 645 F.3d at 521.

On August 5, 2011, Petitioner Veale filed an

affidavit (Doc. 145-1) and memorandum of law (Doc. 145-3) in opposition to the additional sanctions proposed pursuant to the panel's decision of July 7, 2011. In his affidavit, Mr. Veale explained to the Court that the recusal motion was motivated by a sincere (even if erroneous) belief that the panel was predisposed against the Complaint or, at least, that the public might so perceive; that he believed (even if incorrectly) that this predisposition or appearance of predisposition was evidenced by various factors stated in his papers; and that he had neither the desire nor the intention to file a motion simply to harass and disparage the court generally or the panel members in particular. Additionally, he apologized to the court for the intemperance of certain of his arguments.

In his memorandum (Doc. 145-3), Mr. Veale's counsel referenced a survey they had conducted, which briefly set forth the relevant facts and asked whether an appearance of bias would be created

should Judge Walker (who was not named in the survey) be on the appellate panel. Eighty percent of the 100 survey respondents answered affirmatively. (*See* Doc. 145-2.)

On October 14, 2001, the panel issued an order pursuant to which (among other things): (1) "Dennis Cunningham, Mustapha Ndanusa, and William Veale are hereby ORDERED to pay the government double costs in addition to damages in the amount of $15,000..."; (2) the court declined "at this time" to impose sanctions on April Gallop; (3) Petitioner Veale was ordered, "for a period of one year from the date of entry of this order, to provide notice of the sanctions imposed upon him in this case to any court within this Circuit before which he appears, or seeks to appear"; and (4) Petitioner Cunningham was ordered "to show cause in writing within 30 days from the date of entry of this order why he should not be separately sanctioned by being required to provide appropriate notice to any court within this Circuit before which he appears, or seeks to appear, of the sanctions imposed against him in connection with this

appeal." *Gallop v. Cheney* ("*Gallop III*"), 660 F.3d 580, 586-87 (2d Cir. 2011). The panel, in its opinion, did not acknowledge or comment upon the survey reflecting that 80% of 100 respondents believed Judge Walker's "impartiality in this case might reasonably be questioned." The court based its imposition of monetary sanctions on its inherent power, F.R.A.P. 38, and 28 U.S.C. § 1927. *Gallop III*, 660 F.3d at 584.

On November 14, 2011, Dennis Cunningham filed an affidavit and Memorandum in Response to the court's order to show cause of October 14, 2011 (Doc. 162). On February 2, 2012, the panel issued its final opinion in this case. *Gallop v. Cheney*, 667 F.3d

226 (2d Cir. 2012) ("*Gallop IV*"). The panel took note of Mr. Cunningham's acknowledgment that his motion to disqualify "was made as a matter of righteous if overheated advocacy, and not in bad faith" and it further acknowledged his apology to the court for his "aggressive, judgmental, or 'jarring', words and

usages", but found that "these excuses do not adequately explain why a member of the Bar would demand that the members of the original panel and "any other members of the bench of this Circuit who share their feelings" be recused..." 667 F.3d at 230. The panel then imposed on Cunningham the same additional "scarlett letter" sanction it had imposed on Veale, namely, "that Cunningham shall be required, for a period of one year from the date of entry of this order, to provide notice of the sanctions imposed upon him in this case – both here and in our previous opinion entered October 14, 2011 – to any federal court in this Circuit before which he appears or seeks to appear." *Id.* The panel additionally reasserted its prior ruling that both Messrs. Veale and Cunningham pay double costs and a $15,000 fine. *Id.* at 231.

REASONS FOR GRANTING THE WRIT

Mr. Veale, a former Chief Assistant Public Defender in Contra Costa County, California for 32 years and lecturer on criminal trial practice at the University of California, Berkeley, Boalt Hall School of Law for 11 years (Doc. 145-1), and Mr. Cunningham, a

San Francisco and Oakland criminal and civil rights lawyer who has been counsel in numerous successful civil rights cases involving official misconduct over the last 30 years, were sanctioned by the circuit court for filing a frivolous appeal and for filing a motion to disqualify that the court deemed meritless and malicious rather than in the best interests of their clients.

The Second Circuit's *sua sponte* imposition of monetary and nonmonetary sanctions in this case was erroneous as a matter of law, as well as an abuse of discretion, for two reasons: (1) counsel had a legitimate basis for appealing the dismissal of Gallop's Complaint by the district court since the Complaint set forth at least some factual allegations that gave rise to plausible causes of action; thus, appealing the dismissal was neither frivolous nor sanctionable; and (2) that portion of counsels' motion to disqualify that asked any member of the court *en banc* with a

potential bias to recuse himself was not made in bad faith to harass or disparage the court, but rather was based on a number of factors, including Judge Walker's presence on the panel, the court's *sua sponte* order to show cause, the panel's unusual questioning of Petitioners' membership in the Second Circuit Bar during oral argument; and the geographical closeness of the court to the 9/11 attacks, that reasonably led them to question not only the panel's ability to decide their motion to reargue impartially, but also the ability of the *en banc* court to do so.

This Court should grant the writ, first because it presents an opportunity to give the lower courts much needed guidance regarding what constitutes a sanctionable "bad faith" filing and, secondly, because the court's imposition of sanctions in this case unquestionably will chill unpopular advocacy by attorneys, particularly those who would contemplate taking on politically sensitive or unpopular cases.

Twenty-one years ago, this Court held that a federal court has inherent authority to impose

monetary and nonmonetary sanctions "when a party has acted in bad faith, vexatiously, wantonly, or for oppressive reasons." *Chambers v. NASCO, Inc.*, 501 U.S. 32, 45-46 (1991). In the same decision, however, the Court made it clear that this power, "because of [its] very potency ... must be exercised with restraint and discretion." *Id.* at 44. A hallmark of the required "restraint and discretion" is the ability of the court to "fashion an appropriate sanction for conduct which *abuses* the judicial process." *Id.* at 44-45 (emphasis added). This Court has also warned, since *Chambers*, that the power to impose sanctions is uniquely "liable to abuse," because it appeals to "'the most vulnerable and human qualities of a judge's temperament,'" and leaves the offended court "solely responsible for identifying, prosecuting, adjudicating and sanctioning" the conduct in question. *International Union, UMWA v. Bagwell*, 512 U.S. 821, 831 (1994) (internal citations omitted).

Similarly, it is self-evident and has been recognized that F.R.A.P. 38, which provides for the imposition of damages and "single or double costs" where a court of appeals determines that an appeal was "frivolous," and 28 U.S.C. § 1927, which provides for imposition of costs, expenses, etc. for "multipl[ying] the proceedings in any case unreasonably and vexatiously," must not be applied in a way that has a chilling affect on vigorous advocacy or novel appeals. *See, e.g., Mone v. Commissioner of Internal Revenue*, 774 F.2d 570, 574 (2d Cir. 1985) (quoting *Eastway Construction Corp. v. City of New York*, 762 F.2d 243, 254 (2d Cir. 1985)) (recognizing power under statute and "potential for abuse" and stating that the statute should therefore "be construed narrowly and with great caution, so as not to stifle the enthusiasm or chill the creativity that is the very lifeblood of the law'"); *White v. General Motors Corp., Inc.*, 908 F.2d 669, 675 (10th Cir. 1990) (declining to hold sanctions appropriate for appeal even where presentation of issues in district court was bad enough to be sanctionable, since "[s]uch a draconian rule would make sanctions available in nearly every appeal of a case dismissed for failure to state a claim unless the appellant is successful. This would constitute too great a chill of advocacy."); *Lamboy-Ortiz v. Ortiz-Velez*, 630 F.3d 228, 250 (1st Cir. 2010) (noting courts must "exercise particular care in reviewing fee awards in civil rights cases to prevent the chilling of meritorious litigation"); *see also* Danielle Kie Hart, *Still Chilling After All These Years: Rule 11 Of The Federal Rules Of Civil Procedure And Its Impact On Civil Rights Plaintiffs After The 1993 Amendments,* 37 Val. U. L. Rev 1 (2002); Meehan Rasch, *Not Taking Frivolity Lightly: Circuit Variance in Determining Frivolous Appeals Under Federal Rule of Appellate Procedure 38,* 62 Ark. L. Rev. 249 (2009).

Regardless of whether or not the "conspiracy theories" espoused in the Complaint were implausible, the Complaint set forth facts that arguably gave rise to colorable causes of action. Assuming a frivolous appeal is one having no factual or legal basis, appealing the district court's dismissal of the Complaint was appropriate client advocacy, and not a "patently frivolous appeal[]," as held by the circuit court (Doc. 91-1). Gallop asserted, *inter alia,* a *Bivens* claim alleging injuries due to violations of her constitutional rights under the First, Fourth, Fifth, and Ninth Amendments. She set forth in the Complaint two factual allegations in support of those claims that were accepted as true by the district court: (1) that Defendants and others had recent intelligence that there was a serious possibility of a terrorist attack in the near future, if not imminently, and failed to act on that information; and (2) that on the day of the attack, Defendants and others had at least 30 minutes to react between the time the twin towers were hit by airplanes in New York and the attack on the Pentagon, had knowledge of at least one other plane heading towards Washington, D.C., and had prior intelligence that made it likely that the Pentagon would be that plane's target, yet failed to alert Pentagon employees and evacuate the building. *See* Complaint at ¶ 35. These factual assertions could not be – and in fact were not – dismissed as purely speculative, since Gallop supported them with evidence from various sources, including the 9/11 Commission Report and the testimony (before the 9/11 Commission) of then Secretary of Transportation Mineta. Furthermore, these factual assertions did not depend on a conspiracy theory to be the basis for a plausible cause of action. These claims were potentially cognizable under, for example, the Fifth Amendment, which applies "to a narrow band of extreme misbehavior by government agents acting under color of law: mistreatment that is 'so egregious, so outrageous, that it may fairly be said to shock the contemporary conscience.'" *Arar v. Ashcroft*, 585 F.3d 559, 589 (2d Cir. 2009) (quoting *Lombardi v. Whitman*, 485 F.3d 73, 79 (2d Cir. 2007)).

Under these circumstances, as a matter of law, Petitioners did not act unreasonably, vexatiously, or frivolously, when they appealed on Plaintiffs' behalf to the Second Circuit, asserting that the Complaint stated a cause of action that the district court had dismissed without an appropriate *Iqbal* analysis. Surely, if Defendants and other government officials, for whatever reason, ignored recent threats of Al Qaeda terrorism and failed to warn and evacuate people from the Pentagon on 9/11 when they had knowledge that a plane might possibly, or even was likely to, hit the Pentagon, their conduct could be considered "so egregious as to shock the contemporary conscience" and therefore provide the basis for at least a colorable cause of action that the district court had ignored. *Id.*

Rather than send an appropriate message that patently bad-faith, frivolous, and vexatious appeals will not be tolerated, the circuit's imposition of sanctions against Petitioners counsels the Bar to abandon their advocacy on behalf of marginalized plaintiffs or sensitive or unpopular causes when a district court characterizes their complaint as "fanciful," "fantastic" or "delusional."

This Court has warned that the inherent authority to sanction counsel must be exercised with great restraint and discretion. *Chambers*, 501 U.S. at 45-46. Surely that warning was intended, at least in part, to assure attorneys that they can confidently bring novel, untested, and even politically unpopular claims, without fear that their advocacy will be met with sanctions. For the Second Circuit to have sanctioned counsel for appealing an adverse decision under these circumstances sends the opposite message, from a very influential circuit, that the courts need have little tolerance for politically unpopular or novel claims.

Nor was Mr. Veale's motion to disqualify "entirely without color" and, thus, in bad faith. To the extent that his motion sought disqualification of the three-member panel that heard Gallop's appeal, it was based on Mr. Veale's perception that the court was scornful of his argument, not only because of the content and tone of its decision, but based as well on an unusual exchange during oral argument in which his bona fides as a lawyer admitted to practice before the court were questioned. Additionally, the same panel had refused to disqualify Judge Walker, whose presence created at least the *appearance* of a conflict of interest, even recognizing this Court's *dicta* that familial relationship beyond the third degree is not *alone* grounds for disqualification under 28 U.S.C. § 455(a), *see Liteky v. United States*, 510 U.S. 540, 552-53 (1994). Indeed, fully 80% of respondents in the survey conducted by Petitioner Veale's counsel agreed that Judge Walker's participation in this appeal created an appearance of unfairness. (Doc. 145-2.) Yet, in its decision imposing sanctions the Second Circuit did not even acknowledge this survey.

In light of the foregoing, Mr. Veale's request (which was mentioned only in passing in a single sentence of his motion to disqualify the panel) that any members of the court *en banc* who believed they might have a bias against Plaintiffs' assertion of a 9/11 conspiracy disqualify themselves as well, was not unreasonable. The court called Mr. Veale's request futile because it knew of "no precedent for recusing *unnamed* judges" (emphasis in original) based on prejudice "the only evidence of which is manifested in a decision adverse to an attorney's (or a party's) interests." *Gallop II*, 645 F.3d at 521. As discussed above, the adverse decision was not, in fact, the only evidence of potential bias on which Mr. Veale based his request. That the request may also have been unprecedented did not make it meritless, and that it may have been futile was certainly no reason to impose sanctions. Indeed, almost any appeal brought in a circuit court might be deemed "futile" given the small likelihood that any appellant will obtain a reversal.

Additionally, in the opinion of the court, Mr. Veale's actions, "rather than pursuing his client's interests," were "malicious – intended, in bad faith, to use his position as an attorney of record to harass and disparage the court." *Id.* It is self-evident, however, that contrary to the court's finding, it could only be in Ms. Gallop's best interest, as it would be for any litigant, to have an unbiased panel, particularly since this would be her last shot at having her lawsuit go forward. It is difficult to see in whose interest Mr. Veale was acting if not in his client's, since it made no sense to "use his position" as an attorney to incur the wrath of the very court he hoped to convince to grant his motion for a rehearing. Although it is difficult for any court to determine counsel's motivations, certainly an attorney should be presumed to be acting in his client's interest when, if he wins his motion, his client benefits.

The courts obviously may not sanction counsel for bringing appeals or making motions that are objectively reasonable regardless of the likelihood of their ultimate success. On the facts here, the circuit court's imposition of sanctions was inappropriate as a matter of law or, at the least, an abuse of discretion. As this Court and others have noted, the "court" is all too human in that it is composed of no more or less than men and women. As one judge aptly stated:

In the performance of the judicial function, a court like any other person in authority too easily can lose sight of its otherwise dispassionate review of the facts and the law when it considers without a prior exchange of reasoning an assessment of sanctions. "A judge awarding sanctions is often advocating the correctness of his decision and is likely to do so convincingly.... [A court in an] opinion 'has the power to make an attorney's argument seem frivolous.'" Nelken, Sanctions Under Rule 11 – Some "Chilling Problems in the Struggle Between Compensation and Punishment, 74 Geo. L.J. 1313, 1339-40 & n.172 (1986) (citation omitted); see also Weinstein v. University of Illinois, 811 F.2d at 1099 (7th Cir. 1987) (Cudahy, J., dissenting from sua sponte award of sanctions). This tendency can become compelling when the court, in the absence of a request by a party and on its own motion, determines to assess sanctions.

Hill v. Norfolk and Western Ry. Co., 814 F.2d 1192, 1203 (7th Cir. 1987) (Senior District Judge Parsons, dissenting in part).

It has been noted as well that the imposition of sanctions by appellate courts has, for many reasons, "increased markedly." See Hill, 814 F.2d at 1203; Eltech Sys. Corp. v. PPG Industries, Inc., 903 F.2d 805, 811 (Fed. Cir. 1990). This is a troublesome trend and one this Court should address and redress through a grant of certiorari in this case.

CONCLUSION

For the foregoing reasons, the petition for a writ of certiorari should be granted.

Respectfully submitted,

RICHARD WARE LEVITT

LEVITT & KAIZER

40 Fulton Street, 23rd Floor

New York, New York 10038

(212) 480-4000
Attorneys for Petitioners
APPENDIX E
UNITED STATES DISTRICT COURT
SOUTHERN DISTRICT OF NEW YORK ___
APRIL GALLOP, for Herself and as Mother
and Next Friend of ELISHA GALLOP, a Minor, No.

Plaintiff, **Jury Trial Demanded**

DICK CHENEY, Vice President of the U.S.A.,
DONALD RUMSFELD, former U.S. Secretary
of Defense, General RICHARD MYERS, U.S.A.F.
(Ret.), and John Does Nos. 1– X, all in their
individual capacities,
Defendants.

COMPLAINT FOR VIOLATION OF CIVIL RIGHTS, CONSPIRACY, AND OTHER WRONGS
PRELIMINARY STATEMENT

This case arises from the infamous Attack on America of Sept 11, 2001, and especially on the Pentagon; and is premised on an allegation of broad complicity in the attack on the part of key U.S. Government officials, beginning with and led from the top by Vice President Dick Cheney, then-Secretary of Defense Donald Rumsfeld, and Richard Myers, then acting Chairman of the Joint Chiefs of Staff. The plaintiffs allege that these and other government officials, whose identities will be ascertained from their proven or evident relevant roles and activities, and who are named herein as 'John Doe' defendants, together with other known and unknown operatives and functionaries, official and otherwise, engaged in an unlawful conspiracy, or a set of related, ongoing conspiracies, in which the concrete objective was to facilitate and enable the hijacking of the airliners, and their use as living bombs to attack buildings containing thousands of innocent victims; and then to cover up the truth about what they had done.

The defendants' purpose in aiding and facilitating the attack, and the overall object of the conspirac(ies), was to bring about an unprecedented, horrifying and frightening catastrophe of terrorism inside the United States, which would give rise to a powerful reaction of fear and anger in the public, and in Washington. This would generate a political atmosphere of acceptance in which the new Administration could enact and implement radical changes in the policy and practice of constitutional government in our country. Much of their intention was spelled out prior to their coming into office, in publications of the so-called Project for the New American Century, of which defendants Cheney and Rumsfeld were major sponsors. There they set forth specific objectives regarding the projection of U.S. military power abroad, particularly in Iraq, the Persian Gulf, and other oil-producing areas. They observed, however, that the American people would not likely support the actions the sponsors believed were necessary, without being shocked into a new outlook by something cataclysmic: "a new Pearl Harbor". By helping the attack succeed, defendants and their cohorts created a basis for the seizure of extraordinary power, and a pretext for launching the so-called Global War on Terror, in the guise of which they were free to pursue plans for military conquest, "full spectrum dominance" and "American primacy" around the world; as they have doneIn pursuit of the goals of the conspiracy, the named and unnamed defendants knowingly and by agreement committed a series of acts and omissions which were aimed at and did generally accomplish the following objectives:

+ To permit the men they later identified as the hijackers and any immediate accomplices to enter and remain in the country, and carry out the activities, movements and communications needed in their preparations for the hijacking, free from interference by police or counter-terrorist authorities; and then allow the groups of these men to book passage, all on the same day, and board the flights;

+ To cause normal operation of the regular off-course airline flight interception practice of the US Air Force, in cooperation with civil flight control authorities, to be altered, suspended or disrupted in such a way as to remove its protections, at least on that day, and thus permit three of the four apparently hijacked planes to reach their targets and crash into them (or appear to do so...);

+ To cause the normal operation of ground and air defenses which guard the Pentagon
from external attack to be altered, suspended or disrupted in such a way as to remove or negate the building's normal protections, and thus permit an airliner, believed to be hijacked by possible suicide bombers, and following a forbidden, descending flight path, to reach the Pentagon undeterred;

+ To cause and arrange for high explosive charges to be detonated inside the Pentagon, and/or a missile of some sort to be fired at the building, at or about the time the wayward airliner supposedly arrived there, to give the false impression that hijackers had crashed the plane into the building, as had apparently happened in New York;

+ To arrange, thereafter, and fabricate, propound and defend, as part of the conspiracy, an elaborate, highly complex and sophisticated cover-up, centering around the Report of the 9/11 Commission, and continuing to this day. To this end, defendants misappropriated the highest authority of government to block, misdirect and otherwise evade any fair, independent investigation of the evidence, and officially if implausibly explain away the evident wholesale failure of America's defenses with misinformation, omissions and distortions, withheld and destroyed evidence, and outright lies.

In the attack on the Pentagon, in particular, plaintiff avers that the official story, that a hijacked plane crashed into the Pentagon and exploded (causing the plaintiff's injuries), is false. In fact, the bombing was accomplished another way, so as to limit the damage, protect the defendants, and only make it appear that a plane had been crashed into the building. This claim is supported by data from the plane's supposed "black box", released by the National Transportation Safety Board (NTSB), which indicate the plane passed over the building at very low altitude, just as an explosion and fireball were engineered by other means, a planted bomb or bombs and/or a missile. This is supported by the lack of any photographic evidence of a wrecked airliner at the Pentagon, compounded by the record of reported refusal by the U.S. Department of Justice to release some 85 video tapes from surveillance cameras in locations at or near the Pentagon, which it has declared exempt from Freedom of Information Act disclosure.

Whatever way the bombing of the Pentagon was accomplished, however, and whatever else may or may not have been done by defendants to facilitate the hijackings that day, it is clear the defendant top commanders would have had and did have, at a profound minimum, enough foreknowledge, on that day and in the intelligence information they received beforehand, to have sounded a warning in time for plaintiff and others to evacuate the building, and thereby avoid much if not all the death and injury which occurred. In the end, more than half an hour passed after flight controllers first sounded the alert on Flight 77, while all concerned were fully aware of the suicide crashes in New York; plenty of time for the Pentagon to be evacuated. 'Top gun' jet fighter-interceptors under defendants' command, available with time to spare, were not summoned; and the people in the building, including plaintiff and her infant, were not

warned. This was the result of unlawful conspiracy among these highest-level commanders, and others, who acted knowingly and intentionally to have the Pentagon attacked or to allow it to be attacked, without warning, with deliberate indifference to and in reckless and callous disregard for the fundamental constitutional and human rights of plaintiff and her child, and many other people, dead, injured and bereaved.

Plaintiff April Gallop brings this action for herself and as next friend of her son Elisha Gallop now aged 7, who was a two-month-old baby in her arms on that day, her first back from maternity leave. She was a career member of the US Army, a ranking specialist with top secret clearance, who had served six years, two-and-a-half of them in Germany, before being assigned to the Pentagon in 2000. Her desk was roughly 40 feet from the point where the plane allegedly hit the outside wall. As she sat down to work there was an explosion, then another; walls collapsed and the ceiling fell in. Hit in the head, she was able to grab the baby and make her way towards the daylight showing through a blasted opening in the outside wall. There was no airplane wreckage and no burning airplane fuel anywhere; only rubble and dust. Plaintiff and her baby both suffered substantial head and brain injuries, which seriously affect them still today. Plaintiff charges that, because of the conspiracy alleged herein, she and her child and others were injured by acts of terrorism participated in by defendants. Further, as more fully described within at Pars 57-59, she and her child were and subsequently have been denied fundamental rights — including by acts of retaliation against her for raising painful questions about what occurred — as the cover-up continues.

JURISDICTION & VENUE

This Court has **jurisdiction** of this case, as follows:

Under the First, Fourth, Fifth and Ninth Amendments to the U.S. Constitution, as applied to federal officials under the rule of *Bivens v Six Unknown Named Agents*, 403 U.S. 388 (1971); and 28 USC 1331;

Under the federal Common Law — given that the most direct occurrences and mechanisms of plaintiffs' injuries, no doubt including crucial agreements and other communications among various defendants, took place in the Pentagon, a federal enclave — giving plaintiff a right of action in this Court for conspiracy to commit and facilitate actions likely to cause wrongful death, great bodily injury, terror and other loss to plaintiff and others to whom defendants owed a special duty of care; where, instead, defendants acted with reckless and callous disregard for and deliberate indifference to the likelihood of great harm to plaintiff and others, and deprivation of their rights;

Under the Terrorism Acts, 18U.S.Code 2333(a), for acts of terrorism brought about by actions wholly outside the scope of defendants' duties, in perversion of their authority, and beyond the bounds or color of any law; and therefore not exempt or immune under the provisions of Sec. 2337, the application of which to exonerate these defendants would be unconstitutional.

Venue for the case is set by the special provisions of the Air Transportation Safety Act of September, 2001, 49 U.S.C. 40101, Subsection 408(b)(3), bringing all claims arising from events of 9/11 to this honorable Court .

PARTIES

Plaintiff APRIL GALLOP is an American citizen, resident of the State of Virginia, a member until this year of the U.S. Army, stationed at the Pentagon on 9/11, claiming for herself and for her minor child, ELISHA GALLOP, who was just two months old on 9/

11/01, and was with her when the building was hit. Plaintiff respectfully petitions the Court to appoint her as guardian *ad litem* for the purposes of this action and related matters.

Defendants are DICK CHENEY, the Vice President of the United States;

DONALD RUMSFELD, formerly and at relevant times Secretary of Defense of the U.S.; Gen. RICHARD MYERS, then acting chairman of the Joint Chiefs of Staff; all sued in their individual capacities. Additional named, unknown defendants are other persons who were and are co-actors and co-conspirators in sundry phases of the (terrorist) undertaking complained of herein, whose identities, and some of whose precise places or functions in the plot(s) alleged herein are not yet known or fully known, but who certainly include high-ranking members of the Defense Department, the Military, the C.I.A., the F.B.I. and other agencies. Such persons are named and alleged as co-defendants, designated as John Does Nos.1-X and hereby notified of this action, *pro tanto*, to be identified for the record and impleaded by plaintiffs as the particulars of both culpable and innocent acts and omissions by everyone involved in these events become known.

Existence of a Class. Plaintiff notes that a number of other persons suffered injury and loss in the Pentagon on September 11 as she did, and are similarly situated to her, plainly within the provisions of Rule 23, F.R.Civ P., so that she represents a Class, the members of which evidently are also entitled to recover judgment as sought herein. She does not now assert the Class interest; but, where it appears there could be action by the Court affecting this question, and a class could emerge, she wishes to and does hereby reserve the right, subject to the Court's approval, to act as lead plaintiff.

Limitations. There is no time bar to the claims in this action. The Statute does not run against plaintiff's child, as a minor, under Virginia law (Va. Code Ann., §8.01-229). As to the plaintiff herself, defendants and their cohorts and agents, by means of elaborate planned and other ad hoc cover stories, public lying, alteration of records, misappropriation of official authority and other nefarious activities, have concealed and continue to conceal, fraudulently, the truth about the attacks and the way they occurred — and their own participation and complicity in the range of acts and omissions needed, in furtherance of conspiracy, to bring them about. Likewise, the original conspiracy to act secretly in furtherance of terrorism, and lie and dissemble afterwards, in order to foment war and vengeance against the supposed perpetrators, has stayed alive and continued to harm the plaintiff, as she will show.

STATEMENT OF FACTS

Background: Al Qaeda and the 9/11 Attack

14. **As the world knows, four large commercial airliners filled with ordinary passengers were reported hijacked in the northeastern United States the morning of September 11, 2001. Two were evidently crashed into the World Trade Center towers in New York, which later collapsed; a third was said to have hit the Pentagon in Washington DC, and the fourth, supposedly aiming for the White House or the Capitol, was reported crashed in Pennsylvania by its passengers, fighting back against the hijackers.**

15. **The alleged hijackers were quickly identified by US authorities, supposedly from passenger lists, as 19 men of Middle Eastern descent, fifteen from Saudi Arabia, two from the United Arab Emirates, one Egyptian and one Lebanese.** Their pictures, apparent police mug shots, were shown

on TV around the world soon after the attack. It emerged that some if not all of these men were already known to police and intelligence authorities in the US and elsewhere as terrorist suspects. They were said to be associated with Al-Qaeda, a network of radical 'Islamic' militants, led by the renegade Saudi aristocrat Osama bin Laden, and pledged to unremitting 'holy war' against the United States and its people. Al Qaeda was blamed for several previous terrorist attacks, including suicide attacks in which hundreds died, in the Middle East and Africa, and against a U.S. Navy warship in the Persian Gulf. An earlier, precursor group of 'Islamist' terrorists, based in Brooklyn and New Jersey, carried out the first bombing of the World Trade Center, in 1993.

16. At the time the Clinton Administration was succeeded by that of George W. Bush and defendant Dick Cheney, in January, 2001, an extensive, complex U.S. counter-terrorism effort against Al Qaeda was in progress, involving personnel and resources from a number of government agencies, including the FBI, the CIA, the NSA, the U.S. Military, and others, requiring coordination between these agencies at the highest levels. The Chief of Counterterrorism under President Clinton, Richard Clarke, was retained by Bush, but later strongly criticized the Bush Administration for ignoring the Al Qaeda threat, allowing the effort begun under Clinton to lapse, to the point where he felt constrained to apologize to the families of those who died, for the failure he said led directly to the devastation of September 11th. At all events, it is clear from the accounts of Clarke and others that, once Mr. Bush and Defendant Cheney were in office, the effort to combat Al Qaeda was decisively blunted at the top, and at key points down the chain of command.

17. In particular, little or no attention was paid by defendants and others responsible to an increasingly explicit series of warnings, during 2001, that Al Qaeda was hoping and planning to strike inside the US; and that there were concrete plans — which cadres in U.S.

agencies were aware of, and were in fact conducting exercises to prepare for, and defeat — which included attempting to crash planes into important buildings. U.S. investigators were well aware that the man they believed was the enemy network's chief bomb-maker for the 1993 attack on the Trade Center, Ramzi Youssef, had hoped and attempted to bring a tower down in that attack; and that this remained a goal of the group.

18. Responsible intelligence officials were aware that Al Qaeda members were operating inside the U.S., and there were a number of critical investigative leads. Two of the hijackers-to-be lived with an FBI informant in San Diego. The CIA monitored a meeting in Malaysia in 1999, after which two of the participants came to the U.S., where authorities supposedly lost track of them. There were reports from FBI field offices in Arizona and elsewhere that figures on the suspect list were taking or seeking training as pilots — including one who reportedly said he only wanted to learn how to fly an airliner, not how to land or take off — but coordination and follow-up investigation on these and other leads was blocked by John Doe defendant CIA and FBI higher-ups and key players. Notwithstanding such malfeasance, the signs and portents of an imminent attack were very strong in the summer of 2001. As the then CIA chief George Tenet testified, "The system was blinking red."

19. Despite the flow of ominous information to various sections of the US counterterrorism apparatus, however, and the danger to innocent people — and as a result of conspiracy among defendants Cheney and Rumsfeld, and other members of the Government in various positions — the many warnings of a coming attack by Al Qaeda forces (as many as forty messages in all, according to the Commission Report, from eleven different countries) were studiously ignored.

20. That is, defendants and others in the highest circles of the Government knew more than enough beforehand about the threat

and gathering danger of an imminent possible attack by Al Qaeda in the U.S. to understand that they needed to take strong, thorough-going measures to increase the country's protections and alertness. Instead, led by defendants Cheney and
Rumsfeld, and because defendants were callously indifferent to the rights and safety of innocents — including their own people in the Pentagon, plaintiff among them — the government did not re-spond. On information and belief, no special meetings of high offi-cials and agency heads were called, to make sure protections systems were on high alert and functioning properly, and that all needed information was being shared. No special warnings were given to the Federal Aviation Administration, the Immigration Service, the Military and other affected agencies. No consultations were had about possible methods of attack, including specifics about possible hijackings, and the use of planes as missiles to hit buildings, despite operational planning and training which had already occurred at lower echelons. The FBI did not step up surveillance of suspected terrorist individuals or "cells", or immigration checks, or let such people know they were being watched, in order to impede their activities; and it appears that no coordinated, high-level monitor-ing and analysis of the threats, and planning for counteraction, ever took place. Instead, the threat was dismissed, and ignored.

21. It should be noted that plaintiff cannot and does not know with certainty the outlines of the plot at its initiation. The attacks may have been conceived of as a false-flag operation from the be-ginning, with the defendants and their operatives as creators, plan-ners, and executors, with the assistance of others as necessary. Or, defendants may have employed Muslim extremists to carry out sui-cide attacks; or they may have used Muslim extremists as dupes or patsies. The roles of the supposed "nineteen" could have been to hijack the airliners, or simply, unwittingly, to be on the planes

when they were crashed into buildings by remote control. It is also possible that the defendants learned of a plot originated by Muslim extremists, and co-opted or overrode it with their own plan. Whatever lay in the minds of the defendant conspirators at the outset, it is clear that the nineteen men so quickly identified as the hijackers, some if not all of them known terrorist suspects, traveling under their own names, simply walked onto the four planes that morning, with their "box cutters", without hindrance or incident.

Failure of the Air Defense System.

22. Accounts from the FAA and the National Military Command Center vary widely, suffer from internal contradictions, and are in conflict with each other; but credible reports show that FAA flight controllers were aware of a problem with the first plane as early as 8:14 or 8:15 a.m. the morning of September 11th, and evidently called the military for emergency assistance, pursuant to routine, by 8:21 a.m. or thereabouts. They learned the second plane was off course and not responding a short time later. According to reports, United Flight 11 hit the WTC North Tower at 8:46 a.m. and Flight 175 hit the South Tower at 9:03. The Pentagon was hit at or about 9:32 a.m. — although the official version says 9:38 — and the fourth plane crashed in Pennsylvania shortly after 10:00 a.m. High performance jet fighter planes stationed at various bases around the northeastern U.S. — tasked to intercept and deal with unidentified or straying aircraft entering or flying in U.S. airspace under NORAD district command, or otherwise at NORAD's disposal — were available at a moment's notice. None were notified, however, or sent to the right place, until it was too late; at least for the first three planes.

23. No interceptor planes came to stop the supposed hijackers

— shoot them down if necessary — even though the Air Force
has for many years maintained a practice of immediate response in
which the fighters have readily been "scrambled" when aircraft are
seen to go too far off course, or lose radio contact with flight controllers. The interceptor program has been an elite assignment in
the Air Force, even after the Cold War ended, in which pilots fly
regularly, and wait in 'ready rooms' near the hangars, and planes
are kept in top condition, with engines warm and ready for takeoff. The best jets are used, which can reach speeds of 1600-1800
miles per hour, and the personnel are so well trained and practiced
that pilots routinely go from hearing the scramble order to 29,000
feet in less than three minutes. The scramble orders are normally
made by local NORAD commanders in cooperation with the
FAA. Both the FAA and the affected NORAD North East Air Defense Sector (NEADS) military command have radar tracking cov-
erage of the entire airspace, and special telephone hotlines between
them and with higher authority. Nor are these forays rare, reportedly occurring once or twice a week at various U.S. locales during
the past several years. Published Federal Aviation Administration
(FAA) records showed that, between September 1, 2000 and June 1,
2001, interceptor jets took to the air 67 times to check on "in-flight
emergencies" involving wayward planes.

24. No interceptors came to defend the Pentagon, in particular,
and plaintiff and the other occupants, because of actions and failures
to act by defendant Rumsfeld, Defendant General Myers and John
Doe others in concert with them, even though more than an hour
passed between the time the first warning went out to the Military,
at or about 8:21a.m., and the attack on the Pentagon at 9:32; even
though the first tower was hit in a suicide crash in New York at least
46 minutes before the Pentagon was hit; and even though 'combat
air patrol' jets from any of several bases in the region could have
reached the Pentagon — or the path of Flight 77 — in a fraction of

that time.

25. Having pre-arranged a coordinated failure of the Pentagon defenses, and its warning system, the defendants hid and distracted themselves, and otherwise failed to act, just at the time they were needed to ensure defense of the building; and they have dissembled ever since, as part of the conspiracy, in representing where they were and what they did during that time. As with the planes that hit the towers in New York, the Military and the 9/11 Commission, while failing to cast blame, explained away the failure to launch fighter interceptors at the Pentagon as the result of a failure by flight controllers — which FAA personnel deny — to notify the Air Force of the flight emergencies in a timely way. This was cover-up, in furtherance of the conspiracy.

26. Likewise, by the acts of one or more defendants in further-ance of the conspiracy, no defenses at the Pentagon responded ei-ther, no missile or anti-aircraft batteries opening from the ground around the building, or the roof; no sharpshooters deployed with hand-held missiles at stations close by; nothing. And, shockingly, when the towers in New York had already been hit, and Flight 77 (or a substitute, see below) was out of radio contact and headed back towards the capital; and even when the plane approached, and then doubled back and headed toward the building in a long dive, no alarm was sounded.

27. It is evident, particularly with respect to the attack on the Pentagon in which the plaintiff and her baby were injured, that, if the building was hit by a plane that morning, or if, as appears more likely, a plane flew low over the building at the time the bomb(s) went off inside and/or the missile hit, to give the (false) impression of a crash, some form of order or restriction was in force which sus-pended normal operation of the building's defenses. In particular, it is indisputable that the expected response of the fighter-intercep-tors failed completely; and plaintiff avers this resulted from orders

or authorization from within the defendant circle of Rumsfeld and Myers and their helpers, restraining normal operation of the protections system and armaments at the Pentagon — including but not limited to jets available at various bases near the capital.

28. Plaintiff alleges further that such "standdown" orders, in whatever manner or form
they had been prepared or issued, were maintained and affirmed by defendants up to and through that morning, and that defendant Cheney in particular, operating in the underground command bunker (Presidential Emergency Operations Center, or PEOC) beneath the White House, personally affirmed such an order. His word kept the order in force during the period between 9:20 a.m., when he was observed in the Bunker and the moment the Pentagon was hit.

29. In this connection, plaintiff refers the Court to the testimony of then-U.S. Secretary of Transportation Norman Mineta to the 9/11 Commission. Mineta testified that when he arrived at the White House, he was sent to the PEOC, and arrived at around 9:20 a.m., to find Cheney there, and in charge. He said he sat at a table with Cheney for the next period of time, during which a young man came in the room, three times, and informed the Vice President that an "unidentified plane" was approaching Washington, D.C., first at 50, then 30, and then 10 "miles out"; and that, when he reported the distance as 10 miles, the young man asked the vice president, "Do the orders still stand?" Secretary Mineta testified that defendant Cheney responded sharply, "Of course the orders still stand. Have you heard anything to the contrary?" Whereupon the young man left the room; and a few minutes later, the hit on the Pentagon was announced. This testimony by the Secretary has never been contested, discredited or explained away by any U.S. official.

30. Plaintiff alleges that the "orders" were orders not to intercept or shoot down the approaching plane. If the orders had been

to attack the approaching plane, it would have been shot down before it reached the Pentagon — or at least some attempt to stop it would have been made; and the world would know of it. Based on some two hundred years of American military history, the failure would have led to a Board of Inquiry or other public official investigation, to determine how and why the defense apparatus had failed. Individuals would have been called to account, and disciplinary procedures followed resulting in findings of responsibility and demotions or formal charges against those found to have failed the Country. All of these bureaucratic events would have become part of the official record, and known to the public; none of which has happened. There has been no publicly recorded disciplinary action against any military or civilian officer of the United States government as a result of the attacks of September 11th. Such proceedings would have created a great risk that the truth would be exposed.

31. The public record also shows that no meaningful follow-up questioning of Sec. Mineta occurred before the 9/11 Commission; that defendant Cheney has never testified under oath or been reasonably questioned about these events; and that he has given contradictory accounts, one of which---the account he gave to Tim Russert on "Meet the Press" five days after 9/11--- conflicts with The 9/11 Commission Report. The 9/11 Commission Report adopts an unsworn statement by Cheney that he never reached the bunker until about 10:00 a.m.; and contains no reference to Mineta's testimony, ignoring completely this contradiction between the two high government officials. The Commission also ignores the fact that Richard Clarke's book "Against All Enemies" supports Mineta's testimony and hence contradicts the 9/11 Commission's account.

32. Plaintiff charges that, in point of fact, the "orders" referred to were orders not to shoot the plane down, but to let it proceed, and that such orders were given and/or approved by defendants

Cheney, Rumsfeld, and Myers, pursuant to the root conspiracy alleged herein, and transmitted down a chain of command. The normal expected operation of Pentagon defense that day was thus prevented, allowing the attack to succeed, or to "succeed" in creating a false and deceptive scenario of a plane crash.

The Attack on the Pentagon.

At the Pentagon, the plaintiff was at her desk, with her baby, in her office on the first floor, when large explosions occurred, walls crumbled and the ceiling fell in. Although her desk is just some forty feet from the supposed impact point, and she went out through the blown-open front of the building afterwards, she never saw any sign that an airliner crashed through. If Flight 77, or a substitute, did swoop low over the building, to create the false impression of a suicide attack, it was then flown away by its pilot, or remote control, and apparently crashed someplace else. At the building, inside or outside of the wall the plane supposedly hit, there was no wreckage, no airplane fragments, no engines, no seats, no luggage, no fuselage sections with rows of windows, and especially, no blazing quantities of burning jet fuel. The interior walls and ceilings and contents in that area were destroyed, but there was no sign of a crashed airplane. A number of those present inside the building and out have attested to this fact in published reports.

Instead, just when plaintiff turned on her computer — for an urgent document-clearing job she was directed by her supervisor to rush and begin, as soon as she arrived at work, without dropping her baby off at child care until she was finished — a huge explosion occurred, and at least one more that she heard and felt, and flames shot out of the computer. Walls crumbled, the ceiling fell in, and she was knocked unconscious. When she came to, terrified and in pain, she found the baby close by, picked him up, and, with other survivors caught in the area, made her way through rubble, smoke and dust towards daylight, which was showing through an open space that now gaped in the outside wall. When she reached the outside she collapsed on the grass; only to wake up in a hospital some time later.

Plaintiff's injuries could have been avoided, had an alarm been sounded. However, despite the undoubted knowledge of the defendant commanders and operators in the system that an unknown aircraft was headed towards Washington, possibly as part of the apparent terrorist suicide attack begun earlier in New York — and in spite of well-established Pentagon emergency evacuation procedures and training — there was no alarm. On the contrary, plaintiff was directed to go straight to her desk when she arrived at work, and when she got there, and turned her computer on, the place blew up. If an unauthorized non-military plane was headed towards the building, on a day when two apparently hijacked planes had hit the Twin Towers, why wasn't she evacuated, with her baby, instead of hurried inside? Why weren't alarms going off, and all the people in the building rushing to safety? Due to the conspiracy, and defendants' actions and flagrant failures to act, in furtherance of it, one hundred and twenty-five people, members of the Military and civilian employees, died in the bombing; and many more including plaintiff and her child were seriously hurt.

Plaintiff alleges further that, pursuant to the conspiracy, the attack on the Pentagon was contrived to "succeed" in only a very limited way. Destruction, death and injuries, in comparison to what would have occurred if the building had been attacked straight on with a large plane, by enemies bent on causing the greatest possible devastation and loss of life, were kept to a minimum; and the conspirators themselves not put at risk. Certainly the official account of what occurred is full of gross anomalies, which contradict the physical evidence, the scientific and aeronautical evidence, and the laws of physics and aerodynamics. The 9/11 Commission Report is exposed as an artifact of the conspiracy, aimed at covering up the fact that no airliner crashed into the Pentagon, and that it was bombed a different way.

The official account established in the 9/11 Commission hearings is that American Airlines Flight 77, a Boeing 757-200 jetliner, took off from Dulles International Airport at or about 8:20 a.m., and apparently was hijacked at about 8:55 a.m. some two or three hundred miles west of Washington. Radio contact was lost and the plane's "transponder" was turned off. At that point, Flight 77 was traversing an apparent radar "dead zone", located over the southeast Ohio-West Virginia borderland, where another similar plane, fitted with radio control reception equipment, may have been substituted, so as to ensure that the precise maneuvers required by the conspirators' plan could be carried out. Whichever plane it was soon established a flight path leading back towards Washington at high speed, on a downward trajectory, until it was close to the Pentagon. There it began a two-and-a-half-to-three-minute spiral dive, from an altitude of about 8000 feet and in a 330-degree loop, which supposedly carried it into the northwest wall of the building. Experts agree this dive was an aeronautically fantastic maneuver, nearly impossible for a plane of that size, which would require the most skillful and experienced pilot — or remote control.

The returning plane, according to the official version, struck the Pentagon just above ground level. There it disintegrated — even maybe vaporized, according to some accounts, at least in part — but, paradoxically, also plowed inside. Had it simply flown straight into the top of the building rather than making its improbable spiral dive, there would have been far greater damage and loss of life. Had it turned only 150-180 degrees, it could have smashed into the East side of the building, where the office of defendant Rumsfeld was publicly known to be located on the third floor, looking out at the river, with the Joint Chiefs and other high officials all nearby. In contrast, the ground floor area that was blown up held offices like the one plaintiff worked in, many of them empty for a remodeling project, which was said to have included reinforcement to protect against attack. Another part of the destroyed space held financial records.

Also in the official version, the nose of the plane supposedly penetrated the distance of the three outer "rings" of the building, leaving a large, nine- or ten-foot-high round hole — shown in official photographs, without any sign of a plane — in the inner wall of the third ("C") ring. The hole waslocated some *300 feet* from the alleged impact point, through a maze of structural pillars and interior walls. It was also said that the wings of the plane knocked over five lampposts along a nearby road, as it approached the building, which meant the wings were a maximum of 50 feet off the ground as the plane flew past, roughly 300-350 yards away from the near face of the building.

This account is at odds with known evidence, and raises substantial questions about the absence of evidence — and official withholding of evidence — including the following:

There are no photos of a wrecked airplane at the place where the building was hit and set on fire; or of airplane wreckage at the hole in the inner ring where the nose of the plane was originally said by Rumsfeld to have come to rest, or elsewhere inside the building. Moreover, the nose of such a plane contains radar equipment, and the outer shell is made of a porous, composite material that allows the radar to function. Therefore, the nose was not capable of surviving an impact with the outer wall without being crushed, let alone penetrating all the way inside to the C-Ring wall, 300 feet away.

Although this story was later dropped, defendant Rumsfeld has never been publicly questioned about his statement that this is what occurred.

As noted, there is no footage from numerous video surveillance cameras — reportedly 85 different tapes are being withheld by the U.S. Justice Department — which are known or reliably assumed to have been operating at various nearby locations where some or all of the plane and the crash could be expected to have been caught on tape.

The official account says the plane knocked over several lamp-posts with its wings — two on one side of a nearby road, three on the other — which meant the wings were less than fifty feet off the ground as the plane approached, over uneven terrain, and the undercarriage even closer. The earliest photographs, taken before the upper floors fell in, about 30 minutes after the explosion(s), show the front blown off an expanse of the ground floor, no marks on the lawn in front of the impact zone; and several large cable reels standing in front of the building, unscathedThe "black box" flight data recorder identified by the Government as coming from Flight 77, and reportedly recovered from the wreckage at the scene, bears data, according to

pilots who have examined printouts provided by the National Transportation Safety Board (NTSB), which contradict various aspects of the official account, — and indeed the very notion that a plane struck the Pentagon — in crucial ways, viz:

It is a fundamental premise of airliner manufacture and operation that the black box only stops recording data when a flight is terminated — by the pilot turning off the engines at the gate, or by a crash. According to the pilots who studied the printouts, however, the record showing the path of Flight 77, etched with codes which connect it to that plane that day, cuts off, unaccountably, some 4-500 yards short of the building — a point reached after the pitched, diving loop described above — at an altitude of 273 feet.

The Pentagon is roughly 75 feet high. Just as they will confirm the improbability of that dive, expert pilots will attest that for a plane that size to descend from 273 feet, going approximately 500 miles an hour, and then level off inside of a quarter mile without hitting the ground — let alone get down to 50 feet in time to catch the lamp-posts, 300 yards closer — is an aerodynamic and gravitational impossibility.

The Safety Board has released a computer simulation of the flight path of Flight 77, allegedly based on the data from the flight recorder, which contradicts a simulation adopted by the 9/11 Commission. The Commission simulation shows the flight path of the official story, at an angle reflected by the damage inside the building, consistent with the downed light poles, and to the south of two nearby buildings housing the Navy Annex and a Citgo gas station. The NTSB simulation shows the plane headed towards the building on a path north of the two buildings and the line of lamp-posts.

Similarly, in the one fragment of a surveillance tape the Pentagon has released, two of the five frames disclosed appear to show an object, not recognizable as an airliner and apparently trailing a plume of white smoke, moving parallel to and just above the ground towards the Pentagon wall, followed by a bright explosion and a fireball mounting from the front of the building. The NTSB's black box data shows Flight 77 was roughly 200 feet above the top of the Pentagon as it reached its last known position some 400 to 500 yards (2-3 seconds) away. Thus, it could not have hit the building except by diving into it, and so could not have flown parallel to the ground between there and the point of impact. So it appears that, contrary to the defendants' false cover story of an airliner suicide crash, there was a different, additional, flying object, which hit the Pentagon, and was part of the terrorist bombing that caused the plaintiffs' injuries.

Additionally, the FBI identified the hijacker pilot of Flight 77 as "Hani Hanjour", supposedly a known terrorist suspect, who was reported to have received flight training in various places in the months before the attack. His flight instructors, however, reported that Hanjour was such a poor flight student that he was barely able to fly a small Cessna; and then he was so erratic that instructors refused to go up with him, and, just a few months before 9/11, recommended he be washed out and his license taken away. Thus it seems quite impossible that he could have flown the 757 really at all, let alone in its great uncanny dive. There have also been repeated reports since 9/11 that several of the other men named and pictured by the FBI as the hijackers were still alive after 9/11, and living in various locations in the world — including one, Waleed Al-Shehri, who was said to be a working pilot for Moroccan Air Lines, correctly shown in the FBI photo, whose identity and location have been verified by at least one major press outlet, the BBC. This information has not been pursued by U.S. investigators, or media.

Several trained and experienced military personnel at the scene noted the distinctive odor of cordite, a high explosive used in gunpowder, in the aftermath of the attack at the Pentagon. This suggests explosives as the cause for the destruction rather than the impact and fire resulting from burning jet fuel.

One investigator has documented the fact that numerous clocks in the damaged area of the building stopped at 9:32 a.m., as the plaintiff's watch did also, supporting the idea that electrically timed or detonated explosives were used to bring about the intended damage to the building — and that the attack occurred at 9:32, not 9:38.

All the matters alleged in paragraph #40 are known and demonstrable, and most would have been immediately evident to the defendants at the time. As Secretary of Defense, defendant Rumsfeld in particular was in a unique position to determine the truth and fix responsibility. He did neither. That he did not is confirmation of his complicity in the attack--and his indifference to and callous disregard for the injuries and loss of rights suffered by plaintiff and others.

Further, it should be noted that on September 10, 2001, the day before the attack, Defendant Rumsfeld conducted a press conference at the Pentagon in which he publicly announced that auditors had determined that some 2.3 *trillion* dollars in Defense Department funds —$2.300,000,000,000 — could not be accounted for. To plaintiff's knowledge and belief, part of the area of the ground floor of the Pentagon that was destroyed in the bombing is a location where records were kept that would be used to trace those funds, and where people worked who knew about them. On information and belief, there has been to this day no public report concerning the fate of those records, or that money.

In any event, the plainly visible pattern of damage on the outside and in other photographic views makes it clear the building was not hit by a plane. There may have been a missile strike, perhaps penetrating through to the back wall, which helped collapse the section that fell in, possibly augmented by explosives placed inside. Photos taken before the collapse suggest this, showing a single blown-out window section, above the ground floor; and witnesses have reported seeing a helicopter above the building, and disappearing behind it, followed by a big explosion and bright fireball. As noted, a large roundish hole was found in the C-ring wall, some 300 feet inside the building; and there were credible accounts, ignored in the Commission Report, of serious bomb damage in the B-ring, second from the center, and even some reports of dead bodies in the central A-ring, also ignored. As shown on CNN television, a large military aircraft, identified as an E-4B — the so-called "Doomsday Plane", which carries the most complete and sophisticated military command and control apparatus — was circling above Washington at the time the Pentagon was hit. It was in perfect position to coordinate the detonation and/or missile shot with a fly-over; and guide the airliner in its dive by remote control. It was also in perfect position to spot the oncoming plane on its radar and sound an alarm. Significantly, the Department of Defense has denied any knowledge of this airplane flying in that area on that day.

Whatever the cause of the bombing, and the traumatic injuries to plaintiff and others which resulted, the Government, of which the two main defendants were and have been the highest, most powerful officers, pursuant to the conspiracy they led and still lead as alleged herein, has been altogether deceptive in investigating, reporting and explaining the attack and its cause; and defendants, rather than righteously investigate and determine the derelictions which

occurred, have done nothing but lie and cover up.

Defendant Rumsfeld in particular has been deceptive from the start, as where, on September 13, he reported on *Good Morning, America* that the plane "...went in through three rings (of the Pentagon). I'm told the nose is — is still in there, very close to the inner courtyard, about one ring away"; a palpably false statement, contradicted by numerous witnesses, a total lack of photographic evidence, and evident impossibility. Rumsfeld has also contradicted himself several times in describing his whereabouts and movements during the first hour or more of the attack. He does not acknowledge his presence in a teleconference which Richard Clarke said he, Rumsfeld, and others were part of, beginning shortly after 9:00 a.m. — after the Flight 77 emergency was reported, at or about the time the second tower was hit in New York, and more than half an hour before the Pentagon was hit — and he contradicts himself about whether and when he went to the Executive Support Center and/or the National Military Command Center, both within the Pentagon, as events transpired that morning. General Myers also (falsely) denied he was at the Pentagon in the early stages of the teleconference, as reported by Clarke. Tellingly, the tape of the videoconference, which obviously would have been part of any good faith investigation, has been kept secret.

Defendant Rumsfeld also made a striking prediction of the attack, as if speaking compulsively about his secret knowledge, that very morning, and several days later, he publicly referred to the "missile" that hit the Pentagon. In testifying before the 9/11 Commission, the defendant stonewalled and double-talked egregiously, responding to direct questions (some of them personally submitted by plaintiff herself during a hearing open only to survivors), especially about the Air Force fighter-interceptors not showing up, with irrelevant and sometimes incomprehensible ramblings. Consistent with their part in the cover-up, Commissioners failed to question him closely or confront his non-responsiveness.

The Other Planes.

In spite of what the record shows was a regular, timely alert and request to NEADS commanders by FAA flight controllers at Boston for in-flight emergency response regarding United Airlines Flights 11 and 175 out of Boston, as described above in Pars. 22-24, the jets were not scrambled, or properly "vectored", in time to intercept the planes that hit the Towers

in New York — even though there was plenty of time for the interception.

With respect to Flight 93, which was thought to be intended for an attack on the White House or the Capitol, but crashed in Pennsylvania, there remains a great deal of mystery. Much of what supposedly happened was a made-in-Hollywood saga, where the passengers, learning of the earlier suicide crashes, gathered themselves and counter-attacked the hijackers, succeeding in heroic, self-sacrificing measure by crashing the plane (or causing the hijacker pilot to crash it) in a remote field, before it could approach its target. This story was supposedly recounted to persons on the ground by passengers with cell phones; but the science is clear that, at least in 2001, cell phones couldn't operate at the high altitude where the struggle supposedly took place. Also, the FBI, in presenting evidence at the Moussaoui trial in 2006, denied that any of the high-altitude calls that had been reported actually took place. The only cell phone calls confirmed by the FBI were two that reportedly occurred when the plane had descended to 5,000 feet. Thus, the mythic account is suspicious, to say the least.

Moreover, it appears fairly well established that one or more fighters ultimately did go aloft, and reached Flight 93, although this was also comprehensively denied in the Commission Report. There is also good evidence that supposed presidential authority to "engage", meaning shoot down the plane, was given by defendant Cheney at or about 9:50 a.m. that morning, wherewith Flight 93 was indeed shot down with an air-to-air missile from a U.S.A.F. fighter jet.

Finally, there are multiple reports that debris from the plane was found a mile or more from the crash site, an obvious impossibility if the plane simply fell or dove into the ground. Likewise, there is no debris visible in photographs of the crash site, despite a long photographic history of airliner crashes showing plane parts and debris spread around the point of impact. Instead there was a crater, and no sign of the plane. Implausibly, however, the official report said that a visa, in the name of the alleged hijacker identified as the pilot, was recovered near the crater, along with a red headband of the type the hijackers supposedly wore. Again, available evidence shows the official account promulgated under the defendants' illicit influence is, and plaintiffs allege that it is, false and fraudulent, in furtherance of the conspirac(ies) alleged herein.

The Cover-up.

As with the other branches or phases of the conspiracy, wherein a number of John Doe defendants working on different aspects of the organized enablement of the hijacking led by defendants Cheney and Rumsfeld may not have been aware or fully aware of each other's involvement; so too with the cover-up, a complicated operation which those involved have maintained for these seven years, and must continue to see to, indefinitely, on any number of fronts. That is, the skein of misrepresentations, distortions, omissions, contradictions, withheld evidence and outright lies which comprise the fraudulent "official" version, must be and plaintiffs allege that it has been and is assiduously, and fraudulently, maintained by the original perpetrators and various cohorts, who have kept the original conspiracy alive to this day.

In particular, the cover-up — beyond the fact that the simulated plane crash at the Pentagon was itself a cover-up — has been concentrated around the purported investigation and analysis of the attack and its supposed background by the 9/11 Commission, formally known as The National Commission on Terrorist Attacks Upon The United States, and the Report it issued in 2004. There, as extensively shown by a number of critics and commentators, this official organ put forth a supposedly comprehensive account of the attacks, the alleged attackers and their history, and various surrounding events and circumstances, in a version so full of omissions, distortions and outright falsehoods, as to clinch its purpose as a mainstay of the cover-up, in furtherance of the underlying conspiracy alleged herein, and its ongoing success.

Thus the Report gives a careful account and description of some of the many warnings the Government received during 2001 about Al Qaeda's intention to attack — in the United States, possibly with hijacked planes. The Report goes on to describe an interview with President Bush, which occurred only after intense negotiations in which the Commissioners acquiesced to White House conditions requiring that defendant Cheney be permitted to accompany the President, and that no record would be kept and no notes taken. There the President earnestly insisted to his Commission interlocutors that no warning of the attack had come. All contradictions were left unexplored, and ignored in the Report.

Similarly, defendant Rumsfeld — like the President himself, then-National Security Adviser Condoleezza Rice, Defendant Gen. Richard Myers and others — testified and said in public, repeatedly, that no one in the Government security apparatus ever imagined terrorists suicidally crashing planes into buildings. This claim was also absolutely false. In point of fact, the CIA, the NSA, the FAA and NORAD had planned and trained for just such a possibility. Indeed, the record shows training exercises involving such a potential attack had in fact been carried on at the Pentagon in October, 2000 and May, 2001, and that NORAD had begun planning in July, 2001, for a training exercise in which the premise would be that a hijacked airliner was crashed into the World Trade Center. The 9/11 Commission, however — with the same studied indifference it showed towards the Mineta testimony — failed even to mention these contradictions in its Report, let alone explain them away.

In any event, it is in the nature of the acts alleged that the participants would endeavor from the outset to keep their actions — and the meeting of the minds that unleashed them — the deepest and darkest of secrets, forever. Thus the cover-up, even as it continues today, and will be manifest in the litigation of this complaint, was inherently part of the original unlawful agreement, and thereby part of the cause of the injuries and deprivations plaintiffs suffered on 9/11, and continuing injury since that time.

As to the overall plot, with its roots in the command positions and unhinged political fantasies and intentions of the two main defendants, Cheney and Rumsfeld, plaintiff alleges that, necessarily, there were multiple meetings of the minds among the various necessary parties in various implicated locations, positions and phases of the action. Indeed, the narrative reflects an evident form of rolling conspiracy, or multiple successive, interlocking, sub-conspiracies, by which defendants and their cohorts maintain and have maintained the original agreement to cover up the original crime(s) of terrorism, and their part in it, to this day.

VII. Plaintiffs' Injuries.

The injuries, loss and deprivation of rights suffered by Plaintiff April Gallop, her child and others in the bombing of the Pentagon, however it was accomplished, were the result of terrorism, and terrorist acts, and conspiracy to commit terrorism, and to violate constitutional rights, and they include serious head and brain injuries she and her child both sustained when the ceiling caved in on them, as well as the loss and deliberate denial of their rights involved in their being made innocent victims of the attack. Plaintiff's son, Elisha, has had ongoing problems as he has grown older, associated with injury to his brain, and has required continuing medical care and other special help. Both mother and child have had continuing difficulty, pain and suffering as a result, and sustained need for medical care, and financial and other loss; and they evidently will continue to suffer and to need medical and other assistance for the future.

Further, clearly as a result of and in retaliation for her public statement that no airplane wreckage was present in the building after the explosion(s), and for raising other questions, John Doe Department of Defense (DOD) defendants, pursuant to the conspiracy, have wrongfully caused plaintiff to be denied medical care and other benefits she should have received since the attack, and have acted to discourage others from helping her, all to her consequent, actionable loss. Most recently, on being discharged from the Army earlier this year, plaintiff's financial account was closed out with a zero balance. A short time later, however, she was refused service at the VA medical center, on grounds that she supposedly owed the Defense Department more than $14,000; for which no documentation has been provided.

The plaintiff and her child also will experience more general loss, pain and suffering, forever, from what was done to them by high officials of their own government, who, attacking the Country and the Constitution, were willing to see her killed, and did see many others, thousands, killed, simply to further crass political designs. They were and are themselves terrorists, in truth, without whose crucial complicity the Al Qaeda attacks would never have occurred.

PLAINTIFFS' CAUSES OF ACTION

One. **Violation of Constitutional Rights – Bivens**.

Conspiracy. The defendants engaged in an unlawful conspiracy or series of interlocking conspiracies whereby they and various co-conspirators and others took various concrete steps, pursuant to a meeting of the minds around the objective of facilitating and enabling the terrorist attacks, specifically by de-activating and defaulting various normal defense systems and measures, as described and to be shown, so that the Al Qaeda hijackings and bombings of September 11 could succeed. They thereby helped cause the attacks and the resulting injuries to plaintiff, denial of her fundamental rights under the Fourth, Fifth and Ninth Amendments to the U.S. Constitution, and death and injury loss to so many others; entitling plaintiff to judgment against the defendants under the rule of the *Bivens* case, for compensatory damages in such amount as the Jury may determine; and Punitive Damages.

Deliberate Indifference. The concerted actions of defendants in their efforts to facilitate and enable the terrorist attacks of September 11 in various ways as described hereinabove and to be shown, and the defendants' deliberate indifference to the likelihood of serious injury and deprivation of rights arising therefrom, resulted in plaintiff and her child being made unknowing, defenseless victims of the attack, and thereby seriously injured and denied fundamental rights under the Fourth, Fifth and Ninth Amendments to the U.S. Constitution, entitling her to judgment against the defendants, under the rule of the *Bivens* case, for compensatory damages in such amount as the Jury may determine; and Punitive Damages.

Retaliation. The actions taken against plaintiff in retaliation for her speaking out with questions about the official explanations of what happened violated her rights under the First Amendment, entitling her to a further judgment against those responsible for compensatory damages in such amount as the Jury may determine; and Punitive Damages.

Two. **Common Law Conspiracy to Cause Death and Great Bodily Harm.** The plaintiff is further entitled to judgment against the defendants, jointly and severally, for the injuries she and her child received which were caused by the acts and omissions of defendants and others pursuant to the conspiracy(ies) alleged herein, and by breach of defendants' duty of care towards the plaintiff, for compensatory and punitive damages in such amounts as the Jury may determine, and costs and attorneys fees.

Three. **Acts of Terrorism Causing Injury** – 18 U.S.Code 2333(a). The aforesaid acts and omissions of and by defendants were part and parcel of a terrorist attack on the United States, and the Pentagon in particular, resulting from a conspiracy or conspiracies to cause and help cause, facilitate and enable the hijacking and crashing of the planes and other elements of the attack; and these acts resulted in serious injuries to plaintiff and her child, entitling her to judgment against the defendants for compensatory damages as determined by the Jury, treble damages, and Attorneys Fees, under the Terrorism Acts — notwithstanding the provision of Sec.2337, purporting to exempt or immunize U.S. officers and employees acting "within...official capacity or under color of legal authority"; in that the agreements, acts and omissions alleged herein are outside and beyond the reach and compass of any conceivable official capacity or legal authority, actual or colorable, and therefore unconstitutional as applied in this case, as a deprivation of Due Process of Law, and of her right under the Seventh Amendment to have her claim tried by a Jury according to Law.

///

PRAYER FOR RELIEF

WHEREFORE, the plaintiff demands Trial By Jury, and Judgment against all defendants, jointly and severally, for compensatory and punitive damages in such amounts as the Jury may see fit to award; treble damages under 18 U.S.C. 2333(a), and costs of suit, expenses and attorneys fees...

Yours, etc.,

DATED: December 15, 2008.

Dennis Cunningham   (DC 7142)

36 Plaza Street
Brooklyn, NY 10238
718-783-3682
denniscunningham-law@gmail.com

William W. Veale
2033 North Main Street, #1060
Walnut Creek, CA 94596

925-935-3987

centerfor911jus-

tice@gmail.com

APPENDIX F

TAIBBI EMAILS

Mr. Taibbi,

I retired as Chief Assistant Public Defender in Contra Costa County, CA two years ago. You and I have been working in the same area recently. I found your Cheney, et al conversation hysterical. But it didn't answer any of the many questions which have fueled the truth movement. I would like to know if you have ever discussed the case with a trial lawyer who has done the reading. I propose myself, if you have not. Anytime, anywhere.

If you have not, I have those questions which I will put to you only if you have any interest in trying to answer them. Let me know if you care to engage.

Mr. Veale,

Just out of curiosity, tell me what your questions are. But if it's the same old bunk about freefall speed and WTC-7 and all of that shit, don't bother. As a lawyer you should know that you don't prove a conspiracy with "according to the quadratic formula of X, the car couldn't have crashed: therefore the cops cut the brake lines." There isn't a single piece of "evidence" that you could use in court against any specific person in the whole landscape of this movement - which is pretty incredible given the number of Bush-era scandals that were defined by leaks of real, prosecutable criminal behavior. So if you've just got the usual science crap, please don't. But if you want to talk about a real case that you think would get past a judge, be my guest.

MT

Mr. Taibbi,

May I say your Daily Show persona comes through even in the slapdash of email. Have I misunderstood you? On the one hand, you appear to be laughingly dismissive of the very notion of such a conspiracy, but on the other hand, critical of the inability of the evidence to pin it on a person. Someone in the first camp would have no interest in, say, an honest investigation. A person in the second camp would support such an investigation since that is what is normally done in the case of crime.

I will attach my questions should you feel the inclination, but in case I got you right, and you are looking for the goods that put someone in chains, as a prosecutor, it isn't that complicated. You start subpoenaing records and asking questions. For example, of Dick Cheney: what was the order the young man was asking you about not long after Mineta arrived in the PEOC. Who was the young man? How many other people were in the room? A prosecutor finds the young man and then gives immunity, or prosecutes. If the Cheney order was to shoot down the plane (Flight 77), what is the

explanation for no Boards of Inquiry? If the order was to let it be, slap the handcuffs on him. That, in addition to the existence of the master cover story, spawning lies by all the major participants, is what gets you justice, should anyone want it.

What is particularly cute and provocative about your Cheney/Kristol parody is that there had to be a team, though one guy or gal could do it-you did, sitting down trying to figure out what would enhance Matt Taibbi's ability to make light of the suggestion of conspiracy. I call it the curly-cue group-see Lloyd England. What I say is that the most important movie of this century was one made in the last- Wag the Dog.

As to whether there is evidence to get by a judge, you can disparage the science crap all you want, but that is what has been putting my clients in prison for 30+ years. Steven Jones, Richard

Gage, thermate residue, etc. The existence of a conspiracy beyond the Al Qaeda elements is way beyond dispute at this point, if you are open to the possibility, which many people are not. Are you or aren't you?

BV

Attached Questions:

QUESTIONS DEMANDING ANSWERS

1.WHAT PENTAGON DEFENSES WERE SUCCESSFULLY COMPROMISED AND WHY?

2.WHY IS NORMAN MINETA UNDESERVING OF CREDENCE WHEN HE TESTIFIED THAT CHENEY WAS IN THE PEOC GIVING ORDERS CONCERNING THE PLANE THAT HIT THE PENTAGON?

3.HOW DOES THE GOVERNMENT EXPLAIN MOLTEN METAL IN THE RUBBLE OF GROUND ZERO, AND PARTICULARLY WTC 7 THAT WAS NEVER HIT BY ANY AIRCRAFT?

4.HOW DOES THE GOVERNMENT EXPLAIN THE INCONSISTENCY BETWEEN THE FLIGHT 77 FLIGHT PATH DESCRIBED BY THE NTSB AND THE ONE DESCRIBED BY THE 9/11 COMMISSION REPORT?

5.HOW DOES THE GOVERNMENT EXPLAIN THE IMMEDIATE EXHAUSTION OF ENERGY BY THE PROJECTILE THAT ALLEGEDLY CAUSED THE HOLE IN THE E-RING OF THE PENTAGON BUT THAT CAUSED NO MARK ON THE SUCCEEDING WALL, 40 FT AWAY?

6.HOW DOES THE GOVERNMENT EXPLAIN THE PRESENCE OF THERMATE IN SAMPLES OF DUST AND RUBBLE FROM

GROUND ZERO, AND THE EXISTENCE OF THE CORROBORATING SIGNATURE PHENOMENA OF THERMATE- USE IN THE VIDEOS OF THE COLLAPSE OF THE TWIN TOWERS?

7.HOW DOES THE GOVERNMENT EXPLAIN THE MULTI-PLE INSTANCES OF EYEWITNESS TESTIMONY CONCERN-ING EXPLOSIONS IN THE TWIN TOWERS BEFORE THE IMPACTS OF THE AIRPLANES AND BEFORE AND DURING THE COLLAPSES OF THE TOWERS?

8.WHY HAVE OFFICIAL AGENCIES OF GOVERNMENT REFUSED OR NEGLECTED TO INVESTIGATE THE POSSI-BILITY OF CONTROLLED DEMOLITION WITH REGARD TO THE WORLD TRADE CENTER BUILDINGS?

9.WHY DIDN'T THE SECRET SERVICE IMMEDIATELY GET THE PRESIDENT TO A PLACE OF SAFETY AS THE AT-TACKS WERE OCCURRING?

10.HOW DOES THE GOVERNMENT EXPLAIN THE EX-ISTENCE OF CELL PHONE CALLS ON UNITED FLIGHT 93 WHEN SUCH CALLS WERE VIRTUALLY IMPOSSIBLE IN 2001?

11.HOW COULD, AND WHY WOULD, HANI HANJOUR, AN INCOMPETENT PILOT, PERFORM THE MANEUVER HE IS SAID BY GOVERNMENTAL AGENCIES TO HAVE PER-FORMED, WHEN THE ASSUMED MISSION OF ANY ACTIVE TERRORIST IS TO BE AS DESTRUCTIVE AS POSSIBLE

bv

I dealt with most of these questions in a debate with David Ray Griffin that will be coming out soon. They're all absurd, all of them. If your best evidence -- or even one of your eleven best pieces of evidence -- of a conspiracy that massive is the lack of a mark on the E-ring of the Pentagon wall or whatever, that's totally fucking sad.

As for science putting your clients in prison, yes -- scientific evidence of things that actually happened, not evidence of things that did not happen. This business about the phone calls is a classic example. It's preposterous, utterly absurd, to argue that the phone calls did not happen. To believe this would be to believe that all of the ordinary people who received these calls would be willing to take part in the conspiracy that killed their loved ones. If you can believe that someone like Lisa Beamer, insufferable person though she might be, would go through that elaborate fake-out, this 100-IQ New Jersey housewife with no connection to anyone, for the sake of some nebulous conspiracy that cannot possibly benefit her personally, then you're so far gone that nothing I say to you would matter anyway. You really believe that all of those people

would do that? We're not talking about one call. We're talking about a bunch of people. Ted Olsen, his wife dies horribly and violently that day -- and he's going to go along with that crap? What, are you two years old? It's easier to believe in Santa Claus than this stuff.

And please don't tell me you're one of those people that believes in "voice-recog technology" or whatever, that the phone calls were elaborate fakes. That enters no-plane hologram territory to believe that stuff.

Beyond that, your passage about "one guy or gal could do it" made absolutely no sense on any level. I read it five times and couldn't even begin to guess what you were talking about. So please go back, put your tinfoil hat on and enjoy your retirement, which can't possibly have come soon enough.

Sincerely

Matt Taibbi

Outstanding, How about taking the gloves off?

This comes under the heading of "the best defense..." I guess the answer to the question about open to the possibility, is "no." I agree that both sides of this debate have a lot of explaining to do. I have to

resort to the ludicrous, because you and yours are unable to explain the impossible.

How about, just as an exercise in mental conditioning, trying to write down your explanation for what Cheney was ordering or why you don't believe Mineta. Lastly, what is it in the history of the last 70 years that makes our claims inconceivable?

Where do I get to see you eating Griffin for lunch? He doesn't strike me as having sufficient jugular instinct, as opposed to you. Any time you want to take on somebody your own size, let me know.

Veale

Mr. Taibbi;

The exchange below took place a year ago. You are certainly right about that paragraph; Sorry. And I am sorry to bother you now, but since the conclusions have found their way into peer-reviewed journals at least twice at this point, I was wondering if you could address just one small part of the problem: What is the benign explanation for the presence of

thermite and its derivatives in four separate, independently collected samples of dust and debris from Ground Zero? I read your exchange with Griffin and you didn't answer that question.

We are in federal court now, Gallop v. Rumsfeld, Cheney, and Myers. The Defendants' Motion to Dismiss should be decided late in the summer.

Bill Veale

Family, Friends, Acquaintances, and Those From Whom I Have Sought Help;

Alas, the anticipated moment has arrived. Gallop v. Cheney, Rumsfeld, and Myers was dismissed with prejudice by Judge Denny Chin. We have filed our notice of appeal. I write this to inform those who have supported, those who have derided, and those who have averted their eyes. Chin did not spare himself, and those of you who agree with his assessment, that the suit was based in cynical delusion and fantasy, may have your moment. Those of you not so well acquainted with me might take this moment to get to know the depths of our disaster.

Few of you will think this ends the matter for me. I attach the decision and a rebuttal prepared for the centerfor911justice.org website. Read, laugh, cry, continue to avert your eye.... I would be interested in any feedback.

Bv

4/7/10

I just read your complaint. Let me see if I have this straight. Your theory is that the defendants allowed the hijackers to get on the plane, then allowed the plane to fly over the Pentagon, at which point an explosive device was set off simultaneous to the plane's arrival? Do I have this right? I'm quoting from your complaint:

"In the attack on the Pentagon, in particular, plaintiff avers that the official story, that a hijacked plane crashed into the Pentagon and exploded (causing the plaintiff's injuries), is false. In fact, the bombing was accomplished another way, so as to limit the damage, protect the defendants, and only make it appear that a plane had been crashed into the building. This claim is supported by data from the plane's supposed "black box", released by the National Transportation Safety Board (NTSB), which indicate the plane passed over the building at very low altitude, just as an explosion and fireball were engineered by other means, a planted bomb or bombs and/or a missile. This

is supported by the lack of any photographic evidence of a wrecked airliner at the Pentagon, compounded by the record of reported refusal by the U.S. Department of Justice to release some 85 video tapes from surveillance cameras in locations at or near the Pentagon, which it has declared exempt from Freedom of Information Act disclosure."

First of all, I've never heard of a lawyer arguing that a lack of evidence for something was affirmative evidence of anything.

Secondly, can I ask what the defendants' purpose was in effecting a hijacking and flying a wayward liner so close to the Pentagon -- only to explode a bomb inside? Why not just have the plane hit the building? And if the plane didn't hit the building, what happened to the plane?

Thirdly, if this is indeed what you are proposing, can I ask what the hijackers' motive is in pretending to hit the Pentagon on behalf of Dick Cheney and Don Rumsfeld?

MT

4/7/10

Goddamn, Thank you for taking the time.

First, may I say that I do not recommend that anybody try this at home; it is astounding the number of mistakes that were made and only because they have been completely successful does one give them the slightest credit at all.

As a general response, each Macchiavelli is going to have his own "way of going," if you will. If one thinks a lot of curly cues attached to the plan, to make it the more outlandish, and easily dismissible, is a good idea, another is going to kill as many people as possible, and another is going to stay away from Cantor Fitzgerald, because somebody important's friend might get hurt. I have never had Macchiavellian tendencies, so I am mostly guessing, from matters that are factually immobile.

As for the absence of evidence, not to be too dismissive, but my 32 years as a public defender were spent asking juries, "where are the fingerprints?". Whatever my pal Denny said, that my client saw no airplane as she stumbled out of the building is certainly a very serious problem for anyone who believes that there was one. For starters, she was in a position to catch the left engine, all 6 tons at 500+ mph. Second, she was entirely conscious as she made her way out; how did she manage to miss the airplane? And if it vaporized from heat, how, precisely, did she manage to avoid the same fate? You should be aware as well, that a column in front of her, and

a column behind her, were both destroyed. The only explanation for that, and the continued existence of her heartbeat, is 2 explosions, at different times, corroborated by the 2 different times on two stopped clocks.

As to the defendants' purpose, you are a smart fellow, and I think, were I planning it all, I would have made some different decisions, but as I said before, they have been entirely successful. They likely were handed a plan, as in infiltrated the KSM cell, like they did the Blind Sheik's with Emad Salem in 1993. They saw an opportunity to project US power, have wars, build bases, get the Patriot Act, and make a lot of money. So they tweaked what they were given and adapted it to their uses. They blew up the Towers because less than that, 1993 and Oklahoma City, had not granted them the blank check they were looking for. I'm obviously just spitballing here, but maybe they thought running the plane into the Pentagon might have killed too many people, but they wanted to stick to the general plan. They know their abilities a lot better than I do, but it is clear that they scrubbed the radar data to make it look like the plane ran into the Pentagon. We know that because they made a mistake and obliterated the ground clutter along with the track of the overflown plane. We have additional evidence of their ability to scrub radar data from the fact that the E-4B, the Flying Pentagon, that John King of CNN reported on a while back, that was videotaped flying above the White House as the Pentagon was exploding, had its tracks removed as well.

What happened to the overflying plane? Here is

why the Truth Movement can't get any traction. Smart people get to this question in a hurry, and the answer is so disturbing that it disables the thought process. That plane and its occupants were killed as props, and the pictures of the dead bodies were shown to the jury in Moussaoui's trial. The helpful evidentiary value of that fact is that if the airplane that hit the building combusted to nothingness, its occupants would have done the same, which means the dead bodies depicted did not come from the Pentagon. A couple are not that badly burned.

Lastly, the hijackers, or whatever the mechanism was, had very little to do with the precise shape of the final plan and the events of 9/11. There is a lot of evidence that the planes could not have done what they did without remote control. This is more spitballing, of course, but many of your questions and the others I have been presented with in last 5 years, I answer by simply saying, I don't know, but give me subpoena power and I will find out.

There are some fundamental problems that skeptics such as yourself must confront. 1. The Ted Olson story of calls from his wife from Flight 77 was disproved by the FBI with phone records at the Moussaoui trial. 2. In 2001, cell phones didn't work at the altitudes alleged in the United 93 story. 3. Passports can't survive blazing infernos, nor can bandannas. 4. They scrubbed the radar tracks. 5. No defender of the official

story has ever tried to explain how and why Norman Mineta is to be seen as delusional, given the fact that Richard Clark, Condi

Rice, David Bohrer, the White House photographer, and Dick Cheney, at least twice, all agree with Mineta's version of the timing. Which means that Cheney was giving orders, or confirming orders, that had to do with the plane flying toward the Pentagon, that immediately preceded the explosion(s) there. If the orders were to shoot down the plane, there should have been a lot of boards of inquiry that never took place. If they were to let the plane be, Boss Cheney has a lot of explaining to do. When the other side refuses to address your best argument, the jury is entitled, in some instances instructed, to draw adverse inferences. When the other side is cheating, as in the examples I just cited, you know you have a case.

Mr. Taibbi, you have had some fun at my expense before. God bless you; it happens to be the sort of humor I appreciate. In all seriousness, this matter deserves a hearing. You can give it one. Would you please give me some of your time, wherever you say, and pretty much whenever, to discuss it deliberately and methodically and honestly? I will make you the promise that, if you agree, our communications will be confidential until you say otherwise.

Veale

Ah. So they did Oklahoma City, too?

Have you ever thought about this from the point of view of the supposed conspirators? Let's just say they want to fake an act of terrorism at the Pentagon and murder only selected military personnel. Why not just explode a truck bomb outside it? Or plant a bomb in the basement, a la 1993? If you're faking this, are you really going to

1.hijack a plane, remote-buzz the Pentagon, then fly it to some undisclosed location and murder the passengers, making the wounds look like crash trauma

2.do elaborate simulations of cell phone calls from victims

3.plant a bomb or bombs ANYWAY in the building, and make an an elaborate show of making them look like an exploding airplane

4.fake the radar, involving all those people

5.have the Vice President admit to the crime in front of a half dozen people

6.include the Moussaoui prosecutors in the scam, as well as the cleanup crews, the Pentagon hierarchy, the DC police, the FBI, the firefighters, and so on.

Either that or some pissed-off Muslims hijacked a plane to kill a bunch of infidels, which only happens every nine minutes or so. I mean, have you ever been to the Middle East? The part of your theories that make the least sense are those aspects that reject the idea that Islamic fundamentalism is a real threat. These are people who commit mass murder over cartoons. And they're somehow unlikely to have done this? It boggles my mind that you people believe this stuff.

MT

9/21/10

Mr. Veale,

I am deeply troubled by the fact that you appeared at my home yesterday. I think you owe me an explanation -- what you were doing here, and why you felt the need to come without warning.

I'm particularly upset that upon arriving at my building you apparently went straight past my doorman and to my door. If there had been any kind of logical explanation for your appearance at my home you would have at least asked my doorman to ring me before coming up. Arriving at my door unannounced in the manner that you did is highly questionable: extremely rude at best, and at worst threatening.

Please tell me there is some kind of explanation for your bizarre behavior.

MT

9/23/10

Mr. Taibbi;

Thank you for giving me this opportunity to discuss my "bizarre" behavior. Your doorman was not in evidence when I walked in the building, but had he been, I would not have liked my chances at getting a conversation. I have been ignored by some of the most famous names in this country, at least among the politically astute, and in at least one disheartening case, by someone at the other end of the phone with their doorman, having had a day to consider the matter with a legal brief in their possession, read or not, I have no idea.

It is a fact of life that nothing difficult happens, or is accomplished, except eye to eye. I came to your door because I could, and because I must do everything I can. By email I offered you, and asked you for, an opportunity to sit down and talk under any conditions which you might dictate. The result of that was silence. What else could I do but hope you might have a change of heart if you saw me in the flesh? I certainly had no intention of being threatening, quite the opposite. I am only a theoretical threat to what I consider to be the enormous lie that has been told. I vow to combat it any way I can.

Is it rude to come to a person's door unannounced with a request for an interview? It wasn't for the first several millenia; if it is now because we live in fear and have doormen to keep us from the intrusion of the world, it is a sad path we travel. I offer my apology for my ancient and subversive ways with the explanation that in matters of such import, politeness must give way. Or may it be viewed from a different perspective? A traveler has come thousands of miles to see you, and you cannot deign to open the door and look them in the eye?

Let me offer this: I sent out a notice of my head being handed to me by a Federal District Court Judge, and you, of all my non-friends who received it, decided to respond. You could have felt well-rid of me as I gently left your hallway the other night, yet you sent me an email demanding an explanation for my behavior. I know you are concerned for the life of this country, I have read some of your writings (my 24 yr old son is a real fan of yours and steers them to me), my tennis partner is an Imus listener and has a great respect for your brains and your point of view. I allow myself the hope that you are having some trouble with the official story.

Let me ask one final time, please, give me an hour and a half to discuss the matter, at

the time and place of your choosing. This poor misused nation needs your help. I will abide by any rules you lay down; I give you my word which I take seriously.

bv

9/30/10

I don't know why I didn't receive your explanation, but I didn't. In any case I'm not interested in talking with you and must request that you never come near me again. Your theories are deeply misguided and it is my hope that you will see this eventually. I am certainly not willing to argue about them with you and ask only that you reassure me that you never come to my home again. My family was disturbed by the incident. Incidentally, it's a doorman's job to protect residents from unannounced visitors. And unannounced arrivals were only permissible for "millennia" because other forms of communication were not available.

MT

10/1/10

Mr. Taibbi;

And there you have it. I shan't visit you again.
Bv
3/25/11
Jim and Matt,
This will be your formal invitation to 141 Church St in New Haven,
Conn. at 11 AM on April 5th to witness the entirety of the 5 min-
utes the 2nd Circuit has allotted me for oral argument in Gallop v.
Cheney et al. Will the world get tired of playing with me at some
point? I am told it is not only unusual to be given such a short time,
but it is also unusual for it to be heard in New Haven. Why don't
one or the both of you get to bottom of this most recent indignity?
Veale

Sounds like a terrible injustice. The world weeps for you.
MT
4/1/11
Jim and Matt,
So who was assigned our case for Tuesday's argument, ntyc?
Walker, cousin of Bush and either brother or cousin of Wirt
Walker, owner of Securasec or whatever, that ran security for the
WTC. I challenge anyone to make this shit up.
Bv

That's awesome. I burst out laughing hearing that. I'm just imagining how much more you'll complain now to your girlfriend or wife
or whatever about how they're all railroading you and how bored
she's going to be to hear it and how even more secretly desperate
she'll be for you to get a real lawyer job somewhere, forget all this 9/
11 horseshit and buy her some new furniture or take her on a trip to

the Caribbean. She's like at least two years further away from that Caribbean vacation now.

APPENDIX G
Summers and Swann Emails
Authors, I am one of the lawyers who put their 9/11 truth money where their mouth is and sued Cheney, Rumsfeld and Myers for complicity in the attacks. You can imagine I have "issues" with your telling of the tale. Some of them come from spending lots of money hiring, maybe literally, the preeminent physicist of our time from UC Berkeley, so that he/she could grade Jones and Harrit's paper finding nanothermite in the dust. That their paper isn't mentioned in your book is...disturbing. You, of course, couldn't have Known of my expenditures unless you had asked me, which you wouldn't have known to do unless you had looked. Google, that is. My distress to the side, I would do just about anything to be able to discuss our differences in person, or otherwise. Your point about chain of custody is not unimportant. Would you be interested in a longtime trial lawyer's approach to it

Dear Mr. Veale,
Thank you very much for your letter. It is certainly good to hear from someone who,
though critical of some of our work, is interested in engaging in serious discussion.
That said, we are deeply involved in research for another project. I hope you will not be offended if I suggest that we be in touch if and when we are doing further work on 9/11.
Until then, I wish you well with your own endeavors.
Sincerely,
Robbyn Swan
Ms. Swan,

You have been very polite, and in responding at all, almost unique. Phil Shenon was one of the few others to respond, and he actually gave me a little time, but by the time I made contact with him, he was able to say, "it's been a while; I don't remember." As a supplicant, I can be mollified with very little, but your recent memories and decisions are extremely important. So, I ask for anything; lunch, coffee.

In the event that the above request is politely denied, would you respond to two questions: 1. It must have occurred to someone to include the story of nanothermite in your book. Can you tell me what the rationale for its absence was? 2. The Pennsylvania Environmental Protection Agency couldn't find 37,500 gals of jet fuel, in any form, combusted or otherwise, at the site in Shanksville. Can you tell me what went into your decision to leave this information out of your work?

I am enormously indebted for any time you spend.

Bill Veale

Dear Mr. Veale,?Thank you for your further note and reasonable questions.

I am currently living in Europe, but if I get to your area at any point, shall remember your kind offer.

As to your queries:?1) You will find discussion of the thermite issue in chapters 10 & 11 or our book, along with some additional material in the Notes section at the back?2) We wrote the Flight 93 section of our book almost four years ago. I cannot, at this distance, recall the particulars of the issue you mention, nor could I even say whether you are correct as to what the Pennsylvania EPA found or didn't find.

We accumulated many tens of thousands of pages of material in the writing of the 11th Day. At this point, they have all been moved into storage.

If we ever have cause to return to the subject, I'll certainly have a look at the files with your question in mind.?

Best of luck with your research. Sincerely,?Robbyn Swan

Dear Ms. Swan,

I am most grateful for your response. I am afraid I was taught not to stop until the bottom is reached. I have read 10 and 11. As opposed to "thermite," the word "nanothermite" does not appear in your book, whereas it is the focus of the peer-reviewed article which you cite in a footnote, taking note of the disapproval of the contents of the article on the part of the editor of the journal where the article appeared. When you read the article, it must have occurred to you that the scientists were claiming to have found a substance which PROVES controlled demolition, as it most certainly does.

In another context, one might neglect to mention the presence of the perpetrator's DNA in a rape kit. I am one who believes it is possible to tell this horrible story in the way you have, not out of a desire to deceive, but rather because of a hard-wired world view which does not allow that conclusion which is demanded by the evidence, to exist in the mind.

If your intents were to deceive, I doubt you will tell me that. If, however, you never had someone demand an explanation for the choices you made, any existing internal bias could lead to the result you produced. What I see throughout your book is an effort, as a defense lawyer might, to poke some sort of hole in whatever piece of evidence is being referred to. I am more than familiar with the tactic since that has been my business for my adult life.

The palpable resistance felt by most Americans to 9/11 Truth makes people able to disregard evidence if ANYTHING negative can be written or said about it. The search for truth requires much more than that. In this case it requires mental and emotional toughness and considerable courage.

Sadly, when I saw no reference to the work Architects and Engineers for 9/11 Truth have done, I was afraid your book was not going to be what was needed under the circumstances. I write to express concern, but also to try to learn what went wrong.

bv

Dear Mr. Veale,

Ours was an honest, independent investigation aimed solely at getting to and presenting the facts in so far as they are discernible.

If you do not accept that as true - and your letter suggests that you do not - there is nothing that I can say that will convince you otherwise.

In our research for the *Eleventh Day* we uncovered much fresh evidence on ar- eas in which genuine questions still require answers. I hope, at some future date, to be able to give those matters further investigation and would encourage serious researchers to do likewise.

I'm afraid that is all I can add for the time being. Sincerely,?Robbyn S.

APPENDIX H

OFFICE OF THE INSPECTOR GENERAL Complaint

Dear Sir/Madam,

I write to register a complaint with the Office of the Inspector General for the performance of the Justice Department in the matter of the attacks of 9/11 and specifically with regard to the case of Gallop v. Cheney, docket number 08 CV 10881, filed in December of 2008 in the Southern District of New York. I am one of the two lawyers who were responsible for filing the case.

As a review of the papers in the case will demonstrate, instead of defending the defendants, former Vice President Dick Cheney, former Secretary of Defense Donald Rumsfeld, and former Chairman of the

Joint Chiefs of Staff Richard Myers, the criminal division should have been referred the matter for prosecution of those individuals, and others, for the crimes of mass murder, treason, and conspiracy to commit those offenses.

A summary of the most important facts in the case is available at vealetruth.com and 911justice.org in a piece entitled "Conclusion of Gallop v. Cheney" to which is attached a 47-page Affidavit where the evidence is set out. In my view, I and the American people, no less the citizens of the world, given the worldwide devastation created as a direct consequence of the attacks, are entitled to an official effort to address and rebut the evidence contained in the Affidavit.

I write to register complaint and to demand official action on the part of the agency of government statutorily empowered with the investigation of wrongdoing by the Department of Justice. I complain here of the misconduct of the lawyers in the Department of Justice and the special agents and their supervisors in the FBI.

Given the history of this matter, any but the darkest expectations would be unwarranted, so I will include in this letter some reference to a few of the most salient claims upon which our lawsuit was based.

Nanothermite, a compound created in the defense laboratories of the USG, has been found by eminent physicists in at least four, separate, independently collected samples of dust and debris from Ground Zero, establishing without question the destruction of the three buildings in Manhattan by controlled demolition. There is no mention of the compound or this fact in the 9/11 Commission Report.

Over 2000 architects and engineers have declared that the buildings in New York were destroyed as set out in the preceding paragraph.

Secretary of Transportation Norman Mineta testified to the 9/11 Commission that Vice President Cheney gave or confirmed orders which assured that the airplane that was flying toward the Pentagon would accomplish its role in the destruction of the West Wing of that structure. There is no mention`of Mineta's testimony in the 9/11 Commission Report.

Respectfully submitted,

The OIG responded after a couple of months with an unsigned letter saying no further investigation would be conducted.

APPENDIX I

DECISIONS OF THE SECOND CIRCUIT

1 10-1241-cv Gallop v. Cheney UNITED STATES COURT OF APPEALS FOR THE SECOND CIRCUIT August Term 2010 (Argued: April 5, 2011 Decided: April 27, 2011) Docket No. 10-1241-cv APRIL GALLOP, individually and for her minor child, E.G., Plaintiff-Appellant, -v.- RICHARD CHENEY, former Vice President of the United States, DONALD RUMS-FELD, former Secretary of the Department of Defense, General RICHARD MYERS (Ret.), United States Air Force, Defendants-Appellees, JOHN DOES NOS. I-X, in their individual capacities, Defendants. 1 Before: WINTER, WALKER, and CABRANES, Circuit Judges. _____ 1 The Clerk of Court is directed to amend the official caption as set forth above. April Gallop appeals from a March 18, 2010 judgment of the United States District Court for the Southern District

of New York (Denny Chin, Judge) dismissing her complaint asserting violations of her constitutional rights pursuant to Bivens v. Six Unknown Federal Narcotics Agents, 403 U.S. 388 (1971), a common law tort of conspiracy to cause death and great bodily harm, and a violation of the Antiterrorism Act, 18 U.S.C. ' 2333(a). Gallop, represented by counsel in the District Court and on appeal, alleged that defendants, former senior government officials, caused the September 11, 2001 attacks against the United States in order to create a political atmosphere in which they could pursue domestic and international policy objectives and to conceal the misallocation of $2.3 trillion in congressional appropriations to the Department of Defense. We hold that the District Court did not err in concluding that Gallop's claims were frivolous, and affirm the dismissal of her complaint. In addition, Gallop's counsel are ordered to show cause why sanctions should not be imposed under Federal Rule of Appellate Procedure 38, 28 U.S.C. ' 1927, and the inherent power of this Court. 2 WILLIAM W. VEALE (Mustapha Ndanusa, Brooklyn, NY; Dennis Cunningham, San Francisco, CA, on the brief), Walnut Creek, CA, for Petitioner-Appellant April Gallop. ALICIA M. SIMMONS, Assistant United States Attorney (Preet Bharara, United States Attorney; Benjamin H. Torrance, Assistant United States Attorney, on the brief), Office of the United States Attorney for the Southern District of New York, New York, NY, for Defendants-Appellees Richard B. Cheney, Donald H. Rumsfeld and Richard B. Myers. JOSÉ A. CABRANES, Circuit Judge: April Gallop ("Gallop") appeals from a March 18, 2010 judgment of the United States District Court for the Southern District of New York (Denny Chin, Judge) dismissing her complaint asserting violations of her constitutional rights pursuant to Bivens v. Six Unknown Federal Narcotics Agents, 403 U.S. 388 (1971), a common law tort of conspiracy to cause death and great bodily harm, and a violation of the Antiterrorism Act, 18 U.S.C. ' 2333(a). Gallop, represented by counsel in the District Court and on appeal, alleged that defendants, former senior government officials, caused the September 11, 2001 attacks against the United States in order to (a) create a political atmosphere in which they could pursue domestic and international policy objectives and (b) conceal the misallocation of $2.3 trillion in congressional appropriations to the Department of Defense. The District Court concluded that Gallop's claims were frivolous, and dismissed her complaint for failure to state a claim upon which relief can be granted under Federal Rule of Civil Procedure 12(b)(6). We affirm. BACKGROUND As the sentient world well recalls, on the morning of September 11, 2001, "agents of the al Qaeda terrorist organization hijacked commercial airplanes and attacked the World Trade Center in New York City and the national headquarters of the Department of Defense 3 in Arlington, Virginia." Hamdan v. Rumsfeld, 548 U.S. 557, 567-68 (2006). Among the nearly 3,000 civilians that were killed in the attacks were the 6 crew members and 58 passengers of American Airlines Flight 77, which crashed into the Pentagon at 9:37 a.m. See, e.g., The 9/11 Commission Report: Final Report of the National Com-

mission on Terrorist Attacks Upon the United States 8-10
(2004). The attacks of September 11, 2001 constituted the dead-
liest attack on American soil since the bombing of Pearl Harbor on December 7, 1941. On December 15, 2008, Gallop filed a
complaint in the District Court alleging the following facts.
Gallop, a Specialist in the United States Army, was working
in the Pentagon with her infant child, E.G., on September 11,
2001, when a large "explosion" caused the walls and ceiling
to collapse on top of her. Complaint & 6. Although she was
"knocked unconscious" by the initial blast, she regained her
senses in time to exit the building through a hole in the wall
and "collapsed on the grass" outside. Complaint & 34. She
awoke sometime later in the hospital. Id. Both she and her
son, now seven-years-old, sustained lasting "head and brain
injuries" as a result of the explosion. Complaint & 7. Apart
from these factual allegations, the Complaint hypothesizes
a fantastical alternative history to the widely accepted account of the "explosion" that injured Gallop and killed hundreds of other men and women inside the Pentagon. Among
other things, Gallop's complaint alleges that American Airlines Flight 77 did not crash into the PentagonCindeed, that
no plane crashed into the Pentagon. Complaint & 4 ("[T]he official story, that a hijacked plane crashed into the Pentagon
and exploded ... is false."). Instead, the Complaint alleges that
the United States" most senior military and civilian leaders Acause[d] and arrange[d] for high explosive charges to be
detonated inside the Pentagon, and/or a missile of some sort
to be fired at the building . . . to give the false impression

that hijackers had crashed the plane into the building, as had apparently happened in New York." Complaint & 3. 4 Gallop further contends that these officials knew of the September 11 attacks in advance, facilitated their execution, and attempted to cover up their involvement in order to "generate a political atmosphere of acceptance in which [the government] could enact and implement radical changes in the policy and practice of constitutional government in [the United States]." Complaint & 2. In addition, Gallop alleges that the attacks were intended to conceal the revelation on September 10, 2001 that $2.3 trillion in congressional appropriations "could not be accounted for" in a recent Department of Defense audit. Complaint & 42. Gallop claims that defendants' alleged responsibility for the attack that resulted in the injuries she sustained and the deaths of thousands of others entitles her to compensatory and punitive damages for (1) violations of her rights under the First, Fourth, Fifth and Ninth Amendments of the United States Constitution pursuant to Bivens; (2) the common law tort of conspiracy to cause death and great bodily harm; and (3) a violation of the Antiterrorism Act, 18 U.S.C. ' 2333(a), which provides civil remedies to U.S. nationals injured by Aan act of international terrorism."2 2 18 U.S.C. ' 2333(a) provides: Any national of the United States injured in his or her person, property, or business by reason of an act of international terrorism, or his or her estate, survivors, or heirs, may sue therefore in any appropriate district court of the United States and shall recover threefold the damages he or she sustains and the cost of the suit, including attorney's fees. On May 6, 2009, defendants moved to dismiss Gallop's complaint on the following bases: (1) that defendants are entitled to qualified immunity; (2) that the Antiterrorism Act fails to provide a cause of action against U.S. government officials; (3) that Gallop's constitutional claim is untimely, and, in any event, fails to state a claim upon which relief can be granted; (4) that all of her claims are barred under the doctrine of judicial estoppel; and (5) that all of her claims are frivolous. The District Court agreed that the Complaint was 5 frivolous and could not survive a motion to dismiss. See Gallop v. Cheney, No. 08 Civ. 10881, 2010 WL 909203, at *3 (S.D.N.Y. Mar. 15, 2010). Accordingly, without reaching any of the government=s other arguments, the District Court dismissed the complaint with prejudice. Id. On appeal, Gallop argues that the District Court erred in concluding that the complaint failed to make out well-pleaded, non-conclusory factual allegations and erred in declining to provide her leave to amend her complaint. DISCUSSION A. We review de novo the dismissal of a complaint for failure to state a claim upon which relief can be granted. See, e.g., Maloney v. Soc. Sec. Admin., 517 F.3d 70, 74 (2d Cir. 2008). To survive dismissal, Gallop "must provide the grounds upon which [her] claim rests through factual allegations sufficient 'to raise a right to relief above the speculative level.'" ATSI Commc'ns, Inc. v. Shaar Fund, Ltd., 493 F.3d 87, 98 (2d Cir. 2007) (quoting Bell Atl. Corp. v. Twombly, 550 U.S. 544, 555 (2007)). As the Supreme Court explained in Ashcroft v. Iqbal, a complaint that merely "tenders naked assertions devoid of further factual enhancement" fails to meet this standard. 129 S. Ct. 1937, 1949 (2009) (quotation marks and alterations omitted). Moreover, even if the complaint contains sufficiently "well-pleaded" allegations, "only a complaint that states a plausible claim for relief survives a motion to dismiss." Id. at 1950. A court may dismiss a claim as "factually frivolous" if the sufficiently well-pleaded facts are "clearly baseless"Cthat is, if they are "fanciful," "fantastic." or "delusional." Denton v. Hernandez, 504 U.S. 25, 32-33 (1992) (quoting Neitzke v. Williams, 490 U.S. 319, 325, 327, 328 (1989)) (quotation marks omitted). B. 6 After a de novo review, we have no hesitation in concluding that the District Court correctly determined that the few conceivably "well-pleaded" facts in Gallop's complaint are frivolous. While, as a general matter, Gallop or any other plaintiff certainly may allege that the most senior members of the United States government conspired to commit acts of terrorism against the Untied States, the courts have no obligation to entertain pure speculation and conjecture. Indeed, in attempting to marshal a series of unsubstantiated and inconsistent allegations in order to explain why American Airlines Flight 77 did not crash into the Pentagon, the complaint utterly fails to set forth a consistent, much less plausible, theory for what actually happened that morning in Arlington, Virginia. See, e.g., Complaint & 3 (alleging that defendants may have caused "high explosive charges to be detonated inside the Pentagon"); & 21 (alleging that defendants "may have employed Muslim extremists to carry out suicide attacks; or . . . may

have used Muslim extremists as dupes or patsies"); id. (alleging that "four planes" were in fact hijacked on the morning of September 11); & 33 (alleging that "[i]f Flight 77, or a
substitute, did swoop low over the [Pentagon], to create the
false impression of a suicide attack, it was then flown away
by its pilot, or remote control, and apparently crashed somewhere else"); & 40(d)(3) (alleging that apart from Flight 77 "a
different, additional, flying object . . . hit the Pentagon"); &
43 (alleging that there "may have been a missile strike, perhaps penetrating through to the back wall, which helped
collapse the section that fell in, possibly augmented by explosives placed inside"). Furthermore and notwithstanding the
unsupported assumptions regarding the fate of American
Airlines Flight 77, the complaint also fails to plausibly allege the existence of a conspiracy among the defendants. For
example, Gallop offers not a single fact to corroborate her allegation of a "meeting of the minds" among the conspirators.
Complaint & 55. It is well settled that claims of conspiracy
"containing only conclusory, vague, or general allegations of
conspiracy to deprive a person of constitutional rights cannot withstand 7 a motion to dismiss." Leon v. Murphy, 988
F.2d 303, 311 (2d Cir. 1993) (quotation marks omitted). We
therefore agree with the District Court that Gallop's allegations of conspiracy are baseless and spun entirely of "cynical delusion and fantasy." Gallop, 2010 WL 909203, at *5. The
District Court did not err in dismissing the complaint with
prejudice. Although, like the District Court, we do not reach
the question of whether judicial estoppel bars Gallop's com-

plaint, we note that the complaint is facially irreconcil-
able with factual allegations made by Gallop in other actions.
See Gallop v. Am. Airlines, Inc., No. 03 Civ. 1016, Order of Final
Judgment at 2 (S.D.N.Y. Dec. 13, 2007) (dismissing with prejudice Gallop's complaint against various defendants alleging
that American Airlines Flight 77 did crash into the Pentagon
on September 11, 2001); Vadhan v. Riggs Nat'l Corp., No. 04 Civ.
7281, Amended Complaint & 2 (S.D.N.Y. Mar. 23, 2005) (alleging
that defendants "ultimately facilitated ... the terrorists being
able to complete their terrorist deeds on September 11, 2001 by
crashing four United States passenger airlines into the New
York World Trade Center buildings, the United States Pentagon, and into a field in Shanksville, Pennsylvania"); Burnett v. Al Baraka Investment, No. 03 Civ. 5738, Complaint & 9
(S.D.N.Y. Aug. 1, 2003) (alleging that "on September 11, 2001, al
Qaeda co-conspirators ... hijacked American Airlines Flight
77 . . . and crashed it into the Pentagon"). While Gallop=s
counsel asserted at oral argument that Gallop=s inconsistent
claims could be explained by the emergence of new evidence
since her previous submissions, he did not identify any. We
therefore do not know whether Gallop's reconsideration of
the events of September 11, 2001 is the product of new evidence or of new counsel. C. On appeal, Gallop also contends
that she should have been granted leave to amend the complaint. While leave to amend under the Federal Rules of Civil
Procedure is "freely granted," see Fed. R. Civ. P. 15(a), no court
can be said to have erred in failing to grant a 8 request that
was not made. As a result, the "contention that the District

Court abused its discretion in not permitting an amendment that was never requested is frivolous." Horoshko v. Citibank, N.A., 373 F.3d 248, 249-50 (2d Cir. 2004). Moreover, in the absence of any indication that Gallop couldC-or wouldC-provide additional allegations that might lead to a different result, the District Court did not err in dismissing her claim with prejudice. As we have had occasion to explain, "[a] counseled plaintiff is not necessarily entitled to a remand for repleading whenever he has indicated a desire to amend his complaint, notwithstanding the failure of plaintiff's counsel to make a showing that the complaint's defects can be cured." Porat v. Lincoln Towers Cmty. Ass=n, 464 F.3d 274, 276 (2d Cir. 2006). D. Finally, while the government has not moved for sanctions, the record on appeal leaves no doubt that this appeal, to say nothing of the original complaint, was "brought without the slightest chance of success," and therefore should not have been brought at all, even if authorized by the client. Bankers Trust Co. v. Publicker Indus., Inc., 641 F.2d 1361, 1367 (2d Cir. 1981). Pursuant to the terms of Federal Rule of Appellate Procedure 38, 28 U.S.C. ' 1927, and the inherent authority of the Court to consider sanctions on parties who pursue patently frivolous appeals and force this Court to considerCand the government to defendCvexatious litigation, we may, with adequate notice and opportunity to be heard, impose sanctions nostra sponte. See Fed. R. App. P. 38 ("If a court of appeals determines that an appeal is frivolous, it may, after a separately filed motion or notice from the court and reasonable opportunity to respond, award just damages and single or double costs to the appellee."); 28 U.S.C. ' 1927 ("Any attorney or other person admitted to conduct cases in any court of the United States or any Territory thereof who so multiplies the proceedings in any case unreasonably and vexatiously may be required by the court to satisfy personally the excess costs, expenses, and attorneys' fees reasonably incurred because of such conduct."); 9 Chambers v. NASCO, Inc., 501 U.S. 32, 45-46 (1991) (discussing the "inherent power" of the court to impose sanctions on a party who has Aacted in bad faith, vexatiously, wantonly, or for oppressive reasons") (quotation marks omitted); Cooter & Gell v. Hartmarx Corp., 496 U.S. 384, 408 (1990) (discussing the authority of appellate courts to impose sanctions under Rule 38); Revson v. Cinque & Cinque, P.C., 221 F.3d 71, 78-79 (2d Cir. 2000) (discussing the authority of appellate courts to impose sanctions under 28 U.S.C. ' 1927 and under their inherent power to sanction parties and their attorneys); In re JC=s East, Inc., 84 F.3d 527, 532 (2d Cir. 1996) (discussing the authority of appellate courts to impose sanctions under Rule 38); DeLuca v. Long Island Lighting Co., 862 F.2d 427, 430 (2d Cir. 1988) (discussing same); DLC Mgmt. Corp. v. Town of Hyde Park, 163 F.3d 124, 136 (2d Cir. 1998) (discussing the Ainherent power@ of appellate courts to impose sanctions). As in United States v. Potamkin Cadillac Corp., 689 F.2d 379 (2d Cir. 1982), this appeal was an unnecessary imposition "on the government which is forced to defend against the appeal and on the taxpayers who must pay for that defense." Id. at 382. Accordingly, Gallop and her counsel are hereby ordered to show cause in writing within thirty days from the date of entry of this order why they should not pay double costs and damages in the amount of $15,000, for which they would be jointly and severally liable, under Rule 38, 28 U.S.C. ' 1927, and the inherent power of this Court. See, e.g., Knipe v. Skinner, 999 F.2d 708, 711 (2d Cir. 1993) (ordering nostra sponte that counsel show cause why he should not pay double costs and fees under Rule 38).3 The government shall file a letter-brief within three days of Gallop=s counsel=s submission stating its views, if any, on the question of sanctions. 3 As we have previously stated, "since attorney and client are in the best position between them to determine who caused this appeal to be taken," the prudent course for this Court is to impose joint and several liability. Potamkin, 689 F.2d at 382; see also In re JC=s East, Inc., 84 F.3d at 532 (ordering that "appellants and their attorney, who are in the best position to allocate responsibility for bringing this appeal, show cause within thirty days why they should not be sanctioned, with joint and several liability") (citation omitted). 10 CONCLUSION For the reasons stated above, we AFFIRM the judgment of the District Court. Gallop=s counsel are ordered to show cause as directed in the penultimate paragraph of this opinion.

1 10-1241-cv Gallop v. Cheney UNITED STATES COURT OF APPEALS FOR THE SECOND CIRCUIT August Term 2010 (Submitted: June 16, 2011 Decided: July 7, 2011) Docket No.

10-1241-cv APRIL GALLOP, individually and for her minor child, E.G., Plaintiff-Appellant, -v.- RICHARD CHENEY, former Vice President of the United States, DONALD RUMSFELD, former Secretary of the Department of Defense, General RICHARD MYERS (Ret.), United States Air Force, Defendants-Appellees, JOHN DOES NOS. I-X, in their individual capacities, Defendants. Before: WINTER, WALKER, and CABRANES, Circuit Judges. _____ April Gallop moves, through counsel, to disqualify the panel from consideration of her petition for panel rehearing and rehearing in banc of the opinion of this Court in Gallop v. Cheney, ___ F.3d ___, 2011 WL 1565858 (2d Cir. 2011). That motion, along with her petition for panel rehearing, are denied. In addition, Gallop's counsel, William Veale, is ordered to show cause why sanctions should not be imposed under Federal Rule of Appellate Procedure 38, 28 U.S.C. ' 1927, and the inherent power of this Court. William Veale, Walnut Creek, CA, for Petitioner-Appellant April Gallop. PER CURIAM: On June 13, 2011, appellant April Gallop petitioned, through counsel, for rehearing of an April 27, 2011 decision of this Court affirming the judgment of the United States District Court for 2 the Southern District of New York (Denny Chin, Judge). See Gallop v. Cheney, ___ F.3d ___, 2011 WL 1565858 (2d Cir. 2011). In our opinion, we determined, as the District Court had, that Gallop's complaint—which alleged that former senior government officials caused the September 11, 2001 attacks against the United States in order to (1) create a political atmosphere in which they could pursue domestic

and international policy objectives and (2) conceal the misallocation of $2.3 trillion in congressional appropriations to
the Department of Defense—was frivolous. Id. at *3. We also
ordered Gallop and her counsel to show cause why they
should not be sanctioned for filing a frivolous appeal under
Federal Rule of Appellate Procedure 38, 28 U.S.C. § 1927, and
the inherent power of this Court. Id. at *5. While Gallop's
petition for rehearing was pending before this Court, she
moved, pursuant to 28 U.S.C. §§ 144 and 455(a), to disqualify
the panel from consideration of that petition and any other
aspect of her appeal, including the imposition of sanctions.
Gallop argues that this Court's opinion demonstrates an "evident severe bias" arising from the panel's "active personal
emotions" associated with the attacks of September 11, 2001,
which merits disqualification. Motion to Disqualify at 2. A.
Prior rulings are, ordinarily, not a basis for disqualification.
United States v. Yousef, 327 F.3d 56, 170 (2d Cir. 2003) (declining to set a precedent that would "essentially . . . requir[e] .
. . judges to recuse themselves anytime they were asked to
revisit a prior decision"); see also Liteky v. United States, 510
U.S. 540, 555 (1994) ("[J]udicial rulings alone almost never constitute a valid basis for a bias or partiality motion."). As the
Supreme Court has explained, absent a "deep-seated fa-
voritism or antagonism that would make fair judgment impossible," rulings are "[a]lmost invariably . . . proper grounds
for appeal, not for recusal." Id. 3 Here, the only evidence Gallop proffers establishes no more than that the panel ruled
against her. As we have previously held, that alone is insuf-

ficient to establish the sort of extreme antagonism required for disqualification. In re Basciano, 542 F.3d 950, 957–58 (2d Cir. 2008); cf. Berger v. United States, 255 U.S. 22, 28 (1921) (finding extreme bias where a district judge announced that it was difficult "not to be prejudiced against the German Americans" because "[t]heir hearts are reeking with disloyalty"). Gallop's motion to disqualify the panel is therefore denied. B. Having denied Gallop's motion to disqualify the panel, we also deny her petition for panel rehearing. Gallop's petition for rehearing in banc will be considered by the in banc court in the normal course. C. In his affidavit in support of Gallop's motion for disqualification, William Veale—one of Gallop's counsel of record—"demand[s]" not only that the panel, but "any other members of the bench of this Circuit who share their feelings[,] be recused." Motion to Disqualify (Veale Aff. ¶ 2). We know of no precedent for recusing unnamed judges based on a prejudice, the only evidence of which is manifested in a decision adverse to an attorney's (or a party's) interests. Cf. In re Nettles, 394 F.3d 1001, 1003 (7th Cir. 2005) (recusing all district and circuit judges where the defendant acted on a threat to destroy the federal courthouse in which those judges worked by means of a truck bomb); but see Tapia-Ortiz v. Winter, 185 F.3d 8, 10 (2d Cir. 1999) (recognizing that under the rule of necessity, where all judges would be disqualified in a suit brought against every district and circuit court judge in the circuit, none are disqualified). Veale certainly points to none. Indeed, rather than pursuing his client's interests, Veale's actions appear to be malicious—intended, in bad faith, to use his position as an attorney of record to harass and disparage the court. See Tapia-Ortiz, 185 F.3d at 4 11. Such conduct, in our view, is ground for consideration of further appellate sanctions. See In re 60 E. 80th St. Equities, Inc., 218 F.3d 109, 119 (2d Cir. 2000). Accordingly—wholly apart from the order to show cause required pursuant to our decision in Gallop, ___ F.3d ___, 2011 WL 1565858, at *5, for which briefs are now due on July 11, 2011 (for Gallop and her counsel) and July 14, 2011 (for the government)—William Veale is hereby ordered to show cause in writing within thirty days from the date of entry of this order why this Court should not impose additional sanctions pursuant to Federal Rule of Appellate Procedure 38, 28 U.S.C. § 1927, and the inherent authority of the Court, requiring him to provide appropriate notice to any federal court before whom he appears of any sanctions that may be imposed against him by this Court. No extensions of time to comply with this order to show cause will be granted. CONCLUSION For the reasons stated above, Gallop's motion to disqualify the panel is DENIED. The petition for panel rehearing is DENIED. Gallop=s counsel, William Veale, is ORDERED TO SHOW CAUSE as directed in Part C of this opinion.

10-1241-cv Gallop v. Cheney UNITED STATES COURT OF APPEALS FOR THE SECOND CIRCUIT August Term 2010 (Argued: April 5, 2011 Decided: October 14, 2011) Docket No. 10-1241-cv APRIL GALLOP, individually and for her minor child, E.G., Plaintiff-Appellant, -v.- RICHARD CHENEY, former Vice President of the United States, DONALD RUMS-

FELD, former Secretary of the Department of Defense, General RICHARD MYERS (Ret.), United States Air Force, Defendants-Appellees, JOHN DOES NOS. I-X, in their individual capacities, Defendants. Before: WINTER, WALKER, and CABRANES, Circuit Judges. _____ Following this Court's April 27, 2011 order for April Gallop and her counsel of record to show cause why sanctions should not be imposed for filing a frivolous appeal, see Gallop v. Cheney, 642 F.3d 364 (2d Cir. 2011) ("Gallop I"), sanctions are imposed on Gallop's counsel of record pursuant to Federal Rule of Appellate Procedure 38, 28 U.S.C. § 1927, and the inherent power of this Court. One of Gallop's counsel of record, William Veale, is further sanctioned for filing a frivolous and vexatious motion to disqualify the panel "and any like-minded colleagues" from considering Gallop's petition for panel rehearing and rehearing in banc of this Court's opinion in Gallop I, following a July 7, 2011 order to show cause, see Gallop v. Cheney, 645 F.3d 519 (2d Cir. 2011) ("Gallop II"). In addition, Gallop's lead counsel of record, Dennis Cunningham, is admitted pro hac vice for the purpose of this appeal, and is ordered to show cause why he should not be separately sanctioned for his principal role in drafting the relevant filings. WILLIAM W. VEALE (Mustapha Ndanusa, Brooklyn, NY; Dennis Cunningham, San Francisco, CA, on the brief), Walnut Creek, CA, for Petitioner-Appellant April Gallop. 2 ALICIA M. SIMMONS, Assistant United States Attorney (Preet Bharara, United States Attorney; Benjamin H. Torrance, Assistant United States Attorney, on the brief), Office of the United

States Attorney for the Southern District of New York, New York, NY, for Defendants-Appellees Richard B. Cheney, Donald H. Rumsfeld and Richard B. Myers. PER CURIAM: In an April 27, 2011 opinion in the above-captioned appeal, Gallop v. Cheney, 642 F.3d 364 (2d Cir. 2011) ("Gallop I"), this Court (1) affirmed the order of the District Court dismissing plaintiff-appellant April Gallop's complaint as frivolous1 and (2) ordered Gallop and her counsel of record, Dennis Cunningham, Mustapha Ndanusa, and William Veale, to show cause in writing within 30 days why we should not impose sanctions in the form of double costs and a monetary penalty of $15,000, for which they would be jointly and severally liable, for filing a frivolous appeal.2 Gallop I, 642 F.3d at 370-71. Gallop subsequently moved for an extension of time until July 11, 2011 to file a response to our order to show cause, which motion was granted. On June 16, 2011, before responding to the outstanding order to show cause, Gallop moved to disqualify the panel, pursuant to 28 U.S.C. §§ 144 and 455(a), from considering her petition for rehearing and rehearing in banc. See Mot. to Disqualify (Veale Aff. ¶ 2) The motion, which was signed by William Veale,3 stated that the panel should be disqualified due to "evident severe bias, based in active personal emotions arising from the 9/11 attack . . . leading to a categorical prejudgment totally rejecting [Gallop's] Complaint, out of hand and with palpable animus in [its] decision." Mot. to Disqualify at 2. In addition to signing the motion to disqualify, Veale also 1 Gallop v. Cheney, No. 08 Civ. 10881, 2010 WL 909203, at *3 (S.D.N.Y. Mar. 15, 2010) (describing

Gallop's claims as "factually baseless[,] . . . fanciful, fantastic, and delusional"). 2 See Fed. R. App. P. 38; see also 28 U.S.C. § 1927; Chambers v. NASCO, Inc., 501 U.S. 32, 45-46 (1991) (discussing courts' inherent authority to impose sanctions). 3 Although William Veale alone signed the motion to disqualify, Dennis Cunningham claims he was the primary author. See Appellants' Mem. in Response to the Court's April 27, 2011 Order Imposing Sanctions (Cunningham Aff. ¶ 28). 3 provided a supporting affidavit, in which he further demanded not only that "the three panel members" who heard Gallop's appeal recuse themselves from future participation in the case, but also that "any other members of the bench of this Circuit who share their feelings" do the same. Id. (Veale Aff. ¶ 2); see also id. (Veale Aff. ¶ 27) (reiterating that the panel members "and any like-minded colleagues" must be recused). The affidavit was also peppered with disdainful and unsubstantiated conclusions about the panel members' emotional stability and competence to serve objectively. See, e.g., id. (Veale Aff. ¶¶ 3, 19) (alleging that the Court had engaged in a "rank, dishonest wielding of ordained power," and that the participation of one member in particular was so egregious that it "would or should provoke a congressional investigation"). On July 7, 2011, in a second published opinion, Gallop v. Cheney, 645 F.3d 519 (2d Cir. 2011) (per curiam) ("Gallop II"), we (1) denied Gallop's motion to disqualify the panel, (2) denied her petition for panel rehearing, and (3) ordered William Veale to show cause in writing within 30 days from the date of entry of that order why the Court should not impose additional sanctions against him for his role in drafting the motion to disqualify and accompanying affidavit. Gallop II, 645 F.3d at 521-22. Pursuant to the terms of the proposed additional sanctions, Veale would be required to provide appropriate notice to any federal court before which he appears of any sanctions imposed against him in connection with this appeal. Id. On July 12, 2011 and August 8, 2011, respectively, Gallop and her team of attorneys submitted their responses to our orders to show cause of April 27, 2011 and July 7, 2011. A. Dennis Cunningham, Gallop's lead counsel of record, states in his affirmation in response to our April 27, 2011 order to show cause that he is "not currently admitted to practice before this Court" because, although previously admitted, he was "dropped from the rolls without notice." Appellants' Mem. in Response to the Court's April 27, 2011 Order Imposing Sanctions 4 ("Appellants' Mem. Response") (Cunningham Aff. ¶ 28). He states that he was "substantially 'the decider' in [the] development of the case, and author of the pleadings at issue here," and moves to be admitted pro hac vice for the purposes of this appeal, so that in considering sanctions we may "assign [the] blame herein to whom it mainly belongs." Id. (Cunningham Aff. ¶ 28.) Cunningham's motion to be admitted pro hac vice is hereby granted. B. In Gallop I, we affirmed the dismissal of Gallop's complaint by the United States District Court for the Southern District of New York (Denny Chin, Judge); the complaint had alleged that on September 11, 2001, a bomb was detonated inside the Pentagon, that no plane hit the Pentagon, and that various identified United States civilian and military leaders knew about the 9/11 attacks in advance, assisted in their planning, and subsequently covered up the government's involvement. See Gallop I, 642 F.3d at 366-67. We found the District Court's dismissal of the complaint appropriate because it consisted of speculation and conjecture and "fail[ed] to set forth a consistent, much less plausible, theory for what actually happened" on September 11, and further failed to present anything beyond vague and conclusory allegations of conspiracy among the defendants. Id. at 368- 69. We then ordered Gallop and her attorneys to show cause why they should not be sanctioned for forcing the court to consider, and the government to defend, a frivolous and vexatious appeal. Id. at 370-71. The response of Gallop and her attorneys to our April 27, 2011 order to show cause fails to demonstrate that this appeal was anything but frivolous. Like other papers submitted by Gallop and her team of attorneys in this appeal, the response presents only irrelevant information in a jarringly disorganized manner, united solely by its consistently patronizing tone. The response is a comprehensive compilation of every rumor, report, statement, and anecdote that may reveal an inconsistency or omission in an "official version" of the 9/11 attacks, such as the 9/11 Commission 5 Report: Final Report on the National Commission on Terrorist Attacks Upon the United States, available at http://www.gpoaccess.gov/911/pdf/fullreport.pdf.4 Despite this effort, Gallop and her attorneys neglect to explain how or why these random accounts—even assuming they reveal inconsistencies or omissions in the "official" 9/11 story—provide a sufficient basis for pursuing an appeal of Gallop's claims against defendants. As such, the response fails to show why the appeal was not frivolous, see Gallop I, 642 F.3d at 370-71. Moreover, the response contains a robust collection of unsupported accusations of bias against the Court. For example, it accuses the Court of "an untoward, actionably biased judicial response" to Gallop's claims, "angry pre-judgment," and participation (or at least acquiescence) in the "ongoing" government "conspiracy" regarding the events of 9/11. Appellants' Mem. Response at 7, 9, 17-18. 1. Turning first to the question of whether sanctions are appropriate against Gallop, we note that she is not an attorney and thus has not assumed the ethical obligations that her attorneys owe to this Court. Additionally, the record before us reveals that Gallop did not spearhead her litigation strategy, but rather relied heavily upon her attorneys to draft the relevant documents and provide advice in pursuing this litigation. See, e.g., Appellants' Mem. Response at 21 n.13 (describing Cunningham as the "principal author of the plaintiffs' pleadings here and in the district court"); id. (Gallop Aff. ¶¶ 6-7) ("I understand from my attorneys that . . . .") ("[A]s explained by my lawyers . . . .")). Under the circumstances, we decline to impose sanctions on Gallop at this time. Cf. In re Porto, 645 F.3d 1294, 1304 (11th Cir. 2011) ("[T]he rule that the sins of the lawyer are visited on the 4 For example, Veale's affirmation consists almost exclusively of random anecdotes and culminates in a laundry list of publications that could potentially support a conspiracy theory. See generally Appellants' Mem. Response (Veale Aff.). 6 client does not apply in th[e] context [of sanctions], and a court must specify conduct of the [client] herself that is bad enough to subject her to sanctions."). Rather, Gallop is hereby admonished that the submission of future frivolous filings, either as a pro se litigant or one represented by counsel, may result in sanctions being imposed on her by the courts, including the imposition of leave-to-file restrictions, requirements of notice to other federal courts, and monetary penalties. 2. Turning to the question of whether sanctions are appropriate against Gallop's attorneys, the record before us reflects that this team of lawyers "multiplie[d] the proceedings in [this] case unreasonably and vexatiously," 28 U.S.C. § 1927 ("§ 1927"); see also Fed. R. App. P. 38 ("Rule 38") (providing for sanctions where a court of appeals "determines that an appeal is frivolous"). See generally Gallop II, 645 F.3d at 520-22; Gallop I, 642 F.3d at 364-71; Appellants' Mem. Response. The record also reflects that Gallop's attorneys repeatedly and in bad faith accused the Court of bias, malice, and general impropriety. See, e.g., Appellants' Mem. Response at 7, 9, 17-18. Accordingly, pursuant to our authority under § 1927, Rule 38, and the inherent power of this Court, we hereby order, adjudge, and decree that Dennis Cunningham, Mustapha Ndanusa, and William Veale shall pay the government double costs in addition to damages in the amount of $15,000, for which they are jointly and severally liable, within 60 days of the date of entry of this order. It is further ordered that (1) unless such payment is timely made, attorneys Dennis Cunningham, Mustapha Ndanusa, and William Veale shall be required to request leave from this Court before filing any papers with the Clerk of this Court or the clerks of any court within this Circuit; (2) within 24 hours of receipt of the $15,000 penalty imposed on Gallop's counsel of record, the government shall submit an affidavit to this Court confirming its receipt of such payment; and (3) if no payment is made within 60 days of the date of entry of this order, the government shall so 7 certify to this Court, along with a statement regarding additional remedies that may be available under the circumstances. C. On July 7, 2011, we ordered William Veale to show cause why he should not be separately sanctioned for statements made in the June 16, 2011 motion to disqualify and his accompanying affidavit. Gallop II, 645 F.3d at 521-22. On August 8, 2011, Veale filed a response to this second order to show cause, in which he attempts to establish that he filed the motion to disqualify and accompanying affidavit in good faith. See generally Veale Mem. in Response to Court's July 7, 2011 Order to Show Cause ("Veale Mem. Response"). In his affirmation accompanying this response, Veale declares that he "sincerely believed [the motion] was meritorious," id. (Veale Aff. ¶ 5), and denies that it was motivated by a "desire to harass or disparage this Court," id. (Veale Aff. ¶ 6). Although Veale concedes that the motion and accompanying affidavit evinced a "regrettably ... intemperate" tone, he attributes this tone to his "fe[eling] demeaned by th[e] Court's decision and its Order to Show Cause [in Gallop I]," and apologizes to the Court for allowing his personal feelings to influence the tone of his submissions, id. (Veale Aff. ¶ 7). Veale's intemperate tone is less significant to our analysis than the legal futility of his demand that the members of the original panel and "any other members of the bench of this Circuit who share their feelings" be recused, Mot. to Disqualify (Veale Aff. ¶ 2); id. (Veale Aff. ¶ 27 (reiterating that "[t]he Panel members here, and any like-minded colleagues," must recuse themselves)), a demand for which no precedent was presented, nor, as far as we know, exists, Gallop II, 645 F.3d at 521. In the absence of legal support, Veale offered an untested (and presumably untestable) circular explanation: that the panel members found Gallop's conspiracy theory claims to be frivolous because they were experiencing 9/11-related emotions that prevent them from "com[ing] to grips 8 with the concrete factual allegations set forth in the Complaint." Mot. to Disqualify (Veale Aff. ¶ 23). This theory requires the ambitious assumption that the "[o]nly . . . explan[ation]" for the panel's adverse decision is that Gallop's claims were so "abhorrent" that they deactivated the judges' "normal intellectual functions," forcing them to "abandon[] impartiality decisively" in favor of "a reflexive pre-judgment," id. (Veale Aff. ¶¶ 3, 21). Accordingly, in Veale's view, the panel's very rejection of Gallop's claims proves that the panel members—perhaps as a "psycho-emotional matter"—either "will not be" or "cannot be" impartial. Id. (Veale Aff. ¶ 26). Conveniently, the apparent litmus test for whether a judge's normal intellectual functions have been compromised such that he or she must be disqualified from hearing

408 | WILLIAM W. VEALE

Gallop's case is identical to the question of whether a judge agrees with the original panel's determination that Gallop's action is frivolous. But as Veale is surely aware, no party to litigation is entitled to a prescreened panel of sympathetic judges, and we have no patience for Veale's homegrown psychosocial theories contrived to achieve that end. Moreover, we reject Veale's claim that he "sincerely believed [his motion to disqualify] was meritorious and that it was [his] duty as [Gallop's] lawyer to [make it]," Veale Mem. Response (Veale Aff. ¶ 5). We refuse to accept that any attorney acting in good faith, particularly an attorney who claims to have 32 years of trial experience and who avers that he "taught criminal trial practice at the University of California, Berkeley, Boalt Hall School of Law for 11 years," id. (Veale Aff. ¶¶ 1-2), could sincerely believe that he was justified in demanding disqualification of the three panel members "and any like-minded colleagues," id. (Veale Aff. ¶ 27), or that his affidavit was otherwise legally sound and meritorious. Rather, we conclude that Veale allowed his emotional reaction to the Court's adverse ruling to further undermine his legal judgment and interfere with his duty to provide thoughtful and reasoned advice to his client. Enraged and embarrassed by the Court's decision, Veale used the June 9 16, 2011 affidavit to air personal grievances against the Court, rather than to tailor his response to Gallop's best interests. Notwithstanding Veale's insistence in his August 8, 2011 affirmation that he was not "motivated by a desire to harass or disparage this Court," id. (Veale Aff. ¶ 6), his true purpose is revealed in the unusually aggressive—yet entirely unsupported—attacks on the Court in his June 16, 2011 affidavit submitted in response to our April 27, 2011 order to show cause. See, e.g., Mot. to Disqualify (Veale Aff. ¶ 4) (calling the Court's decision "highly emotional" and "angry"); id. (Veale Aff. ¶ 18) (claiming the Court's decision sacrificed "the integrity of the Court, and of history"); id. (Veale Aff. ¶¶ 3, 19) (suggesting the Court had engaged in a "rank, dishonest wielding of ordained power" that "would or should provoke a congressional investigation"). For the foregoing reasons, we conclude that Veale acted in bad faith in demanding the recusal of the three panel members "and any like-minded colleagues," id. (Veale Aff. ¶ 27). Accordingly, we hereby order that Veale shall be required, for a period of one year from the date of entry of this order, to provide appropriate notice of the sanctions imposed upon him in this case to any federal court in this Circuit before which he appears or seeks to appear. Failure to comply with this order may result in additional sanctions. D. Dennis Cunningham, Gallop's lead counsel of record, asserts that he was the "principal author of the pleadings at issue" in this case, including the motion to recuse that resulted in additional sanctions imposed upon Veale, see Part C, ante. Appellants' Mem. Response (Cunningham Aff. ¶ 28). In light of his asserted authorship, along with the disrespectful language he employed in the affirmation he submitted in conjunction with Gallop's response to our April 27, 2011 order to show cause, see, e.g., id. (Cunningham Aff. ¶¶ 23-24 (accusing the Court of "unconscionable," "opportunistic," "cynical," and "scorn[ful]" con-

duct lacking "any pretense of impartiality or objectivity")),
Cunningham is hereby ordered to show cause in writing
within 30 days from the date 10 of entry of this order why he
should not be separately sanctioned by being required to provide appropriate notice to any federal court before which he
appears or seeks to appear of the sanctions imposed against
him in connection with this appeal. Conclusion To summarize: (1) The motion of Dennis Cunningham, Gallop's lead
counsel of record, for admission to our Court pro hac vice, is
hereby GRANTED. (2) Gallop is hereby ADMONISHED that
the submission of future frivolous filings may result in sanctions. (3) Dennis Cunningham, Mustapha Ndanusa, and
William Veale are hereby ORDERED to pay the government
double costs in addition to damages in the amount of $15,000,
for which they are jointly and severally liable, within 60
days of the date of entry of this order. (4) It is further OR-
DERED that (i) unless such payment is timely made, attorneys Dennis Cunningham, Mustapha Ndanusa, and William
Veale shall be required to request leave from this Court before filing any papers with the Clerk of our Court or the
clerks of any court within this Circuit; (ii) within 24 hours
of receipt of the $15,000 penalty imposed on Gallop's counsel,
the government shall submit an affidavit to this Court confirming its receipt of such payment; and (iii) if no payment
is made within 60 days of the date of entry of this order, the
government shall promptly so certify to this Court, along
with a statement regarding additional remedies that may be
available under the circumstances. (5) William Veale is

hereby ORDERED, for a period of one year from the date of entry of this order, to provide notice of the sanctions imposed upon him in this case to any court within this Circuit before which he appears, or seeks to appear. Failure to comply with this order may result in additional sanctions. 11 (6) Dennis Cunningham is hereby ORDERED to show cause in writing within 30 days from the date of entry of this order why he should not be separately sanctioned by being required to provide appropriate notice to any court within this Circuit before which he appears, or seeks to appear, of the sanctions imposed against him in connection with this appeal.

10-1241-cv Gallop v. Cheney UNITED STATES COURT OF APPEALS FOR THE SECOND CIRCUIT August Term 2010 (Argued: April 5, 2011 Decided: February 2, 2012) Docket No. 10-1241-cv APRIL GALLOP, individually and for her minor child, E.G., Plaintiff-Appellant, -v.- RICHARD CHENEY, former Vice President of the United States, DONALD RUMSFELD, former Secretary of the Department of Defense, General RICHARD MYERS (Ret.), United States Air Force, Defendants-Appellees, JOHN DOES NOS. I-X, in their individual capacities, Defendants. Before: WINTER, WALKER, and CABRANES, Circuit Judges. _____ In an order dated October 14, 2011, Gallop v. Cheney, 660 F.3d 580 (2d Cir. 2011) ("Gallop III"), this Court imposed sanctions on counsel of record to plaintiff-appellant April Gallop—Dennis Cunningham, Mustapha Ndanusa, and William W. Veale—for filing a frivolous appeal from a judgment of the United States District Court for the Southern District of New York (Denny Chin, Judge) dismissing her complaint alleging that defendants, former senior government officials, caused the September 11, 2001 attacks against the United States in order to (1) create a political atmosphere in which they could pursue domestic and international policy objectives and (2) conceal the misallocation of $2.3 trillion in congressional appropriations to the Department of Defense. The 2 Court separately sanctioned Veale for filing a frivolous and vexatious motion to disqualify the panel "and any like-minded colleagues" from considering Gallop's petition for panel rehearing and rehearing in banc of this Court's opinion in Gallop v. Cheney, 642 F.3d 364 (2d Cir. 2011) ("Gallop I"). Gallop III further ordered Cunningham, who had described himself as "substantially 'the decider'" in the development of Gallop's case and the principal author of the motion to disqualify the panel—for which Veale, who signed the motion and accompanying affidavit, was separately sanctioned—to show cause why additional sanctions should not be imposed on him for his selfproclaimed lead role in drafting the motion to disqualify. Following this Court's review of the November 14, 2011 memorandum Cunningham filed in response to the order to show cause in Gallop III, we impose additional sanctions on Cunningham pursuant to Federal Rule of Appellate Procedure 38, 28 U.S.C. § 1927, and the inherent power of this Court. In addition, we vacate the sanctions imposed on local counsel Mustapha Ndanusa in Gallop III based on Cunningham's insistence that Ndanusa served a peripheral and subordinate role in Gallop's frivolous appeal. WILLIAM W. VEALE (Mustapha Ndanusa, Brooklyn, NY; Dennis Cunningham, San Francisco, CA, on the brief), Walnut Creek, CA, for Petitioner-Appellant April Gallop. ALICIA M. SIMMONS, Assistant United States Attorney (Preet Bharara, United States Attorney; Benjamin H. Torrance, Assistant United States Attorney, on the brief), Office of the United States Attorney for the Southern District of New York, New York, NY, for Defendants-Appellees Richard B. Cheney, Donald H. Rumsfeld and Richard B. Myers. PER CURIAM: In our fourth opinion in this case, we consider whether Dennis Cunningham, counsel to plaintiff-appellant April Gallop and the purported "decider" in the development of Gallop's action 3 alleging that defendants, former senior government officials, caused the September 11, 2001 attacks against the United States, should be subjected to additional sanctions for his primary role in drafting a frivolous and vexatious motion to disqualify the panel "and any like-minded colleagues" from considering Gallop's petition for panel rehearing and rehearing in banc of this Court's decision in Gallop v. Cheney, 642 F.3d 364 (2d Cir. 2011) ("Gallop I"), a motion for which his co-counsel, William W. Veale, was separately sanctioned in our order dated October 14, 2011, see Gallop v. Cheney, 660 F.3d 580 (2d Cir. 2011) ("Gallop III"). Although Veale alone signed the motion to disqualify and submitted the affidavit in support thereof, Cunningham claimed in a later filing to have been the primary author of those pleadings. See Appellants' Mem. in Response to the Court's April 27, 2011 Order Imposing

Sanctions (Cunningham Aff. ¶ 28). In response to this claim, we ordered Cunningham to show cause why he should not be separately sanctioned for his self-proclaimed lead role in drafting the motion to disqualify the panel. See Gallop III, 660 F.3d at 586. Following our review of the November 15, 2011 memorandum Cunningham filed in response to our order to show cause in Gallop III, we conclude that Cunningham has failed to show cause why we should not impose additional sanctions on him. Accordingly, we impose sanctions on Cunningham pursuant to 28 U.S.C. § 1927, Federal Rule of Appellate Procedure 38, and the inherent power of this Court. In addition, we vacate the sanctions imposed on local counsel Mustapha Ndanusa in Gallop III based on Cunningham's insistence that Ndanusa served a peripheral and subordinate role in Gallop's appeal. BACKGROUND The facts of this case are convoluted, and have been thoroughly summarized in the initial opinion of the United States District Court for the Southern District of New York (Denny Chin, 4 Judge)1 and our three previous opinions. The abbreviated account below includes only those facts necessary to explain the disposition of the issues currently before us. Gallop, represented by counsel in the District Court and on appeal, filed a complaint asserting violations of her constitutional rights pursuant to Bivens v. Six Unknown Federal Narcotics Agents, 403 U.S. 388 (1971), a common law tort of conspiracy to cause death and great bodily harm, and a violation of the Antiterrorism Act, 18 U.S.C. § 2333(a), against defendants, former senior government officials, for allegedly causing the September 11, 2001 attacks against the United States in order to (1) create a political atmosphere in which they could pursue domestic and international policy objectives and (2) conceal the misallocation of $2.3 trillion in congressional appropriations to the Department of Defense. The District Court concluded that Gallop's claims were frivolous, and dismissed her complaint for failure to state a claim upon which relief can be granted under Fed. R. Civ. P. 12(b)(6). See Gallop v. Cheney, No. 08 Civ. 10881, 2010 WL 909203 (S.D.N.Y. Mar. 15, 2010). In an April 27, 2011 opinion, we (1) affirmed the order of the District Court dismissing Gallop's complaint as frivolous, and (2) ordered Gallop and her counsel of record—Cunningham, Ndanusa, and Veale—to show cause in writing within 30 days why we should not impose sanctions in the form of double costs and a monetary penalty of $15,000 for filing a frivolous appeal, for which they would be jointly and severally liable. Gallop I, 642 F.3d at 370–71. On June 16, 2011, before responding to the outstanding order to show cause, Gallop moved under 28 U.S.C. §§ 144 and 455(a) to disqualify the three members of the panel from considering her petition for rehearing and rehearing in banc. See Mot. to Disqualify (Veale Aff. ¶ 2). The motion stated that the panel should be disqualified due to "evident severe bias, based in active personal emotions arising from the 9/11 attack . . . leading to a categorical pre-judgment totally 1 Gallop v. Cheney, No. 08 Civ. 10881, 2010 WL 909203, at *3 (S.D.N.Y. Mar. 15, 2010). 5 rejecting [Gallop's] Complaint, out of hand and with palpable animus in [its] decision." Mot. to Disqualify at 2. Veale signed the motion to disqualify and provided a supporting affidavit, in which he further demanded not only that "the three panel members" who heard Gallop's appeal recuse themselves from future participation in the case, but also that "any other members of the bench of this Circuit who share their feelings" do the same. Id. (Veale Aff. ¶ 2); see also id. (Veale Aff. ¶ 27) (reiterating that the panel members "and any like-minded colleagues" must be recused).2 On July 7, 2011, in a second published opinion, Gallop v. Cheney, 645 F.3d 519 (2d Cir. 2011) ("Gallop II"), we (1) denied Gallop's motion to disqualify the panel, (2) denied her petition for panel rehearing, and (3) ordered Veale to show cause why the Court should not impose additional sanctions against him for his role in drafting the motion to disqualify and accompanying affidavit. Gallop II, 645 F.3d at 521–22. On July 12, 2011 and August 8, 2011, respectively, Gallop and her team of attorneys submitted their responses to our orders to show cause of April 27, 2011 (Gallop I) and July 7, 2011 (Gallop II). In his response to the second order to show cause (July 7, 2011), Veale insisted that he filed the motion to disqualify and the accompanying affidavit in good faith. See Veale Mem. in Response to Court's July 7, 2011 Order to Show Cause ("Veale Mem. Response"). In his affirmation accompanying this response, Veale declared that he "sincerely believed [the motion] was meritorious," id. (Veale Aff. ¶ 5); denied that it was motivated by a "desire to harass or disparage this Court," id. (Veale Aff. ¶ 6); and conceded that the motion and accompanying affidavit evinced a "regrettably . . . intemperate" tone, which he attributed to 2 The affidavit was also peppered with disdainful conclusions about the panel members' emotional stability and competence to serve objectively. For example, it alleged that the panel members found Gallop's conspiracy theory claims to be frivolous because they were experiencing 9/11–related emotions that prevented them from "com[ing] to grips with the concrete factual allegations set forth in the Complaint." Mot. to Disqualify (Veale Aff. ¶ 23). 6 "fe[eling] demeaned by th[e] Court's decision and its Order to Show Cause [in Gallop I]." Id. (Veale Aff. ¶ 7). Veale apologized to the Court for allowing his personal feelings to influence the tone of his submissions. Id. In his affirmation in response to our April 27, 2011 order to show cause in Gallop I, Cunningham described himself as "substantially 'the decider' in the development of [Gallop's] case," and claimed that he was the "author of the pleadings at issue," including the motion to recuse which Veale had signed. See Appellants' Mem. in Response to the Court's April 27, 2011 Order Imposing Sanctions (Cunningham Aff. ¶ 28). In an opinion filed October 14, 2011 (Gallop III), following our review of the responses to the orders to show cause entered in Gallop I and Gallop II, we revisited the appropriateness of sanctions. First, after declining to sanction Gallop, we sanctioned her counsel of record— Cunningham, Ndanusa, and Veale—for filing a frivolous appeal, ordering them "[to] pay the government double costs in addition to damages in the amount of $15,000, for which they are jointly and severally liable, within 60 days of the date of entry of this order." Gallop III, 660 F.3d at 584. Second, we imposed additional sanctions on Veale for filing the frivolous motion to disqualify, pursuant to which Veale is required, for a period of one year from the date of entry of the order, to provide appropriate notice of the sanctions imposed against him in connection with this appeal to any federal court before which he appears. Id. at 586. Finally, we ordered Cunningham to show cause why we should not impose separate, additional sanctions on him for his principal role in drafting the motion to disqualify and accompanying affidavit, for which Veale was separately sanctioned. Id. On November 14, 2011, Cunningham filed a response to our October 14, 2011 order to show cause, Cunningham's Mem. in Response to the Court's October 14, 2011 Order to Show 7 Cause ("Cunningham Mem. Response"), in which he insisted that the appeal and motion to recuse were filed out of zealous advocacy, rather than bad faith. See id. at 10–13. In addition, Cunningham asked that we vacate the sanctions against Ndanusa, who, he claimed, "was not involved in the case until after the complaint was filed, and then served as local counsel only, implementing our needs on the ground, not forging or determining in any way what we said to the Court." Id. at 12. DISCUSSION Pursuant to 28 U.S.C. § 1927, "[a]ny attorney ... who so multiplies the proceedings in any case unreasonably and vexatiously may be required by the court to satisfy personally the excess costs, expenses, and attorneys' fees reasonably incurred because of such conduct." 28 U.S.C. § 1927; see also Fed. R. App. P. 38 ("If a court of appeals determines that an appeal is frivolous, it may ... award just damages and single or double costs to the appellee."); Chambers v. NASCO, Inc., 501 U.S. 32, 45– 46 (1991) (discussing courts' inherent authority to impose sanctions, including "when a party has 'acted in bad faith, vexatiously, wantonly, or for oppressive reasons'" (quoting Alyeska Pipeline Serv. Co. v. Wilderness Soc'y, 421 U.S. 240, 258–59 (1975))). A. Additional Sanctions against Cunningham We turn first to the issue of whether additional sanctions should be imposed against Cunningham for his principal role in directing Gallop's appeal. Accepting Cunningham's claim that he was substantially involved in drafting the motion to disqualify and accompanying affidavit bearing Veale's name, this matter is largely foreclosed by Gallop III, in which we imposed additional sanctions against Veale for filing the motion to disqualify and accompanying affidavit. Despite Veale's insistence that he "sincerely believed [his motion to disqualify] was meritorious and that it was [his] duty as [Gallop's] lawyer to [make it]," Veale Mem. Response (Veale Aff. ¶ 5), we "refuse[d] to accept that any attorney acting in good faith . . . could 8 sincerely believe that he was justified in demanding disqualification of the three panel members 'and any like-minded colleagues,'" Gallop III, 660 F.3d at 585 (quoting Mot. to Disqualify (Veale Aff. ¶ 27)). The memorandum Cunningham filed in response to our October 14, 2011 (Gallop III) order to show cause is similar to the memorandum and affirmation Veale filed in response to our July 7, 2011 (Gallop II) order to show cause. Like Veale, Cunningham insisted that the motion to disqualify "was made as a matter of righteous if overheated advocacy, and not in bad faith." Cunningham Mem.

Response at 12–13. Citing "[t]he evidence of one's own eyes," id. at 6 & 7, Cunningham reiterated his continued belief that the appeal was meritorious. He apologized to the Court for his "aggressive, judgmental, or 'jarring', words and usages" in the motions and supporting papers he drafted, which he, like Veale, attributed "to feeling demeaned, and disrespected by [the] nature and tenor of the Court's judgments." Id. at 4–5. As we explained in Gallop III while reviewing the appropriateness of sanctions against Veale, these excuses do not adequately explain why a member of the Bar would demand that the members of the original panel and "any other members of the bench of this Circuit who share their feelings" be recused, Mot. to Disqualify (Veale Aff. ¶ 2); id. (Veale Aff. ¶ 27 (reiterating that "[t]he Panel members here, and any like-minded colleagues," must recuse themselves)), "a demand for which no precedent was presented, nor, as far as we know, exists," Gallop III, 660 F.3d at 585. For the reasons stated in Gallop III, we conclude that Cunningham acted in bad faith in demanding the recusal of the three panel members and any like-minded colleagues. Accordingly, we hereby order that Cunningham shall be required, for a period of one year from the date of entry of this order, to provide notice of the sanctions imposed upon him in this case—both here and in our previous opinion entered October 14, 2011—to any federal court in this Circuit before which he appears or seeks to appear. 9 B. Sanctions Against Ndanusa In his response to our October 14, 2011 order to show cause, Cunningham urged us to "remit the share of the fine accruing to [Ndanusa]" from our order for Gallop's counsel of record "[t]o pay the government double costs in addition to damages in the amount of $15,000, for which they are jointly and severally liable," Gallop III, 660 F.3d at 584, "because [Ndanusa] was not involved in the case until after the complaint was filed, and then served as local counsel only, implementing our needs on the ground, not forging or determining in any way what we said to the Court." Cunningham Mem. Response at 12. Accordingly, we vacate the sanctions against Ndanusa. Cunningham and Veale remain jointly and severally liable to the government to pay double costs plus damages in the amount of $15,000, and must do so within 30 days of the entry of this order. CONCLUSION To summarize: (1) Dennis Cunningham is hereby ORDERED, for a period of one year from the date of entry of this order, to provide notice of the sanctions imposed upon him in this case to any court within this Circuit before which he appears, or seeks to appear. Failure to comply with this order may result in additional sanctions. (2) It is further ORDERED that the sanctions entered against Mustapha Ndanusa on October 14, 2011 are vacated, without effect on the sanctions entered against Dennis Cunningham and William Veale on that date.3 3 Cunningham and Veale are jointly and severally liable for reimbursing Ndanusa for any funds he already contributed. 10 (3) Pursuant to our October 14, 2011 order, Cunningham and Veale shall pay the government double costs, in addition to damages in the amount of $15,000, for which they are jointly and severally liable, within 30 days of the entry of this judgment.4 We appoint

Judge Brian M. Cogan, of the United States District Court for the Eastern District of New York, to serve as Special Master to ensure full and prompt compliance with the Court's mandate. The mandate shall issue forthwith. 4 According to the Declaration of Alicia M. Simmons, Assistant United States Attorney for the Southern District Court, filed December 16, 2011, the government has received a check from Veale in the amount of $15,000 in satisfaction of the sanctions imposed in our order entered October 14, 2011.

10-1241-cv Gallop v. Cheney UNITED STATES COURT OF APPEALS FOR THE SECOND CIRCUIT August Term 2010 (Argued: April 5, 2011 Decided: February 2, 2012) Docket No. 10-1241-cv APRIL GALLOP, individually and for her minor child, E.G., Plaintiff-Appellant, -v.- RICHARD CHENEY, former Vice President of the United States, DONALD RUMS-FELD, former Secretary of the Department of Defense, General RICHARD MYERS (Ret.), United States Air Force, De-fendants-Appellees, JOHN DOES NOS. I-X, in their individual capacities, Defendants. Before: WINTER, WALKER, and CABRANES, Circuit Judges. _____ In an order dated October 14, 2011, Gallop v. Cheney, 660 F.3d 580 (2d Cir. 2011) ("Gallop III"), this Court imposed sanctions on counsel of record to plaintiff-appellant April Gallop—Dennis Cunning-ham, Mustapha Ndanusa, and William W. Veale—for filing a frivolous appeal from a judgment of the United States District Court for the Southern District of New York (Denny Chin, Judge) dismissing her complaint alleging that defendants, former senior government officials, caused the Sep-

tember 11, 2001 attacks against the United States in order to (1)
create a political atmosphere in which they could pursue domestic and international policy objectives and (2) conceal the
misallocation of $2.3 trillion in congressional appropriations
to the Department of Defense. The 2 Court separately sanctioned Veale for filing a frivolous and vexatious motion to
disqualify the panel "and any like-minded colleagues" from
considering Gallop's petition for panel rehearing and rehearing in banc of this Court's opinion in Gallop v. Cheney, 642
F.3d 364 (2d Cir. 2011) ("Gallop I"). Gallop III further ordered
Cunningham, who had described himself as "substantially
'the decider'" in the development of Gallop's case and the
principal author of the motion to disqualify the panel—for
which Veale, who signed the motion and accompanying affidavit, was separately sanctioned—to show cause why additional sanctions should not be imposed on him for
his selfproclaimed lead role in drafting the motion to disqualify. Following this Court's review of the November 14,
2011 memorandum Cunningham filed in response to the order to show cause in Gallop III, we impose additional sanctions on Cunningham pursuant to Federal Rule of Appellate
Procedure 38, 28 U.S.C. § 1927, and the inherent power of this
Court. In addition, we vacate the sanctions imposed on local
counsel Mustapha Ndanusa in Gallop III based on Cunningham's insistence that Ndanusa served a peripheral and subordinate role in Gallop's frivolous appeal. WILLIAM W.
VEALE (Mustapha Ndanusa, Brooklyn, NY; Dennis Cunningham, San Francisco, CA, on the brief), Walnut Creek, CA, for

Petitioner-Appellant April Gallop. ALICIA M. SIMMONS, Assistant United States Attorney (Preet Bharara, United States Attorney; Benjamin H. Torrance, Assistant United States Attorney, on the brief), Office of the United States Attorney for the Southern District of New York, New York, NY, for Defendants-Appellees Richard B. Cheney, Donald H. Rumsfeld and Richard B. Myers. PER CURIAM: In our fourth opinion in this case, we consider whether Dennis Cunningham, counsel to plaintiff-appellant April Gallop and the purported "decider" in the development of Gallop's action 3 alleging that defendants, former senior government officials, caused the September 11, 2001 attacks against the United States, should be subjected to additional sanctions for his primary role in drafting a frivolous and vexatious motion to disqualify the panel "and any like-minded colleagues" from considering Gallop's petition for panel rehearing and rehearing in banc of this Court's decision in Gallop v. Cheney, 642 F.3d 364 (2d Cir. 2011) ("Gallop I"), a motion for which his co-counsel, William W. Veale, was separately sanctioned in our order dated October 14, 2011, see Gallop v. Cheney, 660 F.3d 580 (2d Cir. 2011) ("Gallop III"). Although Veale alone signed the motion to disqualify and submitted the affidavit in support thereof, Cunningham claimed in a later filing to have been the primary author of those pleadings. See Appellants' Mem. in Response to the Court's April 27, 2011 Order Imposing Sanctions (Cunningham Aff. ¶ 28). In response to this claim, we ordered Cunningham to show cause why he should not be separately sanctioned for his self-proclaimed lead role in drafting the motion to disqualify the panel. See Gallop III, 660 F.3d at 586. Following our review of the November 15, 2011 memorandum Cunningham filed in response to our order to show cause in Gallop III, we conclude that Cunningham has failed to show cause why we should not impose additional sanctions on him. Accordingly, we impose sanctions on Cunningham pursuant to 28 U.S.C. § 1927, Federal Rule of Appellate Procedure 38, and the inherent power of this Court. In addition, we vacate the sanctions imposed on local counsel Mustapha Ndanusa in Gallop III based on Cunningham's insistence that Ndanusa served a peripheral and subordinate role in Gallop's appeal. BACKGROUND The facts of this case are convoluted, and have been thoroughly summarized in the initial opinion of the United States District Court for the Southern District of New York (Denny Chin, 4 Judge)1 and our three previous opinions. The abbreviated account below includes only those facts necessary to explain the disposition of the issues currently before us. Gallop, represented by counsel in the District Court and on appeal, filed a complaint asserting violations of her constitutional rights pursuant to Bivens v. Six Unknown Federal Narcotics Agents, 403 U.S. 388 (1971), a common law tort of conspiracy to cause death and great bodily harm, and a violation of the Antiterrorism Act, 18 U.S.C. § 2333(a), against defendants, former senior government officials, for allegedly causing the September 11, 2001 attacks against the United States in order to (1) create a political atmosphere in which they could pursue domestic and international policy objectives and (2) conceal

the misallocation of $2.3 trillion in congressional appropria-
tions to the Department of Defense. The District Court concluded that Gallop's claims were frivolous, and dismissed her
complaint for failure to state a claim upon which relief can
be granted under Fed. R. Civ. P. 12(b)(6). See Gallop v. Cheney,
No. 08 Civ. 10881, 2010 WL 909203 (S.D.N.Y. Mar. 15, 2010). In an
April 27, 2011 opinion, we (1) affirmed the order of the District Court dismissing Gallop's complaint as frivolous, and
(2) ordered Gallop and her counsel of record—Cunningham, Ndanusa, and Veale—to show cause in writing within
30 days why we should not impose sanctions in the form of
double costs and a monetary penalty of $15,000 for filing a
frivolous appeal, for which they would be jointly and severally liable. Gallop I, 642 F.3d at 370–71. On June 16, 2011, before
responding to the outstanding order to show cause, Gallop
moved under 28 U.S.C. §§ 144 and 455(a) to disqualify the three
members of the panel from considering her petition for rehearing and rehearing in banc. See Mot. to Disqualify (Veale
Aff. ¶ 2). The motion stated that the panel should be disqualified due to "evident severe bias, based in active personal emotions arising from the 9/11 attack ... leading to a categorical
pre-judgment totally 1 Gallop v. Cheney, No. 08 Civ. 10881,
2010 WL 909203, at *3 (S.D.N.Y. Mar. 15, 2010). 5 rejecting [Gal-
lop's] Complaint, out of hand and with palpable animus in
[its] decision." Mot. to Disqualify at 2. Veale signed the motion
to disqualify and provided a supporting affidavit, in which
he further demanded not only that "the three panel members" who heard Gallop's appeal recuse themselves from fu-

ture participation in the case, but also that "any other members of the bench of this Circuit who share their feelings" do the same. Id. (Veale Aff. ¶ 2); see also id. (Veale Aff. ¶ 27) (reiterating that the panel members "and any like-minded colleagues" must be recused).2 On July 7, 2011, in a second published opinion, Gallop v. Cheney, 645 F.3d 519 (2d Cir. 2011) ("Gallop II"), we (1) denied Gallop's motion to disqualify the panel, (2) denied her petition for panel rehearing, and (3) ordered Veale to show cause why the Court should not impose additional sanctions against him for his role in drafting the motion to disqualify and accompanying affidavit. Gallop II, 645 F.3d at 521–22. On July 12, 2011 and August 8, 2011, respectively, Gallop and her team of attorneys submitted their responses to our orders to show cause of April 27, 2011 (Gallop I) and July 7, 2011 (Gallop II). In his response to the second order to show cause (July 7, 2011), Veale insisted that he filed the motion to disqualify and the accompanying affidavit in good faith. See Veale Mem. in Response to Court's July 7, 2011 Order to Show Cause ("Veale Mem. Response"). In his affirmation accompanying this response, Veale declared that he "sincerely believed [the motion] was meritorious," id. (Veale Aff. ¶ 5); denied that it was motivated by a "desire to harass or disparage this Court," id. (Veale Aff. ¶ 6); and conceded that the motion and accompanying affidavit evinced a "regrettably ... intemperate" tone, which he attributed to 2 The affidavit was also peppered with disdainful conclusions about the panel members' emotional stability and competence to serve objectively. For example, it alleged that the panel members found Gallop's conspiracy theory claims to be frivolous because they were experiencing 9/11–related emotions that prevented them from "com[ing] to grips with the concrete factual allegations set forth in the Complaint." Mot. to Disqualify (Veale Aff. ¶ 23). 6 "fe[eling] demeaned by th[e] Court's decision and its Order to Show Cause [in Gallop I]." Id. (Veale Aff. ¶ 7). Veale apologized to the Court for allowing his personal feelings to influence the tone of his submissions. Id. In his affirmation in response to our April 27, 2011 order to show cause in Gallop I, Cunningham described himself as "substantially 'the decider' in the development of [Gallop's] case," and claimed that he was the "author of the pleadings at issue," including the motion to recuse which Veale had signed. See Appellants' Mem. in Response to the Court's April 27, 2011 Order Imposing Sanctions (Cunningham Aff. ¶ 28). In an opinion filed October 14, 2011 (Gallop III), following our review of the responses to the orders to show cause entered in Gallop I and Gallop II, we revisited the appropriateness of sanctions. First, after declining to sanction Gallop, we sanctioned her counsel of record— Cunningham, Ndanusa, and Veale—for filing a frivolous appeal, ordering them "[to] pay the government double costs in addition to damages in the amount of $15,000, for which they are jointly and severally liable, within 60 days of the date of entry of this order." Gallop III, 660 F.3d at 584. Second, we imposed additional sanctions on Veale for filing the frivolous motion to disqualify, pursuant to which Veale is required, for a period of one year from the date of entry of the order, to provide appropriate notice of the sanctions imposed against him in connection with this appeal to any federal court before which he appears. Id. at 586. Finally, we ordered Cunningham to show cause why we should not impose separate, additional sanctions on him for his principal role in drafting the motion to disqualify and accompanying affidavit, for which Veale was separately sanctioned. Id. On November 14, 2011, Cunningham filed a response to our October 14, 2011 order to show cause, Cunningham's Mem. in Response to the Court's October 14, 2011 Order to Show 7 Cause ("Cunningham Mem. Response"), in which he insisted that the appeal and motion to recuse were filed out of zealous advocacy, rather than bad faith. See id. at 10–13. In addition, Cunningham asked that we vacate the sanctions against Ndanusa, who, he claimed, "was not involved in the case until after the complaint was filed, and then served as local counsel only, implementing our needs on the ground, not forging or determining in any way what we said to the Court." Id. at 12. DISCUSSION Pursuant to 28 U.S.C. § 1927, "[a]ny attorney ... who so multiplies the proceedings in any case unreasonably and vexatiously may be required by the court to satisfy personally the excess costs, expenses, and attorneys' fees reasonably incurred because of such conduct." 28 U.S.C. § 1927; see also Fed. R. App. P. 38 ("If a court of appeals determines that an appeal is frivolous, it may ... award just damages and single or double costs to the appellee."); Chambers v. NASCO, Inc., 501 U.S. 32, 45– 46 (1991) (discussing courts' inherent authority to impose sanctions, including "when a party has 'acted in bad faith, vexatiously, wantonly, or for oppressive reasons'" (quoting Alyeska Pipeline Serv. Co. v. Wilderness Soc'y, 421 U.S. 240, 258–59 (1975))). A. Additional Sanctions against Cunningham We turn first to the issue of whether additional sanctions should be imposed against Cunningham for his principal role in directing Gallop's appeal. Accepting Cunningham's claim that he was substantially involved in drafting the motion to disqualify and accompanying affidavit bearing Veale's name, this matter is largely foreclosed by Gallop III, in which we imposed additional sanctions against Veale for filing the motion to disqualify and accompanying affidavit. Despite Veale's insistence that he "sincerely believed [his motion to disqualify] was meritorious and that it was [his] duty as [Gallop's] lawyer to [make it]," Veale Mem. Response (Veale Aff. ¶ 5), we "refuse[d] to accept that any attorney acting in good faith . . . could 8 sincerely believe that he was justified in demanding disqualification of the three panel members 'and any like-minded colleagues,'" Gallop III, 660 F.3d at 585 (quoting Mot. to Disqualify (Veale Aff. ¶ 27)). The memorandum Cunningham filed in response to our October 14, 2011 (Gallop III) order to show cause is similar to the memorandum and affirmation Veale filed in response to our July 7, 2011 (Gallop II) order to show cause. Like Veale, Cunningham insisted that the motion to disqualify "was made as a matter of righteous if overheated advocacy, and not in bad faith." Cunningham Mem. Response at 12–13. Citing "[t]he evidence of one's own eyes," id. at 6 & 7, Cunningham reiterated his continued belief that the appeal was meritorious. He apologized to the Court for

his "aggressive, judgmental, or 'jarring', words and usages" in
the motions and supporting papers he drafted, which he, like
Veale, attributed "to feeling demeaned, and disrespected by
[the] nature and tenor of the Court's judgments." Id. at 4–5.
As we explained in Gallop III while reviewing the appropriateness of sanctions against Veale, these excuses do not adequately explain why a member of the Bar would demand
that the members of the original panel and "any other members of the bench of this Circuit who share their feelings" be
recused, Mot. to Disqualify (Veale Aff. ¶ 2); id. (Veale Aff. ¶
27 (reiterating that "[t]he Panel members here, and any like-
minded colleagues," must recuse themselves)), "a demand for
which no precedent was presented, nor, as far as we know,
exists," Gallop III, 660 F.3d at 585. For the reasons stated in
Gallop III, we conclude that Cunningham acted in bad faith
in demanding the recusal of the three panel members and
any like-minded colleagues. Accordingly, we hereby order
that Cunningham shall be required, for a period of one year
from the date of entry of this order, to provide notice of the
sanctions imposed upon him in this case—both here and in
our previous opinion entered October 14, 2011—to any federal
court in this Circuit before which he appears or seeks to appear. 9 B. Sanctions Against Ndanusa In his response to our
October 14, 2011 order to show cause, Cunningham urged us
to "remit the share of the fine accruing to [Ndanusa]" from
our order for Gallop's counsel of record "[t]o pay the government double costs in addition to damages in the amount
of $15,000, for which they are jointly and severally liable,"

Gallop III, 660 F.3d at 584, "because [Ndanusa] was not involved in the case until after the complaint was filed, and
then served as local counsel only, implementing our needs on
the ground, not forging or determining in any way what we
said to the Court." Cunningham Mem. Response at 12. Accordingly, we vacate the sanctions against Ndanusa. Cunningham
and Veale remain jointly and severally liable to the government to pay double costs plus damages in the amount
of $15,000, and must do so within 30 days of the entry of this
order. CONCLUSION To summarize: (1) Dennis Cunningham
is hereby ORDERED, for a period of one year from the date
of entry of this order, to provide notice of the sanctions imposed upon him in this case to any court within this Circuit
before which he appears, or seeks to appear. Failure to comply with this order may result in additional sanctions. (2) It
is further ORDERED that the sanctions entered against
Mustapha Ndanusa on October 14, 2011 are vacated, without
effect on the sanctions entered against Dennis Cunningham
and William Veale on that date.3 3 Cunningham and Veale
are jointly and severally liable for reimbursing Ndanusa for
any funds he already contributed. 10 (3) Pursuant to our October 14, 2011 order, Cunningham and Veale shall pay the government double costs, in addition to damages in the amount
of $15,000, for which they are jointly and severally liable,
within 30 days of the entry of this judgment.4 We appoint
Judge Brian M. Cogan, of the United States District Court for
the Eastern District of New York, to serve as Special Master to ensure full and prompt compliance with the Court's

mandate. The mandate shall issue forthwith. 4 According to the Declaration of Alicia M. Simmons, Assistant United States Attorney for the Southern District Court, filed December 16, 2011, the government has received a check from Veale in the amount of $15,000 in satisfaction of the sanctions imposed in our order entered October 14, 2011.

CPSIA information can be obtained
at www.ICGtesting.com
Printed in the USA
BVHW040503290921
617684BV00008B/390

9 781087 897530